Critical Perspectives on Educational Policies and Professional Identities

In the field of education, a bridge is often needed between research and practice. This book not only bridges the two but also provides directions for linking research on practice and educational policy. It tells us about practitioners' research in a range of professional settings – it is not fixed in one setting, and it has something to say to professionals in many settings. Whether or not you do research, this book will prompt you to engage with educational policies, navigate the dominant rhetoric and consider solutions emerging from research described in this book. This book explains how societal and political influences shape educational policy. It also suggests how policy may be challenged.

The diversity of approaches is thought-provoking, and there are plenty of ideas and implications that we can take from these chapters: a chapter about research in the primary school setting, for example, can get us thinking about other settings; chapters on the teaching of controversial topics like terrorism and counter-terrorism measures, for example, are helpful in terms of both theory and practice.

More importantly, this book offers a model of supporting doctoral students and researchers to publish their work in order to bring it to a wider audience, where it can actually be of use. Drawing on my own work on communities of writers and writing retreats, the editors decided to co-author and mentor doctoral students, so that students learnt about the publication process. This will not only help educators but will also boost careers. It also means that all this research will not just sit in university archives. Of immediate use to other researchers and Directors of Research will be the chapters where the whole process of writing this book is opened up. So often, the stage of 'writing up' research is unexplained, but this book shows the way to develop a community of writers, a practitioner research community. This is how to sustain research and impact. Writing communities and retreats will sustain practitioner researchers, for whom making time for research and writing is a huge challenge. Moreover, in light of the recent warning about the urgent need for a supportive culture for researchers in Education, from the British Educational Research Association (2023), this book shows how to create such a culture through supportive peer review and dedicated time.

Finally, this book shows how to produce real research outputs that speak for and to educational professionals. Other books may focus on research findings or practical implications; this book does both, while opening up the process of practitioner research and writing. This will have more interest to more readers because of the many individual researcher voices that come through – they tell us how and why they did their research. I hope this will not only prompt more people to read and do practitioner research but also embed the idea of communities that bring researchers and practitioners together.

—***Rowena Murray*, Formerly Professor in Education and Director of Research at University of the West of Scotland, now independent Higher Education consultant**

Critical Perspectives is a vibrant addition to the academic literature, echoing the spirit of Bathmaker and Harnett's influential work while carving its own distinct path. Within its pages, a chorus of practitioner–researcher and established academic voices offer a refreshing perspective on doctoral education that extends far beyond the confines of traditional school or college settings.

This book is a must-read for anyone with a stake in doctoral education, providing a rich tapestry of insights into policy and professionalism across diverse landscapes. From Higher Education to the National Health Service, Further Education and Early Years, the authors unravel the complexities with meticulous detail. What emerges is a vivid portrayal of local concerns with a resounding impact that transcends boundaries, resonating across phases, settings and sectors.

What sets this volume apart is its innovative approach to co-production, seamlessly weaving together emerging and established academic voices in each chapter. This dynamic collaboration opens a portal for the researching professional, inviting them to seamlessly transition into a professional researcher role. The book balances academic rigour with a grounded practitioner focus, effortlessly straddling theory and practice, conceptual and empirical realms, honouring the individual of voice entangled within an extensive ecology of agency.

At its core, *Critical Perspectives* will captivate academics and practitioners with a detailed exploration of the 'messiness and situatedness' inherent in the experience of being and becoming an educational professional. The authors skillfully navigate the intricate landscape of constructing, interrogating, and challenging professionalism, unveiling the limitations of a one-size-fits-all approach with poignant clarity.

This volume is more than a departure; it is a welcome revelation. It serves as a powerful reminder that doctoral training goes beyond providing the technical skills required to manage small-scale research project, urging us to embrace knowledge generation that is applied, transdisciplinary, and deeply contextualized. It serves as a catalyst for change, reminding us that engagement with policy is not restricted to interpretation and enactment but includes the invisible activism of not only inevitable but welcome disruption. *Critical Perspectives* is a vibrant affirmation of the landscape of doctoral education as a realm of endless possibilities and transformative potential.

—***Dr Carol Azumah Dennis*, The Open University**

Critical Perspectives on Researching Educational Policies and Professional Identities: Lessons from Doctoral Studies is a wonderful and unique collection of chapters, perfectly showcasing doctoral students' work. Each chapter is cleverly crafted by a recent EdD graduate and their supervisor and makes a perfect volume of co-produced practitioner research projects, undertaken by EdD students at the University of the West of England. This will be particularly useful for other students at the thesis writing stage because the collection provides a very useful catalogue of exciting and relevant topics covered in previous EdD research. I imagine that 3 audiences will be very interested in this book: EdD students; EdD lecturers and course leaders; other HEIs who provide the EdD.

The book is organized into three core sections, each one dealing with a theme of educational practitioner research. The themes skilfully bring together doctoral research projects from EdD students at UWE, ensuring that their research gets disseminated more widely, as well as in a manageable and accessible collection. Prospective students will be able to see relevant examples of research topics and projects, possibly relating to their own sectors and research interests.

I have not seen any collections like this which relate to the professional doctorate in education. This book makes a valuable contribution to the field and an even more valuable resource for students and academics. A major strength of the book is that it represents the most up-to-date research in the field of education, bringing together relevant, current, and interesting doctoral research projects.

The EdD is fast becoming a very popular route to acquiring a doctorate, particularly for educational professionals. This collection of chapters is a much-needed resource; the research content is varied, interesting and pertinent, and this makes it a significant and important contribution to the field of education and doctoral research.

—***Iona Burnell Reilly*, University of East London**

How much doctoral research in education disappears after the viva? How much illuminating and critical research about the complex interplay of society, professional identity, policy and practice remains forever unread?

Critical Perspectives on Researching Educational Policies and Professional Identities: Lessons from Doctoral Studies is vitally important because it is the first book to provide a space for early career researchers in education to share key aspects of their doctoral methodologies and findings by co-producing chapters with more experienced academics and a highly credible editorial team. The result is a truly fascinating, theoretically informed practitioner-based insight into education policy and practice at all levels using a range of cutting-edge and often creative methodological approaches.

While each chapter stands alone, offering insights for doctoral researchers, early career researchers, their supervisors and more experienced academics into specific subject and age phases of education research, the chapters also resonate with one another, drawing out key themes that help define and articulate close-to-practice research in its current context. The first theme looks at different ways in which educational professionalism is shaped and contested within society; the second theme highlights different perspectives on professional identity and how professional development might be conceptualized over time; the third theme examines the impact of policy on professional identity and practice, highlighting tensions and modes of resistance.

This means that *Critical Perspectives on Researching Educational Policies and Professional Identities: Lessons from Doctoral Studies* is highly relevant and a must-read for all academics and practitioners in education who are interested in articulating their research and its value through exploring and applying theory, innovating with and adapting methodologies and experimenting with forms of representation to reach and impact on new audiences.

—***Professor Tom Dobson*, York St John University, School of Education, Language and Psychology**

As someone who has been involved in doctoral research for many years, it is clear that this book will be an extremely useful resource for students and supervisors of doctoral research. The book showcases, through careful discussion, the issues of educational policy and professional identities within and through doctoral research. The included research is invaluable in informing practice. The book will therefore be extremely useful in understanding how to support researcher development as well as the broader research community and is therefore highly recommended.

—***Professor Carol Fuller*, Institute of Education, University of Reading**

This novel and highly original collection speaks to a range of critical perspectives articulated in the research of a doctoral community at UWE through a rich blend of methodologies.

Each chapter is a collaboration between the doctoral graduates (now early career researchers) and experienced academics who worked as their supervisors. The result is a huge contribution to our understanding of the impact of the doctoral journey on professional identities and practices in education but also to the development of the educational doctorate field itself. This is manifested in Meg Maguire's concluding appraisal of the body of work curated here, observing how this book casts a lens on how practitioner research enabled by educational doctorates disrupts policy and in so doing is policy work in itself. This gives this collection a tactical status, moving beyond 'lessons from' to a form of activism.

This book will be reassuring, inspiring and developmental – politically, conceptually and practically – for anyone involved in an EdD, thinking about doing one or curious about them.

—***Professor Julian McDougall*, Bournemouth University**

Critical Perspectives on Educational Policies and Professional Identities: Lessons From Doctoral Studies

EDITED BY

RICHARD WALLER
University of the West of England, UK

JANE ANDREWS
University of the West of England, UK

AND

TIMOTHY CLARK
University of the West of England, UK

emerald
PUBLISHING

United Kingdom – North America – Japan – India – Malaysia – China

Emerald Publishing Limited
Emerald Publishing, Floor 5, Northspring, 21-23 Wellington Street, Leeds LS1 4DL

First edition 2024

British Library Cataloguing in Publication Data
A catalogue record for this book is available from the British Library

ISBN: 978-1-83753-333-6 (Print)
ISBN: 978-1-83753-332-9 (Online)
ISBN: 978-1-83753-334-3 (Epub)

Printed and bound by CPI Group (UK) Ltd, Croydon, CR0 4YY

INVESTOR IN PEOPLE

We have decided to dedicate this book to Max Weedon, one of the authors in the collection (Chapter 14). Max was tragically killed in a car accident in Barbados on 8th January 2023, just as the process of writing the volume had begun. Max's mother, Kathy Mansfield Higgins, got in touch to tell me the awful news; she had found emails between Max and me discussing ideas for his chapter. In an amazingly brave act, Kathy, herself an academic albeit it an unrelated field, decided to step in and lead the writing of Max's chapter by way of a tribute to him, working with Ciaran Burke who had been Max's internal examiner for his doctoral viva examination in March 2021.

I first met Max when he applied for a place on our EdD Professional Doctorate in Education back in 2015. He was an extremely interesting and deeply passionate man, fiercely intelligent, highly politicized and with a clear sense of social justice. I became Max's Director of Studies for his research, and, most unusually, co-opted two academic colleagues from our Sociology team (Andy Mathers and Sean Creaven) to act as joint supervisors since I felt Max's deep knowledge of social theory was likely to push the boundaries of my own theoretical understanding and test me fully, meaning I wanted some 'back-up', intellectually speaking; I was right to do so.

During his studies Max made theoretical breakthroughs and had insights that seasoned academics would be proud of, as his chapter in this collection demonstrates. Max also wrote for publication during his studies, appearing twice in the British Sociological Association's Discover Society online journal, once writing about his doctoral research into the impact of the Prevent strategy, and once offering his reflections on the outcome of the 2019 UK general election.

Max was also an incredibly modest man, and probably had a wider breadth of experience in the UK education system than anyone else I have worked with on the EdD. He had taught in the primary, secondary, further and higher education sectors, designed further and higher education curricula and been a university governor. But Max had many interests outside of education. We shared a love for football, though we supported rival teams – Liverpool for Max and Spurs for me – a source of much banter and good natured ribbing. I only discovered after his death that Max had co-founded an African charity for HIV orphans. From our conversations over the years I knew that Max loved scuba diving, although I didn't know just how good he was at it, and certainly not that he was a highly qualified instructor (hence his trips to the Caribbean).

I also knew Max had a professional background in music, but didn't know until reading his obituaries just how passionate he was about it, how successful a musician he had been and how important he was to developing the careers of numerous others, largely through the establishment of the BA1 record label whilst teaching music at Bath College. In addition to running a record label, Max had also run a music publishing company, and been both a band manager and a sound engineer.

Having been born in Botswana, Max's own musical journey begun as a young passenger on journeys into the African bush where he was exposed to the captivating sounds of legendary bands from the 1960s and 1970s on the Toyota Hilux tape deck. Classical guitar lullabies at bedtime added to his early musical influences. Upon moving from his country of birth to England, Max was an early adopter of the Sony Walkman, which became his constant companion, filling his ears with melodies day in, day out.

During Max's teenage years, the Stone Roses track 'Fools Gold' ignited a passion for drumming, leading him to form a band called SHC. Their journey saw them supporting renowned acts like Blur and Spiritualized in the early 1990s. However, his musical evolution didn't stop there. He later transitioned to playing the guitar and, along with his band embarked on a new chapter in Brighton, ultimately becoming known as The Just.

Over time Max's commitment to music only grew stronger, culminating in a formal education that included a degree in music production and not one, but two master's degrees in music and songwriting. This extensive knowledge and experience paved the way for him to inspire and nurture the next generation of musicians through teaching and tutoring, ensuring that his passion for music continues to resonate with and through others. He had been instrumental in launching the careers of numerous musicians including chart topping singer songwriter Gabrielle Alpin, X-Factor star singer Lascel Wood, and Radio 1 DJ and music producer Julio Bashmore.

Max's approach to teaching young musicians was to insist they create and produce their own music rather than simply cover the popular music of established acts, and Max took this approach of 'following your passion and forging your own path' into his academic work. Max was a unique individual, and I genuinely feel proud to have known and worked with him during his doctoral studies. He is remembered with great fondness by all who knew and worked or studied with him, and his sudden and premature death a big loss to the academic community.

A charitable organisation, Max Weedon Music (charity no. 1206950) has recently been set up by Max's family in his memory to promote the work of young musicians [www.maxweedonmusic.org]. The charity will make modest awards to help disadvantaged young people in need of a financial helping hand to buy an instrument, or pay for studio time, some coaching, training in mastering and mixing and so on. The charity Trustees are currently working to establish its principles and operating procedures. It is planned to offer the first Awards in the autumn of 2024. Some of the proceeds from the sales of this book will go to support the charity and help continue the good work Max was so passionate about.

For further details please contact: info@maxweedonmusic.org

Richard
[Prof Richard Waller]

Contents

Section 2: Interrogating Approaches to Becoming, Being and Developing as Education Professionals

Section 3: Challenging Education Policy and Practice

List of Tables and Figures

Tables

Figures

About the Editors

Richard Waller is Professor of Education and Social Justice at UWE Bristol. He has taught in further and higher education for nearly 30 years. Richard co-leads UWE's EdD Professional Doctorate in Education and Education PhD programmes. His own research interests cover education, inequality and identity/ies, and he has published widely on these topics.

Jane Andrews is Professor of Education at UWE Bristol. Her research interests focus on multilingualism and learning. Jane teaches on the undergraduate programmes BA (Hons) Early Childhood and BA (Hons) Education. Jane supervises doctoral students and jointly leads the UWE EdD programme. Jane's current research explores integrating creative arts practices into learning and teaching.

Timothy Clark's research focuses on researcher development, including the role of doctoral pedagogy in supporting and influencing methodological decision-making. Following a career as a leader in early years education, he completed an EdD before joining UWE in 2019. He is currently the Director of Research and Enterprise for the School of Education and Childhood at UWE.

About the Contributors

Shamsudin Abikar is a Doctor of Education and for 19 years has been working in mainstream educational settings (primary and secondary) in Bristol in different roles. In 2012, he won the Primary Language Classroom Award for his contribution of how English is taught to primary pupils who learn it as an additional language (EAL learners). Shamsudin presented his research outcomes in and outside of the United Kingdom His research interests include languages and education, multilingualism, identity and learning. He has published many articles including Addressing English Reading Comprehension Difficulties by Somali Origin Pupils in England Primary Schools.

Jake Bacon is a Senior Lecturer in Education at UWE and is the digital lead for the BA Education programme. Jake worked in further education (FE) for 15 years firstly as a sports lecturer, and later as a teacher training coordinator. Jake's EdD, completed in 2017, was titled 'FE Sports Lecturer Professionalism': 'Freedom to Play', or 'Do as I Say?'. Jake's research interests relate to teacher professionalism, working contexts of teachers and digital pedagogy. Outside of work Jake is a volunteer lifeboat Helm at Portishead RNLI, which he has been doing for the last 12 years.

Helen Bovill's research interests focus on identity, in particular non-traditional identity. Helen's recent research is situated in the field of relationships, sex and health education, and prevention and response to violence against women and girls. Helen has taught at UWE for nearly 20 years and currently teaches and supervises postgraduates.

Nicola Bowden-Clissold's primary research interest is in exploring young children's experiences in educational settings, adopting participatory action-based research methodologies. Being passionate about early childhood education, Nicola teaches and supervises in areas of early years, childhood, children's rights and voices and teacher and practitioner provision.

Ciaran Burke is an Associate Professor of Higher Education; his research focuses on social inequalities in higher education and the graduate labour market through a Bourdieusian theoretical lens. His recent work has focused on conceptualizing 'resilience' within a Sociological framework.

Juliet Edmonds' current research interests are engineering education in primary schools, using science literary materials with children, the development of expertise in science teaching and language in science. Her doctoral research explored the ways teachers develop their science teaching and identity in school. She has worked at UWE, educating teachers, for over 20 years. She started her career as a primary teacher in London schools and as an advisory teacher for science.

Georgie Ford has been a figure in the mental health and educational field for over 15 years. Georgie has worked within the NHS and acute settings before moving to education where she has lectured from GCSE to HE level and is a senior fellow of the HEA and SET. Georgie's doctoral research focuses on changing the narrative of mental health in FE. This was presented at the London International Conference of Education and is published in the International Journal for Cross Disciplinary Subjects in Education. Georgie writes for TES and developed an emotional recovery framework for education. Georgie is a Mental Health First Aid and Suicide First Aid instructor and has achieved the Gold Carnegie Award in mental health for her work.

Nicholas Garrick, as a teacher, school leader and consultant, is committed to exploring how people think about learning, teaching and research. As an EYFS and primary school teacher and leader for 23 years, he has led and supported a range of schools locally to organizations and governments in post-conflict and post-disaster countries. As a school leader and consultant, he enables others to seek solutions, and considers creativity, curiosity and enquiry as essential to both leading and learning. As a researcher, Grounded Theory and clean language drive everything he seeks to understand.

Andy Goldhawk's doctoral research explores perceptions of ongoing professional learning for mid-career lecturers in the further education (FE) sector in England. Previously an FE lecturer for 15 years, Andy now works in higher education. Andy's interest in professional learning has since led to the publication of his first book, 'The Super Quick Guide to Learning Theories and Teaching Approaches', by SAGE in May 2023. He has also published in the journal Research in Post-Compulsory Education.

Neil Harrison is an Associate Professor in Education and Social Justice in the School of Education at the University of Exeter. His research interests focus on educational inequalities and marginalization, with a particular theme around young people's decision-making. He enjoys supervising doctoral students across a range of topics, theories and methodologies.

Verity Jones has worked with organizations such as Friends of the Earth, Fashion Revolution, the BBC and Barnardo's to explore themes such as climate and sustainable education, anti-racism and impacts on mental health and wellbeing. Social and environmental justice is a consistent thread through Verity's research and educational practice.

Ben Knight is a Senior Lecturer in Education and former teacher and school leader. He lectures on Initial Teacher Education (ITE), postgraduate, masters and doctoral programmes at UWE, Bristol. His research interests include investigating teaching and learning from a complex systems perspective and applications of complexity theory to education, e.g. exploring ways learning emerges within classroom collectives. He also researches and writes about the importance and development of teacher judgement. Ben is Pedagogy Strand co-leader for UWE's Education & Childhood Research Group and founder and Director of Project Zulu, an international education partnership between UWE and school districts in KwaZulu-Natal, South Africa. Ben's first book titled 'Nurturing Professional Judgement' published by Critical Publishing was published in October 2023.

Meg Maguire is a Professor of Sociology of Education in the School of Education, Communication and Society at King's College London. Her research is in the sociology of education, social justice and policy. Currently she is part of a team working on a five year project investigating how England's vocational education and training (VET) system can better support the school-to-work transitions of the 50% of young people who don't go to university.

Laura Manison's research is centred on class, gender and the perceived choices people make as a result. Her doctoral research explored choice in terms of young working and middle-class women becoming primary school teachers. She works on postgraduate courses in UWE's School of Education and Childhood looking chiefly at learning theory in HE. Before that Laura worked as a primary school teacher, school leader and then led the PGCE in Primary and Early Years Education at UWE. Laura's methodological interest is grounded in narrative inquiry and as her academic work has evolved she has embraced poetic representation and autoethnography to present her own and her participants' narratives.

Kathy Mansfield Higgins is Max's mother. She started her career teaching geography in Botswana and subsequently worked in several African countries in various state-building and governance assignments. Max was born in Botswana and maintained a deep attachment to southern Africa. Kathy now writes short stories and teaches creative writing.

Alexandra Morfaki's research interests lie in the area of inclusion in the early years for children with Special Educational Needs and Disabilities. Her doctoral thesis focused on early years educators' interpretation of inclusion in practice and explored interprofessional partnerships for inclusion and their influence on the formation of the role and identities of early years educators. Alexandra currently works as a Lecturer in early years at Norland College. She initially trained as a reception class teacher and worked in a range of early years settings in the capacity of teacher and manager prior to completing her Doctorate.

Sally Moyle's research interest is in the arena of professional identity, and supporting health practitioners move into new and expanding roles. A nurse by professional background, Sally worked as an Emergency Nurse Practitioner and has been in Higher Education for over 20 years developing new programmes and initiatives to support role expansion across all levels and more specifically

Advanced Practice. She is currently the Pro Vice Chancellor for Health and Science at the University of Worcester.

Tessa Podpadec's research interests include teacher professionalism, educational environments, sustainable futures in education and using creative approaches as research method and pedagogical practice. Most recently she has worked on projects exploring climate change, fast fashion and sustainable education and impacts of racism on mental health and wellbeing.

Catherine Rosenberg's professional interests have included the varying development of students and academics. Her work in academic management and teaching is now focused at postgraduate level on a range of professional development programmes. She supervises postgraduate students on various pedagogical and methodological areas, particularly in relation to narrative inquiry.

Julie Smith's doctoral research investigates the beliefs and practices of high expectation teachers. Julie has taught in secondary schools for nearly 30 years and is currently the Vice-Principal at a school in Gloucestershire, with responsibility for teaching and learning. She has also written for various publications including the Times Educational Supplement, the BERA blog and the Chartered College of Teaching. Julie's educational philosophy is underpinned by a belief in social justice, and as such she is a passionate advocate for non-selective state education, and for the professional learning and development needs of teachers to advance a transformative vision of education.

Karan Vickers-Hulse's research interests focus on the impact of policy and identity. Karan's doctoral research explored the complexities of professional identity formation for trainees on a postgraduate teacher education programme. Karan is a teacher educator and researcher; although much of her work focuses on student teachers, she is passionate about supporting all educators to continue learning in a constantly shifting landscape of policy and practice in education. Karan started her career as a primary school teacher and worked in senior leadership roles in schools in England and Wales before moving to UWE Bristol in 2013. Karan is now the Associate Director of Education in the School of Education and Childhood.

Sarah Whitehouse's research interests are focused on the teaching of sensitive and controversial issues that teachers may face in the classroom. Her doctoral research considered how the history curriculum can cause tensions for teachers when they engage in topics that can be sensitive and or controversial. Sarah's recent research is situated in the field of anti-racist education and issues of social justice. Sarah started her career as a primary school teacher and has worked in higher education supporting trainee teachers for the last 13 years. She is an active and passionate member of the history and geography education community, locally, nationally and internationally.

Marcus Witt began teaching in South India and rural Kentucky before returning to the United Kingdom to complete his PGCE work in primary schools. He now works in initial teacher education. He has a long-standing interest in psychology;

from the cognitive and emotional processes in mathematical learning to the role of personality in children's classroom interactions.

Max Weedon was a passionate and highly gifted teacher and academic. His main love was music in all genres, and he worked with young musicians in the United Kingdom, the Caribbean and Zimbabwe. Another passion was scuba diving, and he was Padi qualified Master Diver and Instructor. It was while diving in Barbados that he died in a car accident in early 2023. As a committed teacher in the United Kingdom, faced with implementing the Government's controversial Prevent policy, Max researched the societal and political motives behind the policy, and its effects on teachers' pedagogic and welfare responsibilities towards their students.

How to access the original doctoral studies

Any of the 14 theses upon which these chapters are based can be found in the UWE research repository using this address, and typing the author's name into the search box: https://www.uwe.ac.uk/study/library/browse-resources-a-z/theses

Acknowledgements

We are grateful for support from the University of the West of England's Faculty Research Investment Scheme to enable us to devote time to curating and developing this collaborative writing project to showcase the wonderful work of some of our recent postgraduate researchers, and to offer others the chance to benefit from their studies.

The collection would not have happened without the enthusiasm and hard work of our chapter authors, their co-authors and all those who have supported them during the writing process, so we want to put on record our thanks to them all. In particular, we would like to thank Kathy Mansfield Higgins, the mother of chapter author Max Weedon, who stepped in to lead the writing of that chapter by way of a tribute to him after his sudden tragic death in a car accident in the early stages of this project.

We are grateful to all of the participants and institutions who agreed to participate in the doctoral studies explored in this collection.

Throughout the development of this project and the writing process we have been fully sustained and supported by Professor Meg Maguire and we thank her wholeheartedly for this.

The anonymous reviewers of the proposal for this volume provided several valuable insights and suggestions to enhance the collection, for which we are grateful.

Finally, we want to thank Emerald Press, in particular Kim Chadwick initially and Kirsty Wood more recently who each saw the value in promoting a collection of co-authored early career researchers' postdoctoral writing. We hope to work with you again in the near future.

Richard, Jane and Timothy

Chapter 1

Educational Policies and Professional Identities: Showcasing Lessons From Doctoral Practitioner Research

Richard Waller, Jane Andrews and Timothy Clark

University of the West of England, UK

The Background to the Collection

The inspiration for this collection can be traced to an earlier book, Bathmaker and Harnett's (2010) edited Routledge volume 'Exploring Learning, Identity and Power through Life History and Narrative Research'. That collection contained 12 chapters, many sole-authored by staff of the University of the West of England (UWE), and most of which focused upon doctoral studies employing qualitative approaches to educational research. Contributors included Richard Waller (RW) and Jane Andrews (JA), two of this collection's editors. RW and JA have co-led UWE's Professional Doctorate in Education (EdD) since 2014, having redeveloped the programme upon appointment to the role.

Unlike the previous collection, this volume only showcases doctoral work, much of which was influenced by UWE's EdD's Researching Educational Policy and Professional Identities (REPPI) module. REPPI explores the interplay between education policy (whether at national, regional or local level) and the professional identities of those working within the education system. These topics are frequently investigated by candidates in the EdD's research phase, and occasionally by our PhD students too (many of whom are practitioner-researchers themselves, including Georgie Ford, the sole PhD graduate whose work features here). That was the case before the REPPI module was developed and introduced in 2014, and has remained so in the decade since. REPPI explores issues, across all education sectors, including the tensions between professional autonomy, personal values and 'performativity', and how they are facilitated or constrained by policy diktats, whether on a macro, meso or micro level, and that is what the chapters here consider.

The notion of pairing early career researchers (ECRs), all of whom were recent doctoral graduates (as lead authors), with a supervisor or other senior colleague

Critical Perspectives on Educational Policies and Professional Identities, 1–8

Published under exclusive licence by Emerald Publishing Limited
doi:10.1108/978-1-83753-332-920241001

with greater experience of academic writing as a co-author, significantly assists the ECR's journeys into publication and aids their development as researchers in the postdoctoral phase of their careers. Anecdotally from our experience as programme leaders, and discussions with those in similar roles elsewhere, we knew that the academic activity of recent graduates from practice-based doctorates such as the EdD often stalled as the demands of their personal lives and professional roles returned to the fore after completing their studies. Curating and developing collections such as this helps strengthen the education research community within and between the university and its partner organisations, offering clear routes into publication for the co-authors. The process of how this happened is outlined later within this chapter.

While there have been several recent books focusing on EdD study (e.g. Emerald's excellent 2020 collection edited by Iona Burnell Reilly and Jodi Roffey-Barentsen), none actually exclusively feature the work of doctoral students themselves. Our book acts as an example of practitioner-researcher doctoral study within various professional settings and emphasises the impact and transferability of the findings across a range of educational sectors. It also highlights lessons that other practitioner-researchers, including those on professional doctorates, can benefit from learning about the process of doctoral research; as such it offers a unique contribution to the literature on doctoral study.

The book concludes with a chapter from a leading academic in the field, Prof Meg Maguire of Kings College, London, who reviews the contribution of the collection in furthering our understanding of educational policies and professional identities, and reflects upon the role doctoral studies can play in exploring such topics.

Setting the Scene: Researcher Development

There is a continuing focus on researchers' development during and after their doctoral studies both nationally, in the United Kingdom, and internationally. In 2023, the British Educational Research Association (BERA) published a review document entitled 'The State of the Discipline' which made the following warning: 'future career trajectories after completion of doctorates are too uncertain', BERA (2023, p. 2). This warning was further qualified with the observation that the career uncertainty was worse for researchers from minoritised backgrounds. The Researcher Concordat (VITAE, 2019) had raised a similar concern, as expressed in its foreword:

> there is still much to do to create the healthy and supportive culture needed to ensure our researchers are given every opportunity to thrive and realise their potential.

Both of these sources signal the need for the routine provision of developmental opportunities to scaffold doctoral graduates between being postgraduate students and the next stage of their research careers. We planned this book project with the goal of generating a supportive culture for postdoctoral students from our institution to work together, turning an aspect of their thesis into a book chapter.

The Researcher Concordat further recommended that in the postdoctoral phase, researchers need time and opportunities to develop their academic identities, reflecting the move from being a supervised doctoral student to being an independent researcher. Attention to how the needs of the researchers of the future can be met was explored in 2019 by an international group of research leaders gathered in Germany. The outcome of that meeting was published as the Hannover Recommendations for Doctoral Education, all of which coincide with our own commitment to continuing support for graduates and, in particular, to equity in doctoral students' experiences.

A distinctive feature of the studies explored in chapters 2 to 15 in this collection is their focus on exploring educational policy, practice and professional identities through research across a range of educational sectors in England. The perspectives of practitioner researchers in education have been highlighted and discussed recently within the work of BERA in their delineation of 'close to practice' research, which is defined as follows:

> Close-to-practice research focusses on issues defined by practitioners as relevant to their practice, and involves collaboration between people whose main expertise is research, practice, or both. (Wyse et al., 2018, p. 34)

We believe that the practitioner-researchers in our collection have identified issues relevant to their practice and are contributing to improving and understanding those practices better. We would also go further, however, in suggesting that the studies offer insights into the policies shaping the practices documented in the specific contexts where the studies were located. These are studies that are close-to-policy as well as close-to-practice and are enhanced through being generated by insider researchers.

In the UK context, the Research Excellence Framework (REF) is used as an accountability tool for reporting on the quality of research outputs, the impact of research and the research environment associated with research-active institutions, usually universities. In a post-REF report (2021) relating to the discipline of education, particular mention was made of the crucial contribution of postgraduate research students to 'the vitality and intellectual life of research units'. We believe that this collection is reflective of that vitality.

Rationale

This text brings together a collection of chapters highlighting lessons relating to educational policy and professional identities arising from the doctoral studies of 14 practitioner-researchers, 13 of whom were EdD graduates and one a PhD graduate. The lessons the studies offer, therefore, come directly from 'researching professionals' (Butcher & Sieminski, 2006) whose research is entangled with, and informed by, their professional roles and expertise (Boud & Lee, 2009). As a result, their contributions prioritise learning within, for and about professional contexts (Fink, 2006), and thus the lessons, and the type of knowledge they generate, have a strong tendency to be applied, transdisciplinary and highly contextualised. The chapters illustrate aspects of the researchers' journeys in navigating the relationships between their workplaces and the academy as sites of learning and knowledge production (Tennant, 2004), but also sites of responsibility and expectation. The nature of these relationships has the potential to create challenges in relation to realising the potential for wider value and impact from professional doctoral research, including through publication (Boud et al., 2021). While models for supporting doctoral practitioner researchers typically prioritise the need for intellectual rigour (Wildy et al., 2015) for busy professionals who may be primarily located outside of the academy, accessing time and support and developing understanding of some of the 'hidden' rules involved in academic production has the potential to present challenges and barriers to traditional forms of academic activity during and postdoctoral study.

In editing this collection, we therefore had two key objectives: First, we sought to bring together a range of high-quality examples of practitioner doctoral research studies which offer valuable, contextualised, insider, perspectives on issues relating to educational policy and professional identity. We believe that these illustrate the often unrealised potential of this form of research and will have value for a range of audiences, including doctoral students, academic colleagues, and education practitioners across a diverse range of contexts. Second, we aimed to utilise the development of this collection as an opportunity to build our practitioner research community, supporting doctoral graduates to share their research findings, to write for publication and to think about their next steps as ECRs. It is worth noting that in the majority of cases, the chapters included here represent the ECR authors' first recognised academic publication of this nature. The following sections will briefly outline how these two central objectives informed the structure of the book and the approach we took to working with the authors during its production.

Structure

The collection is organised into three sections: 'Constructions of the Professional and Society', 'Interrogating Approaches to Being, Becoming and Developing as Education Professionals' and 'Challenging Educational Policy and Practice'. These sections each include chapters addressing topics relating to educational policy and professional identity in a diverse range of contexts, from early years education through to higher and professional education. The structure of the book aims to embrace this contextual diversity, while prioritising a focus on the nature of the contributions and lessons these examples of doctoral studies offer in relation to the collection's substantive focus. We hope that this will encourage readers to reflect on their potential to offer critical perspectives across educational contexts.

Constructions of the Professional and Society

The four chapters in this first section offer insights into the variety of contexts and the various different career points where professionals learn and develop. The contexts represented are early years settings, further education, higher education and the National Health Service (NHS) in England. The studies provide explorations of how professionals negotiate their changing identities, at different career stages and in response to existing or changing policies and practices. The authors use their doctoral studies to expose and explore enduring issues such as power imbalances between professionals, gendered professional identities and two alternative perspectives on hybrid professional identities.

Interrogating Approaches to Being, Becoming and Developing as Education Professionals

The book's middle section contains five chapters set in a range of educational contexts. Two are based in primary schools, one in a further education college and two on teacher education programmes. One primary school focused chapter explores how learning happens in a specific classroom, the other examines the influence of teachers' science backgrounds for those leading the teaching and learning of that subject in their school. The further education focused chapter explores the nature of continuing professional development in the sector, arguing persuasively for a more bespoke approach to provision than currently exists for lecturing staff. The two teacher education chapters centre on different routes into the profession, and how the teacher education programmes pursued impact the process of becoming education professionals.

Challenging Educational Policy and Practice

In the book's final section, the five chapters feature studies seeking to challenge, and illuminate the implications of, a selection of key contemporary educational policies in England. Addressing a range of educational contexts, including primary, secondary, further and higher education, the chapters explore the complexity of policy enactment and the impact this may have on range of stakeholders. As practitioner-researchers, the authors provide important, grounded contributions relating to a range of issues embedded in their own practice and lived experiences and shaped by educational policy in England. These encompass areas including the teaching of sensitive and controversial issues, the enactment of counter-terrorism policy and support for students' mental and emotional health.

Process

The process for developing the collection took place over a period of approximately 18 months and had a pre-planned structure designed to focus on researcher development and building a practitioner-researcher community. The project was allocated some internal funding by the University to support these aspects, and as part of this expressions of interest were invited for an ECR to gain experience as a co-editor, through working with RW and JA as more experienced authors (this role was taken on by Timothy Clark (TC)). A call for abstracts was then issued to recent doctoral graduates from the Department, which resulted in a high level of interest – over 20 were received – and subsequently a selection process to identify the final 14 chapters, which was the maximum number as editors we felt we could accommodate given the collection's word limit. All doctoral graduates were encouraged, but not required, to consider working with a member of their doctorate's supervision team or another colleague with greater experience of academic writing, who could act as a second author and help guide the chapter's development. Two chapters were sole authored by the doctoral graduate alone, 10 by the ECR and one other writer, and two in collaboration with a couple of co-authors. Once the chapters' writing teams were identified, we ran an initial briefing session, at which we provided detailed guidance to all authors, and also facilitated introductions and invited overviews of each proposed contribution. Given the various professional commitments of the authors, this took place as a hybrid session in the evening.

The project then included a number of aspects intended to support our objectives relating to individual researcher development and the strengthening of our wider research community. Firstly, each author was invited to work with their co-author to determine the most constructive approach to their individual roles, and levels of input, into the writing process. Alongside this, they were also paired with the author of another chapter and encouraged to share and discuss their writing, and their challenges, as the work developed, and to provide feedback on each other's drafts as 'critical friends'. Each section of the book also had a lead editor (RW, JA or TC) who acted as a primary point of contact for discussing questions, ideas and requirements throughout the process. At the beginning of the project, a detailed timeline was provided, and this included a series of writing retreat sessions for the authors, providing designated time for writing and promoting further opportunities for connections between contributors. These sessions utilised a format developed by Rowena Murray (Murray, 2012; Murray & Newton, 2009), consisting of designated writing time alongside opportunities to discuss writing objectives and any individual challenges. Authors attending these sessions frequently commented on the significant value they offered in progressing their work. The final key source of support for authors was the production of guidance in response to emerging queries as we progressed. For example, authors were provided with recorded video guidance about getting started on planning their chapters after some had highlighted the potentially overwhelming nature of trying to move from a lengthy doctoral thesis to a distinct chapter which captured key lessons for other postgraduate researchers.

The editing and review process took a similarly supportive approach, with each chapter going through at least three cycles of review and feedback including responses from each of the editors. We developed a feedback template to ensure consistency of editorial approach and that the guidance was clearly structured, enhancing its utility. We 'moderated' our feedback to one sample chapter before the editing and feedback process began in earnest. This aimed to highlight both the strengths of the chapters and areas for potential development, and to adopt a supportive and constructive tone throughout. Regular communications were provided to contributing writers to explain the editing process and authors were encouraged to discuss feedback and revisions with their co-authors.

In addition to these structured aspects for supporting the writing process, we also utilised this collection's development to create additional opportunities for the doctoral graduates to share their work including through conference presentations and other events. Papers arising from this collection were presented at the 2023 BERA and Society for Research into Higher Education (SRHE) conferences, and presentations were given to our university's Education and Childhood Research Group and at postgraduate research seminars. All of these opportunities featured selected authors involved in this book and again in some cases this was the authors' first experience of presenting their work in such fora.

Alongside the valuable contributions, these chapters offer individually, we hope that the collection as a whole, and the editorial process detailed above, will provoke reflections on opportunities for supporting doctoral graduates' and other ECRs' next steps. We also hope to highlight the significant potential of the wealth of knowledge and expertise contained within postgraduate practitioner research of this nature.

References

Bathmaker, A.-M., & Harnett, P. (Eds.). (2010). *Exploring learning, identity and power through life history and narrative research*. Routledge.

Boud, D., Costley, C., Marshall, S., & Sutton, B. (2021). Impacts of a professional practice doctorate: A collaborative enquiry. *Higher Education Research and Development*, *40*(3), 431–445.

Boud, D., & Lee, A. (Eds.). (2009). *Changing practices of doctoral education*. Routledge.

British Educational Research Association (BERA). (2023). *Education: The state of the discipline – A BERA statement*. BERA.

Burnell Reilly, I., & Roffey-Barentsen, J. (Eds.). (2020). *Completing your EdD: The essential guide to the doctor of education*. Emerald Press.

Butcher, J., & Sieminski, S. (2006). The challenge of a distance learning professional doctorate in education. *Open Learning: The Journal of Open, Distance and e-Learning*, *21*(1), 59–69.

Fink, D. (2006). The professional doctorate: Its relativity to the PhD and relevance for the knowledge economy. *International Journal of Doctoral Studies*, *1*(1), 35–44.

Hannover Recommendations. (2019). *Forces and forms of doctoral education 2019*. https://doctoral-education.info/dl/Hannover-Recommendations-DocEd-2019.pdf. Accessed on August 22, 2023.

Murray, R. (2012). Developing a community of research practice. *British Educational Research Journal*, *38*(5), 783–800.

Murray, R., & Newton, M. (2009). Writing retreat as structured intervention: Margin or mainstream? *Higher Education Research and Development*, *28*(5), 541–553.

Research Excellence Framework (REF). (undated). *Overview report by main panel C and sub-panels 13 to 24*. mp-c-overview-report-final-updated-september-2022.pdf(ref.ac.uk). Accessed on November 2, 2023.

Tennant, M. (2004). Doctoring the knowledge worker. *Studies in Continuing Education*, *26*(3), 431–441.

VITAE. (2019). *The concordat to support the career development of researchers*. https://researcherdevelopmentconcordat.ac.uk/. Accessed on November 2, 2023.

Wildy, H., Peden, S., & Chan, K. (2015). The rise of professional doctorates: Case studies of the doctorate in education in China, Iceland and Australia. *Studies in Higher Education*, *40*(5), 761–774.

Wyse, D., Brown, C., Oliver, S., & Poblete, X. (2018). *The BERA close-to-practice research project: Research report*. British Educational Research Association. https://www.bera.ac.uk/researchers-resources/publications/bera-statement-on-close-to-practice-research. Accessed on November 3, 2023.

Section 1

Constructions of the Professional and Society

Chapter 2

Hierarchies of Professionalism in Interprofessional Partnerships for Inclusion: Mapping the Role and Professional Identities of Early Years Educators[1]

Alex Morfaki[a], *Helen Bovill*[b] *and Nicola Bowden-Clissold*[b]

[a]Norland College, UK
[b]University of the West of England, UK

Abstract

Despite the rhetoric emphasising partnership working, there has been a dearth of research related to the educational practices that reify interprofessional partnerships for young children with special educational needs. This doctoral study examined the subtle power shifts in the interactions between early years educators and other professionals against the backdrop of deficit policy discourses and institutional challenges. This research adopted a case study approach and utilised methodological triangulation to unveil educators' phronetic knowledge. The findings point to power differentials and partnership inequities which affect the roles and identities of early years educators. Participants assumed emergent leadership roles that encompassed elements of social pedagogy and pedagogical eclecticism which eschewed medicalised interventions in favour of intuitive pedagogical approaches centred on the child and family.

Keywords: Interprofessional partnerships; early years' educators' roles; identities; special needs; hierarchies of professionalism

[1]This chapter has been developed using extracts from the thesis, Morfaki, A. (2020). *Inclusion in the early years: An exploration of the dilemmas of difference, roles and partnerships in the operationalisation of inclusive practices for children with special educational needs and disability.* Thesis, Faculty of Arts, Creative Industries and Education, University of the West of England.

Critical Perspectives on Educational Policies and Professional Identities, 11–28

doi:10.1108/978-1-83753-332-920241002

Identities and Professionalism Through Insider Research in the Early Years

The professional roles and identities of early years educators have warranted unprecedented attention in recent years as a result of an incessant raft of policy initiatives that aimed to increase childcare provision while professionalising the workforce, improving the quality of care and bridging gaps in attainment (Archer, 2022; Nutbrown, 2021). Ongoing efforts to upskill and professionalise the workforce have been deemed incohesive and inadvertently led to the perpetuation of deficit perceptions of early years educators (Osgood, 2012). Recent reports highlight successive governments' failures to attract and retain staff in the early years sector, which to a large part is attributed to poor working conditions, remuneration and low status (Bonetti, 2018; Pascal et al., 2020).

While issues surrounding qualifications and professionalisation dominate the agenda, distinct areas of practice such as interprofessional collaboration provide unique opportunities to investigate the roles and identities of early years educators, highlighting how the ramifications associated with low status and conditions affect their professionalism. The introduction of Every Child Matters (DfES, 2004) signalled a milestone in the establishment of interagency partnership working, paving the way for integrated working and collaboration to improve welfare and developmental outcomes for children (Oliver et al., 2010). The Special Educational Needs Code (DfE & DoH, 2015) further reinforced the concept of joint working and called for increased collaboration between educators, parents and other professional partners (Hellawell, 2018). This alluded to an expansion of the roles of the early years workforce (Edwards et al., 2012). Cohesive initiatives to provide training opportunities that would prepare the workforce for their new roles and responsibilities were less forthcoming (Richards, 2021).

This chapter reports on the findings of doctoral research conducted in the Southwest of England during 2016–2019 and adopted a qualitative case study approach, which comprised interviews and focus group discussion with 15 early years educators. The aim was to explore interprofessional partnerships for inclusion formulated between early years educators, other professionals and parents within naturalistic settings (Swarnborn, 2010). At the centre of case study lies phronetic knowledge which brings 'together stories from one's horizon of meaning but understood from one's own' (Thomas, 2010, p. 579).

This project moved away from the traditional notions of theory which presupposes the exploration of a process from a distance (Citton, 2012). Instead, it focused on seeking the unpredictability of stories, exploring the fluidity of roles shaped by unspoken values (Egan, 2004) and the challenges emerging through institutionalised struggles (Holland & Lave, 2009) from the proximity afforded by an insider's perspective. The first author was a practising educator at the time of the research, who chose to conduct research with colleagues while acknowledging the ethical dilemmas of researching within one's own cultural and organisational context (Alvesson, 2003). The second and third author constituted the supervising team during the research lending expertise and experience on the subject.

The intentions of an insider educational researcher have been viewed with scepticism (Sikes, 2006) yet an insider perspective could give rise to valuable, situated knowledge that is fully conversant with the complex organisational realities of a community of practice (Brannick & Coghlan, 2007). Such knowledge could serve to deepen the understanding of the perceptions and practices of this community. Although studying one's own professional community presents methodological and ethical challenges, its contribution to doctoral studies has been underestimated particularly with relation to unveiling the tacit values and practices of professionals thus providing insights into areas of practice that remain misunderstood or inaccessible to 'outsider' researchers. Researching with colleagues is neither atheoretical, nor apolitical. While one should be mindful of the ethical implications of misrepresenting voices, the potential for advocacy and the unveiling of the specificities associated with roles and the formation of identities is more likely to emerge from within (Harwood et al., 2013; Osgood, 2012).

Introduction: A Distinct Professionalism?

This chapter utilises stories to unveil the pedagogical and professional praxis of early years educators supporting children with special educational needs and disabilities (SEND) in partnerships with families and other professionals. The expansion of professional boundaries associated with interprofessional partnerships (Edwards et al., 2012) creates action spaces (Boylan & Woolsey, 2015). These spaces afford opportunities for early years educators to carve their own paths and reclaim their professional identity (Dreier, 2009). The challenges encountered and the power asymmetries formulated during interprofessional partnerships are explored to highlight how roles and identities are reformed within the nexus of SEND professionalism.

The development of professionalism and a distinct identity in early years has been viewed as a process which is 'socially constructed and culturally determined' (Simpson, 2010, p. 6), enacted in communities and formulated in practice (Egan, 2004). Identities and roles are interlinked and formed and reformed 'in action' (Holland & Lave, 2009), as early years educators act and interact with others within their community and beyond. This chapter considers how this ongoing process helps early years educators become enculturated into the tacit values that govern their community. The professionalism of early years educators has been considered a top-down approach, dictated in part by government discourse (Archer, 2022; Ball, 2015), enshrined into feminine stereotypes and a historicity of unqualified care (Osgood, 2012). However, voices from studies exploring early years educators' professionalism attest to their capability to develop agentic responses, formulate their own trajectories (Dreier, 2009) and author their professional stories (Payler & Georgeson, 2013; Simpson, 2010; Urreitta, 2007).

The authors of this chapter refrain from adopting a deterministic approach to the formation of agency and identity (Taggart, 2011), which is seen as wholly constrained by sociocultural and institutional challenges. The findings of this research point to early years educators' capacity to overcome challenges and provide meaningful inclusive provision for the children in their care. Equally, we argue that their professional trajectory can reach a glass ceiling (Pascal et al., 2020). Early years educators' contribution to the education of children with SEND has been underestimated and critiqued (HM Government, 2023). The accountability imposed upon them by neoliberal regimes fails to account for the fragmentation of the sector and conflicting attempts by successive governments to re-regulate and de-regulate it (Archer, 2022). This research adds to the voices of prominent researchers in the field (Archer, 2022; Nutbrown, 2021). These voices call upon governments and policymakers to deconstruct the Early Years Education and Care (ECEC) sector in its current state and reconstruct a new field which strives for equity and respect and is underpinned by cohesive and well-funded policy initiatives.

Theorising Early Years Educators' Professional Roles and Identities in Interprofessional Partnerships for Inclusion

The variance of qualifications (Nutbrown, 2021) noted across the early years sector has prevented the introduction of a universal training qualification to support early years educators in the implementation of the SEND Code. Whereas qualified teachers in schools were expected to complete a postgraduate qualification within a specified timeframe when undertaking the role of Special Educational Needs Co-ordinator (SENCo), early years practitioners had to contend with short training courses provided by local educational authorities (Richards, 2021). Only recently has accredited training for Early Years SENCos is been established (DfE, 2022). This 'anomaly' in training between school and Early Year SENCos remains (Layton, 2005). Early years practitioners have been expected to implement the SEND Code and apply the new requirements with variable support provided by local educational authorities (Richards, 2021). This, in combination with the disparate funding arrangements provided to educational authorities (Pascal et al., 2020), accounts for the significant variations observed among settings with relation to their capacity to include children with SEND and support them effectively (Sales & Vincent, 2018).

In their attempts to promote inclusion, early years educators are called to make decisions which are underpinned by ethical considerations and moral dilemmas (Norwich, 2014; Rose & Norwich, 2014). These complex decisions are not taken in isolation and presuppose the involvement of various professionals. The intersection of professionals in the enactment of collaborative inclusive practice is framed within cultural, structural and institutional constraints (Hall, 2005; Salmon, 2004). Despite studies pointing to the importance of shared agendas and aims, these do not materialise unproblematically in practice (Palikara et al., 2019) and invariably lead to the fragmentation of provision which impacts the welfare of children and their families (Sloper, 2004). Ideological alignment may be hard to achieve among professionals of diverse backgrounds who have historically been used to working within different contexts. Boundaries within and between roles and professions become institutionalised and can lead to power imbalances and inequalities among partners (Griffin, 2010). The barriers to multiagency partnerships erected by institutional, cultural and organisational structures have been reported widely in studies that explore social and healthcare professionals' roles (Abbott et al., 2005; Griffin, 2010; Salmon, 2004). In contrast, there has been a dearth of studies exploring the enactment of multi-professional partnerships between early years educators and other professionals (Palikara et al., 2019).

Wenger (2000, p. 233) asserts that learning at the boundaries of communities of practice is enhanced for 'individuals and communities when experience and competence are in close tension'. The established tensions in multiagency partnerships – against a backdrop of incessant educational diktats and ambivalent political agendas – should provide a space for action where early years educators could negotiate their positionality and constitute their own professional identity (Urietta, 2007). In view of the increased demands placed upon the early years workforce to provide inclusive provision for diverse children populations, it becomes critical to map the professional roles and responsibilities of early years educators into new structures.

Methodology

The participants in this study were selected based on their capacity to bring the phenomenon under study (Thomas, 2011) to the fore. The study used narration of critical events and professional stories. Participants were SENCos and early years educators tasked with establishing interagency partnerships to meet the needs of children with SEND and families. They were deployed in settings that fell under the remit of Bristol and South Gloucestershire local authorities at the time of the study.

All 15 participants were qualified educators: four possessed degrees and qualified teacher status (QTS), two held the postgraduate SENCo award and a third was working towards a Master's degree qualification at the time of the study, one held a Foundation degree, three held Early Years Teachers' status and four held National Vocational Qualifications or an NNEB in fields related to early years. The variety of qualifications reflects the disparity and plethora encountered in the early years sector in England and represents participants who held the international equivalent of tertiary education certificates, intermediate (foundation) and bachelors' degrees as well as more generalist postgraduate degrees and specialist postgraduate qualifications.

The theoretical lenses applied to interpret the narratives involved 'bricolage', a concept traced back to Claude Levi-Strauss (Citton, 2012). When applied to theory, bricolage advocates the explication of a process through the adoption of theoretical polytheism which embraces the in-disciplinarity of life which does not conform with the linearity and predictability of a singular theory. The analysis of the data set followed the phases of thematic analysis identified by Braun and Clarke (2006) and was guided by an abductive reasoning approach that combined a dialogue between inductive and deductive logic (Pearce, 2012). The former provided an initial theoretical framework for the coding of tentative themes while the latter enabled the researcher to become surprised by the findings (Thomas, 2010) and review literature, expand upon codes and construct new themes. The themes reflected the experiences of educators and narrated stories that flowed organically and presented plausible evidence (Polkinghorne, 2007).

The research design adopted methodological triangulation (Natow, 2020) through interviews and focus group discussions. The interviews were conducted with seven Early Years SENCos deployed in a variety of early years settings; six of the SENCos were working in private, voluntary and independent settings (PVI) and one in a maintained children's centre. Concurrently, the first author held focus group discussions attended by eight participants in the independent setting where she was employed at the time of the research. The combination of interviews and focus groups discussions can enhance the explication of a process by zooming in and out, thus allowing individual and collective views to emerge and converge or diverge to expose situated nuances (Lambert & Loiselle, 2008). This was pertinent to this study which sought to explore individual professional paths and collective values through the exploration of sensitive topics that interviews foster, and the emergence of contextualised, relational values that focus groups elicit.

Interprofessional Partnerships for Inclusion: Tensions, Hierarchies and the Expansion of Roles

The educators' stories and narratives report the intersectionality of various partners in interprofessional partnerships against the backdrop of funding cuts and variable local authority support. Neoliberal thinking imposed by regulatory frameworks results in enhanced accountability and culpability (Archer, 2022). Subtle tensions are unveiled which often lead to power asymmetries and professional hierarchies. Educators respond by expanding their roles to encompass pedagogical leadership and family advocacy.

Partnership working was welcomed by many participants in this study who felt that their involvement was synonymous with good inclusive practice and resulted in advice that could enhance the environment on offer and support the early years educators in altering provision:

> I think working with outside professionals has been great for me and my experience of them supporting the children – just by having somebody else to come in and look at the environment. We see the environment every day and we think it's accessible for children and inclusive, but an outside professional might have other suggestions to make it more beneficial for the children. (Sian, SENCo)

For other educators, partnership working had come to acquire negative connotations as authorities had reportedly failed to develop an infrastructure that was conducive to developing effective partnerships. This had resulted in some educators becoming suspicious about the involvement of other professionals as they felt that their visits placed them under surveillance:

> I think we've been fortunate in our setting because we were fairly new as a team that came in; our council spent a lot of attention on us and made sure that we were comfortable with things. It's meant that we've got quite good relationships with all those people that are external, where I think a lot of settings see them as the enemy or that they're coming to check on us. (Philippa, Early Years Teacher)

The SEND code (2015, DfE and DoH) although clear in its aspirations on inclusive practice devolved responsibility and accountability of its pragmatic and practical interpretation to local authorities and schools (DfE, 2022; House of Commons, 2019). This resulted in local educational authorities creating organisational structures that differed based on the financial restrictions and the specificities framing implementation in respective micro-contexts (Ofsted, 2022). Subsequently, the support offered to settings could vary widely and miscommunication served to erect attitudinal barriers. Equally, participants demonstrated awareness of how top-down systems of working had introduced performative 'responsibilisation' (Ball, 2003; Hellawell, 2018).

> We are failing in general in the system because obviously you have to prove that you're working, you have to prove that you have observed a child, you have to prove that you have things in place.... (Edith, Early Years Professional)

Successive governments' agendas designate early years educators as 'self-governing professionals' whose value and performance are measured by their ability to quantify their pedagogical contribution and input into measurable outcomes (Roberts-Holmes & Bradbury, 2016, p. 601). This has implications for inclusive pedagogy as its effectiveness is not framed solely within a discourse of increasing participation or belonging. Children are thus objectified and serve to meet political agendas; for children with special educational needs, this could lead to 'othering' as they may not meet these externally imposed goals.

The strategies proposed by other professionals were often embedded within a clinical discourse (Ng et al., 2015) and favoured individualistic approaches (Thomas & Loxley, 2007) over educational interventions which revolved around the child and their interests. Although support and input from other professionals was sought by early years educators, the advice provided was not considered applicable within a pedagogical context. The following extract from a discussion between three professionals demonstrates these frustrations:

Lyra: it's good advice, but it's hard to implement, for instance, the external professional came in and did an activity and took two members of staff. We don't have two spare members of staff or a quiet room. It was a quiet room, the child was the only one in it and there were two staff in there to help him engage in the activity.

Edith: And then you need three people to do it because one is taking the photo.

Beatrice: One is holding to support. Really...

Lyra: Do we have three people to do that?

(Lyra, Early Years Practitioner; Edith, Early Years Professional; and Beatrice Early Years teacher)

Early years educators questioned the feasibility of their application on the basis of the constraints imposed by the regulatory requirements of the curriculum and the realities of the early years classroom environment. Yet their critique was not influenced merely by practical considerations but demonstrated resistance, and agentic responses which are centred on their knowledge of the child and their tacit pedagogical insights:

> Sometimes they've given us advice and we've not agreed with it, we might have tried it for a little while because we're open to trying things. We know the children and if we think something works better and we're still achieving the same thing, then we will go with that. I think we've got the confidence to do that. Sometimes it's not like one strategy works for all children on the spectrum. So, it's knowing children as individually as we know all our children and what works for them. (Patricia, SENCo)

Patricia's account foregrounds the confidence that stems from getting to know the child and promotes tailored personalised approaches that meet their specific needs and interests. The knowledge of the child is deemed to be far more valuable. Her assertion aligns with a social model of disability; it eschews the notion of 'one-size-fits-all' approaches (Watson, 2012). Relationships with children are prioritised and seen to lead to intuitively appropriate strategies. The proclaimed confidence enables the adoption of alternative pedagogical provision which is equally effective while the professional 'openness' allows for other professionals' suggestions to be adopted to include 'trial and error' stances. While the multiplicity of input from other professionals is considered conducive to a holistic approach, it could lead to the educational and developmental compartmentalisation of a child and their exclusion from their community of peers as demonstrated by Sian's comments:

> We work with the individual educational plans so we complete those and that often contains input from professionals, but sometimes we can end up with speech and language targets...and

> physio has given us targets and hearing support has given us targets so the child then ends up with 10 targets that they should be working towards which I feel is too much. It's just streamlining and working with the parents to see what they feel is more important for the child. They are, you know, with their peer groups...they want to follow their peers'. (Sian, SENCo)

The early years educators in this study developed an eclectic approach focused on what they considered important for the child and allowed for their inclusion in the established daily routine of the early years setting. The child's participation and sense of belonging were seen to be threatened by attempts to weave externally imposed, disparate targets into activities. These strategies were not consistent with the child's priorities and posed constraints that threatened their autonomy and prevented the development of ownership over their nursery life (Markstrom & Hallden, 2009). In these cases, early years educators advocated for provision that allowed children to develop their own voice and fostered an ownership in the process of support. In doing so, they clearly acted as child advocates, articulating the distinct values that underpinned their decision-making and guided their pedagogical praxis:

> The speech and language therapist advised us to support, for example, two-word sentences with her, so rather than have the generic picture cards...we took photos of her engaging in these activities; she was eating, she was drinking, she was sitting. We made a copy so that the child could also have some ownership over that and have the same pictures at home as well. (James, SENCo)

The accounts of educators frequently conceptualised the children as co-investors (Sebba et al., 2011) in the process of their own learning. Attempts to implement strategies or introduce resources which were not meaningful were resisted and dismissed. The pedagogical assertiveness and eclecticism (Zierer, 2011) demonstrated, coupled with the confidence expressed, designated early years educators as 'experts' in children.

Despite the proclamations of expertise and the resistance against the attempts of other professionals to decontextualise or 'specialise' provision, participants often questioned decisions and expressed self-doubt over their professional abilities to meet the needs of the child:

> If you read and you research how much happens within the first five years, and in the first five years we are failing them, and then we are sending them to school and then what they were meant to do...we haven't given it to them because none of us is really trained. I have the training, but I am not an expert.... (Samantha, SENCo)

Samantha's sense of failure could be partly ascribed to the ethical dilemmas encountered when faced with complex decisions over a child's care or provision;

these are underpinned by multiple, often contrasting, values (Norwich, 2014) and exacerbated in interactions with other professionals. On one hand, early years educators presented a self-assured stance which actively advocated for the child's educational and personal rights, but on the other they appeared heavily reliant upon the reassurance offered by other professionals (Hall, 2005):

> It would be nice to have that professional support coming in because that team are amazing and they've got resources just to say, "Actually I think you're stepping too far ahead but come back and take a smaller step. That's really useful". (Hayley, SENCo)

Hayley's account may be seen as referring to the professional capital of external professionals and emphasised that their 'decisional capital' (Hargreaves & Fullan, 2013) prevailed in the decision-making process of pedagogical strategy implementation. Successive government initiatives to professionalise the early years workforce have pointed to their professional deficits and lack of skill. This has served to undermine the social capital of the workforce, and juxtaposed it to that of traditional, highly regarded professions. The practitioners' accounts exposed a hierarchy of professionalism. The knowledge of the external professionals was thus valued and elevated to a higher order of professionalism (Thomas & Loxley, 2007), while early years educators were assigned the role of the understudy in the newly founded community of practice established through interprofessional partnerships (Wenger, 2000). Issues of dominance and validation came to the forefront and jeopardised the shared aims of an inclusive partnership which is focused on the child and their families. Despite the challenges encountered and self-doubt, early years educators had developed agentic responses and expanded upon their roles to proactively advocate for children and their families. This strength of advocacy can be seen in James' extract:

> We also had to organise a specific transition meeting for Mum. She did not attend the one for the school, so we really had to say to the school, "Please, please come in, and we'll orchestrate it here." because we were having issues with Mum dealing with anyone outside of nursery. We did manage to get them in and meet with her to explain what would happen and how that transition would look but it was a real challenge. (James, SENCo)

The educators in this study had crafted a working knowledge of the complexities of the system, understood its barriers, and the legislative, cultural and institutional frameworks within which multiagency partnerships were operationalised. Equally, they acknowledged that some parents felt ostracised due to their perceived lack of system knowledge and felt unable to advocate for the child (Hodge & Runswick-Cole, 2008). In these cases, early years educators used their capacity to navigate the system to the advantage of the family by acting as advocates and assuming responsibilities which would pave the way for the gradual involvement of other professionals. The role of the family advocate became crucial in the pursuit of inclusion. Good inclusive practice was not limited to the pedagogy in the early years classroom but extended to encompass social pedagogy:

> I've got some lovely examples of where settings have gone above and beyond and done really different things for different families, which has helped them to feel included, to be able to change their provision, to change the way they do things that suits a parent's needs... I think the family work can be even more important sometimes than what they're providing for the children. (Anna, Early Years Advisor)

As social pedagogues, early years educators' roles widened to support parents and act as mediators, putting strategies into place to enable collaboration between services with the aim of addressing the holistic needs of children and their families. The integrated role of the social pedagogue was evident in the accounts of the early years educators in this study but progressed beyond the care of the child to embrace support for the family (Kyriacou, 2009). The increasing calls for inter-agency collaboration in the field of special educational needs and disability have created an interface of practice which remains undefined yet appears to be operationalised by early years educators in their attempts to bridge gaps created by failures occurring in partnerships. Within this interface, early years educators have emerged as 'brokers' (Claridge, 2018; Wenger, 2000) between communities of practice. They have developed strategies that allowed them to navigate the system while supporting children and their families. Their agentic responses demonstrate resistance and resilience in the face of professional hierarchies while their practices promote pedagogical eclecticism and educational partnerships which place the child and family at the heart of pedagogy.

Mapping the Roles of Early Years Educators

The roles of early years educators in interprofessional partnerships for inclusion are multifarious and subject to intense policy regulation (Harwood et al., 2013). The latter places an ever-increasing set of responsibilities upon them which instal them in emergent leadership positions (Clark, 2012) undertaken willingly to support children and their families. The discourse promoting the ubiquity of inclusion and the rhetoric of effective multiagency partnerships has changed 'what they do and who they are' (Ball, 2015, p. 306) Although SEND policy as an unproblematic discourse may have been assimilated and served to constitute educators as subjects of policy reproduction at ground level – who attested to the significance of early intervention and prevalent policy narratives – the reality of practice distanced them from the domination of government agendas, leading to interpretations demonstrating agency and distinct values.

The ethics of care (Osgood, 2012; Shapiro & Stefkovich, 2005;) demonstrated by the participants were governed by their knowledge of the child as a unique individual, whose specific needs and personal requirements were not compatible with 'one-size-fits-all' approaches and strategies that aim to homogenise populations of children with SEND on the basis of their characteristics or condition (Thomas & Loxley, 2007). They designated themselves as the experts in the child and proclaimed pedagogical practices that were carefully tailored to provide children with a sense of ownership which allowed them to exercise some control and agency in their daily lives. The implementation of external advice which was rooted in medicalised interventions was dismissed in favour of 'craft' pedagogical approaches (Florian & Black Hawkins, 2011) that demonstrated pedagogical eclecticism. Their eclecticism was not based on the arbitrary amalgamation (Zierer, 2011) of disparate professional advice but involved higher order skills that enabled them to carefully select appropriate strategies and interpret medicalised interventions into meaningful pedagogical praxis that was situated and remained relevant to the child and the context.

Early years professionals' ethics of profession were guided by values that demonstrated adherence to an emotional discourse that transcended simplistic notions of care (Harwood et al., 2013) to proactively advocate for families, who were deemed to need support (Hellawell, 2017). Their experience of the system had equipped them with the capability to navigate the heavily bureaucratic processes associated with the implementation of the Code and had placed them in positions of trust, enabling them to take the lead, where required, to support transitions and provide families with an extended system of support in the long term. The role of the social pedagogue displaced the emphasis from children's cognitive and developmental progress and favoured a holistic approach to children's well-being (Kyriacou, 2009).

Early years educators acknowledged that there were distinct hierarchies of professionalism governing the special educational needs field. Their role was not afforded the equivalent status and their views were not granted the gravitas associated with medical professionals. Issues surrounding lower status ascribed to early years professionals persevere and lead to power asymmetries in the operationalisation of partnerships. These enduring constructed hierarchies undermine early years educators' professional standing within the special educational needs episteme (Thomas & Loxley, 2007). Although integrated working points to a model of partnership which favours the involvement of various professionals and their contribution to a child's holistic development, the domination of medicalised professions with relation to special educational needs pose challenges to meaningful inclusive pedagogy.

The internalisation of policy discourses, which on one hand emphasise inclusion for children and on the other promote agendas driven by outcomes (Glazzard, 2013; Hellawell, 2018), pose ethical dilemmas for early years educators. These lead to 'pedagogies of discomfort' (Boylan & Woolsey, 2015) and inquiring stances that serve to challenge professional moral codes and establish new ways of working. When ideology and practice collide (Ball, 2015), educators question and critique their own ontological and professional status. Concurrently, the gap between ideology and provision (Castro & Palikara, 2016) creates spaces for action. The tensions emerging when working at the interface of distinct areas become conducive to learning (Wenger, 2000). Early years educators respond to these opportunities by expanding their roles to encompass work with families and social pedagogy within their remit.

This study is a testimony to the capacity of a historically undervalued workforce to step up to the increasing requirements set upon them while demonstrating a commitment to the needs of the children and their families; their ethics of care have resulted in the conceptualisation of situated moral and professional codes which demonstrate pedagogical adaptability placing the child at the centre of well-informed and caring pedagogy. Their capacity to expand their roles despite the challenges imposed by differing agendas and disparate priorities – against the backdrop of funding cuts and accountability demands – attests to professionalism which is polymorphous and resilient. While the new training addressed to Early Years SENCos is a welcome development, the professionalisation of the early years workforce requires an overhaul of the current system governing the ECEC sector. Current attempts to redress issues related to the professionalisation of early years educators fail to view the larger picture and focus on temporary solutions that perpetuate inequality for all involved: the workforce, families and children with SEND.

The recent consultation on SEND (HM Government, 2023) points to a broken system which despite ongoing efforts to improve it, remains underfunded, poorly governed and highly bureaucratic. Issues surrounding parental distrust, fragmented working practices and educators' accountability will persevere unless governments develop cohesive policy initiatives that address the entrenched issues. The increased responsibilities and implications for the professional roles of early years educators in integrated working cannot be resting on the good will of the workforce but have to be redressed. Collaborative networks, training seminars and fora could serve to build shared understandings of meaningful strategies for young children in the face of distinct agendas and modes of working. However, such initiatives will remain tokenistic unless the government implements a universal early years model, which eschews consumer-led and outcome-driven approaches to childcare and education and moves towards a unified and cohesive approach (Cohen et al., 2021). Until then, early years educators' 'failures' should not be ascribed to their inefficient training or status but reflect on the failure of a whole system to support the early years workforce, the children in their care and their families.

References

Abbott, D., Townsley, R., & Watson, D. (2005). Multi-agency working in services for disabled children: What impact does it have on professionals? *Health and Social Care in the Community*, *13*(2), 155–163. https://doi.org/10.1111/j.1365-2524.2005.00543.x

Alvesson. (2003). Methodology for close up studies: Struggling with closeness and closure. *Higher Education*, *46*(2), 167–193. https://doi.org/10.1023/A:1024716513774

Archer, N. (2022). Uncovering the discursive "borders" of professional identities in English early childhood workforce reform policy. *Policy Futures in Education*. 147821032211380–. https://doi.org/10.1177/14782103221138013

Ball, S. (2003). The teacher's soul and the terrors of performativity. *Journal of Education Policy*, *18*(2), 215–228. https://doi.org/10.1080/0268093022000043065

Ball, S. (2015). What is policy? 21 years later: Reflections on the possibilities of policy research. *Discourse*, *36*(3), 306–313. https://doi.org/10.1080/01596306.2015.1015279

Bonetti, S. (2018). *The early years workforce: A fragmented picture*. [online]. Education Policy Institute.

Boylan, & Woolsey, I. (2015). Teacher education for social justice: Mapping identity spaces. *Teaching and Teacher Education*, *46*, 62–71. https://doi.org/10.1016/j.tate.2014.10.007

Brannick, T., & Coghlan, D. (2007). Defense of being 'native': The case for insider academic research. *Organizational Research Methods*, *10*(1), 59–74. https://doi.org/10.1177/1094428106289253

Braun, V., & Clarke, V. (2006). Using thematic analysis in psychology. *Qualitative Research in Psychology*, *3*(2), 77–101. https://doi.org/10.1191/1478088706qp063oa

Castro, S., & Palikara, O. (2016). Mind the gap: The new special educational needs and disability legislation in England. *Frontiers in Education (Lausanne)*, *1*. https://doi.org/10.3389/feduc.2016.00004

Citton, Y. (2012). From theory to bricolage: Indiscipline and the exemplary gestures of interpretation. *International Social Science Journal*, *63*(207–208), 53–66. https://doi.org/10.1111/issj.12013

Claridge, T. (2018). Functions of social capital – Bonding, bridging, linking. *Social Capital Research & Training*. [online]. https://www.socialcapitalresearch.com/wp-content/uploads/2018/11/Functions-of-Social-Capital.pdf

Clark, R. M. (2012). "I've never thought of myself as a leader but...": The early years professional and catalytic leadership. *European Early Childhood Education Research Journal*, *20*(3), 391–401. https://doi.org/10.1080/1350293X.2012.704762

Cohen, B., Moss, P., Petrie, P., & Wallace, J. (2021). "A new deal for children?" – What happened next: A cross-national study of transferring early childhood services into education. *Early Years*, *41*(2–3), 110–127. https://doi.org/10.1080/09575146.2018.1504753

Department for Education & Department of Health. (2015). *Special educational needs and disability code of practice: 0 to 25 years: Statutory guidance for organisations which work with and support children and young people who have special educational needs or disabilities*. https://assets.publishing.service.gov.uk/government/uploads/system/uploads/attachment_data/file/398815/SEND_Code_of_Practice_January_2015.pdf

Department for Education. (2022). *Early years level 3 SENCO qualification specification*. https://assets.publishing.service.gov.uk/government/uploads/system/uploads/attachment_data/file/1047228/Level_3_Early_Years_SENCO_Qualification_Specification.pdf

Department for Education and Skills. (2004). *Every child matters: Next steps*. DfES.

Dreier, O. (2009). Persons in structures of social practice. *Theory & Psychology*, *19*(2), 193–212. https://doi.org/10.1177/0959354309103539

Edwards, A., Lunt, I., & Stamou, E. (2012). Inter-professional work and expertise: New roles at the boundaries of schools. In *Anon (2012)* (p. 240). SAGE Publications Ltd.

Egan, B. A. (2004). Constructing a professional identity: Some preliminary findings from students of early years education. *European Early Childhood Education Research Journal, 12*(2), 21–32. https://doi.org/10.1080/13502930485209401

Florian, L., & Black-Hawkins, K. (2011). Exploring inclusive pedagogy. *British Educational Research Journal, 37*(5), 813–828. https://doi.org/10.1080/01411926.2010.501096

Glazzard, J. (2013). A critical interrogation of the contemporary discourses associated with inclusive education in England. *Journal of Research in Special Educational Needs, 13*(3), 182–188. https://doi.org/10.1111/1471-3802.12018

Griffin, M. (2010). Getting to know you? Issues of trust and mistrust in understanding community, developing partnerships and delivering policy change in children's services. *Early Child Development and Care, 180*(7), 879–888. https://doi.org/10.1080/03004430802524974

Hall, E. (2005). "Joined-up working" between early years professionals and speech and language therapists: Moving beyond "normal" roles. *Journal of Interprofessional Care, 19*(1), 11–21. https://doi.org/10.1080/13561820400021759

Hargreaves, A., & Fullan, M. (2013). The power of professional capital. *Journal of Staff Development, 34*(3), 36.

Harwood, D., Klopper, A., Osanyin, A., & Vanderlee, M.-L. (2013). "It's more than care": Early childhood educators' concepts of professionalism. *Early Years, 33*(1), 4–17. https://doi.org/10.1080/09575146.2012.667394

Hellawell, B. (2017). A review of parent-professional partnerships and some new obligations and concerns arising from the introduction of the SEND code of practice 2015. *British Journal of Special Education, 44*(4), 411. https://doi.org/10.1111/1467-8578.12185

Hellawell, B. (2018). "There is still a long way to go to be solidly marvellous": Professional identities, performativity and responsibilisation arising from the SEND code of practice 2015. *British Journal of Educational Studies, 66*(2), 165–181. https://doi.org/10.1080/00071005.2017.1363374

HM Government. (2023). *SEND review: Right support, right place, right time government consultation on the SEND and alternative provision system in England.* [Online]. https://assets.publishing.service.gov.uk/government/uploads/system/uploads/attachment_data/file/1063620/SEND_review_right_support_right_place_right_time_accessible.pdf

Hodge, N., & Runswick-Cole, K. (2008). Problematising parent-professional partnerships in education. *Disability & Society, 23*(6), 637–647. https://doi.org/10.1080/09687590802328543

Holland D., & Lave J., 2009),Social practice theory and the historical production of persons, *Action: An International Journal of Human Activity Theory, 2*(2009), 1–15.

House of Commons. (2019). *Special educational needs and disability*. First Report of Session, House of Commons [Online]. https://committees.parliament.uk/publications/2067/documents/19714/default/

Kyriacou, C. (2009). The five dimensions of social pedagogy within schools. *Pastoral Care in Education*, *27*(2), 101–108. https://doi.org/10.1080/02643940902897681

Lambert, S., & Loiselle, C. G. (2008). Combining individual interviews and focus groups to enhance data richness. *Journal of Advanced Nursing*, *62*(2), 228–237. https://doi.org/10.1111/j.1365-2648.2007.04559

Layton, L. (2005). Special educational needs coordinators and leadership: A role too far? *Support for Learning*, *20*(2), 53–60. https://doi.org/10.1111/j.0268-2141.2005.00362.x

Markstrom, A.-M., & Hallden, G. (2009). Children's strategies for agency in preschool. *Children & Society*, *23*(2), 112–122. https://doi.org/10.1111/j.1099-0860.2008.00161.x

Natow. (2020). The use of triangulation in qualitative studies employing elite interviews. *Qualitative Research: Quaternary Research*, *20*(2), 160–173. https://doi.org/10.1177/1468794119830077

Ng, S., Lingard, L., Hibbert, K., Regan, S., Phelan, S., Stooke, R., Meston, C., Schryer, C., Manamperi, M., & Friesen, F. (2015). Supporting children with disabilities at school: Implications for the advocate role in professional practice and education. *Disability & Rehabilitation*, *37*(24).

Norwich, B. (2014). Recognising value tensions that underlie problems in inclusive education. *Cambridge Journal of Education*, *44*(4), 495–510. https://doi.org/10.1080/0305764X.2014.963027

Nutbrown, C. (2021). Early childhood educators' qualifications: A framework for change. *International Journal of Early Years Education*, *29*(3), 236–249. https://doi.org/10.1080/09669760.2021.1892601

Office for Standards in Education (Ofsted). (2022). *The annual report of his majesty's chief inspector of education, children's services and skills 2021/2*. [Online]. https://www.gov.uk/government/publications/ofsted-annual-report-202122-education-childrens-services-and-skills/the-annual-report-of-his-majestys-chief-inspector-of-education-childrens-services-and-skills-202122

Oliver, C., Mooney, A., & Statham, J. (2010). *Integrated working: A review of the evidence*. Children's Workforce Development Council. [Online]. https://dera.ioe.ac.uk/3674/1/Integrated_Working_A_Review_of_the_Evidence_report.pdf

Osgood, J. (2012). *Narratives from the nursery negotiating professional identities in early childhood*. Routledge.

Palikara, O., Castro, S., Gaona, C., & Eirinaki, V. (2019). Professionals' views on the new policy for special educational needs in England: Ideology versus implementation. *European Journal of Special Needs Education*, *34*(1), 83–97. https://doi.org/10.1080/08856257.2018.1451310

Pascal, C., Bertram, T., & Cole-Alback, A. (2020). *Early years workforce review: Revisiting the nutbrown review: Policy and impact*. Sutton Trust.

Payler, J., & Georgeson, J. (2013). Personal action potency: Early years practitioners participating in interprofessional practice in early years settings. *International Journal of Early Years Education*, *21*(1), 39–55. https://doi.org/10.1080/09669760.2013.771322

Pearce, L. D. (2012). Mixed methods inquiry in sociology. *American Behavioral Scientist*, *56*(6), 829–848. https://doi.org/10.1177/0002764211433798

Polkinghorne, D. E. (2007). Validity issues in narrative research. *Qualitative Inquiry*, *13*(4), 471–486.

Richards, H. (2021). EHCP implementation in the early years: Constrictions and possibilities. *Support for Learning*, *36*(2), 204–221. https://doi.org/10.1111/1467-9604.12351

Roberts-Holmes, G., & Bradbury, A. (2016). Governance, accountability and the datafication of early years education in England. *British Educational Research Journal*, *42*(4), 600–613. https://doi.org/10.1002/berj.3221

Rose, J., & Norwich, B. (2014). Collective commitment and collective efficacy: A theoretical model for understanding the motivational dynamics of dilemma resolution in inter-professional work. *Cambridge Journal of Education*, *44*(1), 59–74. https://doi.org/10.1080/0305764X.2013.855169

Sales, N., & Vincent, K. (2018). Strengths and limitations of the education, health and care plan process from a range of professional and family perspectives: Education, health and care plans. *British Journal of Special Education*, *45*(1), 61–80. https://doi.org/10.1111/1467-8578.12202

Salmon, G. (2004). Multi-agency collaboration: The challenges for CAMHS: Multi-agency collaboration. *Child and Adolescent Mental Health*, *9*(4), 156–161. https://doi.org/10.1111/j.1475-3588.2004.00099.x

Sebba, J., Peacock, A., DiFinizio, A., & Johnson, M. (2011). Personalisation and special educational needs. *Journal of Research in Special Educational Needs*, *11*(3), 203–224. https://doi.org/10.1111/j.1471-3802.2010.01189.x

Shapiro, J. P., & Stefkovich, J. A. (2005). *Ethical leadership and decision making in education: Applying theoretical perspectives to complex dilemmas* (2nd ed.).

Sikes (2006). On dodgy ground? Problematics and ethics in educational research. *International Journal of Research and Method in Education*, *29*(1), 105–117. https://doi.org/10.1080/01406720500537502

Simpson, D. (2010). Being professional? Conceptualising early years professionalism in England. *European Early Childhood Education Research Journal*, *18*(1), 5–14. https://doi.org/10.1080/13502930903520009

Sloper, P. (2004). Facilitators and barriers for co-ordinated multi-agency services. *Child: Care, Health and Development*, *30*(6), 571–580.

Swanborn, P. (2010). Case study research: What, why and how? In *Case study research: What, why and how?* (1st ed.). SAGE Publications Ltd. https://doi.org/10.4135/9781526485168

Taggart, G. (2011). Don't we care?: The ethics and emotional labour of early years professionalism. *Early Years*, *31*(1), 85–95. https://doi.org/10.1080/09575146.2010.536948

Thomas, G. (2010). Doing case study: Abduction not induction, phronesis not theory. *Qualitative Inquiry*, *16*(7), 575–582. https://doi-org.ezproxy.uwe.ac.uk/10.1177/1077800410372601

Thomas, G. (2011). The case: Generalisation, theory and phronesis in case study. *Oxford Review of Education*, *37*(1), 21–35. https://doi.org/10.1080/03054985.2010.521622

Thomas, G., & Loxley, A. (2007). *Deconstructing special education and constructing inclusion* (2nd ed.). Open University Press.

Urrieta, L. (2007). Figured worlds and education: An introduction to the special issue. *The Urban Review*, *39*(2), 107–116. https://doi.org/10.1007/s11256-007-0051-0

Watson, N. (2012). Theorising the lives of disabled children: How can disability theory help? *Children & Society*, *26*(3), 192–202. https://doi.org/10.1111/j.1099-0860.2012.00432.x

Wenger, E. (2000). Communities of practice and social learning systems. *Organization*, *7*(2), 225–246. https://doi.org/10.1177/135050840072002

Zierer, K. (2011). Pedagogical eclecticism. *Journal of Educational Thought*, *45*(1), 3–19.

Chapter 3

Professional Identity Within Changing Healthcare Roles: Exploring the Third or Hybrid Space[1]

Sally Moyle[a] *and Richard Waller*[b]

[a]University of Worcester, UK
[b]University of the West of England, UK

Abstract

The ever-changing landscape of healthcare policy has impacted significantly on the development of nursing roles (Lloyd–Rees, 2016), and consequently seen the growth and transformation of existing professions and introduction of new healthcare roles. While the Emergency Nurse Practitioner (ENP) role is now well established within urgent care settings, it has evolved in an adhoc manner, responding to service demand. This has resulted in varying levels of job satisfaction and inconsistency in titles, uniform and scope of practice.

Using photographs or images to describe their perceptions of the role, experience and perceived professional identity, participants reported moving away from their traditional nursing practice into something different that bought new challenges and often conflict. Applying Bhabha's (1994) concept of the 'third space' to our findings suggests that ENPs have adopted a hybrid role that is operating within a 'third (or hybrid) space', where new identity is formed. Our participants' uncertainty around this (and that of others) could negatively impact the development of professional identity during transition into this new role.

[1]This chapter has been developed using extracts from the thesis, Moyle, S. (2017). *Identity crisis within the role of the emergency nurse practitioner? An exploration of autonomy and identity*. Thesis, Faculty of Arts Creative Industries and Education, University of the West of England, Bristol.

Critical Perspectives on Educational Policies and Professional Identities, 29–45

doi:10.1108/978-1-83753-332-920241003

Keywords: Healthcare policy; new roles; third or hybrid space; identity; emergency nurse practitioners

Sally's Professional Story and Context

My interest in professional identity began in the early 2000s when I was developing an academic programme of study for the emerging role of the Emergency Nurse Practitioner (ENP). I had been a practising ENP in the early 1990s and was one of the first to deliver the service in the hospital where I worked, having undergone a brief in-house two-week education programme without formal academic accreditation. I learnt the role 'on the job,' relying heavily on senior doctors to help and guide me. In the mid-1980s, the nursing regulator at that time started to push towards a radical change to nurse education, with a move into higher education (HE) to develop a different type of nurse, one who questioned, critiqued and was able to respond to the complex health system (UKCC, 1999). When I moved into working in HE, I was tasked with setting up one of the first accredited programmes to develop the role. This took the form of a level six and level seven (undergraduate final year and Master's degree, respectively) continual professional development (CPD) short course (which later evolved into a PG Certificate as part of a Master's Degree in Advanced Practice). Since then, role expansion has become commonplace across many disciplines and I have listened with interest and frustration to countless tales from students who are unsure of their role, their title and scope of practice. Today, Advanced Clinical Practice (ACP) is framed around a well-defined, competency-based curriculum (HEE, 2017).

However, practitioners who have moved into these new occupations still cite uncertainty around their role and there remain differences over pay, titles and working conditions (Lloyd-Rees, 2016). While there have been attempts to standardise the role in recent years, there is a body of evidence suggesting that varying levels of scope of practice, lack of standardised education pathways and role clarity exist (Anderson et al., 2020). However, there is less research on how these issues impact on perceived professional identity, and how this relates to job satisfaction, retention and the role's success within an organisation.

Introduction

This chapter explores the concept of professional identity through a group of practitioners (n = 13) who participated in a study conducted by the first author (SM) (and supervised by the second, RW), exploring their experience within the role and perceptions of professional identity. Using photo (or image) elicitation and focus groups to explore their perceptions, several themes emerged in the original study. Concepts such as 'hybridity', 'third space' and transitions are explored in this chapter in light of the findings.

Policy Context

Demand for NHS services continues to increase year-on-year with the population in England predicted to increase by 4.2% over the next 15 years (NHSE, 2023). This, alongside an ageing population, will result in increasing levels of service delivery complexity and a continual rise in multimorbidity and frailty. The recent publication of the NHSE Long Term Workforce Plan (LTWP) (NHSE, 2023) predicts that by 2030, two-thirds of people over 65 will have multiple health conditions and a third of those will have mental health needs. The ever-changing landscape of healthcare has had a significant impact on the development of expanding nursing roles both within the United Kingdom and internationally and has seen the growth and transformation of existing professions and the introduction of new roles (Hoskins, 2011). The LTWP (NHSE, 2023) suggests that new roles such as Advanced Clinical Practitioner (ACP) and Physician Associate (PA) need to grow and will become an integral part of delivering a different model of care by harnessing digital and technological innovations.

At the time of the study, the NHS Five Year Forward View (DH, 2017) demanded a workforce that worked 'across organisation and sector boundaries' promising education and training that '*equips the current workforce with the skills and flexibility to deliver new models of care*' (DH, 2017, p. 30). This was an important policy initiative of that time, with the development of the ENP role and others being a direct response to this and other policy initiatives that precede it.

The ENP role evolved against this backdrop and alongside the gradual development of a formal education programme to support the role. However, the more recent emergence of the ACP (with a well-defined role definition and education programme) has led some practitioners to further question the role definition of the ENP, and it remains uncertain where it sits along the advanced practice continuum. It is evident that despite a lack of standardisation in role definition and scope of practice, the role of the ENP, as noted by Lloyd-Rees (2016), is a well-established role and one that continues to evolve within all urgent care settings both nationally and internationally (Anderson et al., 2020).

Fig. 3.1 is a conceptual map that draws together the evolution of advanced practice against the backdrop of policy drivers for change incorporating the educational developments that have underpinned the evolution of the role to date.

Research Methods

Focus groups were selected as the primary method of data collection, followed by two single semi-structured interviews to offer a different perspective and triangulate results. Data were thematically analysed using Braun and Clarke's (2013) approach. Five broad themes emerged from the data which were further divided into sub-themes. Participants were asked to bring a selection of images which they felt represented their professional identity. Photo (or image) elicitation as a tool for data collection will be discussed later in this chapter. The images themselves were not part of the data analysis, however, participants used them to describe

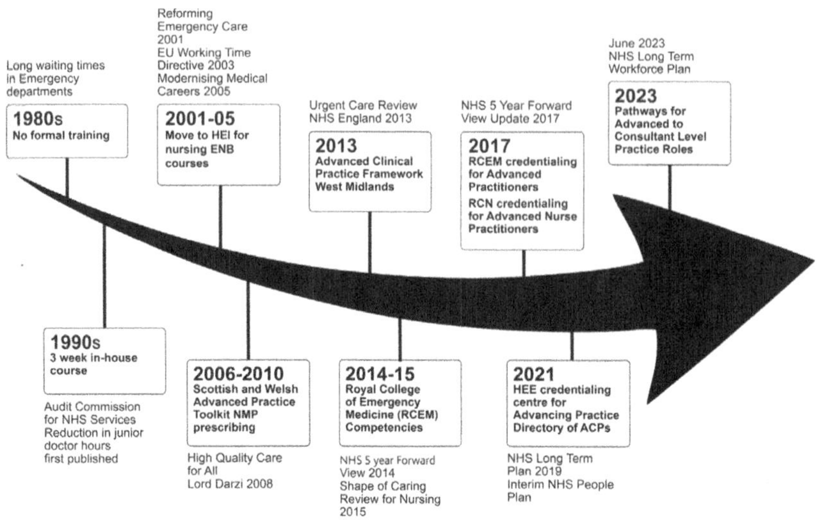

Fig. 3.1. Timeline of the Evolution of Advanced Practice Education and Drivers for Change.

their perceptions of professional identity and bought their voices to the narrative. They were also used to illustrate the theme titles.

The research's aim was to explore aspects of identity and factors influencing it, for example, knowledge, autonomy, relationships and organisational loyalty and, therefore, the focus groups were structured to explore these concepts. Focus groups were selected because their main purpose is to draw upon participants' beliefs, attitudes and feelings by maximising the benefit of group processes (Freeman, 2006). Barbour (2018) explains that group processes can help people explore and clarify their views and attitudes efficiently and encourage participation from those who feel they have little to say. Focus groups, therefore, allowed safe exploration of this, and they were designed to ensure maximum opportunity for exploration of feelings.

The following section highlights the value of participants knowing each other and the relevance of 'insider knowledge', as this was an important aspect for SM as primary researcher, having taught or worked with most of them previously.

The participants in each focus group knew each other. They were selected due to their place of work (rather than being a random sample of ENPs), from across one Emergency Department (ED) and one Minor Injury Unit (MIU). We wanted to explore the experience of ENPs working in two different types of setting (community hospital and acute trust) to compare perceptions around identity (understanding that within the ED there are other health professionals and doctors working together, while at the MIU, ENPs primarily worked alone). We were concerned that if the groups were mixed, it would risk practitioners discussing how their roles differ, rather than concentrating on issues of identity and the influence of colleagues and organisational practise. There are also the practical aspects of getting groups of practitioners from different workplaces together, and the time required to ensure they felt comfortable sharing their experiences. Kruegar and Casey (2014) acknowledge that tensions exist around homogeneity and concede that organisational contexts and practical concerns influence how researchers bring focus groups together. Consequently, the focus groups here were drawn from participants within each organisation separately, rather mixing groups. In addition, the focus groups were small (three and four participants), in part due to pragmatic considerations of releasing staff from clinical shifts and sharing lifts to the focus group location. However, when considering the topic, the experience of participants and potentially intimate nature of sharing their photographs, we felt having smaller groups would facilitate a more informal environment for sharing experiences. The focus group size was tested during the pilot study ($n = 4$), where participants had the opportunity to express their views freely, suggesting the size of group afforded an intimate and safe discussion with all participants having an opportunity to 'have their say'. Participants suggested they felt more comfortable in a smaller group and were able to share photos and experiences freely, producing rich data for analysis.

Insider Knowledge and Ethical Issues

Throughout the research, we were aware of the first author's position within the study. The community of ENPs in the region was relatively small and everyone within that community knew each other, and as ENP programme lead, SM was well-known and highly regarded by them. Participants were keen to be involved in the study, as most had either worked with or had been taught by SM. We were aware this involvement could impact on the research process in terms of subjectivity and bias, with respondents potentially feeling 'pressurised' into consenting to the study due to a perceived power imbalance between the educator-researcher and the participants as past students (Seidman, 2006). Finlay (2002) suggests the researcher should be aware of such bias and endeavour to minimise its impact. To address this, the participants were visited in their place of work, and briefed on the study and given information leaflets. Written consent was gained via email at a later stage, allowing participants to think about their involvement in the study. Social desirability is also a potential problem highlighted within qualitative research, especially when in a group setting, and something that needs careful attention when designing a study. This occurs when participants respond in a manner they think will make them liked or more accepted (Krumpal, 2013). We were aware of this possibility and although traditional characteristics of ED nurses counters such desirability bias (as they are considered open and extrovert (Kennedy et al., 2014), SM attempted to ensure all participants felt comfortable in voicing their opinions by encouraging them to have equal 'airtime' and agreeing ground rules when the discussions started. This was particularly useful when managing a group of participants who are comfortable with each other and is highly recommended.

The position of being an 'insider' within qualitative research can also be beneficial, and actively contribute to the collection and subsequent analysis of data. The participants expressed 'enjoyment' and feeling 'invigorated' at being able to discuss the issues, with some describing it as 'cathartic'. SM's insider knowledge and enthusiasm for the development of the ENP role over many years empowered the participants to feel they could express themselves freely. They described feeling upbeat after the focus group and motivated to develop some form of support network upon returning to work. It is, however, important to acknowledge that SM's professional background undoubtedly influenced how the data were interpreted and this needs further explanation.

It is well recognised within qualitative research methodology literature that the researcher will tell a different story from that told by participants (Braun & Clarke, 2013). Analysis of data involves interpretation, which is informed by the participants' subjective opinions, and the product of analysis often differs from the raw data. For some (Price, 1996), this is disconcerting, and leads to the suggestion of a participatory approach whereby participants are active collaborators in the research process. However, Braun and Clarke (2013) assert that *'the story is our story about the data, not the participants' story, and our story may differ from theirs'* (p. 64). They go on to suggest that it is important to decide whether the analysis will be 'data driven' (the themes will depend on the data), or whether it will be 'theory driven' (the data are approached with specific questions and coded around these). In this study, we decided that the data-driven approach to analysis would be adopted. That is, the emerging themes came from the data. It is important to note, however, that when using this method of data analysis, not all the study's research questions may be answered, as the themes emerge from the data rather than the research questions themselves.

There are other advantages to researching an area with which you are familiar, something linking all professional doctoral researchers. For example, during the focus groups, SM's knowledge of the subject matter enabled the discussion to flow easily since she could interpret colloquial language and acronyms without having to seek clarification. The following quote highlights the advantage of having 'insider' knowledge of the subject matter, since the language used was readily understood and did not need clarification which may have interrupted the conversational flow:

> When I am in navy, I still use my ENP skills, I will request X-rays and do bloods to speed things up, I am part of the nursing team. When I am in black, I am part of the ENP team which is a separate entity. ENP 1

(ENPs in the ED often have dual roles; sometimes they work in the main department as one of the nursing team, and wear navy blue, or they work as an ENP in the minor injury end of the department and wear a black uniform).

Corbin and Buckle (2009) agree, suggesting that the 'insider' researcher can synthesise concepts more quickly. SM was also able to 'push' the discussion on further at times through an ability to interpret the ENPs' understanding of the questions or prompts. RW would not have been able to do this, despite being a significantly more experienced researcher. Corbin and Buckle (2009) recognise that researchers using their own insight and experience have a positive effect on the group dynamic and provide further insight into the participants' responses.

Photograph Elicitation as a Tool for Exploring Participant Perceptions

Images identified by the participants were used as 'prompts' to initiate a discussion about their perceptions of professional identity. It was made clear that they could be either personal photographs or images selected from another source such as the internet. Some participants used their photos (or images) to illustrate their feelings, for example, one participant showed her frustration of the role by showing the group a photo of a woman screaming. Others used them in more general terms, for example, one participant used a picture of a meandering river to demonstrate her 'non-linear' career progression. Studying a group of practitioners who already knew each other was advantageous since they felt more comfortable 'exposing' their images to one another and had already formed relationships within the group and established a level of trust with each other. This had the advantage of not needing time to get to know each other and form relationships that would allow open and honest conversations. Participants were reassured that there were no 'rules' in relation to what type of images they presented. Rather, they were asked to bring any image they felt represented their professional identity. The aim was to create a different conversational dynamic, while adding a layering effect as participants drew on their own photographs and had the opportunity to discuss each other's. During the analysis of the focus group data, participant photographs were used to illustrate the themes that were identified, and to highlight perceptions when they were considered a useful adjunct to the narrative. In this sense, the photographs were as Banks (2000) described, an 'illustration' of the text.

Use of photographs falls into the broad category of visual research approaches and has long been used by anthropologists for documentary purposes or as a tool to aid the research process (Collier & Collier, 1986). Visual aids have been increasingly used within social science research, with most employed to illustrate the narrative rather than analysis of the photograph itself (Banks, 2000). Visual images are also commonly used to elicit information from participants in interviews and are taken either by the researcher for the participant to comment on or by the participants themselves (Heisley & Levy, 1991). Pictures or images used by the participants are considered *'to reflect the participants' views and open a world that the researcher might not otherwise have access to or consider important'* (Warren & Karner, 2005, p. 171). Critics argue there can often be a strong element of bias within this type of data collection because participants may select photographs knowing how they will be represented. However, this could be viewed as similar to a participant answering a question how they think the researcher wants them to. Another method of using photographs is to use pre-existing images. These are more commonly used to reconstruct events, relationships and rituals. Participants might also use pre-existing photographs from the past as a contrast to their current situation, or to indicate a change in their lives (Banks, 2000). Today, many images will undoubtedly come from the internet, allowing participants to expand their ideas and create a different narrative than they might otherwise have with traditional photographs.

Photographs have traditionally been viewed as documenting reality and the 'truth' within research (Bogdan & Biklen, 2006). More recently, however, others suggest that photographs can destabilise the notion of 'truth', and that reality is a 'negotiated version of reality' (Pink, 2005, p. 20), where the researcher and participant bring their experiences together to form the negotiated reality. In this instance, the photographs represent the experience of participants as they see it at that time, which might be different from how someone else views it at another time. Emmison and Smith (2012) suggest that visual data should be thought of not in terms of what the camera can record but of *'what the eye can see'* (p. 4). They argue that photographs are a means of preserving, storing or representing information, rather than a source of data collection. This was certainly true in this study, as the images represented the participants' view at that time. It is quite possible that were the study to be replicated with the same participants, they may well choose different photos and have different stories to tell.

Findings and Discussion

Five themes initially emerged from the data, each with sub-themes. These were considered in light of the literature and theoretical concepts explored within the study. From these five initial themes, three overarching aspects were discussed: the role, career structure and education. Due to word limits in this chapter, only one aspect (the role), which includes concepts of transition, socialisation and the 'third space' as key factors to the role will be discussed here.

The Role

One of the key findings from this study was that participants enjoyed their role and gained a huge amount of satisfaction from the job. Despite acknowledging that they dealt with uncertainty, conflict and a degree of risk management within the workplace, participants described confidence in what they did and were proud of their role:

> The reason I get out of bed in the morning is that I feel important about the job I do and that I feel privileged and trusted to prescribe. It makes my professional identity feel important. ENP 3

> It is something you have earned, we are not just nurses, and not everyone can do it, it is something to be proud of. ENP 7

Participants also reported high levels of job satisfaction and self-confidence relating to delivering high-quality care, clinical expertise and pride from the autonomous nature of the role by delivering the '*whole package*' to patients. Some also reported feelings of uncertainty and frustration and were less confident in other areas of the role including relationships with other nurses, public perceptions of the role, continuing education and career structure, as this participant outlines:

> This is a photo of someone screaming; it represents that we still have to keep screaming about what we do and the role we have. ENP 10

Lloyd-Rees (2016) also examined how ENPs viewed their role in a small qualitative study (n = 8) and found high levels of job satisfaction and motivation despite respondents reporting issues of conflict with other nurses, a lack of understanding of the role outside the ED and concerns around remuneration and lack of clear educational standards for preparing for it.

There is a wealth of literature, for example, Anderson et al. (2020) supporting patient satisfaction within non-medical extended roles, however, there is less literature examining role satisfaction from the emic perspective of the ENP. Hayes et al. (2010) however, identified three variables essential to nurse job satisfaction; inter-personal factors (autonomy, direct patient care, professional relationships and educational opportunities), extra-personal including factors beyond their control such as pay, organisational policy and organisational constraints and intra-personal factors such as personal resilience, education and experience. Desborough et al. (2013) identified similar characteristics in a study examining job satisfaction with a group of ENPs and identified that autonomy within the role was a key factor of satisfaction, but only when coupled with supportive and cohesive professional relationships with both medical and nursing staff. In addition, the ability to deliver high-quality patient care was also identified as a factor supporting positive role fulfilment. Areas that were identified as diminishing satisfaction within the Hayes et al. (2010) study included insufficient access to appropriate education, support and mentorship and lack of role clarity.

Self-confidence and self-esteem are linked to professional identity through the construct of self-concept (Johnson et al., 2012). Positive self-esteem is also linked to positive performance (and job satisfaction) (Bjorkstrom et al., 2008), and as noted previously studies have consistently demonstrated that ENPs perform as well as their medical counterparts in helping reduce waiting times and contributing to patient safety. This suggests that they have a strong sense of self-esteem, confidence and ability around the clinical aspects of the role. Given that self-esteem and confidence impact positively on professional identity, most participants here have a strong sense of professional identity relating to role clarity, clinical expertise and their levels of autonomy. They were, however, less certain about their identity in relation to other 'professional' aspects of their role such as perceptions of others, relationships and education, and their future career options.

The study participants clearly had a sense that they were 'different' from other nurses but were equally clear that they were not doctor substitutes. They tried to articulate what made them different, and for most, the difference was linked to managing risk, litigation and autonomy/responsibility.

> If you make an error or one of your decisions are not sound (that is the risky bit) you know the sharks are underneath you (shows a cartoon picture of a tightrope with sharks circulating underneath). ENP 3

Interestingly, while managing risk and the fear of litigation were important factors in determining what the ENPs did, this did not detract from their overall sense of job satisfaction. These findings are in line with older studies; for example, Tye and Ross (2000) found that managing risk and uncertainty, and a fear of litigation, were factors seen as a barrier to development, and the need for organisational support was apparent. However, despite these barriers, a desire to progress the role boundaries was also evident in both this study and Tye and Ross's (2000).

Our participants also reported feeling disappointed with the lack of understanding of the autonomous nature of the role from senior managers:

> I don't think they (management) understand we do more or less the same the exact same job as our medical colleagues. They don't understand the scope of what we do, but I do think they understand the impact and know a good thing when they see it. ENP 3

> I suppose they see us happily tick away; I don't think they understand us but appreciate we do a good job. I don't think they understand the level of stress and urgent and complex patients we see, even though we give them all the figures. We haven't had huge disasters here and huge incidents and until that happens, they don't understand the level of risk we deal with every day. ENP 6

This was an important finding as retention within the NHS continues to be a challenge (NHSE, 2023) and as job satisfaction is linked to perceived levels of autonomy within the role (Desborough et al., 2013), constraints around this may be impacting on overall job satisfaction and, therefore, impacting on staff retention. In the Pill et al. (2012) study autonomy in decision-making was also identified as a significant component of the ENP's professional identity, but as with others (Desborough et al., 2013), she found factors impeding their autonomy included decisions made by doctors and managers which impacted directly on job satisfaction and arguably influenced their sense of identity.

Role Transition

Participants in this study sensed some sort of 'transition' as they described '*moving away from their traditional nursing roots into something different' ENP 3*. They described being '*somewhere in between' (ENP4)* medicine and nursing, something described elsewhere as moving into the 'third' or 'liminal' space (Bhaba, 1994), whereby practitioners are in moving into new role definitions, boundaries and practices. This is discussed in more detail later in this chapter. Role transition is a key element of successful implementation of the ENP role (MacLellan & Higgins, 2015) as the individual moves from a traditional nursing role into being an ENP as they redefine their role and re-establish themselves within the healthcare team (Santon et al., 2010). Transition involves the nurse moving away from the traditional caring humanistic models of nursing practice and cultures into a sphere of practice incorporating a biomedical model of diagnosis, prescribing and treatment (Santon et al., 2010). The literature examining the transition of nurse to ENP describes the experience as 'uncomfortable', 'difficult', 'stressful' and 'turbulent' (Newhouse et al., 2011).

Some participants in our study identified feeling guilty about the transition as they *'didn't feel like a nurse anymore'* and didn't 'relate to nursing' in the same way.

> Sometimes I feel guilty that I don't feel so much like a nurse anymore, even though that is where you were brought up. That grounding will never leave but I feel like I am almost living beyond that in terms of my role and how I see myself. ENP 2

This echoes the literature around transitioning as ENPs move from a place of comfort and familiarity to a place of unknown territory (MacLellan & Higgins, 2015). Studies have examined the transition of a student nurse into a qualified nurse, and establishing a professional identity within this transition is seen as a key factor in relation to retention and confidence within their new role (Johnson et al., 2012). In the same way that student nurses continue to engage in construction and deconstruction of their identity through clinical practice, interaction with other healthcare professionals and education, it appears that ENPs also undergo a continual change of identity as they transition into a new role through the same processes.

> I think I am separate to both, somewhere in between, so I have a different head to certain nurses, and we have very different opinions to them. I can usually give a good rationale to the nurses on the 'shop floor' why I want to do something, because of the ENP stuff, so I don't necessarily relate to nurses, and I do a bit less nursing (I think) but I am not a doctor, don't want to be one and I don't relate to them either. I think we have our own identity, as an ENP rather than a nurse or doctor, it's a completely separate identity. ENP 4

Bridges (2003) proposes that all transitions have three phases: an ending followed by a neutral zone and finally a new beginning. The first phase (ending) is associated with changing identity as the practitioner loses their status as a nurse but is not yet accepted as an ENP. Bridges describes this loss of identity as the 'in-betweenness', as practitioners describe insecurity and uncertainty and confusion. The second phase (the neutral zone) is described as a period of being 'in limbo' as the ENP feels vulnerable with the new emerging identity and lacks self-confidence. However, also within this phase, new networks are developed and dynamic change and growth takes place. The third phase (new beginnings) involves new attitudes, new values and new identities as the ENP adapts to their role. However, it is important to note that each phase is not time-limited and is a dynamic process with each practitioner moving through the phases at different times and speeds. This has implications for both practitioners and educators when supporting role transition.

Crafter and Maunder (2012) agree, suggesting that the transition process is a period of individual adjustment and an important element in shaping professional identity. They go further, suggesting that each period of readjustment depends not only on the practitioner (and their previous experience and background) but the acceptance and support of the healthcare team within which they work and organisational readiness for such roles in the workforce. In relation to this study, some participants were unsure of their alignment and whether they still felt like 'a nurse'. It would appear from the work of Bridges that some of the ENPs in this study were going through different phases of transition, as some were more experienced than others. It is worth noting here that the acceptance and support of others within the healthcare team also impacts on the transition. Participants in this study, and previous studies (Lloyd-Rees, 2016) described some experiences of conflict from other nurses, uncertainty around teamwork and the perception that senior managers did not understand and support the role, all of which might impact on successful role transition. Previous experience and education preparation is also a key factor in determining successful transition and the development of identity.

Role Socialisation

Professional socialisation is the process whereby individuals acquire and integrate into their lives the expected knowledge, behaviours, skills and attitudes, values, roles and norms deemed appropriate and acceptable to their chosen profession (Pilhammar-Andersson, 1993). Professional identity arguably develops through a process of socialisation, and within health professions, this most commonly takes place during (or before) an educational programme (Wilson & Startup, 1991). If we relate the 'transition' of ENPs to the process of socialisation, ENPs are adapting their 'attitudes', 'values' and 'norms' (Oermann, 1999) as they move into their new roles and re-evaluate their position. It is arguable that the description that participants offered in this study around feelings of 'guilt', 'being separate' and feelings of 'uncertainty' are characteristics of a socialisation process (or transitional process), whereby practitioners are evolving into a new role with a different identity. However, it is worth remembering that both the notion of socialisation and transformation assumes that the role the ENP is moving into has an established and well-defined identity, with the practitioner 'knowing' when they have reached it.

The ENP role has evolved in an ad hoc manner over 30 years, without any formal educational requirements, and with a range of titles and varied role definitions (Anderson et al., 2020). It seems that for many practitioners, working under the umbrella term of 'advanced practice' the lack of role clarity and uncertainty of definition has stopped them successfully transitioning into the third phase. This, in turn, has impacted on their professional identity and understanding of what they are, and left them situated in the second phase feeling isolated, uncertain or 'in limbo' (Bridges, 2003).

The 'Third Space'

Given these concerns, an alternative and arguably more relevant approach to the transitional model described above is offered here, that of the 'third space'. The 'third space' or 'in-between space' describes a phenomenon occurring when two different cultural systems come into contact, and those operating within this space often combine elements of both to create something unique (Jacobs & Brandt, 2012). Our participants articulated feeling that they draw on elements of both nursing and medicine to perform the role. One participant suggested, when showing a picture of a steep bridge, that it represents the 'meeting of minds, between the medical and nursing sides of me' *ENP2*

> It has evolved for me (shows picture of a bridge). This represents the meeting of minds if you like between the nursing and medical side of me. In order for me to do and be the practitioner I have had to merge the nurse and the medical side. ENP 2

This resonates with the work of Bhabha (1994), who suggested that identity within the third space is not an affirmation of a pre-given identity. Similarly, Chulach and Gagnon (2015, p. 55) assert that *'identity for ENPs is actively constructed within a dominant discourse on knowledge, expertise, autonomy and healthcare'*, which aligns with the perceptions of our participants as they continue to use their nursing knowledge and their newly acquired medical knowledge to formulate 'a different knowledge'.

Participants here explained a sense of feeling different and with 'a different head to other nurses' ENP4. This echoes the description of the third space which has been described as *'a "boundary zone" where two cultures meet, hybrid identities take shape and new discourses are created'* (Verbaan & Cox, 2014, p. 2). Our participants also described areas of conflict and tension between themselves and other nurses.

As one noted, junior nurses do not treat them in the same way as they do doctors:

> You don't get treated in the same way as they (the shop floor/ cubicle nurses) treat the doctors, which irritates me. It shouldn't be about 'he is a doctor', or 'she is an ENP', it's about the role you are fulfilling. You do get some that are quite reluctant. I do utilise them for bloods and things, it's not always easy. ENP 2

Similarly, participants highlighted reluctance among some junior nurses to carry out tasks given to them by ENPs. This tension is frequently reported in the literature (e.g. Lloyd-Rees, 2016), and often attributed to a change in role boundary and misunderstanding of roles, as exampled by this participant:

> I don't think I truly understood the role until I started doing it so why would they understand. It's like when you were studying to be a nurse you thought you knew what you were going into and then when you qualify it's like 'oh my god!' ENP 4

However, the notion of the third space goes further, suggesting that as traditional values and practices are scrutinised by others, resulting in cultural clashes (between nurses and doctors and between nurses and ENPs), there is constant renegotiation as boundaries change and redefined identities and cultures emerge with new values, philosophies and practices (Chulach & Gagnon, 2015). Further to this, Rashotte (2010, p. 51) argues that during this period of redefining identity, ENPs often encounter challenges from others related to their constructed identity through their decision-making, clinical expertise and an undermining of their years of experience. This further accounts for the conflicts described in this study (and the literature), and was clearly articulated by one respondent:

> If you don't give them the answers they want, they (junior nurses) will go and ask a doctor, they go up the hierarchy. They put them in a higher esteem. I think they might understand the role, but the role is not valued as highly as it should be. ENP 4

Bhabha (1994) suggests that this failure to recognise expertise and experience, coupled with a lack of recognition for the health outcomes that ENPs can provide, may result in a projected distorted identity for the ENP. Practitioners operating within this space need the skills to strategise and navigate through this turbulent discourse, and as the participants in this study alluded to this can be challenging, leading to feelings of guilt and uncertainty.

Conclusion

Revisiting the study several years later has been a valuable experience and given insight into how to support practitioners moving into new and often complex roles and situations. The assumption that taking on a new (advanced) role with greater autonomy is a simple linear process needs rethinking as practitioners in this study (and others) found the transition difficult, often involving conflict with other colleagues and uncertainty with new (or different) professional identities emerging. Bringing the work of Bhabha (1994) and the concept of the third or hybrid space into the discussion supports this notion and understanding this from the emic perspective of the practitioner could enable educationalists and employers to better support the transition.

Reflecting on the research process has given SM insight into her position as a novice researcher. Having insider knowledge was inevitable given the subject matter and while acknowledging potential challenges, it was certainly a positive position as it allowed her to get close to the subject matter without having to translate language, acronyms and colloquialism during the focus groups. In addition, working with the community of practitioners she knew enabled her to navigate the group dynamics, alongside the practical aspects of getting to the venue and ensuring a safe space which was easier than if the participants were unknown. This is certainly something we would encourage other novice researchers to consider when selecting their participants and method of data collection.

References

Anderson, H., Birks, Y., & Adamson, J. (2020). Exploring the relationship between nursing identity and advanced nursing practice: An ethnographic study. *Journal of Clinical Nursing*, *29*, 1195–1208.

Banks, M. (2000). Visual anthropology: Image, object and interpretation. In J. Posser (Ed.), *Image-based research. A sourcebook for qualitative researchers* (pp. 9–23). Routledge Falmer.

Barbour, R. (2018). *Doing focus groups* (2nd ed.). SAGE Publishing.

Bhabha, H. (1994). *The location of culture*. Routledge.

Bjorkstrom, M., Athlin, E., & Johansson, L. (2008). Nurses' development of professional self-from being a nursing student in a baccalaureate programme to an experienced nurse. *Journal of Clinical Nursing*, *1710*, 1380–1391.

Bogdan, R., & Biklen, S. (2006). *Qualitative research for education. An introduction to theory and methods* (5th ed.). Pearson Pub.

Braun, V., & Clarke, V. (2013). *Successful qualitative research: A practical guide for beginners*. SAGE.

Bridges, W. (2003). *Managing transitions: Making the most of change*. DeCapo Press.

Chulach, T., & Gagnon, M. (2015). Working in a 'third space': A closer look at hybridity, identity and agency of nurse practitioners. *Nursing Inquiry*, *23*(1), 52–63.

Collier, J., Jr., & Collier, M. (1986). *Visual anthropology. Photography as a research method*. University of New Mexico Press.

Corbin Dwyer, S., & Buckle, J. (2009). The space between: On being an insider-outsider in qualitative research. *International Journal of Qualitative Methods*, *8*(1), 54–63.

Crafter, S., & Maunder, R. (2012). Understanding transitions using a sociocultural framework. *Educational and Child Psychology*, *29*(1), 10–18.

Department of Health. (2017). *Next steps on the NHS five year forward view*. Crown Copyright.

Desborough, J., Parker, R., & Forrest, L. (2013). Nurse satisfaction with working in a nurse led primary care walk-in centre: An Australian experience. *Australian Journal of Advanced Nursing*, *31*(1), 11–19.

Emmison, M., & Smith, P. (2012). *Researching the visual* (2nd ed.). SAGE.

Finlay, L. (2002) Negotiating the swamp: The opportunity and challenge of reflexivity in research practice. *Qualitative Research*, *2*(2), 209–230.

Freeman, T. (2006). 'Best practice' in focus group research: Making sense of different views. *Journal of Advanced Nursing*, *56*(5), 491–497.

Hayes, B., Bonner, A., & Pryor, J. (2010). Factors contributing to nurse job satisfaction in the acute hospital setting: A review of recent literature. *Journal of Nursing Management*, *18*, 804–814.

Health Education England (HEE). (2017). *Advanced clinical practice framework*. https://advanced-practice.hee.nhs.uk/. Accessed on October 9, 2023.

Heisley, D., & Levy, S. (1991). Autodriving: A photo elicitation technique. *Journal of Consumer Research*, *18*, 257–272.

Hoskins, R. (2011). Interprofessional working or role substitution? A discussion on the emerging roles in emergency care. *Journal of Advanced Nursing*, 1–8.

Jacobs, H., & Brandt, C. (2012). Opening up a third space to innovate curricula. *The Journal of Social Sciences*, *8*, 420–428.

Johnson, M., Wilson, I., & Young, H. (2012). Professional identity and nursing: Contemporary theoretical developments and future research challenges. *International Nursing Review*, *59*, 562–569.

Kennedy, B., Curtis, K., & Waters, D. (2014). The personality of emergency nurses: Is it unique? *Australasian Emergency Nursing Journal*, *17*(4), 130–145.

Kruegar, R., & Casey, M. (2014). *Focus groups. A practical guide for applied research* (5th ed.). SAGE.

Krumpal, I. (2013). Determinants of social desirability bias in sensitive surveys: A literature review. *Quality and Quantity*, *47*, 2025–2047.

Lloyd-Rees, J. (2016). How emergency nurse practitioners view their role within the emergency department: A qualitative study. *International Emergency Nurse*, *24*, 46–53.

MacLellan, L., & Higgins, I. (2015). Nurse practitioner role transition: A concept analysis. *Journal of the American Association of Nurse Practitioners*, *27*, 389–397.

Newhouse, R., Staniik-Hutt, J., White, K., Johantgen, M., Bass, E., Zangaro, G., & Weiner, J. (2011). Advanced practice nurse outcomes 1990–2008: A systematic review. *Nursing Economics*, *29*(5), 230–251.

NHS England. (2023). *NHS long term workforce plan*. https://www.england.nhs.uk/wp-content/uploads/2023/06/nhs-long-term-workforce-plan-v1.2.pdf. Accessed on September 09, 2023.

Oermann, M. (1999). Developing a teaching portfolio. *Journal of Professional Nursing*, *15*, 224–228.

Piil, K., Kolbaek, R., Ottmann, G., & Rasmussen, B. (2012). The impact of the expanded nursing practice on professional identity in Denmark. *Clinical Nurse Specialist*, 329–335.

Pilammar-Andersson, E. (1993). The perspective of student nurses and their perceptions of professional nursing during the nurse training programme. *Journal of Advanced Nursing*, *18*, 808–815.

Pink, S. (2005). *Doing visual ethnography*. SAGE.

Price, J. (1996). Snakes in the swamp: Ethical issues in qualitative research. In R. E. Josselson (Ed.), *Ethics and process in the narrative study of lives* (pp. 207–215). SAGE.

Rashotte, J. (2010). Knowing the nurse practitioner: Dominant discourses shaping our horizons. *Nursing Philosophy*, *6*, 51–62.

Santon, S., Mihaly, L., Alhusen, J., & Becker, K. (2010). Taking charge of the challenge: Factors to consider in taking your first nurse practitioner job. *Journal of the American Academy of Nurse Practitioners*, *22*(7), 356–360.

Seidman, I. (2006). *Interviewing as qualitative research: A guide for researchers in education and the social sciences*. Teachers College Press.

Tye, C., & Ross, F. (2000). Blurring boundaries: Professional perspectives of the emergency nurse practitioner role in a major accident and emergency department. *Journal of Advanced Nursing*, *31*(5), 1089–1096.

United Kingdom Central Council. (1999). *Fitness for practice*. UKCC.

Verbaan, E., & Cox, A. (2014). Occupational sub-cultures, jurisdictional struggle and third space: Theorizing professional service response to research data management. *The Journal of Academic Librarianship*, *40*, 211–219.

Warren, C., & Karner, T. (2005). *Discovering qualitative methods. Field research, interviews and analysis*. Roxbury Publishing Company.

Wilson, A., & Startup, R. (1991). Nurse socialisation: Issues and problems. *Journal of Advanced Nursing*, *16*, 1478–1486.

Chapter 4

The Impact of Symbolic Violence on the Perceived Choices of Trainee Primary School Teachers: A Poetic Perspective[1]

Laura Manison and Catherine Rosenberg

University of the West of England, UK

Abstract

This chapter explores the theme of symbolic violence (Bourdieu, 2001; Thapar-Björkert et al., 2016), a central theme in my doctoral thesis.

My thesis looked at the experiences of a group of female undergraduate students in their first year of Initial Teacher Education in Primary Education at the university where I teach. I explored the perceived choices my participants made in terms of choosing to become primary school teachers, arguing that symbolic violence is a controlling force in society so powerful and insidious that 'individuals do not question their own role in the production and reproduction of domination and subordination' (Thapar-Björkert et al., 2016, p. 9). Through class and gender, primary school teaching has insidiously presented itself to be a *suitable profession* for young women.

I position myself as a woman from working-class origins who made the choice to become a primary school teacher and who has recognised the impact of symbolic violence. As a result, some of this chapter is written from an autoethnographic perspective. My overarching methodological approach is narrative inquiry and I have used poetry to present my data throughout. My co-author, Catherine, was one of my doctoral supervisors and we were drawn together by our shared investment in narrative and the impact of early experiences on our subsequent selves. For this chapter, we present our own

[1]This chapter has been developed using extracts from the thesis, Shore, L. M. (2022). *Primary school teaching: A classed and gendered profession. Poetically exploring the narratives of female trainee primary school teachers.* Thesis, Faculty of Arts, Creative Industries and Education, University of the West of England, Bristol.

Critical Perspectives on Educational Policies and Professional Identities, 47–64

doi:10.1108/978-1-83753-332-920241004

narrative poems describing the impact of symbolic violence on our own lives alongside that of the participants.

Keywords: Class; gender; symbolic violence; narrative; poetry; autoethnography

Introduction – Setting the Scene

This chapter was born of my – Laura's – interest in the perceived choices that young working-class and middle-class women make to become primary school teachers. I was joined in the writing of this chapter by my former doctoral supervisor, Catherine, our shared interest in narrative methods having brought us together. My doctoral thesis, using narrative inquiry as a methodology, and underpinned by my data, the literature and reflections on my own formative experiences as a young woman, argues that primary school teaching is a classed and gendered profession. My study focused on the perceived 'choices' made by female students to pursue a degree in primary initial teacher education; the sample is presented later in this chapter. As the project developed, my research presented a growing and increasingly convincing argument for the insidious influence of symbolic violence in impacting women's 'choices' – a misrecognition of social coercion as active choice. Scott (2012, p. 531) discusses the concept of misrecognition in identifying symbolic violence, describing it as 'the linchpin in solidifying an amenable relationship between the dominant and the dominated, the haves and have-nots, the powerful and the power-deprived'. What started as one of my theories took on a significance I have since been unable to leave alone and is the aspect of my thesis developed further in this chapter. As my research progressed, I found it increasingly difficult to accept that symbolic violence is not writ large in our collective consciousness; it 'is generated through the subtle inculcation of power relations upon the bodies and dispositions of individuals' (Thapar-Björkert et al., 2016, p. 9). As a society, we are complicit in its hold.

The concept of professional identity and how it interweaves with personal identity is at the heart of the premise of symbolic violence as an invisible force and was a consideration throughout my thesis – an exploration of the perceived 'choices' made by female undergraduate trainee primary school teachers to enter the profession. My data demonstrate how participants had embraced the mantle of teacher from an early age, seeing this as a growing personal identity which, as their teacher education and experience in school settings progressed, shifted towards an embryonic professional identity. Nias (1989) discusses how primary school teachers' personal and professional identities are often conflated in the individual, as was evident in the interviews with participants focusing on themselves as student teachers. Identity is constantly revised and reassessed (Nias, 1989), and I argue that for my participants, this is particularly relevant in establishing themselves simultaneously as students and emerging professionals in a work-based context. Riessman (2008) discusses how the sense of shifting identity – which I had identified my participants were experiencing – aligns with the increased presence of narrative as a credible methodology, particularly in the research field of identity. She suggests identity can no longer be an assumption or 'truth' but must be consciously constructed by individuals and, 'in postmodern times… can be assembled and disassembled, accepted and contested and indeed performed for audiences' (Riessman, 2008, p. 7). Throughout my doctoral research, it became clear how my own experiences had impacted my professional identity and how, as I progressed through my career, my ontological position as a working-class female teacher, then teacher-educator framed how I approached my work and the values that I brought to it. My research had made explicit the concept of symbolic violence for me some time ago, but it became apparent that my participants were insidiously and unknowingly embracing it as part of their personal and professional identity. Having been told by family and friends how good they are with children, their data demonstrate how this had become central to their perceived identity, thereby allowing symbolic violence to embed.

Theoretical Framework – Beyond Bourdieu

My doctoral thesis was underpinned by Bourdieu's (2021) concept of capitals: a way of examining societal inequalities through a lens not based solely on economic advantage but instead taking account of gender, education and class as embedded, yet often invisible forces governing individuals in society. I identified my themes as cultural, economic and social capital, and the later concept of emotional capital (Nowotny, 1981; Reay, 2004). Yet it is indicative of how my work shifted in emphasis that what started as a focus on Bourdieu's capitals almost reframed itself in terms of the centrality of the concept of emotional capital in the context of the data collected from my participants. From a close examination of emotional capital, the relevance of symbolic violence to my work took shape. I embraced the work of Steedman whose book *The Tidy House* (1982) is an elongated story created by three working-class eight-year-old girls about the lives they expect to grow into, framed by an idea of the house they expect to live in. *The Tidy House* powerfully demonstrates how symbolic violence ensures that the girls quietly understand their educational and aspirational limitations. The girls 'play houses' and while Steedman does not present them as passive victims of working-class culture, ultimately the story the children collectively create is a 'symbol of the inevitability of women's lives' and a presentation of the 'ambivalence of motherhood' (Steedman, 1982, p. 33). The voice Steedman gives these children is mitigated by the limitations of their immediate circumstances, and symbolic violence is 'imperceptible, insidious and invisible' (Thapar-Björkert et al., 2016, p. 8). The little girls' futures are imperceptibly but clearly mapped and limited even before they become women. It might be said that both their personal and professional identities are conflated: they are *training* to be mothers. In this chapter, we argue that symbolic violence continues to embed itself insidiously in the lives of women and this particularly resonates for women from working-class backgrounds.

A Methodological Journey

Professional doctorates, representing several years of the writer's life and often written alongside the demands of the professional 'day job' are frequently referred to as a journey, and a journey that will peak, trough and shape-shift along the way. My own was no exception. I have referred above to the way my substantive theoretical underpinning shifted from an overarching emphasis on Bourdieu's capitals to an almost revelatory illumination of how symbolic violence operates in society. However, this was not all that changed. My work is underpinned by my own experience as a working-class woman, the first to attend university and from a family who, while wanting the best for me, were not able to help me guide my choices in terms of higher education: I was what Ball et al. (2002) refer to as a *contingent chooser* – a student from a working-class background whose pathway to higher education was largely self-directed.

As my writing progressed, I had unequivocally embedded myself in my study. Additionally, I had identified narrative inquiry as my preferred methodology with a growing fascination for poetic representation as a powerful means of presenting my data. This fascination was crystallised by the impact that Riessman (2008), Kim (2016) and Richardson (1995) had had on my work and was an opportunity to revisit approaches learnt as an English Literature undergraduate student. As my understanding of narrative inquiry embedded, I began to consider the additional methodological tool of autoethnography. While it was not initially obvious to me that autoethnography – and naming it as autoethnography – had placed itself as central to the project, it had become urgent and non-negotiable, and it took a conversation with Catherine to make me see that. Once I had reached this realisation, everything made sense and:

> All I needed to do was to include my story alongside all the other stories being deposited in my vault. You would never have guessed this little provocation could start an avalanche. It was just a little whisper, a call, a crack. But. . .. (Douglas & Carless, 2013, p. 93)

But the whisper, call or crack meant that I had the bare bones of a thesis. I talked at length with Catherine about this and about how our different backgrounds had resonated with each other. We talked about how we had found our way in the world when young women while also doing our best to suppress the imposter syndrome (Clance & Imes, 1978) which so often taps the shoulder of women who have shifted class or expectations of upbringing. It, therefore, made sense for this chapter to be a collaboration between Catherine and me because the symbolic violence I am writing about is one that is deeply resonant for us both, albeit present in different ways. A further commonality was that Catherine, like me, had also studied English Literature as an undergraduate and also went on to use narrative inquiry with her students leading to her own EdD study.

Narrative methodology is not for everyone, and I recall in that first EdD session the rolling of eyes as some peers refused to embrace it as a serious way of approaching research. However, my world was changed listening to Catherine lay herself bare as she read from her autoethnographic writing. I was enormously excited at these new possibilities for my work; being vividly presented to me was life beyond case study which in one afternoon transformed my assumptions about what research is. My excitement grew further as I immersed myself in narrative and embraced poetry as a legitimate method. The appeal of poetry for me was underpinned by Richardson's (1995, p. 704) assertion that:

> Poetics strips those methodological bogeymen of their power to control and constrain. A poem as "findings" resituates ideas of validity and reliability from "knowing" to "telling". Everybody's writing is suspect – not just those who write the poems.

Both Catherine and I had poems to tell about ourselves, about our journeys to where we are today. We acknowledge the subjectivity of our work and embrace it as 'suspect' while celebrating it as a powerful and moving medium through which to present and understand our stories:

Fairies by Catherine
When I was six, I ran away to be with the fairies.
They lived at the far end of the field beyond our garden.
I took a plastic bag containing only my best dress
To be beautiful in their company.
Nobody noticed I had gone.

Twelve years on I left to be with the fairies.
My plastic bag contained only the lightest of loads.
Mini-sized parcels of self-confidence, self-belief and self-worth.
Other students arrived loaded with trunks,
Heavy with family tradition and expectation,
The self-confidence spilling out over the edges for all to see.

And did I ever meet my fairies? I have glimpsed them: yes.
They have been the few who have danced through my life.
Leaving a delicate but discernible imprint.
They have helped me weave the story of who I am.

The Only Slave by Laura
The Latin teacher said,
Next week
We'll have a Roman feast.
We'll all dress in togas (white sheets from home)
And lie on sofas (our desks)
Be fed grapes (I started to feel uncomfortable)
And drink goblets of wine (wine?)

Lying on the desks in sheets – wow!

Then the Latin teacher said
I just need a couple of you to be the slaves,
To go around the class feeding grapes to the other girls.
Don't worry though, you'll get grapes too.
I don't remember what happened next but what I do remember,

Palpably and painfully
Is that I was a girl who didn't fit,
Who wore Salvation Army sale clothes
And that I had to volunteer to be a slave before I was volunteered.
The discomfort that I had felt earlier had manifested.

When I was 14 years old
I did not have the social capital to lie on a desk and be fed grapes by someone whose brilliant white socks stayed up without elastic garters.
I don't remember the feast; only that I was a slave, **the** *slave: no one else volunteered.*
They were better than me,
They were from a different class.
I was the only slave.

We found using poetry to be a liberating way of identifying and naming how, through experience and upbringing, we both had experienced symbolic violence. Mirroring this, through the representation of my data as poetry in the doctoral thesis, I was able to foreground the experiences of my participants.

This is also the direction in which this chapter travels. Once data have been acknowledged as a construct, reproducing the data as poetry liberated my thinking further. This introduction sets the scene for this chapter in which data are presented as poetry and framed where appropriate with autoethnography. In this chapter, we hope to show how language in the form of careful poetry can be used to unmask and make visible the insidious impact (Thaper-Bjorkert et al., 2016) of symbolic violence (Thaper-Bjorkert et al., 2016). The poetry presents the words my participants spoke; words might have been taken out, nothing has been inserted or substituted nor has the word order has been changed. We hope to use this engaging narrative method to engage readers with this critical subject matter.

Ethical Considerations

In terms of my substantive research and in the spirit of narrative methodology, the desire to listen to stories and remain reflexive in terms of my own 'background' and positionality was at the heart of my work. My aim was to 'gather data not change people' (Patton, 2002, p. 405) alongside my overarching intentions of searching for new knowledge and understanding of a phenomenon (Jupp, 2006). Both perspectives are supported by qualitative research's claim to, through the creation of new ways of knowing, make positive future impact. Clandinin and Connelly problematise the issue of ethics in the context of narrative inquiry in their discussion of how attempting to *completely* address ethical considerations prior to the commencement of research is not wholly satisfactory because of the organic nature of the methodology. To do this 'works against the relational negotiation that is part of narrative inquiry' (Clandinin & Connelly, 2000, p. 170). Over time, some of the principles at the heart of my research shifted and this I discussed with the participants. That their data were to be presented as poetry was a principal discussion area and one they were all fascinated by; yet ultimately none wanted to see the end result. This was potentially because they were all at an advanced stage of their degrees by this time. However, when I reflect on this – and particularly with the benefit of hindsight – I acknowledge that it was incumbent on me as researcher to address issues around member checking and to have potentially tried harder to encourage them to engage. On a more personal level, Catherine and I are both aware of the references we have made to our own families in this chapter and have worked hard to adhere to the principle of 'do no harm' (BERA, 2018). That said, we are aware that while we have discussed experiences that are at the heart of the making of us as women, our families may have different perspectives.

The Sample

Table 4.1 presents participant data illustrating and developing my argument for the often-unseen impact of symbolic violence. My sample comprised of young (no more than two years away from post-GCSE education) women who self-identify as working or middle-class. They were all in their first year of primary initial teacher education degree at the university where I teach. To ensure clarity and context, the table demonstrates the backgrounds of the participants I have chosen to use in this chapter. My subsequent discussion will refer to these participants by pseudonym followed by their self-identified social class, both indicated in parentheses and in bold text (i.e.: *name, w/c* or *m/c*):

Theorising Marginal Voices

We argue that symbolic violence can be used to theorise how marginalised voices are not heard in the milieu of the dominant discourse (Thapar-Björkert et al., 2016). We earlier contextualised this by our opening autoethnographic poems; mine describes an early experience of being marginalised by social class and Catherine's how she was marginalised by familial expectations. Against the backdrop of our poetry, this chapter looks initially at symbolic violence as a societal factor insidiously favouring dominant groups and individuals, and the discussion in this section addresses this to provide a credible and convincing argument that symbolic violence is a prevalent and enveloping phenomenon in our society. We then narrow the focus to how it can be argued that symbolic violence, in the context of choices for women, is a powerful pervasive force potentially leading young women into primary school teaching via discourses of caring (Acker, 1995). We illustrate this with my data indicating how participants claim to *love children* and how they were told *You like children/you want to be a primary school teacher*. In this section, we make the argument that symbolic violence is intrinsically interwoven with the concepts of embedded and contingent choosers and 'hot knowledge' (Ball et al., 2002) – the understanding of how higher education 'works' is passed down to young people from family and family contacts where family and social networks can share information about institutions and qualifications based upon the family's own experience or that of others in their network.

Table 4.1. Participant Data.

Participant Name	Years Since Leaving Secondary School	Social Class Participant Self Identifies With	Highest Educational Level of Mother	Highest Educational Level of Father	Occupation of Mother	Occupation of Father
Polly	3	Middle	Degree	Doctorate	Senior nursing sister and ward leader	Detective in a police force
Kate	0	Working	None	None	Teaching assistant	Retired car park attendant
Lucy	0	Working	Apprenticeship	O levels	Self-employed cleaner	Electronics engineer
Anna	0	Middle	degree	HE diploma	Occupational therapist	Farmer
Emma	2	Middle	GCSE	GCSE	Retail (visual merchandiser)	HGV night driver
Carrie	3	Working	GCSE	None	Shop assistant	Kitchenhand
Kitty	0	Working	None	None	HCA in care home	Factory worker

Symbolic Violence – Society's Invisible Force

Bourdieu (2001, p. 1) describes symbolic violence as 'a gentle violence, exerted through the most part by the purely symbolic channels' and for my participants, and for Catherine and me, it was an experience impacting our childhood, our choices and who we are as adult professional women. My data demonstrate how my participants had internalised the mantras of being told that they were good with children. My own classed and gendered identity made me feel never quite good enough and the autoethnographic poetry presented in the introduction and below demonstrates symbolic violence at the hands of trusted adults, and for Catherine enacted by familial values. These familial values coveted a model of womanhood encompassing 'marrying well', homemaking, material acquisition and child rearing, echoing Steedman's (1982) girls 'playing houses', with little value placed on academic learning, career aspiration or any form of reflective criticality. With this absence of endorsement, stepping into a new space as the first in her family to go to university was unsurprisingly fraught with self-doubt and a lack of entitlement for Catherine, and the building of confidence was a fragile endeavour. Meanwhile, an early memory for me of symbolic violence at the metaphorical hands of a trusted adult was an incident in a primary school assembly where our genuinely loved and respected head teacher was talking about foreign travel in his morning assembly. Reay (2017) discusses how class shame has become embedded in working-class psyche. As demonstrated in the poem below, the shame I felt was palpable and, reflected in the clarity with which I still recall this incident, treacherous:

Spanish Seas by Laura
In primary school
Mr Leonard
A generally good bloke,
An understanding and fair head teacher,
Did an assembly about foreign travel.
He asked all the children who had
been abroad
To put up their hands.
In the mid-70s many families with a 'liveable' income could take their
Big Holiday
Abroad.
Largely to Spain.
The envy.
A Spanish sea of hands shot into the air.
Mr Leonard said, as there are so many of you let's make it easier,
So, STAND UP
If you have never ***been abroad****.*

The parquet floor was scuffed and so were my shoes.
And my white socks would not stay up on their own.

The playtime that followed was a very miserable one for me, my brother and a couple of other unremembered kids.
The kids whose parents barely scraped that 'liveable' income.

This autoethnographic poem demonstrates how easily working-class children can be made to feel 'other' by casual and thoughtless assumptions made by advantaged adults. I argue that symbolic violence works to limit expectation; my data demonstrate that time and again for my participants symbolic violence has played a part in how they conceptualise themselves.

Teaching was never an option for me. In terms of my family's working-class expectations in the early 1980s that would have been too grand, my symbolic violence took the form of an office job. My mum had been a successful and well-regarded secretary, a world away from the long hours of factory and cleaning jobs of her parents forced to make ends meet in the context of the economic challenges of the 1930s and 1940s. She had worked hard to achieve this and was proud and wanted this for me. My quiet rebellion rejected this expectation as I silently resisted learning how to type and do shorthand. I did not know what I wanted for myself – that came much later – but I knew that I did not want *this*, her life, and subsequently the suffocating straight jacket of office work that I had seen friends 'succumb' (in my eyes) to. The friends were all women, all went to their offices dressed the same, their bosses were all men and – like my mother's experiences 30 years earlier – joked about resignedly deflecting the unwanted attention of those men. Thapar-Björkert et al. (2016, p. 148) discuss how feminist research has highlighted the breadth of symbolic violence towards women in terms of emotional and psychological violence in society, stating how repeated actions 'subordinate certain groups of people, [and] mask[s] the underlying power relations'. Thapar-Björkert et al. (2016, p. 148) go on, citing Bourdieu and Wacquant, to give the example that 'the dominance of men is legitimated as the natural order of things in which women are consigned to inferior social positions'. Of course, I was not familiar with the theory of symbolic violence, but I knew that unwanted physical advances in the workplace were wrong, and that this was not going to happen to me. For Catherine, the more deeply she engaged with her own education, the more removed she felt from her own family value sets and the more critically she engaged with them. Born into a competitive large family environment, she found herself entered for the wrong competitions and speaking the wrong language. She recognised that what was not said by those around her had often had as big an impact on her development as what had been said, albeit that much of this was unconscious as symbolic violence so often is:

Lost Words by Catherine
It was nobody's fault
I did not speak until nearly four
Having two older sisters to speak for me
And no one to listen.

It was nobody's fault
I looked inwards instead of outwards
And took refuge in stories
Preferring to inhabit those worlds.

It was nobody's fault
They did not notice
And encourage my differences
Too focused on replicating
shared patterns
and beliefs.

It was nobody's fault
They did not
question
reflect
and notice
Times changing.

It is nobody's fault
That we stand together
but apart
Family without knowing
Loving but not understanding.

'Choosing' to Teach?

My doctoral thesis starts with a statement, not a question, and asserts that primary school teaching is a classed and gendered profession; I explore and demonstrate this assertion through the narratives of my participants and the literature demonstrating the strength of the argument. My thesis examines the ways in which primary school teaching has been viewed as women's work, engaging with the work of Reay (2017), Plummer (2000) and Maguire (1997). These women from working-class backgrounds identified how they were marginalised and limited in terms of choices of profession, and all identify their own experiences as framed by both gender and class. For them teaching, for a 'bright' working-class girl, was a more of an assumption than a considered choice. Symbolic violence legitimises these everyday assumptions and repackages them as choice, and my data illuminate how symbolic violence appeared to impact my participants' perceived choices. As a result, these choices and decisions revolve around discourses of caring (Vogt, 2002) and are foregrounded in the literature relating to the expectations for and of young women in the world of work (for example, Acker, 1995; Maguire, 2005). This is particularly resonant for working-class women because of the traditional and historical positioning of females at the centre of the home not the workplace; discourses of caring subsequently become embedded cultural scripts (Acker, 1995). This positioning resonates for both Catherine and me. While aspiration for me was limited by the 'glass ceiling' of typing in an office, for Catherine, the very idea of women working was not one that was regarded as a serious option in her family.

As a result of symbolic violence, the prospect of women working with and being 'good with children' becomes natural and obvious and embedded in the daily rituals of life (Thapar-Björkert et al., 2016). My data demonstrate that Polly has always been 'good with young children' and Kate has been told by family and others that 'you like children/you want to be a primary school teacher'. Maguire (2005, p. 6) states:

> The gendered nature of being a teacher... is conflated with discourses of caring and discourses of mothering. For this reason, it is perhaps not difficult for women to imagine a future where they work with children. From there, it is an easy step to start imagining being a teacher.

This gendered perception of primary school teaching is demonstrated overtly in some of my working-class participants' data represented as poetry below:

Helping a child
To understand something
That was definitely
    Something I wanted to do,
For a degree
*For my life. (***Lucy w/c***)*

That's a good girls' job.
    They said.
My brother said
It's not a job for him.
Men don't work with little kids. **(Kitty w/c)**

I have noticed this -
    Females are a lot more dominant
        In teaching.
Educating
    As a career thing
I never really noticed before university
How few men there are. **(Emma m/c)**

Maybe teaching is seen as a motherly role
Perhaps that's old fashioned.
    But it sort of requires
        Empathy
And typically feminine traits.
Obviously
    Times are changing.
It's more socially acceptable
    For men to have empathy
And it's more encouraged.
    For men to express emotions
Maybe that is why more men.
Are going in for it. **(Carrie w/c)**

Alongside the working-class voices, I have presented is securely middle-class Polly. Polly does not discuss how primary school teaching is women's work, nor does she ponder the lack of men on her course. She presents, however, a subtle awareness of how symbolic violence works in society and is playing out in her life:

Everyone's always told me
I'm good with young children.
That's what I've been told.
From my mum
From my family friends
When they say to you
You're really good with children
What do you think you're going to do with that?
There was no option
        To say
                You know what?
I'm going to become a firefighter! **(Polly m/c)**

To return to the concept of professional identity, it might be argued that Polly's identity is being established while still a child herself – *what do you think you are going to do with that?* – working in tandem with an almost wry acknowledgement of how symbolic violence is playing out in her life.

The Lens of Choice – Embedded and Contingent Choosers

Ball et al. (2002) demonstrate how familial input into young people's choices around higher education is an important indicator of their subsequent success and, I argue, have the potential to mitigate the impact of symbolic violence. Ball et al. (2002, p. 337) discuss contingent choosers who are 'typically a first-generation applicant to higher education…' whose family can provide emotional but not practical support, and this is apparent in the narratives of my working-class participants and in the stories of Catherine and me. In contrast to this are middle-class embedded choosers for whom university attendance was never a binary choice but an expectation that Ball et al. (2002, p. 342) name as being 'part of a cultural script, a '*normal biography*'. Embedded choosers are also endowed with hot knowledge, a phenomenon located securely in middle-class habitus where family or social networks can share 'first or second-hand recommendations or warnings related to specific institutions based on some kind of "direct" experience' (Ball et al., 2002, p. 337). Both middle-class Anna and Polly discuss how their parents had input and interest in their potential career choices. The parents of both women were insistent that they must be sure that they are making the right choices at this early stage. Anna presents her mum as vehement:

My mum always,
Wanted,
To make sure
That I was making the right decisions.
So even before the week I moved to uni

She was saying:
Are you sure this is what you want to do?
Are you sure this is what you want to do?
She made sure I had spoken
To the right people
And asked the right questions
Beforehand.
To make sure
I was sure.
I was sure though.
My dad
He was more laid back.
And he thought
That if I knew what I wanted to do
Then I would do that… **(Anna m/c)**

In earlier data, Anna had situated her father as working-class, in contrast to her semi-professional mother's middle-class status. As being partially endowed with appropriate hot knowledge and cultural capital to get to university, but with a parent who has no understanding or experience of higher education, Anna is closer to the position of a contingent chooser. Maguire (2001) identified such participants as 'hybrids' whose class identities and identifiers may not be fixed in the way that Polly's is. My data and the research I have situated it in suggest that the further away from embedded chooser status an individual is, the more vulnerable they are in terms of symbolic violence.

Polly is the child of two successful professional people whose support for her future has been explicit from a very early age. Polly's embedded chooser status is unquestionable and while perhaps demonstrating an awareness of symbolic violence as discussed above, she is also very clear about the importance of being sure about her choices from the perspective of *both* parents:

They were really supportive,
Really pleased.
A bit
Are you sure?
Not a paramedic?
Not paediatric science?
Not in a telly-off sort of way
Not trying to discourage me.
But… Are you making the right decision?
Make sure you're sure. **(Polly m/c)**

Reay (2002, p. 29) discusses how 'middle-class mothers push their children towards high academic performance' in a way that working-class families because of their lack of access to sufficient funds of capital, and particularly cultural capital, are unable to do. Both of Polly's parents have attended university, as has Anna's mother. Their parents were anxious to ensure that Polly and Anna were 'sure' that they wanted to train to be teachers, and at *this* university. By presenting my working-class participants' tendency to align themselves to working with children from a young age themselves, I have described how cultural scripts are embedded in the concept of symbolic violence. For Polly and Anna, the cultural script has shifted: 'Choice is part of a cultural script, a "normal biography"' (Reay et al., 2005, p. 112). And choice, I argue, affords a degree of distance from symbolic violence.

What is also of significance in my data was the middle-class participants' narrative in terms of the course and the learning, which I see as an indication of how symbolic violence enacts itself differently across social classes. This sits in contrast to my working-class participants whose reasoning is situated in the narrative of working with children and their parents wanting them to be 'happy' as evidenced in, for example, Lucy and Kitty's data:

Both of my parents.
Their main thing.
Is that they want me to be happy
In what I choose. ***(Lucy)***

They always said
Do what you want
You must do what you want.
As long as you're happy.
That's the important thing. **(Kitty w/c)**

Both Anna and Polly, meanwhile, had different perspectives. Anna stated, in terms of her choice to follow this specific route into teaching (as opposed to doing a non-vocational degree followed by the one-year postgraduate course) 'I thought a three-year course would be better and more beneficial/In terms of learning about the pedagogy'. Similarly, when talking about friendships and fitting in on the course, Polly felt that at the heart of her experience:

It's about the learning.
You feel like a student because you've got to learn
.... So you do feel a little more like a student than a professional
You've still got to be learning.
But some of the time you are teaching
I think you get a bit of a muddled identity. **(Polly m/c)**

While terminology such as 'pedagogy' and 'identity' is used by the teaching team from the outset of the degree, my professional experience tells me it takes more than just the month these undergraduate student teachers had been with us for the term to embed. Polly and Anna are demonstrating hot knowledge beyond that of their peers in this example and appear to grasp of the 'rules of the game'. Bourdieu (1998, p. 25) discusses 'the game' in terms of the invisible social barriers middle-class students pass through to achieve and experience beyond academic success at university, and how an understanding of 'the rules of the game' is embedded for middle- and upper-class families, enabling them to 'make better educational investments and earn maximum returns on their cultural capital'. In contrast, working-class families are not able to imbue their children with this degree of insight and Reay et al. (2005) discuss the 'uneven playing field' that is, therefore, created. For my working-class participants and for Catherine and myself, lack of knowledge of, let alone understanding of the game, allowed symbolic violence to play an early and resonating part in the formation of our personal and initial professional identities.

Conclusions

In this chapter, we have argued that symbolic violence is a powerful and insidious force which pervades society in an invisible and destructive way. We looked firstly at the 'big picture' of symbolic violence and how it impacted us both from an early age and then narrowed our lens to look at how it impacts young women finding their way in society and making choices about their future. What resonates as we close this chapter is the role that the people we are closest to play in deepening the impact of symbolic violence in our formative years. We discussed how the prevailing discourse in Catherine's family favoured homemaking as the role for women, while mine viewed women's work as a very particular and binary phenomenon – an office, not a factory. Both were damaging perspectives and it could be argued that Catherine and I were the ones who 'got away'. However, we still carry those formative years and attitudes with us; they remain prevalent in our families and haunt us still.

Our concluding thoughts are ultimately that it is education that can challenge symbolic violence. Education shines a light on the insidious processes that permeate society and allows us to reflect upon and question the expectations that we have grown up with, both in terms of family and institutions. A casual glance at the media, at social media and at the significantly higher number of women than men on our primary education degrees demonstrates that there are still deeply embedded attitudes and cultural scripts (Acker, 1995), suggesting that primary school teaching largely remains *women's work*. However, as educators, it is our responsibility to encourage consistent critical reflection, not only on the practical aspects of students' practice but also on their motivations for wanting to teach young children. This is how we as academics have the 'power' and privilege to help nurture the teachers of tomorrow, educating the children they teach and challenging dominant discourses in the classroom. It is education that helped both Catherine and me to identify and ultimately resist the impact of the symbolic violence that was part of our formative years. For me, despite my lack of confidence, I worked hard, it took a while, but I quietly resisted the office. As a contingent chooser, I did not engage with higher education until I was in my mid-twenties, but I found my way myself, it just took a little longer than for many others. Catherine also identifies as a contingent chooser, and states that 'education has enabled me to interrogate my own upbringing and recognise symbolic violence which I have been at pains not to replicate with my own children – their upbringing is significantly different to mine.'

The work that we have engaged in together, indeed the journey we have travelled, has made us each understand ourselves and our own stories far more powerfully than had we been going solo. Beyond our academic reading, the discussions we have had as women and as daughters have had real impact on us as authors. The conversations I have had with Catherine have made me see the value of my own story right from the beginning of my doctoral journey, and now I see the story as an important part of my life as an academic. Meanwhile, Catherine has found that accompanying me throughout my journey has deepened her own understanding of the role of symbolic violence in her life and helped her to come to terms with familial patterns which cannot be changed, as seen in her second poem written for this chapter. As is common with narrative enquiry, the process has been of inherent personal value to us both.

References

Acker, S. (1995). Carry on caring: The work of women teachers. *British Journal of Sociology of Education*, *16*(1), 21–36.

Ball, S., Reay, D., & David, M. (2002). 'Ethnic choosing': Minority ethnic students, social class and higher education choice. *Race, Ethnicity and Education*, *5*(4), 333–357.

Bourdieu, P. (1998). *Practical reason*. Polity.

Bourdieu, P. (2001). *Masculine dominations*. Stanford University Press.

Bourdieu, P. (2021). *Forms of capital*.

British Educational Research Association (BERA). (2018). *Ethical guidelines for educational research* (4th ed.). https://www.bera.ac.uk/researchers-resources/publications/ethical-guidelines-for-educational-research-2018

Clance, P. R., & Imes, S. A. (1978). The imposter phenomenon in high achieving women: Dynamics and their therapeutic intervention. *Psychotherapy Theory Research and Practice*, *15*(3), 241–247.

Clandinin, D. J., & Connelly, F. M. (2000). *Narrative inquiry: Experience and story in qualitative research*. Jossey-Bass.

Douglas, K., & Carless, D. (2013). A history of autoethnographic enquiry. In S. Holman-Jones, T. E. Adams, & C. Ellis (Eds.), *Handbook of autoethnography* (pp. 84–107). Routledge.

Jupp, V. (2006). *The Sage dictionary of social research methods*. SAGE.

Kim, J.-H. (2016). *Understanding narrative enquiry*. Sage.

Maguire, M. (1997). Missing links: 'Working class' women of Irish descent. In P. Mahoney & C. Zmroczek (Eds.), *Class matters: 'Working class' women's perspectives on social class* (pp. 87–101). Taylor & Francis.

Maguire, M. (2001). The cultural formation of teachers' class consciousness: Teachers in the inner city. *Journal of Education Policy*, *16*(4), 315–331.

Maguire, M. (2005). 'Not footprints behind but footsteps forward': Working class women who teach. *Gender and Education*, *17*(1), 3–18.

Nias, J. (1989). Teaching and the self. In M. S. Holly & C. S. McLoughlin (Eds.), *Perspectives on teacher professional development* (pp. 155–171).The Falmer Press.

Nowotny, H. (1981). Women in public life in Austria. In C. Fuchs Epsein & R. Laub Coser (Eds.), *Access to power: Cross-national studies of women and elites*. George Allen and Unwin.

Patton, M. Q. (2002). *Qualitative research and evaluation methods*. SAGE.

Plummer, G. (2000). *The failure of working-class girls*. Trentham.

Reay, D. (2002). Mothers' involvement in their children's schooling: Social reproduction in action. *Improving Schools*, *5*(3), 23–33.

Reay. (2004). Gendering Bourdieu's concepts of capitals? Emotional capital, women, and social class. *The Sociological Review*, *52*(s2), 57–74.

Reay, D. (2017). *Miseducation: Inequality, education and the working classes*. Policy Press.

Reay, D., David, M. E., & Ball, S. (2005). *Degrees of choice. Social class, race and gender in higher education*. Trentham.

Richardson, L. (1995). Narrative and society. In J. Van Maanen (Ed.), *Representation in ethnography*. SAGE.

Riessman, C. K. (2008). *Narrative methods for the human sciences*. SAGE.

Scott, B. (2012). Caring teachers and symbolic violence: Engaging the productive struggle in practice and research. *Educational Studies*, *48*(6), 530–549.

Steedman, C. (1982). *The tidy house*. Virago.

Thaper-Bjorkert, S., Samelius, L., & Sanghera, G. (2016). Exploring symbolic violence in the everyday: Misrecognition, condescension, consent and complicity. *Feminist Review*, *111*(1), 144–162.

Vogt, F. (2002). A caring teacher: Explorations into primary school teachers' professional identity and ethic of care. *Gender and Education*, *14*(3), 251–264.

Chapter 5

Further Education (FE) Sports Lecturer Professionalism: 'Freedom to Play', or 'Do as I Say?'

Jake Bacon and Tessa Podpadec

University of the West of England, UK

Abstract

This chapter discusses what the working practices and professionalism of sports lecturers can tell us about the challenges of professionalism in further education (FE). This chapter draws on Jake's doctoral research in which he interviewed five sports lecturers working in FE colleges in England, about their identities and practices. In this chapter, Jake talks about his own experiences as a sports lecturer in FE and how his increasing disillusionment with his role led him to undertake doctoral research in this field. We explore constructions of professionalism within FE, and we show that through a process Jake identified and labelled as 'competitive mediation', the sports lecturers he interviewed used their experiences as elite sports people to navigate the highly performative environments in which they were working. The positives and negatives of using this strategy for them, their learners and wider society are explored in this chapter. We suggest that although Jake's research focused specifically on sports lecturers in FE settings, his insights can be applied more widely, we reflect on the importance of considering the impact our own diverse lived experiences may have on our sense of professionalism as researchers and practitioners.

Keywords: Professionalism; performativity; further education; sports lecturers; competitive mediation

Critical Perspectives on Educational Policies and Professional Identities, 65–83

doi:10.1108/978-1-83753-332-920241005

Readying the Pitch: Introduction to the Research Study

This chapter considers what a study of the working practices and professionalism of sports lecturers in further education (FE) can tell us about the challenges of professionalism. It also explores the extent to which the factors that can lead to a successful professional sporting identity, for example, competitiveness, discipline, teamwork, can influence one's work as a lecturer. The chapter draws on the EdD research Jake completed in 2018, which focused on the lived experiences of five sports lecturers who taught on A level Physical Education and BTEC Sport courses at a range of FE colleges in the South West of England. Although this chapter is based on Jake's research, we (Jake and Tessa) have written it collaboratively, as we have both worked in FE for many years and, as such, have an appreciation of the challenges faced by FE lecturers. We also share a passion for sport, both academically and practically. Jake has worked as a sports lecturer, and Tessa has taught courses on performance psychology with a focus on sporting performance. We have also both enjoyed competing in a variety of sports.

We anticipate that this chapter will appeal to practitioners and researchers working in further education and to practitioners in higher education (HE) and the secondary sector wanting to understand more about professionalism in their settings. Because we are focusing on FE sports lecturers' experiences, we have used sporting metaphors and analogies to help situate our writing in both academic and sporting fields. The literature we refer to includes sources from the time of Jake's original research (2011–2017) and some newer sources which provide a contemporary account of FE lecturer professionalism and working contexts. However, the conclusions reflect the contextual time period of Jake's original research.

Jake will now take up the story.

Pitch Inspection: What Is FE?

FE, located between secondary and HE, has been described as the 'everything else' sector due to the breadth of its provision (Panchamia, 2012). When I carried out my EdD research, FE had a broad remit:

> It {FE} comprises all post-compulsory education and training for 16 to 19-year-olds and adults that is not delivered in higher education institutions. This includes basic skills, A Levels, NVQs, foundation degrees, diplomas, apprenticeships, work-based training, and personal and community learning. (Panchamia, 2012, p. 2)

Given the range of provision, both across FE colleges and within individual colleges, the scale of FE can easily be overlooked by people unfamiliar with the sector (James et al., 2007). Because of this diversity of provision (Hodgson & Spours, 2019), FE has always been in a constant state of change (Howard, 2009). This is due not only to FE having to react to central steering from changing governments (Hodgson & Spours, 2019), but also because of the continual need for FE institutions to offer a variety of provision, 'which is visible in college-to-college variation and also across the range of activity within individual colleges' (James et al., 2007, p. 9), in order to meet the needs of local and regional demands (Hodgson & Spours, 2019). Consequently, pleas for periods of stability have been ignored due to the politically motivated climate within FE to innovate and make changes (Daley et al., 2015), leading to conditions where 'political priorities are imposed, promoted, scrutinised and complied with' (Hayes, 2007, p. 63).This wide-ranging provision continues today (DfE, 2023); there are currently 257 general FE, 70 sixth form and 16 specialist designated colleges in England (AoC, 2022), with the number of young people in full-time education and training set to continue increasing (GOV.UK, 2023). Since the 1980s, the proportion of 16–18-year-olds in full-time education has increased from 40% in 1985 to 85% in 2020 (DfE, 2022). A forecasted 17% growth in the number of 16–17-year-olds in England between 2019 and 2024 equates to 200,000 more young people in FE (ONS, 2022). As a result, the economic and political pressures on the FE sector are unlikely to improve any time soon (Sibieta & Tahir, 2021).

Making the Team: My Experience in FE

In this section, I (Jake Bacon) discuss some of my own experiences as a sports lecturer in FE, as I fully subscribe to the view that it is unethical '…to offer a version of someone's life…without making clear the nature of the gaze that is being brought to bear upon it' (Sikes, 2010, p. 13). Between 2007 and 2018, I was a sports lecturer in various FE colleges in South West England. Sport had always been an important part of my identity. I lived and breathed sport throughout my school life. Physical Education (PE) was my favourite subject, my PE teachers were my favourite teachers, and I have continually played sport throughout my life, having represented my county in rugby and in athletics. After leaving school, I achieved a BSc (Hons) in Sport Studies, an MA in Sport, Culture and Society and a PGCE in Post Compulsory Education. On starting work at an FE college, being a sports lecturer was at the heart of my identity. I was initially very proud to say this to my family and my friends. I wore my teaching identity like a badge of honour. It was clear I had constructed my professional identity as a lecturer in accordance with my context in FE and personal experiences on and off the sports field, and this identity shaped my motivation, commitment and professional goals (Day et al., 2006; Rosenfeld et al., 2022). I felt I had a profession for life; I wanted to work hard every day, progress up the pay scales and make a difference to my learners, my colleagues and my community. I wanted my learners to develop their talents and abilities, and I wanted to help them make their way in the world (Robinson, 2019).

However, it became increasingly clear to me that working in FE embodied a contradictory tension resulting from the sustained underfunding of the FE sector (Sibieta & Tahir, 2021). The places where I worked, along with all FE institutions, were under significant and constant pressure to increase income and reduce costs (Hodkinson et al., 2007), which I felt was at odds with my desire to provide a rounded education for my students. This neoliberal marketised agenda

(Illsley & Waller, 2017) had turned my students into inputs and outputs, no more than 'bums on seats', of interest only because of the funding they brought in and the exam results they achieved (Coffield & Williamson, 2011). This tension had implications for the lived experience of lecturers working in those institutions. I experienced a disconnect between what I understood the purpose of education to be, and what I was being expected to do in my daily working contexts. My task was to make my learners successful exam-passers, and not individuals who were:

> ...Eager to learn and grow in the real-life world of work, leisure and relationships, [who required]...a rich set of useful, general-purpose habits of mind that will stand them in good stead whatever they want or need to turn their hand to. (Claxton, 2010, p. ix)

Instead, I felt my students were regarded as '...assets that must complete if the input of resources including staff time are to be justified' (Illsley & Waller, 2017, p. 481). My teaching role had been 'reduced to [an] empty ritual' (Coffield & Williamson, 2011, p. 46). I was expected to operate according to routines and procedures (Thomas, 2013) rather than acting and reacting as a reasoned professional.

The need to get my students through their exams meant I found myself teaching to the test and narrowing my delivery. At the time, I felt strongly that this was not meeting my needs as a teaching professional or providing my learners with what they needed to thrive in complex modern societies (Biesta, 2015). Indeed, my practice could be interpreted as reflecting a sterile vision of learning (O'Neill & Adams, 2012) which fitted neoliberal marketised agendas (Illsley & Waller, 2017). However, I felt obliged to teach like this because of the 'culture or...system{s} of terror' (Ball, 2017, p. 57), which I perceived to be operating in my institutions. It felt like the government were '...yanking firmly on the reins of public education' (Robinson, 2015, p. 9) and imposing systems to hold me and my colleagues accountable and levying penalties if we did not make the grade. I consequently experienced genuine fear that I would lose my job if I did not achieve positive outcomes related to my employment targets, reflecting a sort of football manager's syndrome where there is a continual pressure to raise one's game or face the sack (Frankel, 2010).

Regulatory bodies, like Ofsted, also fuelled institutional fear in the FE colleges I worked in and continue to do so today (Brady & Wilson, 2022). Clearly, there are documented benefits of Ofsted interventions, including national monitoring of educational quality, thematic reviews of educational practice and challenges to poor practices (Coffield, 2017). However, I found that fear of Ofsted inspections led to a regime of hyper-accountability, which employed '...judgements, comparisons and displays as means of control, attrition, and change' (Ball, 2017, p. 57). Ofsted was effectively a punitive enforcer of government policy (Coffield, 2017), and as teachers, we were expected to be continually 'Ofsted ready' able to:

> ... [deliver a] curriculum devised by 'experts'; to make sure that the whole curriculum has been 'covered' in ways designated by the government; to be endlessly flexible; to be unthinkingly responsive to the government 'initiative of the week'; and to be permanently ready to be inspected. (Coffield & Williamson, 2011, pp. 63–64)

At the time, I found this situation to be stressful and disempowering (Perryman, 2007). Consequently, my morale and the engagement of my students were impacted because of my education establishment's emphasis on meeting outcomes and official targets (O'Neill & Adams, 2012), at the expense of individuality, imagination and creativity (Robinson, 2015). You could say I was scared that if I indeed did 'drop the ball', I would lose my place within the team.

The Game Plan: Understanding Professionalism in FE Contexts

Throughout my FE career, I often felt my knowledge of the social, cultural, historical and political factors which have shaped, and continue to shape FE, was under-developed. I wanted to understand what had become of the idealistic professional I started as, and more importantly, why this disillusionment had happened. This fuelled my ambition to undertake further studies and enrol onto an EdD. My experiences as both an FE lecturer and a sportsperson led me to think that understanding how sports lecturers conceptualised professionalism in relation to both the educational contexts in which they worked and their sporting experience would be able to shine a light on professionalism more generally.

When I started my EdD, I found that professionalism in FE was an elusive concept (James & Gleeson, 2007) and often neglected the voices of educators like me. Early research into professionalism within FE presented two contrasting notions of the FE professional – as either the recipient or the agent of change (Gleeson et al., 2005). The former refers to issues of structure, explaining how professionals are framed by external factors; the latter refers to agency where professionals construct meanings out of the contexts in which they work (Gleeson et al., 2005). Similarly, Bathmaker and Avis (2005) refer to professionalism as having two tiers, what Feather (2014) calls a 'Janus Identity', where there is a clear dichotomy between managerialist perspectives of professionalism on the one hand and more democratic understandings on the other.

However, these understandings of teacher professionalism were challenged (James & Gleeson, 2007; Wallace & Hoyle, 2005). Further research has suggested that teachers' professional behaviours can often be categorised into compliance, non-compliance and mediation (Wallace & Hoyle, 2005), where compliance refers to a willingness to follow management instructions, and non-compliance (resistance) is where staff resist what they are required to do. Between compliance and non-compliance is a middle-ground (mediation) which '...does not oversimplify, and ... recognises the ambiguity and irony of the situation while also giving due regard to the sincerity of the endeavour among many professionals as they try to work round externally imposed requirements' (James & Gleeson, 2007, p. 133). As such, teaching professionals are neither simply de-professionalised because of structures nor strategic operators seeking to challenge structural constraint, rather, their professional practices are mediated and co-produced outcomes of structure and agency (Gleeson & Knights, 2006). In this context, practitioners filter institutional policy messages in various ways, mediating the demands placed upon them (James & Gleeson, 2007), often inventing creative solutions from contradictory policy-practice messages (Gleeson et al., 2005). It was this concept of mediation and specifically a notion of teachers keeping alive an idea of who they are and where their heart is (James & Gleeson, 2007) which became a very influential aspect of my research.

My review of the literature, together with my own experiences, led to the following research questions:

- What were the contexts in which FE sports lecturers in the South West of England worked?
- How did the sports lecturers work in their contexts, and how did they define their sense of professionalism with reference to the contexts they worked in and the jobs they did?

Time for Kick Off: Methodology

Insider Research

Like many EdD researchers, I considered myself to be an insider because I was already a member of the community or group I was investigating (Brannick & Coghlan, 2007; Humphrey, 2012). There were clear and significant advantages to researching as an insider: as a sports lecturer working in an FE college, I had good knowledge of the context I was researching, I could establish higher levels of rapport with research participants (Lor & Bowers, 2018) and as I was researching a field in which I was immersed, I was '...conversant with the formal and informal rules governing the webbing of the human interaction under investigation so that the innermost secrets could be revealed' (Sugden, 1996, p. 201, as cited in Gratton & Jones, 2010, p. 194). Thus, I was able to record a high level of detail in my narratives because I was able to question my participants more thoroughly through being aware of the complexities of their work. However, I also appreciated that being an insider meant that I could be biased by my own experiences or expectations of what the participants' narratives might contain, overlooking what we were all taking for granted (Mannay, 2010).

Participants

The participants in my research were all from medium-sized FE institutions in the South West of England, which were graded as at least 'good' according to Ofsted's FE inspection framework.

Ethics

I adhered to the relevant BERA Guidelines (2011; 2018); however, I took the stance that it is not sufficient to take refuge in the protection of ethics review procedures and ethical codes because they do not allow for individual circumstances (Sikes, 2010). I took particular care to protect the identities of my participants and the institutions in which they worked, and therefore, each participant was given a pseudonym (as detailed in Table 5.1 above). Ultimately, my intention was to represent my participants' lives and stories in a respectful manner.

Table 5.1. Research Participants.

Pseudonym	Teaching	Sporting Expertise
Jack	All levels – Foundation through to HE	Elite basketball player
James	All levels – Foundation through to HE	Elite tennis player/coach
Justin	Vocational sport including adult gym instructor	Elite cyclist
Bethany	Level 3 and HE	Elite rugby player
Elsa	Level 3 and HE	General sporting experience netball, hockey, athletics

A surprising and unintended outcome from this research was that participants found participating in the study beneficial, and indeed, some found the process quite therapeutic. A typical response came from Justin who said:

> Well, it's nice to talk about it because it's...nice to. . .give your views and stuff like that really. It's stuff that...you might do on a day-to-day basis and don't ever really think about because...you are doing it automatically...It's that reflective...process...It's quite nice really.

Taking part in the research appeared to offer the participants an 'outlet to reflect on experiences and share feelings with a neutral, interested party' (Rossetto, 2014, p. 484). This unexpected finding raised the question as to whether they had such opportunities to discuss and share their experiences in their working practices.

Method

I used narrative research as a methodological tool to explore the ways in which these educators understood the environments in which they worked. Narrative research enabled me to show 'how individuals assign meaning to their experiences through the stories they tell' (Moen, 2006, p. 60). This approach allowed me to understand the 'complexities and contradictions' (Flyvbjerg, 2006, p. 37) the research participants experienced, revealing the ambiguity in their accounts, rather than tidying it away (Bathmaker & Hartnett, 2010). This meant that their individual cases retained more of the noise of real life (Hodkinson & Hodkinson, 2001, as cited in Bathmaker & Hartnett, 2010), and because of this they helped me to understand complex interrelationships. This was important for my research because I anticipated that the factors which impacted the professional practice of the sports lecturers would be varied and complex.

Procedure and Sampling

I first emailed all FE colleges in the South West of England (via relevant line managers of sports lecturers) an online qualitative questionnaire in the hope of providing prompts for future interviews. The questions explored what the sports lecturers understood the purpose of education to be, what they understood by the terms 'performance management' and 'professionalism' and how these related to their professional contexts.

I received eight completed questionnaires from sports lecturers in four different FE institutions. I emailed these individuals to see if they would consent to participating in a single one-hour interview. Five individuals consented to be interviewed. The length and location of interviews were often dictated by the limited availability of the sports lecturers, with most taking place in their lunch breaks at their workplace. I was already acquainted with my research participants through working in the same institutions as them, but I had more of a removed connection with them (Costley et al., 2010) because the sports lecturers were not in the same departments in which I was working, and I did not have day-to-day contact with them. Ultimately, the interviews were social encounters and not merely a process of collecting data (Roiha & Iikkanen, 2022).

Analysis

I analysed the interview transcripts using thematic analysis, organising the raw data into conceptual categories (Gratton & Jones, 2004) and using coding to develop a logical structure for the data (Patton, 2002). I then wrote individual narratives for each research participant as well as identifying over-arching themes. The main themes were:

- Family views of education and personal school experiences;
- Individual routes into teaching;

- Prior expectations for working in the FE sector together with any disparities experienced;
- Lecturer perceptions of performance management and professionalism;
- Perceived impacts of sporting experiences on professional practice.

Back of the Net: Findings and Discussion

This section focuses on a small portion of the findings from my EdD, specifically the thematic narratives concerning firstly performance management and professionalism (theme 4 above) and secondly the concept of 'competitive mediation', a term I developed in my EdD which helps elucidate the impact of sporting experiences on the professional practices of FE sports lecturers (theme 5 above).

Professionalism and Performance Management in FE Contexts (Theme 4)

When considering the participants' understanding of professionalism, the dominant response was that performativity and accountability (Ball, 2017) were central to their job role, and these structural constraints were part of how they defined their professionalism. There was some surprise at the disparity between what had been taught on their PGCE courses (that FE was about developing learners), and what they were asked to do as FE sports lecturers. For example, Jack said:

> ...There is so much more of an emphasis placed on grades, retention numbers, as opposed to the development of the student.

This over-emphasis on statistical success was talked about by many of the participants. Justin recognised limitations in such practices when he said that he felt his students were:

> ...Possibly missing out on a much broader outline or subject matter.

The participants suggested that they felt unable to offer a person-centred education, having instead to provide a limited education which they felt did not meet the needs of their students. Furthermore, there was a level of acceptance of this target-driven culture, a view typified by Jack who said he felt these expectations were just part of the job:

> And those expectations are that you abide, or...adhere, to the standards. I think that if you are not prepared to then, either there's a big internal issue, or you are in the wrong profession.

The sports lecturers I talked with made specific links between performance management and their understanding of their professionalism. Many of the respondents saw their role as primarily preparing students for exams and making sure that the students stayed on the course. For example, Jack referred to how he focused less on student development and more on assessment preparation:

> . . .It's more focused towards preparing them for an assignment, preparing them for an exam, making sure they are progressing towards their target grades and succeeding them. It's all about assignments and retention numbers.

The importance of retention and student outcomes was echoed by many of the participants. James, for example, said that he saw his role as being to:

> . . .Retain as many students as possible. . .at the end of the day, they are a number and what is seen at the end is a number. . .how many did you retain? How many were successful? The value added, the high grades that you achieved and, my professionalism is that I am aiming to achieve those targets.

This response from James reflects a view of professionalism as a target-driven code of practice or service level agreement (Evans, 2007), similar to that described by Coffield and Williamson (2011) where lecturers were driven by college management to see students as no more than numbers.

The participants talked about the relationship between the target-driven environment they worked in and the levels of accountability they experienced. For example, Bethany talked about how she was required to focus on underperforming students to ensure they achieved their target grades. She referred to how she felt responsibility for the results of her students:

> I think about students that are...underperforming, what am I going to do?...I'm accountable to my line manager, what...to do if they don't get their...target grade.

Similarly, Jack explained that he needs:

> . . .To be showing that I can work to certain standards. In terms of having students meet their grades...showing that I am doing a good enough job to get them through college targets and, yes...job security.

The sense that these sports lecturers had that they needed to get good results to maintain job security reflects a culture of terror (Ball, 2017) operating within their FE institutions. This could also be likened to 'football managers' syndrome' (Frankel, 2010), whereby constant improvement is required. For example, Elsa described her fear about being reprimanded if she did not do what was expected of her by her manager:

> ...I don't want to be told off. I don't like being told off, being told I've done something wrong...Or be spoken to officially, I don't want that.

Similarly, James said:

> ...I don't want to be below the national benchmark if I can avoid it because I have to go to a meeting where it might be quite uncomfortable with the Principal....

As a result of working in such contexts, this caused considerable pressure and stress for the sports lecturers. Bethany talked about the constant worry she experienced in her job:

> Generally underperforming students...make you worry, Ofsted make you worry, management make you worry.

Consequently, some of the sports lecturers said that they often complied with what they were being asked to do, so that they did not rock the boat (Gleeson & Shain, 1999). This was reflected by Justin's response to performance management in his own institution:

> ...You are almost becoming a victim of the system. You are having to drive towards hitting certain criteria, so statistically your grades don't suffer. And that's very clear with course management meetings...They are looking at making someone accountable....

However, not all accountability was seen as negative. Some participants suggested that having high levels of performance management in their job roles provided useful feedback for developing their own practice. Jack described performance management as:

> ...That process of making sure that you are doing what you are supposed to be doing....

Jack suggested that just as monitoring the performance of students was useful for both teachers and for the students themselves, performance management by educational institutions could be informative for staff members in terms of assessing their progress and achievement, as well as benefitting the institution.

Perceived Impacts of Sporting Experiences on Professional Practice (Theme 5)

In my EdD, I coined the term 'competitive mediation', to describe the relationship between the contexts in which the FE sports lecturers in this research worked and their unique and specific sporting experiences. As discussed earlier, FE practitioners often filter institutional policy messages, to mediate the demands placed upon them (James & Gleeson, 2007), inventing creative solutions to contradictory policy-practice messages (Gleeson et al., 2005). They do this to keep alive an idea of who they are and where their heart is (James & Gleeson, 2007). It was clear that for the sports lecturers I interviewed, there was a coming together of the demands of their professional working contexts and their experiences from playing competitive sport, and it is this process that I called 'competitive mediation'. The sports lecturers interviewed said that what they were being asked to do in their professional practice was not necessarily separate and distinct from their identity as a sportsperson. For example, it was apparent that they were sometimes comfortable with working in a performance-driven culture because this matched their competitive sporting experiences. Indeed, some of the participants felt that as a result of these experiences, they possessed the necessary skills to function within the imposed and rigid structures of their institutions.

This was typified by Jack who said he had an affiliation for the performance management cultures in FE. He talked about his sporting experience and how he was very results-driven and competitive, and this competitiveness related well to his teaching:

> ...I mean, performance under pressure has always been something I have gradually got used to. I think playing sport has prepared me for observations, [and] assessments... ...Like being able to stand in front of a crowd and talk clearly...Has been developed as an athlete, as being part of a team....

Jack also made links to what he viewed as a complementary relationship between teaching observations and sports performance:

> I feel that if I hadn't played sport...I'd feel more anxious being observed....

Jack went on to say that when playing sport, he enjoyed having clear results of progression, and he could see that he was improving in certain aspects. He went on to refer to his competitiveness and stated that:

> ...I think it's more a result of competitiveness being developed as an athlete, which has then transferred into most things that I do.

Similarly, Bethany said she saw complementary links between her sporting experiences and her FE working practices:

> I think it's good for me...Because of my sports background, I probably want to be better than an indicator, so it probably gives me the motivation to move on, but I think that...I am guilty sometimes because I want to be the best.

While Bethany complied with the performance management required by her college, she was also able to mediate these demands by thinking and acting creatively, in a way which reflected her ideas of who she was (Gleeson et al., 2005) – in this case as a sportsperson. She responded to the performative demands of her college by seeing the process into a competition between her colleagues and herself – she wanted to be 'the best'. The creative solution Bethany devised is a good example of how competitive mediation allowed the sports lecturers to use their lived experiences as sports people to function in their working environments.

There was also evidence in interviews to suggest that the sports lecturers narrowed their delivery to prepare students for passing their specific assessments, meaning they taught to their tests. However, this was not necessarily perceived by them to be wholly negative because this practice matched their competitive nature. This was typified by Jack, an elite basketball player:

> ...By no means do I think being results driven is a bad thing...I am very results driven as well. I do enjoy seeing that I have done a good job. So, in terms of working in Further Education and being competitive, seeing my students attain better grades would be rewarding.

Some sports lecturers talked about how their experiences as elite sports people influenced the strategies they employed to deal with the context in which they worked. For example, Justin talked about how his experience as an elite cyclist drove his professional performance, and how the skills he developed when working as a personal trainer could be transferred into teaching:

> ...This is...because...I want to be the best I can be in cycling...I try to apply everything I do with training and with racing...to my professional career...I think that to be good at sport, you have to be logical, you almost have to be bordering on obsessive and it's about...these little things that you are going to be doing, and I think if you can apply those to your professional life...that's how the cross-over happens.

Justin also spoke about how he tried to instill these values into his students:

> I would say to my sports students that if you want to do really well at your sport, how do you get good at sport?...So how can you expect to do well in your work if you are not putting in the extra time, you are not doing the extra sessions, you are not doing that extra bit of work at home?.

These responses from Justin indicate that he was filtering institutional policy messages and mediating the demands that were placed upon him (James & Gleeson, 2007). It was apparent that Justin was complying with what he was being asked to do by college management, while keeping alive an idea of who he was and where his heart was (James & Gleeson, 2007).

The Final Whistle: Conclusion and Recommendations

Jake's study joins the growing body of research which claims that the traditional systems of education, generally, and FE, specifically, are not designed to meet the current needs of individuals or society (Robinson, 2015). Education in a culture of performativity (Ball, 2017) suppresses individuality, imagination and creativity (Robinson, 2015). Professionalism in post-16 education continues to be a key concern for policymakers due to its 'established links to competence, morale and staff continuity' (Tully, 2022, p. 66). However, professionalism remains an elusive concept. One interesting development in this field is Eaude's (2023) view of professionalism as a contractual understanding, reflecting neoliberal contexts. Eaude's understanding of professionalism is based on compliance, which restricts staff autonomy and means regulatory agencies have control over professions. Eaude argues that this creates dissonances for those lecturers who see their roles as being broader and often interferes with their professional judgement. This view of professionalism was apparent in the responses of the sports lecturers Jake interviewed, but we would argue that professionalism in education is more complex than Eaude suggests. The concept of competitive mediation shows that ideas of professionalism are personally negotiated by individual lecturers through both their lived experiences beyond the classroom and their working context. As such, we suggest that a new definition of FE professionalism is required, aimed at uniting the sector, rather than fracturing it (Plowright & Barr, 2012). Such a definition should be based on practical reasoning, judgement and wisdom and would include a value-based professional code of ethics as opposed to a managerial and prescribed focus (Plowright & Barr, 2012). Ultimately, all FE staff, but particularly principals and senior managers, should operate their institutions firstly as centres of excellence in education and secondly as businesses (Coffield, 2008). Such a shift in priority would '…maximise...the professionalism of tutors...the agency of learners, but also the relationship between tutors and learners…' (Coffield, 2008, p. 1).

Post-Match Analysis – What We Have Learned From Jake's Doctoral Journey

After writing this chapter, we (Tessa and Jake) have reflected together on the lessons we have learned from Jake's doctoral journey. Jake's EdD thesis concluded that the FE sector was moving away from democratic understandings of education due to the social, political and economic pressures of the time (Coffield & Williamson, 2011). Since then, financial downturns, the COVID pandemic, international conflicts and Brexit (Sibieta & Tahir, 2021) have further impacted FE. The FE sector remains under sustained pressure, job security is increasingly precarious (Wang et al., 2018; UCU, 2022), pay levels continue to decline relative to teachers in school settings (Sibieta & Tahir, 2023) and staff workloads are seen as increasingly unmanageable (UCU, 2022). We believe there is now a greater need to research the experiences of FE lecturers and would agree with Tully (2022) that unless FE institutions and government prioritise professionalism, the staffing difficulties will continue and teaching in FE will not be seen as a desirable career.

Although Jake's EdD focused specifically on sports lecturers in FE settings, insights from his work allows us to reflect more widely on identity and professionalism in the context of our careers as researchers/practitioners. There is a definite sense that Jake conducted his doctoral research in order to understand more about himself and his professional context. However, it is possible that all research (Jamieson et al., 2023) gives us the opportunity to understand more about ourselves, if we undertake a process of what Mortari (2015) calls 'radical reflection'. This involves exploring how our diverse identities may be constructing our taken-for-granted beliefs, which seem so obvious to us that we do not need to state them explicitly. Jake's research shows how important it is to explore how these potentially hidden identity-related factors impact on our professional identity as researchers and practitioners whether this is through reflexive writing about our personal experiences and background or our intersecting social positionings and ideological perspectives (Braun & Clarke, 2022), identity mapping (Jacobson & Mustafa, 2019) or keeping a reflexive research journal (Nadin & Cassell, 2006). Jake's research is a further reminder of the importance of acknowledging our place within the research process, that our assumptions, beliefs and experiences inevitably influence the way we negotiate our professional settings. Jake focused on the influence of being an elite athlete, but we could also consider the impact that being an artist, angler or accountant might have on our own professional activities.

References

Association of Colleges. (2022). *Data sources*. https://www.aoc.co.uk/research-unit/data-sources

Ball, S. (2017). *The education debate* (3rd ed.). Policy Press.

Bathmaker, A., & Avis, J. (2005). Becoming a lecturer in further education in England: The construction of professional identity and the role of communities of practice. *Journal of Education for Teaching*, *31*(1), 47–62. https://doi.org/10.1080/02607470500043771

Bathmaker, A., & Hartnett, P. (2010). *Exploring learning, identity and power through life history and narrative research*. Routledge.

Biesta, G. (2015). What is education for? On good education, teacher judgement, and educational professionalism. *European Journal of Education*, *50*(1), 75–87. https://doi.org/10.1111/ejed.12109

Brady, J., & Wilson, E. (2022). Comparing sources of stress for state and private school teachers in England. *Improving Schools*, *25*(2), 205–220. https://doi.org/10.1177/13654802211024758

Brannick, & Coghlan, D. (2007). In defense of being "native": The case for insider academic research. *Organizational Research Methods*, *10*(1), 59–74. https://doi.org/10.1177/1094428106289253

Braun, V., & Clarke, V. (2022). *Thematic analysis: A practical guide*. SAGE.

Claxton, G. (2010). *What's the point of school? Rediscovering the heart of education*. Oneworld.

Coffield, F. (2008). *Just suppose teaching and learning became the first priority*. https://www.voced.edu.au/content/ngv%3A11274

Coffield, F. (2017, November 2). *The research evidence for and against OFSTED*. British Educational Research Association. https://www.bera.ac.uk/blog/the-research-evidence-for-and-against-ofsted

Coffield, F., & Williamson, B. (2011). *From exam factories to communities of discovery. The democratic route*. Bedford Way Papers.

Costley, C., Elliott, G., & Gibbs, P. (2010). *Doing work based research*. Dawson Era.

Daley, M., Orr, K., & Petrie, J. (2015). *Further education and the twelve dancing princesses*. Institute of Education Press.

Day, C., Kington, A., Stobart, G., & Sammons, P. (2006). The personal and professional selves of teachers: Stable and unstable identities. *British Educational Research Journal*, *32*, 601–616. https://doi.org/10.1080/01411920600775316

Department for Education. (2022). *Participation in education, training and employment age 16 to 18*. https://explore-education-statistics.service.gov.uk/find-statistics/participation-in-education-and-training-and-employment

Department for Education. (2023). *What is further education*. https://www.teach-in-further-education.campaign.gov.uk/what-is-fe-teaching/

Eaude, T. (2023). Reclaiming teaching as a profession based on autonomy and trust. *The Forum*, *65*(2), 72–82. https://doi.org/10.3898/forum.2023.65.2.07

Evans, L. (2007). *Developing the European Educational Researcher: Towards a profession of 'extended' professionality*. https://citeseerx.ist.psu.edu/document?repid=rep1&type=pdf&doi=dc1db136edb1f80bb1bbfc2be4dabac7fe9a62d8

Feather, D. (2014). Professionalism: Doing a good job. *Research in Post-Compulsory Education*, *19*(1), 107–118. https://doi.org/10.1080/13596748.2014.872940

Flyvbjerg, B. (2006). Five misunderstandings about case-study research. *Qualitative Inquiry*, *12*(2), 219–245. https://doi.org/10.1177/1077800405284363

Frankel, H. (2010). *We need a result*. https://www.tes.com/magazine/archive/we-need-result

Gleeson, D., Davies, J., & Wheeler, E. (2005). On the making and taking of professionalism in the further education workplace. *British Journal of Sociology of Education*, *26*(4), 445–460. https://doi.org/10.1080/01425690500199818

Gleeson, D., & Knights, D. (2006). Challenging dualism: Public professionalism in 'troubled times'. *Sociology*, *40*(2), 277–295. https://doi.org/10.1177/0038038506062033

Gleeson, D., & Shain, F. (1999). Under new management: Changing conceptions of teacher professionalism and policy in the further education sector. *Journal of Education Policy*, *14*(4), 445–462. https://doi.org/10.1080/026809399286288

GOV.UK. (2023). *Further education courses and funding*. https://www.gov.uk/further-education-courses

Gratton, C., & Jones, I. (2004). *Research methods for sport studies*. Routledge.

Hayes, D. (2007). Schools and classrooms. In J. Sharp, S. Ward, & L. Hankin (Eds.), *Education studies – Issues based approach*. Learning Matters.

Hodgson, A., & Spours, K. (2019). Further education in England: At the crossroads between a national, competitive sector and a locally collaborative system? *Journal of Education and Work*, *32*(3), 224–237. https://doi.org/10.1080/13639080.2019.1596231

Hodkinson, P., Anderson, G., Colley, H., Davies, J., Diment, K., Scaife, T., Tedder, M., Wahlberg, M., & Wheeler, E. (2007). Learning cultures in further education. *Educational Review*, *59*(4), 399–413. https://doi.org/10.1080/00131910701619316

Hodkinson, P., & Hodkinson, H. (2001). The strengths and limitations of case study research. In A. Bathmaker & P. Hartnett (Eds.), *Exploring learning, identity and power through life history and narrative research*. Routledge.

Howard, U. (2009). *FE colleges in a new culture of adult and lifelong learning*. (IFLL Sector Paper 7). National Institute of Adult Continuing Education.

Humphrey, C. (2012). Dilemmas in doing insider research in professional education. *Qualitative Social Work*, *12*(5). https://doi-org.ezproxy.uwe.ac.uk/10.1177/1473325012446006

Illsley, R., & Waller, R. (2017). Further education, future prosperity? The implications of marketisation on further education working practices. *Research in Post-Compulsory Education*, *22*(4), 477–494. https://doi.org/10.1080/13596748.2017.1381291

Jacobson, D., & Mustafa, N. (2019). Social identity map: A reflexivity tool for practicing explicit positionality in critical qualitative research. *International Journal of Qualitative Methods*. 160940691987007–. https://doi.org/10.1177/1609406919870075

James, D., Biesta, G., Colley, H., Davies, J., Gleeson, D., Hodkinson, P., Maull, W., Postlethwaite, K., & Wahlberg, M. (2007). *Improving learning cultures in further education*. Routledge.

James, D., Biesta, G. J. J., Hodkinson, P., Postlethwaite, K., & Gleeson, D. (2007). Improving learning cultures in further education? In D. James & G. Biesta (Eds.), *Improving learning cultures in further education. Improving learning* (pp. 3–20). Routledge.

James, D., & Gleeson, D. (2007). Professionality in FE learning cultures. In D. James, G. Biesta, H. Colley, J. Davies, D. Gleeson, P. Hodkinson, W. Maull, K. Postlethwaite, & M. Wahlberg (Eds.), *Improving learning cultures in further education*. Routledge.

Jamieson, M. K., Govaart, G. H., & Pownall, M. (2023). Reflexivity in quantitative research: A rationale and beginner's guide. *Social and Personality Psychology Compass*, *17*(4), 1–15. https://doi.org/10.1111/spc3.12735

Lor, M., & Bowers, B. J. (2018). Perceptions of insider v outsider researchers. *Nursing Research*, *67*(3), 222–230. https://doi.org/10.1097/NNR.0000000000000027

Mannay. (2010). Making the familiar strange: Can visual research methods render the familiar setting more perceptible? *Qualitative Research*, *10*(1), 91–111. https://doi.org/10.1177/1468794109348684

Moen, T. (2006). Reflections on the narrative research approach. *International Journal of Qualitative Methods*, *5*(4), 56–69. https://doi.org/10.1177/160940690600500405

Mortari, L. (2015). Reflectivity in research practice: An overview of different perspectives. *International Journal of Qualitative Methods*, *14*(5), 1–9. https://doi.org/10.1177/1609406915618045

Nadin, S., & Cassell, C. (2006). The use of a research diary as a tool for reflexive practice: Some reflections from management research. *Qualitative Research in Accounting and Management*, *3*(3), 208–217. http://doi.org/10.1108/11766090610705407

O'Neill, J., & Adams, P. (2012). Damned to mediocrity': Political targets, bureaucratic intent, classroom performativity and the child as cipher. *New Zealand Journal of Teachers' Work*, *9*(1), 1–5.

ONS. (2022). *National population projections: 2020-based interim*. Office for National Statistics. https://www.ons.gov.uk/peoplepopulationandcommunity/populationandmigration/populationprojections/bulletins/nationalpopulationprojections/2020basedinterim

Panchamia, N. (2012). *Choice and competition in further education*. The Institute for Government. http://www.instituteforGovernment.org.uk/publications/choice-and-competition-further-education

Patton, M. Q. (2002). *Qualitative evaluation and research methods* (3rd ed.). SAGE.

Perryman, J. (2007). Inspection and emotion. *Cambridge Journal of Education*, *37*(2), 173–190. https://doi.org/10.1080/03057640701372418

Plowright, D., & Barr, G. (2012). An integrated professionalism in further education: A time for phronesis? *Journal of Further and Higher Education*, *36*(1), 1–16. https://doi.org/10.1080/0309877X.2011.590584

Robinson, K. (2015). *Creative schools*. Viking Penguin.

Robinson, K. (2019, April 22). *Standardisation broke education. Here's how we can fix our schools*. Wired Magazine. https://www.wired.co.uk/article/education-personalisation

Roiha, A., & Iikkanen, P. (2022). The salience of a prior relationship between researcher and participants: Reflecting on acquaintance interviews. *Research Methods in Applied Linguistics*, *1*(1). 100003–. https://doi.org/10.1016/j.rmal.2021.100003

Rosenfeld, I., Yemini, M., & Mamlok, D. (2022). Agency and professional identity among mobile teachers: How does the experience of teaching abroad shape teachers' professional identity? *Teachers and Teaching: Theory and Practice*, *28*(6), 668–689. https://doi.org/10.1080/13540602.2022.2097216

Rossetto, K. R. (2014). Qualitative research interviews: Assessing the therapeutic value and challenges. *Journal of Social and Personal Relationships*, *31*(4), 482–489. https://doi.org/10.1177/0265407514522892

Sibieta, L., & Tahir, I. (2021). *Further education and sixth form spending in England*. Institute for Fiscal Studies. https://ifs.org.uk/publications/further-education-and-sixth-form-spending-england

Sibieta, L., & Tahir, I. (2023). *What has happened to college teacher pay in England?* Institute for Fiscal Studies. https://ifs.org.uk/publications/what-has-happened-college-teacher-pay-england

Sikes, P. (2010). The ethics of writing life histories and narratives in educational research. In A. Bathmaker & P. Hartnett (Eds.), *Exploring learning, identity and power through life history and narrative research*. Routledge.

Sugden, J. (1996). Boxing and society. In C. Gratton & I. Jones (Eds.), (2010). *Research methods for sport studies* (2nd ed.). Routledge.

Thomas, G. (2013). *Education: A very short introduction*. Oxford University Press.

Tully, P. (2022). Joining the dots: Theorising professionalism in the English further education sector. *Research in Post-Compulsory Education*, *27*(1), 66–97. https://doi.org/10.1080/13596748.2021.2011510

UCU. (2022, June). *Workload survey 2021: Data report*. University College Union. https://www.ucu.org.uk/media/12905/UCU-workload-survey-2021-data-report/pdf/WorkloadReportJune22.pdf

Wallace, M., & Hoyle, E. (2005). *Education leadership: Ambiguity, professionals and managerialism*. SAGE Publications.

Wang, W., Mather, K., & Seifert, R. (2018). Job insecurity, employee anxiety, and commitment: The moderating role of collective trust in management. *Journal of Trust Research*, *8*(2), 220–237. https://doi.org/10.1080/21515581.2018.1463229

Section 2

Interrogating Approaches to Becoming, Being and Developing as Education Professionals

Chapter 6

Teaching and Learning as Complex Phenomena: Implications for Policy and Teacher Professional Identity

Ben Knight[a] *and Neil Harrison*[b]

[a]University of the West of England, UK
[b]University of Exeter, UK

> One shouldn't complicate things for the pleasure of complicating, but one should also never simplify or pretend to be sure of such simplicity where there is none. If things were simple, word would have gotten around.... (Jacques Derrida, 1988, p. 119)

Abstract

Widespread support exists for the view that teaching is a complex task (Schulman, 2004), that learning is a complex, dynamic phenomenon and that classrooms are 'complex systems' (Hardman, 2010). Systems behaving in complex, emergent ways cannot be successfully 'managed' by rigid, scripted practices but demand flexibility, responsiveness and in situ judgement. However, these dispositions appear only fleetingly, if at all, on professional standards rubrics and statutory descriptors of effective teaching. Discretionary judgement is implied but rarely emphasised. Drawing on the first author's doctoral study of 'emergent learning' in a primary school classroom, we demonstrate the importance of pre- and in-service teachers developing expert in-the-moment professional judgement to navigate the emergent and complex nature of classroom learning and argue that professional judgement should enjoy a more prominent, less tacit, position in pre-service initial teacher education (ITE) and in-service Continuing Professional Development (CPD). This chapter briefly describes and presents findings from the doctoral research which focused on how learning emerges bottom-up through classroom interactions, discusses the implications of this

Critical Perspectives on Educational Policies and Professional Identities, 87–104

doi:10.1108/978-1-83753-332-920241006

for teachers and concludes by setting an agenda for future research into teachers' experiences of agency and autonomy.

Keywords: Teacher judgement; autonomy; classroom complexity; agency; professional identity

Introduction

The above quotation from Derrida captures one of the biggest challenges facing school leaders, teachers and education policymakers. Educating people in groups is a complex endeavour, the outcomes of which are always to some extent unpredictable. Pupils are all unique, teachers and head teachers are too and schools themselves are diverse, context-sensitive communities. Teaching and learning have a non-linear, non-mechanistic, stochastic relationship rendering them relationally complex and their outcomes difficult to control. Despite these characteristics of school education however, the authorship, implementation and enactment of education policy has an inescapable 'pretence of simplicity' about it (in which we are all complicit to some extent) which appears, especially to those doing the educating, somewhat out of step with things we know about learning and the challenges of teaching. In short, teaching and learning are complex phenomena, but policy all too often portrays them, and their outcomes, as simple and directly controllable. For teachers, whose daily professional experiences involve managing classroom complexities, such simplifications and the expectations which accompany them can prove detrimental to the development of professional identity and judgement.

This chapter draws on professional experience and recent doctoral research undertaken by the first author (BK) into classroom learning. It explores the complexities inherent in classroom teaching and the professional attributes which complex classroom contexts demand from teachers. It presents and discusses arguments about over-simplifications and reductionist portrayals of teachers' work in education policy which contrast with the experiences of many teachers. The second author (NH) was part of the supervisory team for the study which provides the springboard for this chapter. Together, we argue that teaching is a good deal more complex than its portrayal in policy typically suggests and discuss some of the consequences this has for teacher professional identity.

The Doctoral Study

The research project, entitled *Complex Adaptive System Behaviours in Small Group interactions: A Year 4 Classroom Case Study of Learning as* 'Emergence' (Knight, 2022), used Complexity Theory as a conceptual framework to explore ways learning emerged through small group activities in a year 4 (8–9 year olds) primary classroom, in England. The study, which received ethical approval from the university, collected mixed methods data. This included video observations analysed using mixed methods social network analysis (MMSNA) (Froehlich et al., 2020), pupil self-reports of learning incidents, pupil interviews and researcher field notes. These were integrated to create four learning narratives, stories which could be told about the learning journeys of small groups of pupils who collaborated on a classroom project over five consecutive days. The learning narratives captured instances of learning, their antecedents and consequences for the small groups and the wider class. Each narrative included a sociograph graphic representation of pupil interactions in a given episode of small group activity, showing types and frequencies of interactions, critical learning incidents in the episode and influential group members (see Figs. 6.1 and 6.2 for examples). Self-reported learning data and extracts from pupils' interview reflections on their learning were integrated to reveal examples of learning emerging bottom-up from the complex interactions between the pupils. Analysis of whole class video episodes contextualised the small group structure, and together, they showed how pupils move between centralised (teacher-led), decentralised (small group) and distributed (whole class) organisational principles. Interactive (Fig. 6.1) and learning incident (Fig. 6.2) data were integrated to identify and analyse when and how learning emerged out of pupil interactions. In Fig. 6.1, nodes represent pupils and edges represent direction and frequency of their interactions. The relative size of each node illustrates each pupils' influence calculated as 'degree centrality' (Grunspan et al., 2014). Nodes with higher incoming than outgoing utterances are considered more influential. Fig. 6.2 illustrates how observed learning incidents were categorised and documented through the duration of each recorded group work

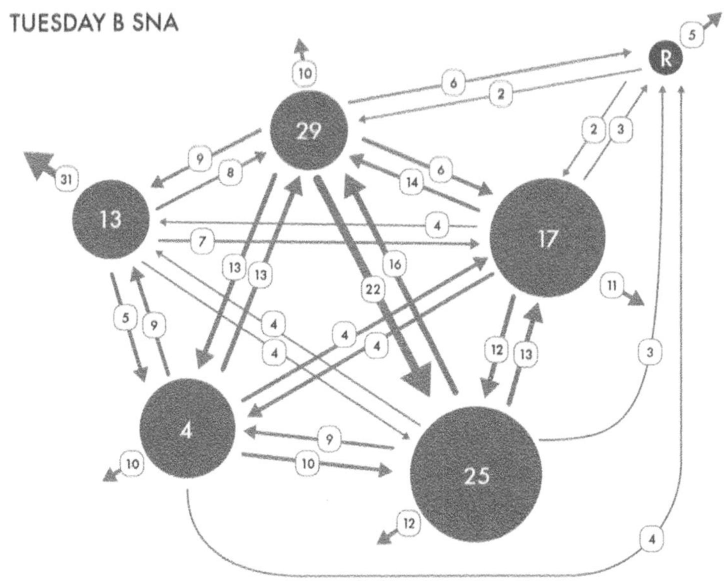

Fig. 6.1. Example of Sociograph Graphic Representation of Small Group Interactions.

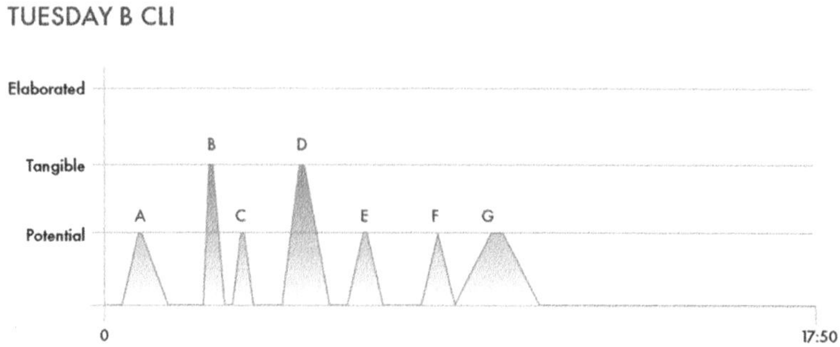

Fig. 6.2. Critical Learning Incident (CLI) Graph Showing When Learning, Categorised as Potential, Tangible or Elaborated, Was Evident During a Group Work Episode.

episode. It shows that towards the end of this episode, there were three observable learning incidents, one 'potential' meaning that learning may be about to emerge, one 'tangible' meaning that learning was evident and one 'elaborated' meaning that learning was not only evident but developed through explanation or discussion. These incidents were then described and analysed using 'thick description' (Geertz, 1973) including transcriptions of dialogue and descriptions of social dynamics and body language. Still images accompanied the written analysis to form vignettes within each learning narrative.

The key findings of the study were:

- That learning can be described as a complex, 'emergent' phenomenon, materialising bottom-up, at least in part as a consequence of pupil–pupil interactions.
- That 'emergent' learning appears largely incomplete, contingent and only partially formed. It rarely appears in elaborated or distilled forms without teacher intervention.
- That environments conducive to 'emergent' learning allow for: the collision of ideas; the distribution of influential (salient) pupils; the articulation of partially formed ideas; shifts between centralised, decentralised and distributed organising structures; pupil autonomy; timely and sensitive teacher intervention.
- That a complex system framing can encourage classroom researchers to think about and look at learning and teaching in ways traditional approaches do not and assist in identifying characteristics of learning which may be inaccessible to constructivist and technocratic approaches.

The study looked at ways learning emerges bottom-upwards when pupils collaborate in small groups. The findings suggest that interactive learning, which is ubiquitous in primary education in many countries, is a complex affair and that learning surfaces in diverse ways and because of a range of networked influences.

This chapter is primarily concerned with the implications of this complexity for teachers, teaching and policy formulation.

Teaching and Learning as Complex Phenomena

Arguments that classroom learning and teaching are not straightforward processes are not difficult to locate in the research and professional literature. As Davis and Sumara (2006) point out, any teacher will attest to not being entirely certain about the outcomes of their teaching due to the unpredictability of learners' responses. Eisner (1985, p. 104) described teaching as 'an inordinately complicated affair' and others including Tripp (1993) conceptualise teachers' work in terms of managing uncertainty and problematising changeability. Alexander et al. (2009, p. 176) point out, 'One cannot begin to understand the true nature of human learning without embracing its interactional complexity.' Schulman (2004, p. 504) puts it in categorical terms, 'teaching [. . .] is perhaps the most complex, most challenging, and most demanding, subtle, nuanced and frightening activity that our species ever invented'. The case is also captured succinctly by Schön, who described teachers' work as operating in the 'swampy lowlands' of everyday life. For him,

> [. . .] the problems of real-world practice do not present themselves to practitioners as well-formed structures. Indeed, they tend not to present themselves as problems at all but as messy indeterminate situations. (1987, p. 4)

Naturally, classroom teaching requires advance planning, known objectives and likely strategies for achieving them, however teaching is not a scripted activity; it could never be due to the inherent complexity, and resulting unpredictability, of learning collectives. Although superficially many classrooms may appear to function with a reasonably high degree of regularity, the interactions of learners' diverse personalities, motivation levels, moods, interests and personal histories, along with variations in home or external factors, including even the weather, will always inject novelty into classroom systems rendering them more indeterminate and contingent than they may appear. Using the analogy of a clock mechanism, Radford (2008) points out that even the most deterministic systems have degrees of unpredictability when viewed at high enough resolution. If one looks closely and for long enough at teaching and learning in any given classroom, the complexity of the teacher's work comes into relief.

The learning end of the teaching–learning nexus is no less complex. In any given school cohort, 'the persistence of inequities in student achievement' (Sinemma et al., 2017, p. 12) speaks to a range of factors influencing variation in learning outcomes. These include inherited and environmental predispositions such as cognitive ability, personality, confidence, task commitment and risk-taking tendencies along with home and school ecosystems. Research from several domains offer insights into learner factors and their effects on learning.

For example, Bronfenbrenner's (1979) ecological systems theory presents a framework for describing community and environmental influences on individuals' development. Research into the emergence of gifts and talents in school age learners (Renzulli, 1986) has highlighted common elements which typically correlate with high performance, including general cognitive ability, environment, personality, self-confidence and chance. Studies from the field of psychology (e.g. Gardiner & Jackson, 2015) illustrate how personality influences learning behaviours and outcomes. Studies of class emotion and mood (Canovi et al., 2019) reveal how pupil interactions, on/off-task behaviours and learning can be influenced by interpersonal features including regulation, negotiation and resistance, which all interact with curriculum teaching in complex ways.

In the doctoral study upon which this chapter is based, classroom complexity showed itself in a number of ways. Firstly, it was evident that learning, which remains stubbornly conceived in policy as a matter of teacher transmission (Knight, 2017), has complex, emergent qualities. That is, it surfaces from the bottom-up as a result of the collision of ideas and interaction of diverse pupil characteristics. This was seen in the spontaneous patterns of interaction and organisation which arose among pupils, eliciting novel ideas and conditions which occasioned learning. Sometimes these emerged as consequence of pupil conflict, sometimes through discussion and disagreement and sometimes pupils sharing their knowledge and understanding. The study also revealed how the interplay of pupils' personalities and personal dispositions created conditions which both prompted, and prevent, learning. In each case, the various points of difference between the pupils, combined with sufficient autonomy for interactions in small groups, created the space, openness and unpredictability which can both elicit and inhibit learning and which teachers typically have to manage.

Sullivan (2009) has pointed out that changes in classroom behaviours, to routines and to expectations and to pupil learning, are often instigated by teachers but can also be triggered from within the pupil collective. Even in the most tightly managed classrooms where learning and routine are largely teacher orchestrated, the collective influence of pupil interactions create complexity, generating teaching and learning landscapes where pupils learn partly because of, partly in spite of and sometimes irrespective of teachers' actions.

Secondly (and related to the previous point), it was evident that learning shared a stochastic relationship to teaching, or as Doll (1993) put it, learning may be anticipated but not predicted since teaching is 'ancillary' to learning, 'not causative'. This was evident in the study by the fact that teaching and learning rarely shared spatio-temporal contiguity, i.e. learning rarely appeared on cue during or shortly after teacher input but often at surprisingly long intervals afterwards. There was also evidence that pupil learning was constructed via a networked array of antecedents and contexts, including direct instruction, positive and negative group interactions, school and home environments. This was seen across the integrated data sets, from the video observation data which showed how learning was prompted by a diversity of interactive behaviours, from the pupil interview transcripts where references to the origins of learning were common and from the self-report moment of learning data which showed time lapses between learning activities and visible learning emerging. These findings are unlikely to surprise any classroom teacher, used as they are to the daily reality that learning is non-linear and learners construct their understandings gradually, in fits and starts by drawing on multiple sources and resources. However, as the next section explores, in policy learning remains stubbornly conceived as a simple, automatic product of teaching.

Education Policy and the Simple View of Teaching and Learning

If curriculum, professional standards and accountability policies give clues to their authors' perspectives, then while these findings may not surprise teachers, they may surprise some policymakers. The doctoral study concluded highlighting that managing classroom complexities to create optimal conditions for the emergence of learning demands sensitivity and judgement about productive levels of pupil autonomy. This requires a good deal of teacher confidence and expertise, including comfort with uncertainty, sensitivity to teachable moments, activation of propositional and procedural knowledge and discretionary judgement. This represents a considerable challenge, even for experienced teachers, and as Burn et al. (2015, p. 14) point out, the challenge for pre-service teachers is even greater,

> If we are to support beginners effectively, we first need to acknowledge just how complex the task of teaching is. If we do not adequately recognise the challenges involved [...] then we will fail to prepare our trainees for the shock of that discovery.

Since policy guides so much of what happens in schools, classrooms and in teacher education, 'adequately recognising the challenges involved' also requires acknowledging them in policy. In the next section, we explore some of the policy frameworks which tend to marginalise, or ignore, the complexities of teaching and learning and position them (albeit indirectly) as straightforward propositions.

A popular portrayal in policy and public discourse present teaching and learning as simple, linear and mechanistic processes, reflecting a technical rationalist view of teaching. In this conception, teachers apply instrumental solutions to address well-formed problems and Schön's *messy, indeterminate situations* are nowhere to be seen. National agendas in England concerning teaching and learning, pupil progress, curriculum, professional standards and teacher development are typically driven by this input–output conception. In the dominant policy discourse, Ofsted's category of 'Outstanding' teaching is narrowly defined as the meticulous planning of lessons to reliably meet specific, predetermined objectives (Eaude, 2012), and despite years of reform, the language of policy still implies a transmission and absorption model of teaching and learning. We refer to this as the 'simple view'. The simple view of teaching and learning is not articulated explicitly in any single policy; however, it hangs invisibly, but uncomfortably, around such concepts as 'best practice' and 'effective teaching' and phrases such as 'pupils should learn that...' and 'teachers must...'.

To illustrate this further, in the principal statutory policy for regulating standards in teaching in England (The Teachers' Standards – DfE, 2021), each of the eight codified expectations are preceded by the phrase 'A teacher must...'. The constituent examples under each standard are dominated by imperative verbs, including 'have', 'demonstrate', 'establish', 'impart', 'use' and 'know'. These language choices, while usefully unambiguous, paint a picture of effective teaching as something teachers simply do or do not do. Conspicuous by their scarcity from this policy are references to reflection (which appears once) or judgement (which does not feature), both of which are central to achieving the aims set out in the standards themselves. Accepting that articulations of expected practice may naturally emphasise outcomes more than processes, we nevertheless argue that the inclusion of process language would characterise teaching more accurately. For example, point three of Standard 7 (DfE, 2021, p. 12):

- *Manage classes effectively, using approaches which are appropriate to pupils' needs in order to involve and motivate them.*

Would more closely resemble reality if it was worded:

- *Make judgements about effective ways to manage classes, evaluating and selecting suitable approaches in order to involve and motivate pupils.*

Point one of Standard 5 (DfE, 2021, p. 11):

- *Know when and how to differentiate appropriately, using approaches which enable pupils to be taught effectively.*

Could be more accurately expressed:

- *Judge when and how to differentiate appropriately, using approaches which enable pupils to be taught effectively.*

Expressed as it is in the policy, this point sends a clear message to pre-service teachers, teacher educators, existing teachers and their managers that effective practice in this area is simply a matter of 'knowing' (or not knowing) what to do. It also tacitly implies that once a teacher 'knows', that knowledge will be relevant in all contexts. However, by leading with the language of judgement, a different message could be signalled about the nature of teaching, that it is a contingent, context-sensitive and complex affair, that effective practice is always a question of reflection and judgement, not possessing (or not possessing) fixed knowledge. In another example, this time from the Early Career Framework (ECF) (DfE, 2019a, 2019b), references to teacher reflection and judgement are similarly scarce. Encouragingly, reflection appears twice, however judgement makes no appearances. Likewise, in the Core Content Framework (CCF), the curriculum for initial teacher education (DfE, 2019a, 2019b), whilst it is encouraging that reflection is mentioned five times, teacher judgement is not mentioned at all. Cordingley et al. (2019) pose a valid question about whether professional standards and competency descriptors promote or restrict teacher autonomy. We argue here that such policies could promote autonomy if the language of autonomy was employed. As can be seen from the examples above, it is not only what *is* said in policy about teaching and learning which may create this simplistic view and restrict teacher autonomy, what *is not* said is also influential.

A similar portrayal of teaching and learning is also mirrored in media and public discourse. Television, online and print media routinely present narratives about school exam results, league tables and 'best' or 'worst' performing schools (Pattinson, 2020), with performance usually cast as solely a function of 'good' or 'poor' teaching (Tait, 2016). This leads to the popular notion that if teaching is 'Outstanding', learning will (or should) be too. The human tendency to seek simple, causal explanations and simple solutions to complex phenomena is well known to complexivists and anthropologists. However, they might argue, as Mencken (cited in Ciotti, 1983) does, that 'for every complex problem, there is a solution that is simple, obvious, and wrong' (p. 37). Journalists too are well aware of the necessity to simplify, which goes some way to explain the reduction of learning to a linear product of teaching in the media. As Levin (2004) points out, 'anything beginning with "This is a complex issue" is likely to result in most people ceasing to pay attention' (p. 278). We believe that the combined result is one in which teachers often cannot recognise the realities of their daily work reflected in the policies which govern it or, we speculate, in the wider cultural landscape within which they operate.

Oversimplification of Teaching and Learning: Implications for Teacher Identity and Development

The reality of the classroom teaching is that teachers are tasked to manage, co-ordinate, choreograph a formidable and diverse assortment of mutually influential factors in the interest of learning. It is problematic if teachers' everyday professional experiences appear at odds with depictions of teaching in public and policy discourse, e.g. to parents, school leaders and in the media. What might be described as the routinising of teaching (Mahony & Hextall, 2000) leads to the view that if teachers would just get it right (or to use the language of the Teachers' Standards 'know' how to do it), pupils would all make desired progress. The concept of 'getting teaching right' is an interesting one. As noted previously, it is rarely expressed explicitly. However, the presumption that when learning outcomes are disappointing teaching must have been too (and vice versa), lurks like a residue underneath much of the policy discourse about teaching and learning.

Hardman (2015), rightly in our view, describes this as a failure of simple causal explanations to adequately account for the complexities of school and classroom learning. While there is no question that quality and appropriateness of teaching strongly influences learning, to paraphrase Derrida, if things were that simple, we would all know about it by now.

Why does this matter? According to Suarez and McGrath (2022), a key factor influencing the development of teacher professional identity is their collective and individual belief about their practice. This includes beliefs about the nature and expectations of their role, self-efficacy and autonomy. According to the Organization for Economic Cooperation and Development (OECD, 2020), teacher professional identity is multifaceted, including factors such as the status of the profession, responsibility and autonomy and societal value of the profession. These components speak directly to the challenge discussed in the previous paragraph. If teaching and learning are viewed as simple in policy and societal discourse, and professional competency descriptors expressed as simplified imperatives, it seems less likely that teachers will feel that the complexities of their work are understood and valued in policy or wider society.

A key finding from the doctoral study, evident in the critical learning incident data, was that visible learning emerges infrequently and often only in 'potential' forms (see Fig. 6.2). However, as already discussed, the view that teaching causes learning and that effective teaching causes better learning more frequently hovers tangibly over much education policy and policy discourse. This finding illustrates a potential mismatch between the ways teaching and learning are portrayed in policy and the reality in classrooms, as observed in the first author's doctoral study. There are obvious risks associated with a rift between policy portrayals and teachers' everyday experiences. A study conducted in Cyprus by Karousiou et al. (2019) showed that teachers can and do feel threatened by policy which contradicts or appears to undermine their values, experience or identity. The potential threat posed by the simple view of teaching and learning common to multiple education policies in England is the discouragement to exercise professional judgement, the stifling of professional autonomy and sense of professional mistrust. For teachers, there is also the burden of being held publicly accountable for a phenomenon (learning) over which they cannot exercise full control. Hargreaves and Fullan (2012) refer to the sense of being permitted and encouraged to exercise autonomy and judgement as professional capital and note with some disappointment that while it appears to thrive in some professions (including medicine, law and social work), it remains elusive in teaching.

A key recommendation from the doctoral study was that since learning is emergent, indeterminate, contingent and characterised by uncertainty, then teaching should be flexible, sensitive to classroom conditions and to some extent improvised. Since learning cannot be relied upon to appear for all pupils on cue during or immediately after teaching input, teachers must be both permitted and able to develop and follow their instincts and exercise their judgement in response to learner dispositions and the dynamic nature of classroom environments. They must enjoy sufficient professional capital. Schön's invoking of real-world practice being 'messy and indeterminate' (1987, p. 4) offers a descriptive explanation of why this is necessary,

In 'messy indeterminate' classroom situations (daily occurrences in most classrooms), teachers may draw on a variety of resources, including routine (Tripp, 1993) and standardised knowledge (Heilbronn, 2008), but they will also inevitably draw on their own interpretation, their instinct and judgement. This is what Dewey (1960) referred to as 'intelligent action', the ability to act in what Schön (1983) referred to as 'no right answer' circumstances. Complex, unpredictable endeavours (like teaching) in complex, dynamic environments (like classrooms) demand this. Teachers are required to make a multitude of judgements throughout a typical day. These include decisions about instruction and explanation, about timings and pace, about seating plans, the movement of pupils, scaffolding support and the management of behaviour, to name just a few. A teacher's professional identity is determined to some extent by their professional capital, and we argue that to build a healthy and productive identity, teachers must see themselves as professionals with both the competence and sufficient latitude to judge what is best.

The 'What Works' Mindset and the Allure of Policy Simplification

The simple view of teaching and learning is really just one co-traveller with the broader policy phenomenon often referred to as 'what works' (Biesta, 2007). This is perhaps exemplified by the creation and prominence of the Educational Endowment Foundation (EEF) as the principal contemporary funder of educational research and its close alignment with policymaking – schools are expected to absorb its findings and implement practices that exemplify them. 'What works' can best be thought of as a mindset, or epistemology, in which evidence of impact and effectiveness is prioritised and learning is characterised as discrete, measurable, products. 'What works' seeks concrete and universal answers to questions like *what should teachers do to optimise (individual) learning outcomes?* There is much to praise about approaches to policy which foreground evidence over ideology, unevidenced assumptions or individual perspectives. Davies (2004, p. 3), for example, champions a 'what works' approach because it:

> helps people make well informed decisions about policies, programmes and projects by putting the best available evidence at the heart of policy development and implementation.

Sayer (2020) attributes the rise of 'what works' in the 1990s to criticisms that education research lacked the rank and rigour of medical research. While on the face of it building policy initiatives informed by evidence appears infinitely sensible, 'what works' is not without its critics, particularly in the field of education. One obvious necessity when creating evidence-informed public policy is that the evidence in question should be credible, reliable and robust. This is more easily achieved in clinical fields where random controlled trials (RCT) are the norm because controlling biomedical variables is relatively straightforward compared to those in social contexts like education. As a result, Davies' 'best available evidence' is often not as robust or reliable as one might like, a point made by Harrison and McCraig (2017). The many context-sensitive variables which create the complexity we discuss in this chapter make schools and classrooms challenging contexts for RCTs.

'What works' is predicated on certain assumptions. Firstly, that it is actually possible to discover what will work in an abstract and decontextualised way. Secondly, that what might work can be usefully translated into teaching approaches that will result in improved pupil outcomes a high percentage of the time, and with little or no risk of worsened outcomes. Thirdly, that what works in one classroom will permanently work, work in all classrooms and with a compelling proportion of learners. Fourthly, that education practice can be neatly compartmentalised ('what works' for special educational needs and disability [SEND], for teaching reading, or teaching mathematics, or managing behaviour, or preventing radicalisation) without mutual-exclusivity or conflict of interest between practices. Fifthly, that there are valid measures and definitive timescales by which the 'what' can be adjudged to have 'worked', and that any gains are sustained (Pawson, 2013).

Understanding what does and does not work in education relies on our ability to make causal attributions (Koopmans, 2016). The first and second of the above assumptions are at the heart of the causality simplification issue, and Byrne's (1998) assertion that in the social world, 'outcomes are determined not by single causes but by multiple causes, and these causes may, and usually do, interact in a nonadditive fashion' (p. 20) rings true here. This, along with similar arguments from Geyer (2012) among others, suggests that even the idea of discovering 'what works' is an impossibility. The reason for this is that complex social systems, such as schools or the teaching and learning within them, are highly contextual and do not behave in ways conducive to illumination via evidence from RCTs. This is something that the EEF itself is beginning to appreciate (Edovald & Nevill, 2021).

Identifying teaching practices which research indicates may accelerate pupil learning on average is one thing. To presume such practices will 'work' everywhere, or that they will not actually have a negative effect for some, is probably expecting too much. In explaining why 'what works' does not always work, Biesta (2016, p. 194) criticises the 'prevalence of quasi-causal thinking about educational practice and its improvement', suggesting that by ignoring the complexities of educational contexts policymakers end up asking the wrong questions and confusing educational improvement with the effectiveness of educational action. A legitimate concern for all invested in improving education is that if we are not naming the challenges accurately enough, or asking the right questions, we have little prospect of meeting them, and that is a problem. As illustrated in earlier examples, the fact that there is no mechanistic causal relationship between teaching and learning (or a magic wand) has not prevented policy from evolving as if there is. Logical extensions of the 'what works' approach include concepts like 'fixing' schools (Lingenfelter, 2015) or 'ensuring' pupil progress. However, the approach of presuming that tweaks to professional standards, curriculum or accountability frameworks will result in wholesale improvements in pupil outcomes is yet to bear significant fruit.

Of course, education policy, especially at national scale, will always be somewhat reductionist and can never portray all the realities of the classroom as teachers experience them. National policy must, to some extent, be presented in terms of causes and effects, the causes mostly being pedagogical enactments and the effects (in theory) being improved outcomes; this is the raison d'etre of national education, after all. While there are cogent arguments in favour of greater devolution of local policymaking to schools and greater autonomy for school leaders and teachers, we accept the cause-effect model as a basic reality of centralised national policymaking. Inherent in this is a belief that some pedagogic practices *will* be more effective, more of the time and in more places, than others.

Complexity reduction is inevitable and necessary in large-scale policymaking. Simplicity is also a necessity. Humans are hardwired to reduce complex entities and systems into manageable and digestible forms (Gelman & Kaylish, 2006). The inclination to present educational issues as simple and fixable is as understandable as it is alluring, particularly for politicians, whose longevity and status is built on being perceived to be effective. However, it does come at a cost. When teachers, and those who educate and manage them, adopt the mindset that what 'works' can be handed down nationally in bite-sized chunks rather than discovered locally and historically, the first casualties are likely to be teacher autonomy, reflection and professional judgement, building blocks of professional identity.

While accepting that policy will have a built-in and unavoidable simplicity, we agree with Hardman (2010, p. 8), who argues that 'policy makers would do well to recognise the limitations of their insights'. We are not arguing that 'nothing works' or 'everything works', but rather that government and its agencies need to better appreciate contextualised nuances and the value of everyday teacher judgement, with a greater acceptance that classrooms are places where learning emerges and is not purely a linear and unproblematic consequence of teaching defined by reductionist ideas of the 'only right way' of doing things.

We believe that asking teachers to enact policies which appear at odds with their experiences of teaching and learning, or which appear to characterise their work in ways they do not recognise, does little to create a positive, empowered or self-motivated workforce and goes some way to explaining the current recruitment and retention crisis in England (Worth, 2023). Equally, education policy which seems disconnected from realities on the ground in classrooms is also vulnerable to neglect. This is illustrated by data from Karousiou et al. (2019) showing that teachers will resist policy initiatives which they perceive to undermine their professional identity. Knight (2017) has argued that there is a need for more accurate depictions of teachers' work and its relationship to pupils' learning. It is our contention in this chapter that inaccurate portrayals of teaching and learning in policy, and the knock-on effects in media and public discourse, may actually discourage teachers from adopting the sorts of professional identity, mindsets and behaviours which may lead to improvements in pupil learning.

Conclusion and Ways Forward

The doctoral research on which this chapter builds showed that learning is unpredictable, contingent and sensitive to context and local system interactions. A key conclusion from the doctoral study was that learning clearly has emergent qualities, meaning that it can, and often will, emerge bottom-up through autonomous distributed and decentralised pupil interactivity. An implication of this is that teaching demands what we refer to as 'managed complexity'. This requires teachers to embrace the heterogeneity and involution of classroom teaching and learning, to exercise judgements about what seems best for their pupils in this moment, and hold less tightly to what ought to 'work'. Another conclusion from the study, and something of an elephant in the room, was that because of the emergent and contingent nature of learning, teachers, while influential, can only exercise partial control over it. We argue that if this was more widely understood, acknowledged and reflected in teaching and teacher education policies, those policies could more authentically represent teaching as teachers experience it and better prepare novices to manage its complexities. As we have argued above, applying even small tweaks to policy language which move it away from categorical imperatives and implications of simplicity, while foregrounding reflection and judgement, would go some way to achieving this.

This matters because portrayals of teaching in policy influence the how it is nurtured in teacher education (Knight, 2023), how it unfolds in the classroom and, crucially, how teachers view their professional work and professional selves. Within the frameworks of curriculum and standards of professional conduct, teachers should be encouraged to view themselves as trusted autonomous agents, expected to, and capable of, making discretionary judgements in the interests of pupil learning. Making judgements, learning from them, adapting them, experiencing them bear fruit and reflecting consciously on one's own growing expertise are key elements of professional development and professional identity formation. Trusted teachers are also self-motivated teachers. Small changes in policy language have the potential to unlock the professional and decisional capital on which professional identity and self-motivation grows, provided the language is backed up by permission to exercise judgement.

Given the recruitment and retention crisis currently unfolding in the teaching profession in England and the fact that the number of new teachers entering the profession barely keeps pace with the numbers leaving it (DfE, 2023), efforts to create professional trust, agency and positive identity among teachers should be a policy priority. This means acknowledging the inherent complexities of learning and teaching to all with a vested interest, but perhaps most importantly teachers themselves. To build on the important observation from Derrida with which the chapter opened, we have been pretending to be sure about the simplicity of learning and teaching for quite long enough. No word has spread about the magic wand producing pupil learning on cue; therefore, it is time to acknowledge that teaching is, to repeat Elliot Eisner's words (1985, p. 104), 'an inordinately complicated affair' and give teachers the trust and latitude they need to judge how best to navigate that complexity.

To support this, we believe further research is necessary into the complexities of classroom teaching and learning. This chapter has drawn on research evidence from a single doctoral study undertaken in one classroom. As such, it offers some initial illustrations of ways learning emerges through pupil interaction, upon which others may build. The study has implications for teaching and teachers, but it also highlights the need to develop new insights into teachers' work, the ways in which it shows itself to be far from simple, predictable or scriptable and the ways teachers wrestle with professional autonomy and agency.

Lessons for Doctoral Students

The principle lesson emerging from this study was that since classrooms, like all social settings, are complex, unpredictable environments with many moving parts classroom research plans must be flexible, and researchers must be responsive to changing conditions and be able to adapt in situ when collecting data. In short, like teachers, researchers must be both permitted to and capable of exercising judgement.

References

Alexander, P., Schallert, D., & Reynolds, R. (2009). What is learning anyway? A topographical perspective considered. *Educational Psychologist*, *44*(3), 176–192. https://doi.org/10.1080/00461520903029006

Biesta, G. (2007). Why "what works" won't work: Evidence-based practice and the democratic deficit in educational research. *Educational Research*, *57*(1), 1–22. https://doi.org/10.1111/j.1741-5446.2006.00241.x

Biesta, G. (2016). Improving education through research? From effectiveness, causality and technology to purpose, complexity and culture. *Policy Futures in Education*, *14*(2), 194–210. https://doi.org/10.1177/1478210315613900

Bronfenbrenner, U. (1979). *The ecology of human development: Experiments by nature and design*. Harvard University Press.

Burn, K., Hagger, H., & Mutton, T. (2015). *Beginning teachers' learning: Making experience count*. Critical Publishing.

Byrne, D. (1998). *Complexity theory and the social sciences*. Routledge.

Canovi, A., Kumpulainen, A., & Molinari, L. (2019). The dynamics of class mood and student agency in classroom interactions. *Journal of Classroom Interaction*, *54*(1), 4–25.

Ciotti, P. (1983). Freaked out by technology: A student of the '60s takes a new look at what moved the new left. *Reason: Free Minds and Free Markets*, August edition 1983, 34–37.

Cordingley, P., Crisp, B., Johns, P., Perry, T., Campbell, C., Bell, M., & Bradbury, M. (2019). *Constructing teachers' professional identities*. Educational International & UNESCO.

Davies, P. (2004). *Is evidence-based government possible?* Jerry lee lecture presented at the 4th annual Campbell collaboration colloquium, Washington, DC.

Davis, B., & Sumara, D. (2006). *Complexity and education: Enquiries into learning, teaching and research*. Routlege.

Department for Education (DfE). (2019a). *ITT core content framework*. https://assets.publishing.service.gov.uk/government/uploads/system/uploads/attachment_data/file/974307/ITT_core_content_framework_.pdf

Department for Education (DfE). (2019b). *Early career framework*. https://assets.publishing.service.gov.uk/government/uploads/system/uploads/attachment_data/file/978358/Early-Career_Framework_April_2021.pdf

Department for Education (DfE). (2021). *The teachers' standards*. https://assets.publishing.service.gov.uk/government/uploads/system/uploads/attachment_data/file/1040274/Teachers__Standards_Dec_2021.pdf

Department for Education (DfE). (2023). *School workforce in England*. https://explore-education-statistics.service.gov.uk/find-statistics/school-workforce-in-england

Derrida, J. (1998). *Limited Inc*. Northwestern University Press.

Dewey, J. (1960). *The quest for certainty*. Capricorn Editions.

Doll, W. (1993). *A post-modern perspective on curriculum*. Teachers College Press.

Eaude, T. (2012). *How do expert primary class teachers really work? A critical guide for teachers, head teachers and teacher educators*. Critical Publishing.

Edovald, T., & Nevill, C. (2021). Working out what works: The case of the education endowment foundation in England. *ECNU Review of Education*, *4*(1), 46–64.

Eisner, E. (1985). *The art of educational evaluation*. Falmer Press.

Froehlich, D., Rhem, M., & Rienties, B. (2020). *Mixed methods social network analysis. Theories and methodologies in learning and education*. Routledge.

Gardiner, E., & Jackson, C. (2015). Personality and learning processes underlying maverickism. *Journal of Managerial Psychology*, *30*(6), 726–740.

Geertz, C. (1973). *Thick description: Toward an interpretive theory of culture. The interpretation of cultures: Selected essays*. Basic Books.

Gelman, S. A., & Kalish, C. W. (2006). Conceptual development. In D. Kuhn & R. Siegler (Eds.), *Handbook of child psychology, Vol. 2: Cognition, perception and language* (pp. 687–733). Wiley.

Geyer, R. (2012). Can complexity move UK policy beyond 'evidence-based policy making' and the 'audit culture'? Applying a 'complexity cascade' to education and health policy. *Political Studies*, *60*(1), 20–43. https://doi.org/10.1111/j.1467-9248.2011.00903.x

Grunspan, D., Wiggins, B., & Goodreau, S. (2014). Understanding classrooms through social network analysis: A primer for social network analysis in education research. *CBE-Life Sciences Education*, *13*(2), 167–178. https://doi.org/10.1187/cbe.13-08-0162

Hardman, M. (2010, August 23–27). Is complexity theory useful in describing classroom learning? [Conference presentation]. *European conference on educational research (ECER)*, Helsinki, Finland 2010.

Hardman, M. (2015). *Complexity and classroom learning*. Unpublished doctoral dissertation, Canturbury Christchurch University.

Hargreaves, A., & Fullan, M. (2012). *Professional capital: Transforming teaching in every school*. Routledge.

Harrison, N., & McCaig, C. (2017). Examining the epistemology of impact and success of educational interventions using a reflective case study of university bursaries. *British Educational Research Journal*, *43*(2), 290–309.

Heilbronn, R. (2008). *Teacher development and the development of practical judgement.* Continuum.

Karousiou, C., Hajisoteriou, C., & Angelides, P. (2019). Teachers' professional identity in super-diverse school settings: Teachers as agents of intercultural education. *Teachers and Teaching*, *25*(2), 240–258.

Knight, B. (2017). The evolving codification of teachers' work: Policy, politics and the consequences of pursuing quality control in initial teacher education. *Teacher Education Advancement Network (TEAN) Journal*, *9*(1), 4–13.

Knight, B. (2022). *Complex adaptive system behaviours in small group interaction: A year 4 classroom case study of learning as 'emergence'.* Unpublished doctoral dissertation, University of the West of England. https://uwe-repository.worktribe.com/output/9030663

Knight, B. (2023). *Nurturing professional judgement: A critical guide for teachers and teacher educators.* Critical Publishing.

Koopmans, M. (2016). Ergodicity and the merits of the single case. In M. Koopmans & D. Stamovlasis (Eds.), *Complex dynamical systems in education* [Online] (pp. 119–139). Springer.

Levin, B. (2004). Media–government relations in education. *Journal of Education Policy*, *19*(3), 271–283.

Lingenfelter, P. (2015). *"Proof", policy and practice: Understanding the role of evidence in improving education.* Stylus Publishing.

Mahoney, P., & Hextall, I. (2000). *Reconstructing teaching: Standards, performance and accountability.* Routledge.

OECD. (2020). *TALIS 2018 results (Volume II): Teachers and school leaders as valued professionals.* OECD Publishing. https://doi.org/10.1787/19cf08df-en

Pattinson, R. (2020, February 11). Pain in the class: Primary school axes teacher because kids' SATs results were too good. *The Sun* [online]. https://www.thesun.co.uk/news/10944050/primary-school-axes-teacher-sats-results-too-good/. Accessed on 16 April 2023.

Pawson, R. (2013). *The science of evaluation: A realist manifesto.* SAGE.

Radford, M. (2008). Complexity and truth in educational research. In M. Mason (Ed.), *Complexity and the philosophy of education* (pp. 137–149). Wiley-Blackwell.

Renzulli, J. (1986). The three-ring conception of giftedness: A developmental model for creative productivity. In R. J. Sternberg & J. E. Davidson (Eds.), *Conceptions of giftedness* (pp. 53–92). Cambridge University Press.

Sayer, P. (2020). A new epistemology of evidence-based policy. *Policy & Politics*, *48*(2), 241–258. https://doi.org/10.1332/030557319X15657389008311

Schön, D. (1983). *The reflective practitioner: How professionals think in action.* Ashgate.

Schön, D. (1987). *Educating the reflective practitioner: Toward a new design for teaching and learning in the professions.* Jossey-Bass higher education series. Jossey-Bass.

Schulman, L. (2004). *The wisdom of practice: Essays on teaching, learning and learning to teach.* Jossey-Bass.

Sinnema, C., Aitken, G., & Meyer, F. (2017). Capturing the complex, context-bound and active nature of teaching through inquiry-oriented standards for teaching. *Journal of Teacher Education*, *68*(1), 9–27. https://doi.org/10.1177/0022487116668017

Suarez, V., & McGrath, J. (2022). *Teacher professional identity: How to develop and support it in times of change*. OECD Education Working Paper No. 267.

Sullivan, J. (2009). *Emergent learning: The power of complex adaptive systems in the classroom*. Unpublished doctoral dissertation, Boston College.

Tait, P. (2016, March 22). *The importance of great teaching on children's success*. The Telegraph. https://www.telegraph.co.uk/education/educationopinion/12201014/The-importance-of-great-teaching-on-childrens-success.html

Tripp, D. (1993). *Critical incidents in teaching: Developing professional judgement*. Routledge/Falmer.

Worth, J. (2023, Mcrah 23). *We need a long-term strategy to tackle this recruitment crisis*. Times Educational Supplement (TES). https://www.tes.com/magazine/analysis/general/teacher-recruitment-crisis-teacher-training-itt-teacher-pay

Chapter 7

Mastering Professional Practices: Primary School Science Teacher Identity and Development[1]

Juliet Edmonds

University of the West of England, UK

Abstract

This chapter explores the way three teachers developed their primary science teaching in English schools, in an educational climate where training policies and financial pressures result in few opportunities to do so, meaning many schools resort to in-school support. The training needs of primary teachers vary according to their experience and backgrounds. This research project used a combined model of Lave and Wenger's (1991) community of practice with Bourdieu's social theory model (1999, 2004), specifically on science capital, to explore the opportunities for primary science development as well as teacher agency and identity within the primary school. The research consisted of three case studies of primary teachers, using co-teaching and semi-structured interviews to develop a greater understanding of teachers' beliefs and development in science teaching. Thematic analysis was used to organise and interpret the data using the theoretical framework outlined. The combined theoretical models proved useful in considering the 'science capital' as part of their identity as a teacher; they contributed to a school or field. The nature and amount of science capital had an impact on the potential for their science teaching development as well as their identity and agency within the school community of practice.

Keywords: Identity; case study; science capital; primary science; CPD

---

[1]This chapter has been developed using extracts from the thesis, Edmonds, J. (2018). *The beliefs, practices and development of three teachers of science in the primary school*. Thesis, Faculty of the Arts, Creative Industries and Education, University of the West of England, Bristol.

Critical Perspectives on Educational Policies and Professional Identities, 105–120

Published under exclusive licence by Emerald Publishing Limited
doi:10.1108/978-1-83753-332-920241007

Introduction

As an initial teacher educator for over 25 years, I have focused on developing new primary science teachers whom I hope are capable, inquisitive and open to developing their skills and knowledge further in schools. Having sent them off to their new jobs, I have been curious about how the teachers evolve during their first few years of teaching. As the status of science in the primary school has been influenced by government policy, e.g. dropping national assessment, so have opportunities for training in science reduced for practising teachers. However, despite this, some teachers apparently have a defined identity as a teacher of primary science, whereas others appear to reluctantly engage in primary science activities in the classroom.

This chapter recounts my multiple case studies of three teachers in Bristol primary school settings to explore their developing science teacher identities, beliefs and practices. I will first explain the context of the research, the theoretical framework, methodology and findings of the study. I will then discuss my proposed novel model, using a combined theoretical framework of Lave and Wenger and Bourdieu, to analyse what teachers bring to their science roles and how that impacts their identity, beliefs and ways they work within their school communities of practice to develop their expertise in teaching science. Firstly, I will consider the national context of primary science teaching and policies surrounding training in England at the time of the research in 2015–2016.

The National Context

Over the last 20 years, the importance of science in the primary school curriculum has declined. Since the removal of national testing of science in the primary school at the end of Key Stage 2 (aged 10–11 years), science has a reduced status within primary schools in England (Ofsted, 2021). It is often treated as a foundation subject or taught using a cross-curricular topic-based approach (CFE, 2017). The state of science provision in primary schools is compounded by 29% primary teachers having 'A' level qualifications in any sciences (Wellcome Trust, 2017). Many teachers feel unconfident in teaching science, especially practical science activities, yet the curriculum requires practical investigative-type activities to be taught to children in schools (CFE, 2017; Dillon et al., 2000).

However, Ofsted (2013) found in their review of secondary and primary teaching that there was a direct correlation between a school's commitment to science Continuing Professional Development (CPD) and children's achievement in it but recognised there was little science support for schools (Ofsted, 2021). When CPD was available, it was found that the training was often a poor match to the needs of the teachers and lacked contextual elements of subject-specific training that change practice (Cordingly & Buckler, 2014). Schools are suffering from a reduction in funding in real terms (Weale, 2022) which has an impact on the money available for teachers' professional development. Often school training tends towards the generalistic to cover many subjects at the same time for financial reasons, for example, generic subject leadership training (Colclough, 2018; Wellcome Trust, 2014).

The current situation of little local science CPD in schools might appear to necessitate the use of peer support and training in schools. School-based training using peers has been identified as a preferred learning context by teachers in their early careers (Grosemans et al., 2015; Richter et al., 2011) using socially constructive and situated learning principles (Brown et al., 1989; Lave, 1996; Lave & Wenger, 1991; Wenger, 2010). This could support the development of school communities of practice to provide school-based training in their local context. Yet is it an effective model for teachers with differing experiences and a range of school levels of expertise in primary subjects?

In this current primary school context, I conducted case studies of three teachers of primary science in the Bristol area aiming to explore how their science capital influenced the way they developed their practice, teacher identity and beliefs about effective teaching in science in their own communities of practice, primarily the school. Science capital can be defined as the qualifications, contacts, understanding and experiences of science that a person has (Archer et al., 2012; Bourdieu, 2004). All these aspects have an impact on the confidence, knowledge and professional identity in science of teachers.

Professional Identity

The professional identity of the case study science teachers was explored within the research. I explored their personal histories in relation to science, finding out about their science capital through science experiences, qualifications and primary science roles in school, all of which make up their identities as teachers of primary science.

However, identity is a contested construct. Schwartz et al. (2012) suggest that identity is not just the 'who are you' but the 'who you act as being' in interpersonal and group interactions, plus the recognition these groups or individuals give you in return. They also argue that the definition will change in emphasis depending on one's theoretical perspective and field of study. Wood and Jefferies (2002) meanwhile divide the construct of identity into three distinct areas: social identities assigned by others to define people as a social object; personal identities assigned by oneself; and self-concept or the '*overarching view of oneself as a physical, social, spiritual, or moral being*' (p. 90).

The identity of a primary science teacher may not even be one individual social identity. Clark and Groves (2012) suggest that the identity and emotions of a primary teacher cannot be separated from the primary science teacher identity, the teacher of children or the school leader, as these identities are all entwined and dynamic. The nature of primary teaching and the culture in English primary schools can foster an identity as a generalist, whose main role is to teach young children (ibid.)

Identities will be formed by personal histories and will also be influenced by teaching experiences themselves. Teacher identities are not static entities; they change continually. Learning to teach can be seen as cognitive but also affective (Turner Bisset, 2001). The combination and learning that takes place between these aspects of the job shapes and teaches the teacher about teaching itself. Smith (2007) proposes that a teacher's identity and subject knowledge will continue to grow throughout their career if they continue to teach science.

Theoretical Framework

In exploring the case study teachers' identities and development as teachers of primary science, the role of their personal science capital and their school communities of practice was explored to research their impact. To support understanding of this development, I drew on the work of Lave and Wenger (1991) who focus their theories on the learning and the acculturation of a student into a subject or skill through the activity of a community. They describe the community of practice (CoP) as a group of individuals with the following features: a common enterprise, which is understood and recognised by participants and a community which functions with a:

> mutual engagement which aligns individuals working together; and a 'shared repertoire' of communal resource. (Wenger, 1998. p. 73)

A CoP may be local and on a small scale or even national on a large scale; for example, in schools, it may be a year group team, while nationally it may be the Association for Science Education. Members of communities may belong to different communities simultaneously.

Lave and Wenger's (1991) 'legitimate peripheral participation' theorises the process of learning through the trajectory of a new individual coming into a CoP. They define legitimate peripheral participation as follows:

> Learners inevitably participate in communities of practitioners and that the mastery of knowledge and skill requires newcomers to move towards full participation in the socio-cultural practices of the community. (Lave & Wenger, 1991, p. 29)

They describe how a newcomer to a community, like a new teacher, functions on the peripheries of the community initially. They state that such novices perform minor task and associate with other novices, ordinary members and even masters of the community. In talking, being and acting out the essential task of the community, the novice learns the task, makes sense of the knowledge and is provided with models by the masters. The learning happens, and the novice changes, resulting from the shared practices, negotiated understandings and functions of the community.

A significant criticism of Lave and Wenger's work on the CoP and legitimate peripheral participation (1991; Wenger, 1998) is that the authors neglect to consider the contribution of the individual, their experience and beliefs and what they bring to a workplace (Cox, 2005; Cobb & Yackel, 1996; Hodkinson & Hodkinson, 2003, 2004). As Hodkinson and Hodkinson state, '*there is a risk of seeing only the social, because the individual is subsumed within it*' (2003, p. 3). These authors argue the dispositions of individuals, and the social and cultural capital brought to the workplace are undervalued in the work of Lave and Wenger (1991). This difference between individuals could also be an important factor when viewing the power relationships within a workplace and the varying degrees of influence that individuals may have within a CoP.

To recognise and evaluate the social and cultural science capital that a teacher brings to a school CoP, I have also drawn on the theories of Pierre Bourdieu (1999, 2004). Bourdieu's social practice theory model needs to be considered in its three constituents: habitus, capital and field (Maton, 2008). It is the relationship between these three aspects that makes the model useful.

Bourdieu's 'habitus' describes the social structures that shape a person's present and future practices (Bourdieu & Emanuel, 1996). Bourdieu sees habitus as a property of individuals, groups or institutions, which acts on a person to produce their views, values, tendencies and beliefs. Habitus is not static as a person's habitus is always changing in response to life events and the people around them. It is influenced by, and in turn influences, the present social space or 'field' that a person inhabits.

The field is a 'social space' where interactions, transactions and events occur (Bourdieu, 2004). A field could be a primary school, shop or public house; however, on a bigger scale, it could also be a national political party. The nature of the field is described by Bourdieu as being inherently competitive, even combative. Thomson (2012) compares Bourdieu's field to that of a football field, bounded by size and physical conditions that affect all players but unequally because of what each player brings to the game, the different skills attributes and experiences that the players bring to the field, described as 'capital' by Bourdieu.

Bourdieu also coins the term 'science capital' (1999, 2004). As part of his theory of habitus, he suggests that the elevated status of science in society can inevitably create economic, cultural and symbolic inequalities among individuals. Bourdieu breaks down capital into economic capital like money and possessions; cultural capital such as taste, knowledge and language; symbolic capital like qualifications and other credentials; and social capital such as personal contacts and networks (Thomson, 2012). Bourdieu (2004) describes how science capital can be built up and transferred or exchanged into other types of capital within society through qualifications, interest and participation in science by family and friends and through participating in science in the wider world. Although in his original writings, he was referring to the situated science societies of industry and research, the theory has resonance for teachers with science backgrounds operating in a world where very few hold that science capital. This social practice model recognises the differences in 'capital' a teacher brings to a school but also the influence of the school on the teacher's views, beliefs and practice.

The argument above proposes that the socialcultural theories of situated learning in communities of practice, located within the socio-constructivist theory of learning, may offer a useful framework for analysing the learning and especially the development of teacher practices and identity within the school environment. My use of this framework comes with an awareness that there are conditions within the school environment, such as time pressures, which make the theoretical model less applicable in schools which do not prioritise time for staff to work together.

Bourdieu's model of social practice implies that a new teacher with strong science capital, joining a school with a CoP consisting of other teachers also with strong science capital, will have less power and influence than if they had joined a school with members with little science capital. However, power within the field of the school may also be impacted by social and economic capital in other areas of expertise such as management and leadership. The use of the two theories facilitated a more accurate representation of the process of development of the science teacher in the primary school. Having developed a theoretical framework, I now needed to design a congruent research approach for my study that would allow me to explore the framework and the field in which the teachers worked. Other postgraduate research (PGR) students will need to do likewise for their research.

Methodology and Methods

To analyse the impact of the communities of practice in school on the teachers' science teaching development and agency in the school, I carried out three qualitative, evaluative case studies of primary teachers with an interest in science.

To collect data on the participants' science capital, I initially carried out semi-structured interviews, with each teacher discussing their background and identity in science, their parents' connections with science, their science qualifications and what they believed effective science teaching was.

I then co-planned and taught a series of science teaching sessions with each teacher drawing on what they thought was effective science teaching and learning. This gave me and the case study teachers a common set of experiences in the classroom to discuss and evaluate. It also allowed me to be present at times when the class teachers 'reflect in action' on the learning in the classroom (Schön, 1987). Thoughts on these teaching sessions were captured through reflective diaries by me and the case study teachers.

I am aware that there will always exist an 'otherness', in the form of a power differential between researcher and research participant (Fine, 1994; Katsiaficas et al., 2011), yet compared to other research approaches in education, this seems most likely to be reduced through the co-teaching scenario, which is perhaps something for fellow PGR researchers to consider. During the research, I occupied and moved between multiple identities of 'teacher', 'researcher' and 'teacher educator'. I was in a 'teacher' role when co-planning and co-teaching the science sessions in the classroom, 'researcher' when interviewing the case study teachers and, in one teacher's eyes, I was 'still the teacher educator he wanted to impress'. I found the role as co-teacher the most comfortable one, despite having been out of the everyday classroom for many years, due to the reduced power differential it necessitated. I found it was a situation where the teacher could discuss their views about science teaching in a natural arena where they had greater personal agency.

In follow-up interviews, I focused on the teachers' self-evaluation of their teaching and learning strategies and how they developed their primary science practice. We discussed how they were developing in their science teaching and their CPD activities: what courses had helped, what support they got from school, whether they used the internet to develop their teaching and what support they might need in the future. This was to explore the strategies the teachers used to develop their expertise in science once in school. The interviews were transcribed and analysed through thematic analysis (Braun & Clarke, 2006) using themes as they emerged to me, as well as themes identified by the research questions.

Ethical approval for the research was gained from the university following BERA (2018) guidelines and data were anonymised and files kept password protected. The participants were given information sheets and consent form about the research which explained the project and the process of removing their data from the research by a specified date they choose to withdraw. The interview data were shared with the participants giving them the opportunity to change or clarify what they had said.

The Three Case Study Teachers

All three case study teachers worked in Bristol primary schools at the time of the research. The case studies were drawn from teachers I had contact within my role as an initial teacher education lecturer. The teachers were working with children aged eight to 11 years (in Key Stage 2).

Nathan did not have science qualifications beyond the General Certificate of Secondary Education (GCSE). Neither of his parents worked in science careers. His father had a keen interest and broad knowledge of science and carried out scientific investigations with Nathan when he was a child, such as launching rockets. Nathan had worked as a teaching assistant in an early years setting before training. He identified himself as a science specialist on his PGCE course. He was in his newly qualified year when the research started in a three-form entry school, in year three. The other year three teachers had told Nathan they disliked teaching science and did not like doing practical investigations. Nathan had consequently avoided planning practical activities for these colleagues. Nathan had not received any science-based CPD since finishing his PGCE.

Karen did not have parents in science careers, but she reported they were 'nature loving'. She took biology 'A' level and a BSc. in psychology. She had been teaching for three years when the research started and was the science lead in her one-form entry school in year five. Karen had attended one session on science enquiry on her Newly Qualified Teacher (NQT) provision but had not found it very useful. Karen was the newly appointed science lead within her school. She had not taken any staff meetings or monitoring in science when the research started.

Shamah trained as a primary/secondary (Key Stage 2/3, children aged 7–13 years) science teacher and worked in a two-form entry school in year 6 and had been teaching for over six years. Her father was a doctor, and her mother and brother both worked in science-related careers. She had a degree in biological sciences and had retrained and worked as a histologist, researching the microscopic anatomy of biological tissues. She was the science leader for her school and in her role attended the Association of Science Education annual meetings, as well as the Big Bang Fair, an event to encourage students into Science, Technology, Engineering and Maths (STEM) careers, and local events run by universities and subject organisations. Her school was in an area of Bristol where many of the parents worked in the aerospace industry. Shamah had led training for her school staff and contributed to professional magazines for teachers.

Findings

Nathan

Nathan was a new member of staff in a three-form entry school; he worked with two other teachers, each with a couple of years' experience of teaching. Nathan planned the science provision for the year 3 group.

Nathan expressed a desire that the science should be taught in a more exploratory manner. This appeared to be drawn from his experiences in the Early Years classroom. However, he felt reluctant to use this approach as it would not be popular with the other year 3 teachers.

Nathan was also using teaching strategies that he had seen used by the other year 3 teachers in his planning and teaching even if they were incongruent with his beliefs about effective teaching and learning. He stated:

> The other thing that I do that is ...maybe not be seen as best practise. We have got flip charts on Power point things, and I make slides that I have made for that lesson and there are bits when we can talk and bits where we write down.

The children had to guess the answers under the blanked-out sections. The answers were then revealed.

When I returned to interview Nathan, after teaching together, it was a new academic year. Nathan had a mentor, a senior teacher in the school who was supporting his development in behaviour management and planning and teaching. Nathan reported that this was generic mentoring and not support for individual curriculum areas such as science.

He had completed his NQT year before our last session teaching together. Nathan appeared to be excited when I arrived for our interview after school. He had been chosen to be part of the science group whose remit was to develop science throughout the school. He described:

> Learning hubs...so there are two, four, six, probably eight of us...in the science team so we are all going to be working together like how we can improve the teaching of science.

Nathan seemed to be delighted that the school had recognised his interest in science and given him some wider responsibility.

Analysing the CPD science teaching support being given by the school, using the model of Lave and Wenger (1991), Nathan appeared to be on the outer edges of the school CoP, the periphery, when I first visited him in school. He had only been a staff member for a couple of terms. Nathan did not see himself as a 'master' of teaching or teaching science; he was often self-deprecatory about his teaching practice. This may be a feature of his personality, but it also may be that he did not yet feel confident in his own practice or identity. However, he appeared to demonstrate that he had been influenced by the pedagogy of the Early Years CoP that he had been part of as a teaching assistant. Nathan's science capital was recognised by giving him the responsibility of planning the science for the year group, albeit from a science scheme, a set of resources with activities, assessments mapped against the curriculum. However, it was not enough to allow him to influence or develop his teaching and learning strategies in the way he felt was congruent with his beliefs about teaching and learning in science. There was no community support for his teaching science in his first year. He was influenced by the practice of his peers.

Karen

Karen had a view of her subject knowledge in science as being secure, she stated '*I consider myself good at science*'. She stated that on her PGCE, she saw science as being her strength, indicating she felt more confident with the subject knowledge and pedagogy than perhaps other subjects. However, she expressed less confident views about her practice. She made casual comments during our teaching and planning about whether she structured the lessons too much and whether she should allow the children more freedom in investigations/enquiry. She demonstrated a lack of confidence in her teaching as she stated of her investigative work:

> But I always find science investigations quite chaotic. They never seem as if they are perfect.

In considering school support for her development of effective practice in science, she stated she planned her science provision with her partner teacher; '*We bounce ideas off each other a lot*'. She described in detail the way she and her partner teacher worked together, identifying themes, pedagogies and inspiration. She reported that the school had a collegial atmosphere. She told me how she had been on holiday with some of the teachers. This indicated a close community, perhaps conducive to a school CoP.

Karen demonstrated insecurity about her current science teaching practice and whether she was doing things right or not and how she should develop in the future. In the second interview, Karen reported that she had experienced an observation by the head teacher and that she did not get the 'outstanding' grade for the observation she wanted. She was upset and baffled as to how she could have further improved her lesson stating:

> So yeah, it would be really interesting to see kind of 'outstanding' science lessons where children are planning and carrying out science investigations. Because I don't think I know what they look like. If that was not it, I am not sure what they look like.

In discussing her role as a science leader in the school, Karen talked about developing science teaching in the school. She had been made the science leader that year and appeared keen to develop her role further. She stated she wanted to extend the shared understanding of planning in science through '*peer planning cross phase*'. She also wanted teachers to team-teach and carry out observations on one another as they never '*get to talk about it*', referring to their teaching. She was perhaps indicating that she wanted to develop a primary science-focused CoP within the school community.

Karen seems to have entered primary teaching with a positive family habitus towards science, forming her identity through her cultural science capital. She had symbolic science capital from her psychology degree and a few years of teaching experience. In a school with little expertise in science, she had the role of science leader. She seemed to have no 'master' in the school, a teacher with expertise in science teaching, to learn from and develop her practice (Lave & Wenger, 1991; Wenger, 1998). Karen declared she was confident in her subject knowledge in science but appeared to have had her confidence in her pedagogical skills in primary science reduced by the head teacher's observation. She had confidence in her ability to manage and organise the class. Karen appeared unsure of how she could develop in her role as science lead as there were no 'master' of science within the school to help her develop.

Shamah

Shamah seemed to have a positive, assured view of herself as a teacher of science; she appeared confident in her credibility in teaching science, probably arising from her strong economic, symbolic and science social capital saying:

> I can offer more with my background.

This science credibility, coming from a previous identity as a research scientist, appeared to be important to Shamah. When describing her first teaching practice with a year 10 class, she described how the children know all the answers to their science quiz, but she mentioned:

> So, I threw in a couple of chemical compounds, and they did say 'I don't know what that one is'.

At the time of the research, Shamah was the school's science subject leader. She had another member of staff from Key Stage 1 (aged five to seven years) shadowing her, but she was the main primary science staff member. She seemed to re-assert this saying of the other staff member '*I'm science leader across the whole school but he does more with Key Stage 1*'. She appeared to see herself nurturing him; she suggested that he was getting a lot out of the experience, learning from her. She talked of staff meetings at her school where she fed back on innovation in science pedagogy she had seen. She mentioned the 'playground science' that she had seen at a talk and how all the staff used the teaching strategy in science week. Shamah stated that she arranged the whole school science week on an annual basis.

For her professional development and that of the wider school, Shamah seemed to actively seek out and learn about pedagogical innovations through external science communities of practice. She stated that she regularly attended the Association for Science Education Annual (ASE) conference. She described several new pedagogical strategies she had seen there:

> ASE conference is like gold, so I learn a lot from there and this time I went for two days and tried to go to as many workshops as I could, and they are just fantastic.

She appeared to have attended sessions in areas not directly appropriate to herself but that she felt would benefit the school, for example, she stated she attended a session on Early Years science even though she taught in the seven- to eleven-year-old phase. Shamah seemed to have started to extend her influence in primary science to other schools and organisations. She had written an article in Primary Science, the *ASE* magazine, and talked at conferences and to Initial Teacher Education students.

Shamah was the person in her school who provided the CPD support, and the school appeared to have an active CoP for science education. The definition by Wenger (2000) states that a CoP would describe the way the school staff worked with Shamah from her account, but this research is unable to judge the effectiveness of this community. Shamah was working in, what Lave and Wenger (1991) would describe, the role of a 'master in primary science'. Shamah seemed to take responsibility for the day-to-day organisation, as well as the development of, and influence on, practice, however effective.

Wenger (2000) talks about individuals, like Shamah, as 'brokers of boundaries.' She seems to travel across the boundary of her own school's CoP to other communities and gains knowledge, objects and practices that she brought back to her own community and vice versa. Wenger argues that brokering knowledge is 'delicate' as it requires the broker to have the credibility to be listened to but a distance to be able to offer something different and novel (2000). Shamah appears to have a background in a science career to bring her credibility and identity and as part of other external communities of practice, enabled by the head teacher and her enthusiasm to be able to offer new pedagogies to her staff. Wenger (2000) also describes brokers of boundaries as those who enjoy making connections and the transfer of knowledge. Shamah appeared to be adept at making connections and the transfer of knowledge and practices, 'the import and export' (Wenger, 2000, p. 235).

Discussion

The position and identities of case study teachers in their school communities of practice appear to be affected by their amount and type of science capital. Lave and Wenger's model (1991) has been criticised for not recognising the differences in power and agency in individuals (Eraut et al., 2002) or the conditions which give equal access to learning in a CoP (Cox, 2005; Cobb & Yackel, 1996; Hodkinson & Hodkinson, 2003, 2004). My research indicates that science capital impacts the teachers in the case studies' power and agency within their communities of practice. The teacher, Shamah, with a large amount of science capital, appeared to have more agency to influence her school community and other national communities of practice in science than the other case studies. This may arise from the confidence in her identity which her science capital has given her or her longer teaching experience.

The theoretical model of the communities of practice and theories of situated learning combined with Bourdieu's theories of social practice has been used in this research to analyse the case study teachers' beliefs and ability to access learning and influence within a CoP. Theories on communities of practice and the way teachers learn from those communities do not recognise new teachers' previous experience and science capital on their position and learning in the community. The greater the science capital, the less the teacher appeared to be influenced by the teachers at the peripheries and the more they had an impact on the school, like Shamah advising the head teacher and leading school science initiatives. This is explored further below.

The amount and type of science capital and the teacher's relative position in their school and external communities of practice also appear to be bound up with their identity as a science teacher and the degree of agency within their school. As Swartz et al. suggest (2012), identity is not just who you see you are but who others see you as and who you act as. Nathan, with low science symbolic capital but some cultural capital in science, was at the peripheries of both his school and wider primary science communities of practice and appeared to be unconfident in his own practice and beliefs. He seemed to be susceptible to taking on the practices of his colleagues at the peripheries of the community, which may, in turn, impact on his beliefs (Nias, 1989; Turner- Bisset, 2001). Nathan appeared to have limited access to learning about science teaching from others and is influenced by his fellow year groups' teachers, even if he did not agree with their approach to teaching the subject. He lacked the influence to challenge practices and was only required to plan from a published science scheme. He gained more agency when invited to join the science working group.

Karen, with stronger science symbolic capital in her field, seemed to experience self-doubt over her practice when only given a 'good' grade from her observation; she appeared to be conscious of how the other staff might see her. She appeared to desire to influence her general school CoP but seemed to feel that she needs to be judged as an 'excellent' science teacher to act like a 'master' leading a primary science community. She was not part of an external science CoP but indicates she would have liked to be and envisaged the benefits of such a community. In both the cases of Nathan and Karen, within-school verification affected their identity as science teachers. Shamah, with strong science capital for her field, had a secure self-identity and expressed few doubts about her beliefs or practice and sees herself as spreading good practice within her school and in the wider science education community. She had taken on a role of developing other teachers as experts of science. With substantial symbolic, cultural and social capital, Shamah appeared to have a position of power and influence over science within her school science CoP and was beginning to influence other primary science communities of practice with her own beliefs about science education.

Conclusion

This research has implications for the type of training and support needed by primary teachers of science within a school CoP. Communities of practice on their own appear to have limited impact on new teachers of science unless schools contain individuals with expertise in science teaching from whom the new teacher can learn or contact external communities. New teachers in schools without expertise can easily pick up teaching strategies contrary to their own beliefs of effective teaching to 'fit in' with current school pedagogy. If schools are relying on 'informal' training through their communities, there is a risk of the new staff developing incongruent science practices, such as Nathan using a PowerPoint reveal rather than other pedagogies he believed were more effective for learning. The loss of teachers from the profession and the lack of teachers with science expertise in schools means there are few teachers who new staff can learn from to develop their practice in science.

This study highlights the importance of the first few years in a teaching role on the development of practice in science teaching. The extension of the early career teacher period policy, introduced in the United Kingdom from 2023, is to be welcomed. However, the access of new teachers to quality CPD and expertise in science teaching may still be an issue in many schools due to financial restrictions and the demise of local authorities. The research supports an argument for local, school-based CPD to involve and engage the existing teachers' community of practice alongside the novice teacher encouraging discussion and mutual development of science teaching. This strategy could enhance the practice of more stablished teachers as well as reduce the impact of less desirable science teaching practices on the early career teacher.

A model that uses Bourdieu's social theory to explore the science capital a teacher has in conjunction with an understanding of the state of the CoP or 'field' for a curriculum subject, like science. The model could be a useful frame of understanding the needs and potential of a NQT in schools and a greater understanding of the strategies to help them develop their teaching in primary science.

Reflecting on my research approaches, a lesson for me was the use of combined theoretical frameworks to better represent my research field. Another insight was that I found co-teaching with the case study teacher an effective way to explore their beliefs and practices as well creating a more balanced power differential between us. I learnt a great deal about their thinking when preparing and teaching science lessons that informed my research but also that enhanced my professional role in teacher education in sharing with students strategies that can be effective in further developing Early Career Teacher (ECT) science practice.

References

Archer, L., DeWitt, J., Osborne, J., Dillon, J., Willis, B., & Wong, B. (2012). Science aspirations and family habitus: How families shape children's engagement and identification with science. *American Educational Research Journal*, *49*(5), 881–908.

Bourdieu, P. (1999). The specificity of the scientific field. In M. Biagioli (Ed.), *The science studies reader* (pp. 31–50). Routledge.

Bourdieu, P. (2004). *Science of science and reflexivity*. University of Chicago Press and Polity Press.

Bourdieu, P., & Emanuel, S. (1996). *The rules of art: Genesis and structure of the literary field*. Polity Press.

Braun, V., & Clarke, V. (2006). Using thematic analysis in psychology. *Qualitative Research in Psychology*, *3*(2), 77–101.

British Educational Research Association [BERA]. (2018). *Ethical guidelines for educational research* (4th ed.). https://www.bera.ac.uk/researchers-resources/publications/ethicalguidelines-for-educational-research-2018

Brown, J. S., Collins, A., & Duguid, P. (1989). Situated cognition and the culture of learning. *Educational Researcher*, *18*(1), 32–42.

CFE. (2017). *State of the nation report of UK primary science education*. CFE.

Clark, J. C., & Groves, S. (2012). Teaching primary science: Emotions, identity and the use of practical activities. *Australian Educational Researcher*, *39*(4), 463–475.

Cobb, P., & Yackel, E. (1996). Constructivist, emergent, and sociocultural perspectives in the context of developmental research. *Educational Psychologist*, *31*(3–4), 175–190.

Colclough, C. (2018) *Science specific professional development: What our members say*. Education in Science.

Cordingley, P., & Buckler, N. (2014). Who you gonna call? – Using specialists effectively. *Professional Development Today*, *16*(2), 62–67.

Cox, A. M. (2005). What are communities of practice? A comparative review of four seminal work. *Journal of Information Science*, *31*(6), 527–540.

Dillon, J., Osborne, J., Fairbrother, R., & Kurina, L. (2000). *A study into the professional views and needs of science teachers in primary and secondary schools in England*. Council for Science and Technology.

Eraut, M., Maillardet, F. J., Miller, C., Steadman, S., Ali, A., Blackman, C., & Furner, J. (2002). *Conceptual analysis of research questions: Do the concepts of "learning community" and "community of practice" provide added value?* https://files.eric.ed.gov/fulltext/ED466030.pdf. Accessed on January 12, 2021.

Fine, M. (1994). Dis-stance and other stances: Negotiations of power inside feminist research. *Power and Method: Political Activism and Educational Research*, 13–35.

Grosemans, I., Boon, A., Verclairen, C., Dochy, F., & Kyndt, E. (2015). Informal learning of primary school teachers: Considering the role of teaching experience and school culture. *Teaching and Teacher Education*, *47*, 151–161.

Hodkinson, P., & Hodkinson, H. (2003). Individuals, communities of practice and the policy context: School teachers' learning in their workplace. *Studies in Continuing Education*, *25*(1), 3–21.

Hodkinson, P., & Hodkinson, H. (2004). A constructive critique of communities of practice: Moving beyond Lave and Wenger. In *Seminar paper presented at 'integrating work and learning –Contemporary issues' seminar series 2004, 11th May*. The Australian Centre for Organisational, Vocational and Adult Learning.

Katsiaficas, D., Futch, V. A., Fine, M., & Sirin, S. R. (2011). Everyday hyphens: Exploring youth identities with methodological and analytic pluralism. *Qualitative Research in Psychology*, *8*(2), 120–139.

Lave, J. (1996). Teaching, as learning, in practice. *Mind, Culture and Activity*, *3*(3), 149–164.

Lave, J., & Wenger, E. (1991). *Situated learning: Legitimate peripheral participation*. Cambridge University Press.

Maton, K. (2008). Habitus. In M. J. Grenfell (Ed.), *Pierre Bourdieu: Key concepts*. Routledge.

Nias, J. (1989). *Primary teachers talking: A study of teaching as work*. Routledge.

Ofsted. (2013). *Maintaining curiosity*. HMSO.

Ofsted. (2021). *Research review series: Science*. HMSO.

Richter, D., Kunter, M., Klusmann, U., Lüdtke, O., & Baumert, J. (2011). Professional development across the teaching career: Teachers' uptake of formal and informal learning opportunities. *Teaching and Teacher Education*, *27*(1), 116–126.

Schön, D. A. (1987). *Educating the reflective practitioner: Toward a new design for teaching and learning in the professions*. Jossey-Bass.

Schwartz, S. J., Zamboanga, B. L., Meca, A., & Ritchie, R. A. (2012). Identity around the world: An overview. *New Directions for Child and Adolescent Development*, *2012*(138), 1–18.

Smith, R. G. (2007). Developing professional identities and knowledge: Becoming primary teachers. *Teachers and Teaching: Theory and Practice*, *13*(4), 377–397.

Thomson, M. (2012) Field. In M. J. Grenfell (Ed.), *Pierre Bourdieu: Key concepts*. Routledge.

Turner Bisset, R. (2001). *Expert teaching. Knowledge and pedagogy to lead the profession*. David Fulton.

Weale, S. (2022). Schools in England face funding crisis as costs soar, study warns. *The Guardian*. Accessed on August 2, 2022.

Wellcome Trust. (2014). *Primary science: Is it missing out?* Wellcome Trust.

Wellcome Trust. (2017). *The science context for primary initial teacher training*. Wellcome Trust.

Wenger, E. (1998). *Communities of practice: Learning, meaning, and identity*. Cambridge University Press.

Wenger, E. (2000). Communities of practice and social learning systems. *Organization*, *7*(2), 225–246.

Wenger, E. (2010). Communities of practice and social learning systems: The career of a concept. In *Social learning systems and communities of practice* (pp. 179–198). Springer.

Woods, P., & Jeffrey, B. (2002). The reconstruction of primary teachers' identities. *British Journal of Sociology of Education*, *23*(1), 89–106.

Chapter 8

Voices From the Staffroom: Impacts of Further Education Policy on CPD in the Sector[1]

Andy Goldhawk

University of the West of England, UK

Abstract

This chapter discusses the findings of doctoral research into further education lecturers' and middle managers' perceptions of how Continuing Professional Development (CPD) in the sector is planned and implemented. Thematic analysis revealed that mandatory CPD is perceived to: involve conflicting purposes between those planning it and its recipients (deriving from divergent understandings of professionalism and the role of CPD among stakeholders); and be characterised as mostly generic, didactic, and ineffective, leading lecturers to compensate by engaging in additional, separate forms of CPD. This chapter demonstrates the value of practice-based doctoral study in enabling the voices of educators to be positioned at the centre of an exploration of their own professional learning.

Keywords: Further education; FE; education policy; CPD; continuing professional development; professionalism

Introduction and Context

This chapter discusses the findings of my doctoral research into further education (FE) lecturers' and middle managers' perceptions of how Continuing Professional

---

[1]This chapter has been developed using extracts from the thesis, Goldhawk, A. L. (2020). *The view from the deck – Exploring lecturers' and middle managers' perceptions of English FE sector professional development: A case study evaluation.* Thesis, Faculty of Arts, Creative Industries and Education, University of the West of England, Bristol.

Critical Perspectives on Educational Policies and Professional Identities, 121–138

doi:10.1108/978-1-83753-332-920241008

Development (CPD) in the sector is planned and implemented. I firstly give a brief history of fluctuating policies salient to CPD in English FE over the last 50 years. I then consider how this policy context has contributed to differing conceptualisations of 'professionalism' in FE among stakeholders, and how these differing understandings impact CPD in the sector. To achieve the latter, I discuss the following three themes derived from my doctoral research:

(1) conflicted understandings of the purposes of CPD;
(2) the generic character of mandatory CPD learning content;
(3) learning as a personal endeavour and the 'compensatory principle'.

In discussing my work, I also intend to highlight issues and offer guidance to other postgraduate research students. My research stemmed from wanting to investigate three aspects: what had led to, in my experiences, the prevalence of a passive, knowledge transmission approach to mandatory CPD sessions; perceptions of educators towards such CPD; and how (else) colleagues engaged with professional learning. This third aspect was inspired by frequent comments from colleagues that most mandatory CPD was in their view irrelevant to their professional learning needs, and often incongruent with their preferred means through which to learn. Indeed, throughout my 15 years teaching in different FE colleges, mandatory CPD was almost always characterised as didactic and generic (meaning not calibrated for lectures in particular subject areas, career stages or with specific professional learning needs). Further, I wanted to position FE lecturers' and middle managers' perceptions at the centre of an exploration of their own professional learning. This would counter what Taubman (in Daley et al., 2015) identified as a lack of respect for the expertise and views of professional lecturers in FE and a historical context in which research in the FE sector has been largely invisible (Solvason & Elliott, 2013).

I framed my research in a social constructivist epistemology, by way of investigating CPD through the perspectives of FE lecturers and middle managers. The inclusion of this second group enabled me to give voice to those charged with the practical organisation of mandatory CPD but often without the agency to determine its focus. Taking place across 2018 and 2019, this research was timely: Kennedy (2014, pp. 2–3) argues (and it remains the case at the time of writing in 2023):

> [...] the state of the literature on teachers' CPD as a whole is partial in its coverage, is fragmented, and is under-theorised. [...] studies which look at how the concept of professionalism can be mobilised to influence the profession as a whole in relation to CPD is much less evident.

Terms Used

The terminology relating to CPD in FE has evolved over time. Earlier terms used for ongoing professional learning in education include 'in-service education and training' (INSET) and 'staff development' (Billing, 1982), with both terms still sometimes applied in secondary education into the 21st century (see O'Brian & Jones, 2014). Lee (1990) describes 'staff' development as a narrow concept, in effect a 'function of management' which prioritises equipping educators to satisfy the corporate needs of the organisation. This inference draws parallels with later terms used in salient policy discourses, such as 'workforce training' (see ETF, 2018).

In this chapter, I use the term CPD as defined by Avalos, 2011 (in Postholm, 2012, p. 406), to mean 'teachers' learning, how they learn to learn and how they apply their knowledge in practice to support [their students]'. It was also the term mostly used by participants in this research. I use the word 'lecturer' to refer to educators in the FE sector: in my experiences in the sector the use of both 'teacher' and 'lecturer' was contested among colleagues, and there appeared no clear preference. There is also an inconsistent application of the terms within literature addressing the sector (Goldhawk & Waller, 2023).

A Brief History of FE Policy

FE lecturers' CPD had remained a peripheral concern until the 1970s (Lee, 1990). The James Report (HMSO, 1972) marked a watershed moment in FE (Aubrey & Bell, 2017; Broad, 2015) in calling for substantial increases in 'training' for practising lecturers in the sector to address their development needs. The report suggested a range of both formal and informal CPD, from evening team meetings to higher degrees and even secondment to other work sectors (HMSO, 1972). Provision for CPD in FE increased throughout the 1970s following the James Report (Broad, 2015). Then in 1977, a parliamentary sub-committee focused on the 'in-service training' of FE lecturers recommended formal teacher 'training' for practising lecturers in FE (as had the 1972 James Report) as, unlike with school teachers, qualifications had not been required to teach in FE, resulting in fewer than half of FE lecturers holding a formal teaching qualification at that time (Lee, 1990). Despite this recommendation, there remained no policy requirement for a teaching qualification until 2001 (HMSO, 2001).

Amid this 'golden age' in the early 1970s of increased recognition and investment in CPD activities in FE (Broad, 2015), an apparent tension had been identified in attempting to address the divergent needs of government policy, FE organisations and individual lecturers, through CPD. Elliot-Kemp and Williams (1980, as cited by Lee, 1990) suggest that addressing these differing needs was incompatible, as individualised CPD could not result in organisational improvements. However, this position failed to recognise how CPD interventions at an individual level, such as one-to-one coaching, can serve to both support organisational agendas and the professional learning interests of lecturers (Bennett & Bush, 2014; Lofthouse, 2019).

A lecturer-centred approach to CPD was also considered problematic in relation to resourcing. Addressing common themes within CPD was considered more cost efficient than seeking to attend to diverse individual learning needs (Hopkins, 1986). Such concern for efficiencies echoed the developing neo-liberal policy cultivated by successive governments since the late 1970s which had introduced a discourse justifying reduced public expenditure (Lucas & Crowther, 2016). Over 40 years later, mandatory CPD was similarly characterised by the participants in my doctoral research, most of whom articulating a prevalence of generic learning content (or, 'common themes'), unrelated to the divergent professional learning needs of those in attendance (given varying professional backgrounds, qualifications and teaching experiences). The neo-liberal policy discourse of efficiencies in CPD within the sector informed, I argue, the development of a managerialist concept of professionalism (Tummons, 2014) for FE lecturers and a narrow conceptualisation of the purpose of CPD, as discussed later.

By the mid-1980s, a top-down approach to organising CPD had become pervasive (Broad, 2015), shifting away from individualised CPD and towards a managerialist culture (Smith & O'Leary, 2013). In the late 1980s, organisational and policy agendas were further prioritised in CPD, amid a period of considerable policy change (Broad, 2015). The 1988 Education Reform Act and the Training and Enterprise Councils required:

> [...] colleges to act as businesses in what will be a strongly competitive environment. This will mean that FE colleges will need to conduct curriculum audits [...] in order to assess market position. (Lee, 1990, p. 111)

In alignment with this dominant discourse (Gee, 1996) and subsequent to the 1992 Further and Higher Education Act, incorporation occurred in the sector in April 1993, relocating financial control from local education authorities to college managers and governors. FE colleges were now responsible for funding and planning CPD, with the government 'taking a laissez-faire approach' to CPD (Broad, 2015, p. 18). Broad (2015) classifies CPD in the years following incorporation as characterised by 'knowledge transmission', meaning external 'expert'-led didactic sessions delivered to FE lecturers, who are given the role of passive recipients of information considered important by senior management (Kennedy, 2014).

The goal of incorporation was to create a marketised, competitive and nationally standardised and regulated FE sector (Lucas, 2004b). The period following incorporation marked a further divergence in priorities between FE college management and FE lecturers (Randle & Brady, 1997). College leaders now took a managerialist approach: prioritising performance metrics such as retention and achievement figures, with CPD focused on ensuring compliance to short-term organisational goals (Broad, 2015). Concerns for professional autonomy and addressing individual professional learning needs had been side-lined (Orr, 2008). Further, the efficiencies required by incorporation led to significant staff redundancies, worsened conditions of work, increased workloads and a substantial increase in part-time and temporary lecturers in most colleges (Hodgson, 2015; Lucas, 2004a). Engagement with CPD for this enlarged part-time lecturer workforce was highly restricted as such staff were less likely to be able to attend during their work hours, and as specific provision for CPD was rarely provided for these employees (Lucas, 2004a). The part-time participants in my study echoed this problem in connection with their limited engagement with mandatory CPD.

From 1997, successive New Labour governments embraced the preceding Conservative policy of developing a marketised FE sector and designated the FE sector specifically as the central vehicle responsible for ensuring a globally competitive workforce (see DfES, 2002, 2006; DfEE, 1998; Foster, 2005). This discourse was now interlaced with the language of social justice and widening participation (Aubrey & Bell, 2017) and urgent messages of an apparent need to address the requirements of globalisation (Leitch, 2006; Simmons, 2010). To ensure the FE sector workforce could meet these responsibilities (Orr, 2008), legislation was introduced requiring that, from 2001, FE lecturers were obliged to hold a teaching qualification (HMSO, 2001), and from 2007, FE lecturers were mandated to gain Qualified Teacher Learning and Skills (QTLS) status (HMSO, 2007a). Between 2008 and 2012, FE lecturers were also required by legislation to participate in, and record, 30 hours CPD on an annual basis (HMSO, 2007b). In 2007, mandatory paid membership of the Institute for Learning (IfL) was introduced, an organisation purporting to validate the professional status of FE lecturers and support CPD opportunities in the sector (IfL, 2012).

Some policy changes during this period had the potential to solidify the professional identity and status of FE lecturers, including the mandatory teaching qualifications, the introduction of QTLS status and interlinking the adult education sector with public discourses of professionalism (Aubrey & Bell, 2017). However, the implementation of these policy reforms were underpinned by increased surveillance and auditing through scrutiny from both Ofsted and the IfL. Furthermore, the codification of professional behaviours through extensive formal descriptors defined professionalism in restrictive, managerialist terms (Aubrey & Bell, 2017).

During the Conservative-Liberal Democrat Coalition Government, the Lingfield Review (2012) however regarded these requirements as overly prescriptive, and it marked the end of this mandatory completion of a teaching qualification and the requirement to log CPD. Membership of the IfL once again became voluntary. Implementing the recommendations of the Lingfield Review therefore marked a further policy swing, this time from policy diktat to de-regulation (Aubrey & Bell, 2017; Gleeson et al., 2015): responsibility for lecturers' CPD was once more devolved to FE leadership teams. In 2014, the IfL was replaced by the Education and Training Foundation (ETF). A branch of the ETF, the Society for Education and Training (SET), focuses on teaching quality and professionalism in the sector (SET, 2018).

Contrasting Conceptualisations of Professionalism

Differing conceptualisations of FE professionalism frame the role and expectations of lecturers according to divergent ideological positions, in turn informing the perceived purposes of CPD for this workforce. Literature considering notions of professionalism and professional identity in FE is abundant (for example, Daley et al., 2015; Gleeson et al., 2015; Hodgson, 2015; Tummons, 2014), perhaps reflecting its contested nature.

James and Biesta (2007, p. 127) rightly assert: 'what constitutes professionalism in FE is an elusive concept', in part due to the wide-ranging composition of professional biographies of the FE lecturer workforce. Definitions of professionalism in FE are also emergent, in that the profession is comparably new (Tummons, 2014) and cannot, therefore, be simply defined against features of professionalism ascribed to older professions (Atkins & Tummons, 2017). For instance, unlike in law, health or teaching in the state primary and secondary sectors, FE lecturers do not currently require qualifications to practise (teaching), which Millerson (cited in Atkins & Tummons, 2017) identified as a key characteristic of what defines a profession. Thus, some lecturers begin working in the sector with no formal training, qualifications or experiences in teaching (ETF, 2019). Commonly, however, FE lecturers hold qualifications or possess industrial experiences in the subject areas they teach (James & Biesta, 2007). Those within the FE lecturer workforce, particularly in vocational curriculum areas, are therefore often characterised as having a dual professionalism, with the former industry career role, such as hairdressing or catering, often remaining their principal professional identity (Gleeson et al., 2005).

Discourses of professionalism in FE can be situated within distinct ideological paradigms. The first two considered in this section, the managerialist and utilitarian paradigms, tend to be where policy discourses of professionalism are located, whereas the third, emancipatory paradigm, tends to represent academic and practitioner discourses (Tummons, 2014).

Discourses within the managerialist paradigm conceive professionalism to comprise lecturer compliance, audit and performativity, income generation, inspection frameworks and through adherence to pre-defined standards or criteria (Atkins & Tummons, 2017; Aubrey & Bell, 2017; Daley et al., 2015). Various iterations of professional standards (see ETF, 2014, 2022; FENTO, 1999; LLUK, 2006) define professionalism through descriptors of 'occupational performativity' rather than 'a philosophy of professionalism' (Atkins & Tummons, 2017, p. 362), perhaps because unlike in other education sectors, FE professional standards are rooted in a vocational philosophy of occupational competencies (Lucas & Nasta, 2010) based on industry definitions. Such wording indicates that policy considers the sector through a vocational lens, with the same professional standards applying to academic subjects. The question as to the appropriateness of these standards across sector provision is thus raised.

Managerial professionalism is derived from above (McClelland, 1990, as cited by Lucas & Nasta, 2010) and imposed from the outside (Evans, 2008) through policy diktat and inspection. These restricted and restrictive notions of professionalism represent an ideology whereby employees are not trusted to independently perform their roles in an effective manner (Robson, 1998), akin to de-professionalisation (Gleeson & Shain, 1999; Randle & Brady, 1997).

The utilitarian paradigm narrowly defines professionalism (in FE) as comprising generic teaching skills, in the event diminishing the importance of subject expertise (Atkins & Tummons, 2017). Finally, discourses within the emancipatory paradigm recognise lecturers' professional expertise, agency and autonomy; apply democratically ascribed standards (Atkins & Tummons, 2017; Tummons, 2014); and involve engagement with communities of practice (Wenger, 1998). Emancipatory discourses represent professionalism in FE as emergent and developmental in nature, due to the frequently part-time and casual nature of much FE work which elongates the timeframe in which professional identity is formed (Tummons, 2014). Emancipatory discourses of professionalism coincide with elements of what Taubman (in Daley et al., 2015, p. 107) identifies as a traditional understanding of professionalism, which comprises:

> [...] a specific group of workers with a defined body of knowledge and expertise and a set of values and ethics [...] professionals were allowed to act autonomously and exercise their judgment.

Professionals in this sense operate with independence from outside interference, and their practices are informed and enriched through engagement with CPD (Taubman in Daley et al., 2015).

It must be recognised that these paradigms are not always evident in isolation from one another. For instance, the LLUK standards (2006) appeared to recognise the expertise of the lecturer, in encouraging the autonomous selection and application of learning theory to inform teaching practices, while elsewhere invoking aspects of managerial professionalism in appealing for adherence to organisational quality systems (Tummons, 2014). Atkins and Tummons (2017, p. 363) draw on Gee (1996) to argue that in the current FE standards expressed by the ETF (2014), teachers are indicated as having responsibility for their own CPD, a feature of emancipatory professionalism, but are not involved in 'the discursive constructions of professionalism within which they are enroled as social actors'.

Effects on Professional Learning in FE

This section summarises three themes deriving from my thematic analysis (Braun & Clarke, 2006) in which divergent perceptions of what constitutes professionalism for FE lecturers in turn frame differing understandings of the purpose and form of CPD. I conducted ten semi-structured interviews with FE lecturers who teach across academic and vocational disciplines and four middle managers. The three themes summarised here address the following research question: what are lecturers' and middle managers' perceptions of how professional development in FE is planned, implemented and evaluated?

This research was framed by social constructivism, an epistemology that emphasises 'that the world is constructed by human beings as they interact and engage in interpretation' (O'Leary, 2010, p. 6). This positioning in turn informed my choice of methodological approach, that of 'personalised' evaluation (Kushner, 2000). Evaluation research predominantly concerns the effectiveness of particular programmes, although as Newby (2014) suggests, this is not always the case: evaluation can also focus on processes or activities. Indeed, the evaluation in this research concentrated on FE CPD activities for lecturers and middle managers. Kushner (2000) argued that personalising evaluation recognises that participants' own lives, beliefs, values and work contexts is important: measuring activities against their objectives is meaningless unless we also consider how those objectives relate to the lives of people.

This was also case study research: the case of professional development in an FE college in England. Flyvbjerg (2006) considers a strength of case study research to be that it facilitates the development of context specific knowledge, a form of knowledge that characterises an expert level of understanding in a particular field. As a single case, I could not make generalised claims of knowledge for the whole sector. However, As Flyvbjerg (2006, p. 224) contends: 'concrete, context-dependent knowledge is [...] more valuable than the vain search for predictive theories and universals'. Rather than a search for generalisable features or conclusions relating to CPD, I sought a depth of understanding to obtain a 'nuanced view of reality' which offers context specific knowledge (Flyvbjerg, 2006, p. 223).

The research adhered to all salient aspects of the British Education Research Association (BERA, 2018) ethical guidelines and the ethics policies and procedures both of the University of the West of England and at the site where the research was conducted. Nonetheless, Ryan (2007) as cited by Seale et al. (2013) recognises limitations with generic guidelines when applied to 'insider research': research conducted in the researcher's own place of work. Kvale (1996) argues that the power is located predominantly with the researcher who chooses the questions, steers the discussion and analyses the data. Munro et al. (2004), however, maintain that it is the participant who chooses their answers and the level of detail given, thus holding power. These choices may be affected by interviewees' positions in the organisation, the researcher's usual job role, the interviewees' and researcher's roles in relation to each other or organisational politics (Munro et al., 2004). Elsewhere, Mercer (2007) describes a danger of distortion with interview answers that may occur in light of personal concerns or ambitions or by the need for a participant to continue a professional relationship with the researcher subsequent to the interview. My position was that the means by which power is held and applied as identified by both Kvale (1996) and Munro et al. (2004) both occur.

A means to address such power imbalances, at least in part, is to involve participants at the data analysis stage (Sikes, 2006). I invited participants to review transcribed data to ensure its accuracy in representing their views and as part of developing an ethic of care which 'realigns the notion of power [and] eliminates the potential for exploitation in work-based projects' (Costley & Gibbs, 2010, p. 44). Participants were asked to verify, amend and contest my accounts of their interview answers (Costley & Gibbs, 2010) and check transcripts, albeit still providing only 'snap-shot approval' (Sikes, 2006). The research also incorporated transparency through ongoing openness, clarity and reflection with regard to the purposes of the investigation, the roles of those involved and the boundaries in which data were collected (Finlay & Gough, 2003). I therefore attempted to mitigate the ethical concerns inherent in insider research, while recognising that ethical 'grey areas' will inevitably remain.

Theme 1. Conflicting purposes: a planner/recipient disconnect underpinned by contrasting understandings of professionalism in FE.

The data indicated there are contrasting understandings between the participants and planners of mandatory CPD (most frequently identified as the senior leadership team at the College) regarding the underlying purposes of CPD. All participant names cited below are pseudonyms. Stuart summarised these different understandings: for him, CPD means developing and reflecting on teaching and learning practices (this comprising the occupational and personal aspects of professional learning as defined by Fraser et al., 2007), whereas he felt the planners of CPD perceive this time to be for relaying organisational messages and diktats:

> People being told to do things. Organisational updates. You know, these aren't professional development. These are something that you do, it's important. . .but they're not to do with your development as a teacher. . .they don't lead to any increase in your professionalism, they don't help you engage with your profession, they don't change your craft.
>
> Policy update [training] looks like a PowerPoint slide. . .it may nominally have an activity. . .the activity is broadly to fill time. . .it doesn't lead to reflection. . .except reflection of what you could be doing in that time.

This disconnect, I argue, stems from conflicting understandings of professionalism in FE, reflected in a differently understood purpose for CPD. Stuart's perceptions suggest an understanding by planners of mandatory CPD that its purpose is to enact a culture of managerial professionalism (Tummons, 2014), whereby professionalism means compliance to pre-defined, organisational standards or priorities. This articulation is then manifested in a transmission approach to CPD that locates lecturers as passive recipients of directives that facilitate desired compliance to organisational priorities.

In contrast, for the participants, the purpose of CPD is nearly always described as to enable individualised professional learning that relates to either developing pedagogical practices or subject-specific knowledge:

> [Derek] the stuff that is related to your teaching and that is related to your subject area...on a personal level, that's the stuff that I find a most stimulating and most useful....

> [Jack] What I see it as is responding to the needs of individuals [lecturers].

> [Maya]...keeping up with what is going on in your area of specialism....

These perceptions represent a position whereby lecturers identify professionalism to be emancipatory: professional expertise, agency and autonomy is recognised (Tummons, 2014). It has also been found elsewhere (Goodall et al., 2005) that teachers consider effective CPD to involve transformative activities that facilitate the development of everyday teaching practices. Jack voiced his frustrations with mandatory CPD that ignores any notion of emancipatory professionalism:

> ...if it's top-down CPD, you're just wasting people's time. It has to be bottom-up...there is a belief that people don't know what CPD they need, they need to be told. No they don't, they need to be given a voice and at least, at least have that voice be heard.

Theme 2. The generic character of mandatory CPD learning content. The second theme represents a perception, prevalent across the data, that the content and form of mandatory CPD is usually generic. This means that mandatory CPD mostly involves learning content that is general and mostly introductory in nature and not specific to curriculum areas, career stages or any other individual (rather than collective) learning needs. Such CPD was predominantly considered as inappropriate or irrelevant to their particular learning needs. Poppy discussed her concerns with generic, all-encompassing CPD activities. Poppy goes so far as to suggest such sessions do not even constitute CPD:

> I've been to various ones [mandatory CPD sessions]...where it's supposed to be about, I don't know, something like setting targets and you think, but I'm already setting targets effectively and I agree we can always improve what we're doing, but with something as limited as that, I don't see that as professional development...quite often they're a bit too broad so they're not, they don't really apply to who I teach quite often, then that leaves me feeling a bit deflated.

Poppy's final comment suggests that rather than a conduit to professional learning, generic CPD can conversely lead to lecturers' time being wasted and even a negative impact on workforce morale. Likewise, Milo argued that generic CPD sessions tend to constitute a waste of time and are often patronising:

> ...it tends to be across-the-board rather than specific training...if some of it is irrelevant to you, which a lot of it tends to be...in whole college development days, I just tend to switch off and feel

> frustrated rather than want to engage. The last CPD was about SMART targets and I was learning how to do that fifteen years ago and I just feel that it wasn't relevant. . .that was a waste of time because it really wasn't teaching us anything new.

Derek also considered that generic CPD is problematic as it does not meet individual or team learning needs that are likely to vary according to subject area and career stage:

> CPD should be much more individually tailored or at least tailored to within your department or your area rather than college wide...it's very difficult on a consistent level over a period of years to find stuff that generically is for every member of teaching staff useful, you might have one [a colleague] that's taught for 40 years up against someone who's come into their very, very first teaching post and they're gonna have different requirements.

Generic content was not always described in negative terms, however. For instance, David found that he had learned from these development sessions:

> . . .health and safety. . .every child counts. . .you have to learn these. . .how to organise the class so they don't get bored. . .how to write lesson plans. . .how to write schemes of work. . .British Values. . .

Although an experienced vocational subject specialist, it may be that David has found such mandatory CPD useful as he did not himself hold a teaching qualification in either his subject area or in adult teaching. It appears that CPD concerning generic aspects of teaching and learning content may be useful, therefore, to colleagues who have not previously acquired such knowledge through teaching qualifications.

The predominant position among the participants, however, was of negativity towards generic CPD, considered inappropriate to their learning needs. This position is perhaps best illustrated by the following two comments:

> [Derek]. . .one-off generic day. . .there's only so many generic things that you can do which will interest everyone. . .I've been here ten years and I've seen stuff getting repeated.

> [Milo] [the planners make] sweeping statements that everyone should be doing this. . .we all have different needs, don't we?

In regard to Derek's comment, although repetition of learning content may not itself be inherently problematic, as it may benefit lecturers new to the College, the issue is that a lecturer who has worked at the College for a decade has been required to attend multiple sessions over the years, covering the same content.

Thus, the pursuance of managerial professionalism by the planners of mandatory CPD at the College means a transmission approach intended to convey generic content. Further, this CPD was nearly always described as planned without the involvement of those mandated to attend, and so not addressing professional learning needs as they perceived them.

The case can be made that generic CPD may be appropriate in some circumstances for a transmissive purpose, such as to convey organisational messages or introduce a new college system or procedure. Further, although most participants in this research gave mostly negative views, David's opinions provide a counterpoint. It would be inaccurate to conclude, therefore, that CPD described as generic is unanimously perceived as ineffective in all instances.

Theme 3. Learning as a personal endeavour and the compensatory principle.

Unsurprisingly, participants choose to engage in non-mandatory CPD they perceive to address learning needs in relation to the subject areas in which they teach, specific pedagogical aspects, or for other personal interests, such as in the pursuance of promotion. Some informal, unplanned CPD occurs at the College, according to the participants, through incidental conversations with colleagues, for instance. For the most part, however, non-mandatory CPD was cited as taking place in participants' personal time and can be considered learning as a personal endeavour. I use this wording to emphasise that choices of engagement with non-mandatory CPD are informed primarily by the values and agency of the individual themselves and often occur outside of work time. Yahya discussed a range of engagements with non-mandatory CPD activities, expressing at the same time his underpinning reasons for such engagements:

> . . .conversations in the staffroom...conversations I would say with colleagues who work in other institutions as well because I find them useful because that's the touch with reality...what's happening on the coal face. Online...I'll go to different awarding bodies and I'll watch webinars...just to keep my practical knowledge up, and I've done a lot of that recently with all the changes.

Part of learning as a personal endeavour encompasses what I refer to as 'the compensatory principle'. This means that the purpose of engagement with non-mandatory development is often also to compensate, or fill in the gaps, in professional learning missed by the generic mandatory CPD discussed above. Such instances of compensatory engagement were articulated particularly for the purpose of crucial subject-specific learning or updating:

> [Maya] I'm very reliant on doing the research [on updates in the curriculum] myself in my own time. . .which is not actually a very good feeling.

> [Milo]...I've done CPD that I've arranged myself in relation to my subject or my own training...it's always been...stuff I've had to do off my own back and normally paying for [it] myself because of funding shortages.

The need for such engagement by these participants is symptomatic of the underfunded FE sector in which these lecturers work (Hodgson, 2015; Lucas, 2004a; Lucas & Nasta, 2010; Robson, 1998), located within a dominant discourse (Lucas & Crowther, 2016; Simmons, 2010) whereby little time or resource is afforded to participants' engagement with professional learning outside of activities that respond directly to the immediate priorities of organisational goals. For Jane, the effect of this restriction of support for non-mandatory, participant-instigated CPD is stark:

> Unfortunately it's resulted in me leaving my particular post [at the College] to search employment elsewhere, which can offer me development. I was looking to go down a more quality route...I'm looking for progression, I want something else.

Jane's career motives for additional engagement with CPD were not recognised through financial support or time remittance; thus, Jane determined that she could only pursue her ambitions elsewhere. The result was the loss of this experienced lecturer and subject specialist for the College and her students. This circumstance also indicates that the personal motivations and interests of lecturers appear to be side-lined when they do not directly concern organisational priorities (Avis, 2009).

Additional themes developed in my thesis responded to the second research question: what are FE lecturers' perceptions of what constitutes effective CPD? Effective CPD was perceived to involve learner agency; a learning focus that addressed discrete learning needs relating to subject knowledge, pedagogical knowledge and other professional interests salient to the individual; reflective practice; and learning within a community and, more widely, landscape of practice (Wenger, 1998, 2014). The latter, more recently coined term refers to engagement in learning across communities of practice. These features are nearly always absent from the passive, transmissive CPD characterising mandatory college CPD described earlier.

Concluding Remarks

I have made the case from my doctoral research that generic, mandatory CPD at the College represents the enactment of a restrictive, managerial concept of professionalism. This may be somewhat expected, given that mandatory CPD in FE is located in a political context of neo-liberal performativity (Simmons, 2010) which 'locates the teacher within a complex web of organisational managerialism' (Lloyd & Davis, 2018, p. 92) centred on satisfying policy demands for accountability and regulation (Ball, 2003; Mockler, 2013). Mandatory CPD as experienced by the participants in this research rejects notions of teacher autonomy, ownership and relevance to individuals' learning needs and tends to result in reduced teacher motivation (echoing Appova & Arbaugh, 2018; Varga-Atkins et al., 2009).

Kyndt et al. (2018) consider that a prerequisite of learning is the involvement of adults' agency in determining their own learning focus. This argument is consistent with a humanist, andragogical approach, based on the proposition that adult learners want to be in control of their own learning (Knowles, 1975). It also resonates with the argument from critical pedagogy that learning should occur through a spirit of co-enquiry, rather than characterising students as '*tabula*-rasa' (meaning a blank slate), in need of expert knowledge delivered through transmissive means, a dynamic Freire termed 'the banking method' (Freire, 1970).

Aligned to these features, the participants engage in informal learning that represents their own enactment of emancipatory professionalism. There was a clear preference for CPD characterised as enabling transformative learning (Fraser et al., 2007) that recognises and incorporates the personal, occupational and (often) social aspects of professional learning.

My doctoral research enabled me to give voice to those in the staffroom in FE. It addressed to some extent the paucity in research of CPD for mid-career FE lecturers. I made recommendations relating to both mandatory and non-mandatory CPD. For the former, I suggested, for instance, that there be a range of opt-in CPD sessions with distinct learning foci. For non-mandatory CPD, I proposed that colleagues' engagement be somehow recognised by organisations, and that the FE lecturer community of practice be supported and explicitly celebrated by leadership teams. In these ways, the needs and priorities of both the organisation and individuals might be both addressed.

References

Appova, A., & Arbaugh, F. (2018). Teachers' motivation to learn: Implications for supporting professional growth. *Professional Development in Education*, *44*(1), 5–21.

Atkins, L., & Tummons, J. (2017). Professionalism in vocational education: International perspectives. *Research in Post-Compulsory Education*, *22*(3), 355–369.

Aubrey, K., & Bell, L. (2017). Teacher education in further education 2000–2010: Subversion, avoidance and compliance. *Journal of Further and Higher Education*, *41*(2), 99–111.

Avis, J. (2009). *Education, policy and social justice: Learning and skills*. Continuum.

Ball, S. (2003). The teacher's soul and the terrors of performativity. *Journal of Education Policy*, *18*(2), 215–228.

Bennett, J. L., & Bush, M. W. (2014). *Coaching for change*. Routledge.

Billing, D. (1982). *The role of staff development*. SCEDSIP.

Braun, V., & Clarke, V. (2006). Using thematic analysis in psychology. *Qualitative Research in Psychology*, *3*(2), 77–101.

British Educational Research Association. (2018). *Ethical guidelines for educational research* (4th ed.). BERA. https://www.bera.ac.uk/publication/ethical-guidelines-for-educational-research-2018

Broad, H. J. (2015). So many worlds, so much to do: Identifying barriers to engagement with continued professional development in the further education and training sector. *London Review of Education*, *13*(1), 17–30.

Costley, C., & Gibbs, P. (2010). *Doing work based research*. SAGE.

Daley, M., Orr, K., & Petrie, J. (2015). *Further education and the twelve dancing princesses*. UCL.

Department for Education & Skills. (2006). *Professionalisation of the learning and skills sector*. DfES.

Department for Education and Employment. (1998). *The learning age: A renaissance for a new Britain*. The Stationery Office.

Department for Education and Skills. (2002). *Success for all: Reforming further education and training*. Department for Education and Skills.

Education and Training Foundation. (2014). *Professional standards for teachers and trainers – England*. Education and Training Foundation. https://www.et-foundation.co.uk/wpcontent/uploads/2014/05/ETF_Professional_Standards_Digital_FINAL.pdf

Education and Training Foundation. (2018). *Training needs in the further education sector*. Education and Training Foundation. https://www.et-foundation.co.uk/wp-content/uploads/2018/04/1331_Training-NeedsAnalysis-Final-.pdf

Education and Training Foundation. (2019). *Further education workforce data for England*. Education and Training Foundation. https://www.et-foundation.co.uk/wp-content/uploads/2019/05/SIR26-WorkforceData-report.pdf

Education and Training Foundation. (2022). *Professional standards for teachers and trainers – England*. Education and Training Foundation. https://www.et-foundation.co.uk/professional-standards/teachers/

Evans, L. (2008). Professionalism, professionality and the development of education professionals. *British Journal of Educational Studies*, *56*(1), 20–38.

FENTO. (1999). *Standards for teaching and supporting learning in further education in England and Wales*. FENTO.

Finlay, L., & Gough, B. (2003). *Reflexivity: A practical guide for researchers in health and social sciences*. Blackwell.

Flyvbjerg, B. (2006). Five misunderstandings about case-study research. *Qualitative Inquiry*, *12*(2), 219–245.

Foster, A. (2005). *Realising the potential: A review of the future role of further education colleges*. DfES.

Fraser, C., Kennedy, A., Reid, L., & McKinney, S. (2007). Teachers' continuing professional development: Contested concepts, understandings and models. *Journal of In-Service Education*, *33*(2), 153–169.

Freire, P. (1970). *Pedagogy of the oppressed*. Continuum.

Gee, J. (1996). *Social linguistics and literacies: Ideology in discourses* (2nd ed.). Routledge Falmer.

Gleeson, D., Davies, J., & Wheeler, E. (2005). On the making and taking of professionalism in the further education workplace. *British Journal of Sociology of Education*, *26*(4), 445–460.

Gleeson, D., Hughes, J., O'Leary, M., & Smith, R. (2015). The state of professional practice and policy in the English further education system: A view from below. *Research in Post-Compulsory Education*, *20*(1), 78–95.

Gleeson, D., & Shain, F. (1999). Managing ambiguity: Between markets and managerialism – A case study of 'middle' managers in further education. *The Sociological Review*, *47*(3), 461–490.

Goldhawk, A., & Waller, R. (2023). Voices from the deck: Lecturers' and middle managers' perceptions of effective FE sector professional development. *Research in Post-Compulsory Education*, *28*(3), 485–504.

Goodall, J., Day, C., Lindsay, G., Muijs, D., & Harris, A. (2005). *Evaluating the impact of continuing professional development (CPD)*. Department for Education and Skills.

HMSO. (1972). *Teacher education and training: Report by a committee of inquiry appointed by the secretary of state for education and science, under the chairmanship of Lord James of Rusholme*. HMSO.

HMSO. (2001). *The further education teachers' qualifications regulations*. HMSO.

HMSO. (2007a). *The further education teacher's qualifications (England) regulations*. HMSO.

HMSO. (2007b). *The further education teachers' continuing professional development and registration (England) regulations*. HMSO.

Hodgson, A. (2015). *The coming of age for FE? Reflections on the past and future of further education colleges in England*. UCL.

Hopkins, D. (1986). *In-service training and educational development: An international survey*. Croom Helm.

Institute for Learning. (2012). *IfL review of CPD*. Institute for Learning.

James, D., & Biesta, G. (2007). *Improving learning cultures in further education*. Routledge.

Kennedy, A. (2014). Understanding continuing professional development: The need for theory to impact on policy and practice. *Professional Development in Education*, *40*(5), 688–697.

Knowles, M. S. (1975). *Self-directed learning: A guide for learners and teachers*. Prentice Hall.

Kushner, S. (2000). *Personalising evaluation*. SAGE.

Kvale, S. (1996). *Interviews: An introduction to qualitative research interviewing*. SAGE.

Kyndt, E., Gijbels, D., Grosemans, I., & Donche, V. (2018). Teachers' everyday professional development: Mapping informal learning activities, antecedents, and learning outcomes. *Review of Educational Research*, *86*(4), 1111–1150.

Lee, M. (1990). Conceptualising staff development in further education. *British Journal of In-Service Education*, *16*(2), 107–115.

Leitch, S. (2006). *Prosperity for all in the global economy: World class skills*. HMSO. http://dera.ioe.ac.uk/6322/1/leitch_finalreport051206.pdf

Lifelong Learning UK. (2006). *New overarching professional standards for teachers, tutors and trainers in the lifelong learning sector*. LLUK.

Lingfield, R. (2012). *Professionalism in further education: Final report of the independent review panel*. Department for Business, Innovation and Skills.

Lloyd, M., & Davis, J. (2018). Beyond performativity: A pragmatic model of teacher professional learning. *Professional Development in Education*, *44*(1), 92–106.

Lofthouse, R. (2019). Coaching in education: A professional development process in formation. *Professional Development in Education*, *45*(1), 33–45.

Lucas, N. (2004a). *Teaching in further education: New perspectives for a changing context*. Institute of Education.

Lucas, N. (2004b). The 'FENTO fandango': National standards, compulsory teaching qualifications and the growing regulation of FE college teachers. *Journal of Further and Higher Education*, *28*(1), 35–51.

Lucas, N., & Crowther, N. (2016). The logic of the incorporation of further education colleges in England 1993–2015: Towards an understanding of marketisation, change and instability. *Journal of Education Policy*, *31*(5), 583–597.

Lucas, N., & Nasta, T. (2010). State regulation and the professionalisation of further education teachers: A comparison with schools and HE. *Journal of Vocational Education and Training*, *62*(4), 441–454.

Mercer, J. (2007). The challenges of insider research in educational institutions: Wielding a double-edged sword and resolving delicate dilemmas. *Oxford Review of Education*, *33*(1), 1–17.

Mockler, N. (2013). Teacher professional learning in a neoliberal age: Audit, professionalism and identity. *Australian Journal of Teacher Education*, *38*(10), 35–47.

Munro, A., Holly, L., Rainbird, H., & Leisten, R. (2004). Power at work: Reflections on the research process. *Social Research Methodology*, *3*(4), 289–304.

Newby, P. (2014). *Research methods for education* (2nd ed.). Routledge.

O'Brian, J., & Jones, K. (2014). Professional learning or professional development? Or continuing professional learning and development? Changing terminology, policy and practice. *Professional Development in Education*, *40*(5), 683–687.

O'Leary, Z. (2010). *The essential guide to doing your research project*. SAGE.

Orr, K. (2008). *Room* for improvement? The impact of compulsory professional development for teachers in England's further education sector. *Journal of In-Service Education*, *34*(1), 97–108.

Postholm, M. B. (2012). Teachers' professional development: A theoretical review. *Educational Research*, *54*(4), 405–429.

Randle, K., & Brady, N. (1997). Managerialism and professionalism in the Cinderella service. *Journal of Vocational Education and Training*, *49*(1), 121–139.

Robson, J. (1998). A profession in crisis: Status, culture and identity in the further education college. *Journal of Vocational Education and Training*, *50*(4), 585–607.

Seale, C., Gobo, G., Gubrium, J. F., & Silverman, D. (Eds.). (2013). *Qualitative research practice*. SAGE.

Sikes, P. (2006). On dodgy ground? Problematics and ethics in educational research. *International Journal of Research and Method in Education*, *29*(1), 105–117.

Simmons, R. (2010). Globalisation, neo-liberalism and vocational learning: The case of English further education colleges. *Research in Post-Compulsory Education*, *15*(4), 363–376.

Smith, R., & O'Leary, M. (2013). NPM in an age of austerity: Knowledge and experience in further education. *Journal of Educational Administration and History*, *45*(3), 244–266.

Society for Education and Training. (2018). *CPD*. https://set.etfoundation.co.uk/professionalism/cpd/

Solvason, C., & Elliott, G. (2013). Why is research still invisible in further education? *Journal of Learning Development in Higher Education*, *6*(1), 1–17.

Tummons, J. (2014). The textual representation of professionalism: Problematising professional standards for teachers in the UK lifelong learning sector. *Research in Post-Compulsory Education*, *19*(1), 33–44.

Varga-Atkins, T., Qualter, A., & O' Brian, M. (2009). School professionals' attitudes to professional development in a networked context: Developing the model of 'believers, seekers and sceptics'. *Professional Development in Education*, *35*(3), 321–340.

Wenger, E. (1998). *Communities of practice*. Cambridge University Press.

Wenger, E. (2014). *Learning in landscapes of practice*. Routledge.

Chapter 9

Teacher Training in England: Exploring Trainee Teachers' Perspectives on Their Professional Identity Formation[1]

Karan Vickers-Hulse and Marcus Witt

University of the West of England, UK

Abstract

This chapter outlines research conducted by Karan Vickers-Hulse (KVH) as part of an educational professional doctorate; Marcus Witt (MW) was one of her supervisory team. Participants were from two initial teacher education (ITE) routes (School Direct and university-led) leading to a PGCE primary teacher qualification. The research was set within the context of continuously evolving policy on the training of teachers and the subsequent impact on developing a professional identity. The introduction of new ITE routes in England (DfE, 2015) aimed to offer a wider range of pathways into teaching, attract more applicants and mitigate the impact of teacher shortages. The research discussed in this chapter explored the experiences of trainees on these routes and the impact on their professional identity formation. This chapter begins with an overview of the literature in the field of professional identity formation, followed by a discussion of the chosen methodology and methods. This chapter concludes with several recommendations for teacher training providers as well as recommendations for future research that may be useful for doctoral students interested in the field of professional identity formation.

This chapter provides an illustration of doctoral case study research and insights to how practitioner research can capture the localised impact of policy shifts.

[1]This chapter has been developed using extracts from the thesis, Vickers-Hulse, K. (2020). *Teacher training in England: Exploring views of trainee teachers, from two different training routes, on the formation of their professional identity*. Thesis, Faculty of Arts, Creative Industries and Education, University of the West of England, Bristol.

Critical Perspectives on Educational Policies and Professional Identities, 139–156

doi:10.1108/978-1-83753-332-920241009

Keywords: Professional identity; teacher training; mentoring; policy; relationships

Introduction

This chapter focuses on professional identity formation and explores the space between *becoming* a primary school teacher and *being* a primary school teacher. The research sought to explore trainee teachers' feelings about the formation of their professional identity during initial teacher education (ITE). Data were gathered at a time of change in the ITE model which resulted in a reshaping of partnerships between schools and universities and the composition and content of courses. These changes followed several reforms to teacher education, including the Carter Review (DfE, 2015), which resulted in the growth of school-based ITE routes such as School Direct (SD) (MMU, 2016). For this study, SD is defined as a school-led route into teaching that is run by a partnership between a lead school, other schools and an accredited ITE provider. Core PGCE (Core) provision is defined as led by a university as the accredited provider. Conroy et al. (2013) raised concerns about maintaining professional identity when faced with institutional change, and Loughran and Menter (2019) described the move to school-led training as a shift away from complex professional conceptions and pedagogical expertise. This chapter examines the findings of research that explored how trainee teachers viewed the complexities of developing an autonomous professional identity in this landscape.

Research Questions

Jackson and Mazzei (2012) suggest that research questions enable researchers to make the familiar strange which is a useful consideration for those exploring an area they know well. Through the voices of seven trainee teachers on SD and Core PGCE programmes at a university in the South West of England, the research aimed to address the following questions:

Research Question 1

What do trainee teachers say about what affects the development of their professional identity?

Subsidiary Question:
How have past experiences in a trainee's personal and professional life shaped their values and beliefs?

Research Question 2

To what extent do two different ITE routes offer challenges and opportunities for trainee teachers in the development of their professional identity?

Subsidiary Questions:
What do trainees say about the challenges and opportunities of SD and Core PGCE routes to teaching?
What experiences in placement schools have shaped trainee teachers' professional identity?
Does policy change have an impact on trainees' day-to-day work as a primary school teacher?

Literature Review

Doctoral students read widely in their field of interest enabling them to 'document, analyse and draw conclusions about what is known about a particular topic' (Machi & McEvoy, 2016, p. 4); the literature review demonstrates how knowledge about a particular topic leads to a problem or a question. This review summaries key literature to explore how important themes within it were reshaped and refined throughout this study. Reviewing literature on teachers' professional identity highlighted its centrality to, and impact on, teachers' practice in the classroom as well as their commitment to the role (Cohen, 2009).

Professional Identity

The notion of identity is multifaceted and includes personal, professional and collective identity (Wright et al., 2018). The existing body of knowledge on professional identity is substantial and reveals that there is no single definition (Alsup, 2006; Beauchamp & Thomas, 2011). *Teachers'* professional identity has become a separate field of research, the concept of which has been interpreted in different ways (Beijaard et al., 2003). Hill's (1994) observations linked personal and professional identities and tied the acquisition of a strong professional identity to job satisfaction and developing an identity within society. Van der Wal et al. (2019) discovered that the formation of a stable and positive professional identity was important to feeling motivated in the job role and affected the way that teachers felt and acted daily.

An added complexity for participants in this study was that many had formed professional identities in previous careers and were expected to 'transfer' skills to a new profession. Colliander (2018) argues that people moving between professions need to 'transform' rather than 'transfer' their existing professional identity. Although challenging, this can be positive, as trainees can draw on pre-existing professional identities to interpret new norms and respond to them appropriately (Buchanan, 2015). Maclure (1993) believes that professional identity formation continues throughout a teacher's career but is most intense while training. Before completing the transition to 'qualified teacher', trainees are expected to engage in professional communities and begin the process of professional identity formation (or *trans*formation as described above). Without the complex knowledge and experiences of qualified practitioners, this can lead to the constant creation and recreation of their place within their current context (Wenger, 1998). Gee (2000, p. 99) suggests this 'lack of complex knowledge' results in tensions and challenges in professional identity formation, particularly as trainee teachers can feel they already possess the necessary personal qualities and just need to be shown what to do, rather than recognising the importance of their own experiences in the construction of their professional identity. Burn (2007) reflects that refinement within the two contexts of university and school placements create a trainee's professional identity, and these experiences and challenges help trainees *become* a teacher.

Mentoring and Reflective Practice

Colliander (2018) identifies the actions and attitudes of key colleagues in placement schools as critical in supporting trainees to become teachers and form a robust professional identity. Colliander (2018) and Bullough (2005) believe the relationship a trainee has with their mentor can support or hinder their growth in learning. Hobson et al. (2008) state that school-based practice is central to supporting the initial preparation and professional identity construction of trainee teachers. As well as being evident in policy, research suggests that effective mentoring is essential in trainee development (Carter & Francis, 2001; Lindgren, 2005). Korthagen and Evelein (2016, p. 241) provided evidence that meeting trainee teachers' needs (the 'inner side of teaching'), was related to how they taught, (the 'outer side of teaching'). Their findings call for more attention to the link between 'personal' and 'professional' identities and pinpoint the connection to mentoring to achieve this.

Loughran and Menter (2019) note that mentoring is important for the development of trainees' professional identity, and this can extend beyond the technical practice seen in classrooms to include reflection. Kervin and Turbill (2003) found that reflecting on experiences gave trainee teachers the confidence to act upon new learning they gained. Rawlings-Smith (2020) suggests that reflective practice becomes second nature, but the process of *how* this happens is difficult to teach. Trainees should be supported to reflect, not only in the moment, which Schön (1983, p. 53) refers to as 'reflection *in* action', but, after a situation, which Schön (1983, p. 53) refers to as 'reflection *on* action'. A mentor can support trainees to transform reflections of experiences into possible classroom actions (Korthagen et al., 2006), which is often overlooked (Thompson & Pascal, 2012). Khalid (2014) and Coldwell and Twiselton (2019) found that the quality of placement experiences and the relationships built with mentors were vital to shaping trainees' sense of professional identity, valuing themselves as professionals and affecting their commitment to the profession.

Learning Communities

Trainees have limited autonomy when selecting placements, and Wright et al. (2018) identify that feelings of conflict, competition and 'outsiderness' are not unusual as trainees learn to negotiate a new environment. Avalos (2011) suggests that adjusting a newly developed professional identity can be useful due to trainees' interactions with different communities and cultures. Negotiating position, expectations and interactions is an important facet of developing trainees' professional identity (Colliander, 2018), even though it may require trainees to sit with discomfort in the process. Wenger-Trayner and Wenger-Trayner (2015) state that trainees and teachers' shared focus on pupil outcomes helps trainees to orient and locate themselves within communities of practice in schools. Colliander (2018) sums up the benefits of negotiating these communities and states that, above all, the professional identity formation of trainees is *enabled* by opportunities to engage in a variety of communities of practice in different settings.

Theoretical Framing

An adapted version of Fig. 9.1: Beijaard et al.'s (2013, p. 124) model of professional identity formation was used as the theoretical framing for the study on which this chapter is based.

Their model outlines the complex process that trainees go through from the perspective of building knowledge and discusses the idea of evolving as a professional through combining collective, private, public and individual knowledge. Wenger (1998) argues that individuals develop an identity as they become a valid member of a community of practice, where learning happens in collaboration with others and through activities situated in that community. Gee's (1999) conceptualisations of identity based on the work of Wenger (1998) show the positive outcomes of trainees' involvement in different learning communities. Wright et al. (2018) state that having a sense of belonging to a community

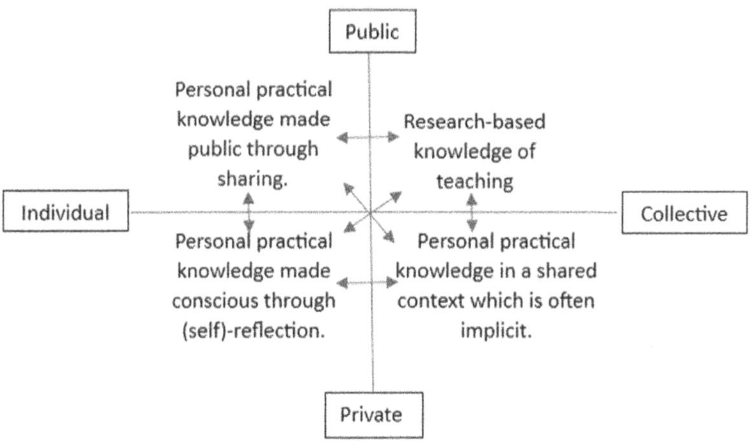

Fig. 9.1. Representation of Professional Identity Formation From a Teacher's Knowledge Perspective. Adapted From Beijaard et al. (2013, p. 124).

requires the ability to be able to participate in several different ways: personally, professionally and socially. Moore and Hofman (1988) found that striving for quality in a school demonstrated a highly developed professional identity and that teachers' positive perception of 'self' negated any poor working conditions or role-related stress. Framing these debates was significant in considering the methodological choices made and ethical considerations within this study.

Methodology and Methods

For this study, the researcher's position was qualitative and interpretivist. Mertens' (1998) definition of the interpretive paradigm is the belief that realities are multiple, socially constructed and influenced by history and culture. The interpretivist paradigm aligns with researchers who value people's words and recognise that there are multiple realities and contexts that can be explored in qualitative research.

It is hoped that the following discussion will be of use to readers who are contemplating a case study methodology in their own work. A case study methodology was used with interviews as the method of data collection. By choosing a case study as a methodological approach, researchers can provide multiple perspectives (Hamilton & Corbett-Whittier, 2013), while preserving the 'wholeness and integrity of the case' (Punch, 2009, p. 153). Choosing a methodology that is fit for purpose is an important consideration when selecting methodology and methods (Menter et al., 2011). A case study involves uncovering the particularities of a subject (Yin, 2013) and generates insights into 'the dynamics present within single settings' (Eisenhardt, 1989, p. 534). The case study approach provides the researcher with the opportunity to 'study complex phenomena within their contexts' (Baxter & Jack, 2008, p. 544). Case studies have had an ambiguous place in education research (Reinharz, 1992) mainly due to their lack of generalisability; however, other postgraduate researchers should note that there is value in case study research when the following apply:

- Aspects of the case are not yet fully understood (i.e. trainees on two different training routes within one institution).
- The case is a persistently problematic research area which has been widely researched yet is difficult to describe reliably (i.e. professional identity formation).
- The case study can help us understand the case in a particular context (i.e. in one institution but other institutions may benefit from findings).

Perhaps most simply, a case study as a design frame means concentrating on one element and looking at it in detail, rather than parts (Thomas, 2016). In this case study, the 'element' refers to trainees within a higher education institution who were on a postgraduate teacher training route. As well as Reinharz's (1992) views above about the acceptability of a case study, Foucault (1981) referred to what he called a 'polyhedron of intelligibility' which emphasises looking at an area of interest in a three-dimensional way to build a rich and balanced picture of the case being studied. A rather poetic description from Thomas (2016) resonated as justification of the case study as a design tool for this research study:

> In a case study you should be able to smell human breath and hear the sound of voices.... much is gained as we add a separate viewpoint – one that moulds and melds the experiences of others through our own understanding. (Thomas, 2016, p. 7)

So, the researcher's voice and viewpoint remained important within the methodological approach to view the case from several angles. However, a case study is designed to allow researchers to understand the distinctiveness of a case which means making theoretical assumptions about what is typical within the population chosen. When considering the case and participants, it was necessary to consider resources and time. While purposive sampling was considered, this was dismissed and replaced with a sample from the population to allow the construction of a framework to answer the research question (Mason, 1996). A case study will not allow researchers to generalise or make assumptions that their findings are relevant elsewhere. However, if researchers are interested in the particulars of a case due to being intimately connected with it, or it is in an area they are interested in, situated in an institution or field they are familiar with, then it may be the right choice for their study. As recognised by Miles and Huberman (1994, p. 27): 'qualitative researchers usually work with small samples of people, nested in their context and studied in depth'. Therefore, this case was made up of a group of PGCE trainees across one academic year in one institution. The sample included core (university-led) and SD (school-led) trainees on the PGCE primary programme.

Cohen et al. (2011) recommend a sample size of no fewer than 30 participants; yet Robson (2011, p. 270) views a sample as a 'selection from the population' where a sample is used to represent the case. All trainees were invited to express an interest in being part of the research, with a need for only a small sample to interview in depth as a case study. This could be termed 'convenience' sampling which is commonly employed in both qualitative and quantitative data collection. The participants in the study were in the cohort being studied and were easily accessible to the researcher as someone in the education department (Lewis-Beck et al., 2004); contextual details for each participant can be seen in Table 9.1. Bell and Olsen (2016) state that samples such as this, although selected for convenience, are still representative of the broader cohort population; however, this means that the results are not able to be generalised but are simply representative of the case. Each participant was given a pseudonym and agreed to have their data published.

The method of data collection used in this study was interviews; this aligned with the social constructionist approach to the construction of knowledge as a way of understanding reality through experiences and perspectives. By not seeking to treat participants' accounts as true pictures of reality, it was possible to

Table 9.1. Research Participants and Contextual Data.

Pseudonym	Age	Gender Identity	Contextual Information	Training Route
Tom	31	Male	Parent. Worked as music teacher.	Core
Vicky	32	Female	Parent. Worked in finance.	SD
Louise	24	Female	Worked as a teaching assistant.	SD
Toby	23	Male	Worked as a teaching assistant.	SD
Sally	45	Female	Parent. Worked as solicitor.	SD
Layla	23	Female	Travelled after university before joining course.	Core
Jack	27	Male	Worked as a teaching assistant.	Core

interpret their responses as 'plausible accounts' of *their* reality (Silverman, 2010). Data collection involved three individual interviews with each participant, where a set of questions and areas for discussion were prepared but the conversation was allowed to flow. For the fourth and final interviews, focus groups were conducted due to logistics and participant need, and all participants were interviewed together. Thomas (2016) points out that adapting methods is common practice in qualitative research as the participant–researcher relationship progresses. This study was constructed with a clear timeline of data collection – moving from the individual interviews to the focus group conducted at the end of the study.

Ethical Considerations

The British Educational Research Association (BERA) highlights the main principle of ethics as responsibility to participants and state that researchers should 'operate within an ethic of respect for any persons involved in the research they are undertaking' BERA (2018, p. 5). The rights of individuals participating in this research were supported by these ethical principles. Ethical clearance was sought from the institution prior to participant recruitment or data gathering. Establishing quality research relationships is complicated by power, perception, ethics and value systems. However, working with a small sample allowed for a rich selection of data and made it easier to focus on building relationships. The fact that participants were able to select participation was intended to avoid selective sampling and the issue of bias, as outlined by Punch (2009), who believes these issues are prevalent as we are inevitably drawn towards subjects who share the same interests, values and beliefs as us. Acknowledging, reflecting and refining approaches and methods throughout the research process and being reflexive, attempted to mitigate these issues. Researchers conducting research within their own field must be open to intensive scrutiny, and values, beliefs and personal interest must not only be declared but challenged on an ongoing basis (Van Heugton, 2004).

Before beginning the first interviews, time was taken to fully explain, in writing and in person, the purpose of the study and what participation (or non-participation) would mean. Duncan and Watson (2010) state that research participants may not always understand the issues at stake and could go on to regret any disclosures made during the research process. Researchers have a duty of care to protect participants and ensure transparency with regards to research aims throughout the study and not just at the beginning. In summary, it is the researcher's responsibility to be open and honest and find ways to ensure that participants are aware of all possible and potential outcomes of their involvement.

Data Analysis

The approach to data analysis chosen for this study was Braun and Clarke's (2006) thematic analysis as this aligned with research questions and methodological choices. Braun and Clarke (2006) state that thematic analysis offers an accessible and flexible approach to analysing qualitative data. Thematic analysis is a widely used approach in interpretative studies (Javadi & Zavea, 2016) but it has its critics, e.g. St Pierre and Jackson (2014) who believe that its simplicity is a potential weakness. However, as Rubin and Rubin (2005) point out, it can be an exciting approach as themes and concepts arise as data are revisited and the researcher has an active role in the process of research and identifies the themes. The fact that a researcher is actively seeking out the information from data rather than waiting for it to 'emerge' fitted with the interpretivist approach and allowed the acknowledgement of decisions made with regards to analysis of data. Despite its critics, Javadi and Zavea (2016) believe that the theoretical freedom that comes from thematic analysis ensures that it is a flexible research tool that allows researchers to gather data in a rich way. Thematic analysis works well for researchers who like to have a structure to follow but also need some flexibility in their analysis; Braun and Clarke's model allows for both.

Key Findings and Recommendations

Five key themes were identified following a review of the literature and the data analysis process:

(1) motivation,
(2) managing workload,
(3) training route,
(4) relationships,
(5) identity.

Although there were links between issues raised within each theme, these were kept separate for the purpose of presenting findings, and links were made in discussion of the analysis and subsequent recommendations for practice. The research aimed to draw out unique aspects to contribute to the existing body of knowledge about professional identity formation in trainee teachers. Examples of responses taken from data gathered in the final focus-group interview are shown below.

Motivation

Trainees were at the end of their training when the final interview was conducted, and it therefore focused on looking forward and reflecting on their time on the course. Toby reflected on the transition from his previous role as a teaching assistant to that of a teacher; he had stated in previous interviews that being a teaching assistant is what had motivated him to become a teacher.

> Toby (Core)
> *And I think the transition from being TA for a year to then suddenly having command over the entire class was something I had to learn to do. Because as a TA ...you know, the unspoken hierarchy or whatever. And I think it was just learning to sort of command respect and build up that rapport with the children that's...yeah, that I already had to some degree, so it wasn't too much of a transition to make thankfully from that experience.*

Toby uses the word 'transition' to describe moving from one role to another which links to Buchanan's (2015) notion of transformation. Despite having an existing professional identity as a teaching assistant, Toby had to navigate the new expectations of his role as a trainee teacher and recreate his place within the classroom (Wenger, 1998).

Managing Workload

Participants identified that just making it to the end of the training demonstrated a certain level of resilience (during their training 10% of the cohort had dropped out). Louise highlighted the ups and downs of the training and how personal discipline had supported her in meeting deadlines.

> Louise (School Direct)
> *I think, you know like some of the undergraduate students who come to school as well, like they just seem so bright and breezy, and then you're thinking 'I'm doing your entire degree in 9 months' and they're like 'are you really stressed', and I was like...at times I felt really stressed and other times I was like 'no, it's alright, I just get on with it' like you know, crack on, don't stress about it, because you know if you keep stressing and putting things off you won't ever do it.*

In some cases, workload can be a barrier to developing reflection. Schön (1983, p. 53) highlights the importance of 'reflection *on* action' where trainees reflect on a situation after it has happened. Times of stress that Louise refers to above can result in insufficient time or headspace for deep, meaningful reflection that impacts practice. However, when discussing workload, it was evident that Louise demonstrated a high level of reflection as she was able to see challenges faced as a way to develop practice. This links to Kervin and Turbill's (2003) ideas that reflecting on experiences (both positive and negative) gives trainees the confidence to act upon their new learning and eventually leads to reflective practice being second nature (Rawlings-Smith, 2020).

Training Route and the Impact on Identity

It was thought that participants may respond differently to questions regarding their training route when in a group environment, but responses were consistent with those from individual interviews. SD participants expressed surprise at the limited input they had for some areas of learning.

> Vicky (School Direct)
> *Like phonics...can you imagine teaching phonics with only half a day's training?*

There seemed to be an agreement that the course had not met the trainees' expectations.

> Louise (School Direct)
> *We're going to take you, we're going to mould you, we're going to train you, you know when any jobs come up, we'll let you know. I wasn't told. (Friend) told me that there were two vacancies at my first training school, I didn't even know. I was told I would be in UWE 6 days...6 days!*
>
> Sally (School Direct)
> *And it's how they're sold, like the partnerships, it's just complete... false advertising.*
>
> Toby (School Direct)
> *I was under the illusion that we'd have more time in school as well, which just simply isn't the case at all.*

Although Wright et al. (2018) identified that trainees have limited autonomy when selecting placements, they do have the ability to select which training route they choose. SD trainees' responses indicated that, despite recruitment and advertising suggesting that they would be welcomed into and become part of the community within the school, or schools they were joining, they felt like outsiders. As mentioned in the literature review, Wenger (1998) believes that individuals develop an identity as they become a valid member of a community. Therefore, this lack of belonging to the community had an impact on their professional identity formation.

The Impact of Relationships on Forming an Identity

Having reached the end of their training, participants were able to look back over the nine months and reflect on what had affected relationships with mentors and children.

Participants mentioned the impact that moving placement schools had on their practice, as they often preferred one of the schools they had been placed in over another.

> Layla (Core)
> *So, I got rated a 'good' and I'm really annoyed about it because I think if I had been in my second placement school for the longer placement I would have got 'outstanding'.*

> Jack (Core)
> *But I found it...well both I really enjoyed, but the second one I was in I did pretty well with, but they were difficult. But I was given more opportunity to do what I wanted to do.*

Moving schools for the second placement was identified as having an impact on relationships. Louise and Layla both referred to 'liking' their school contexts.

> Louise (School Direct)
> *I think changing schools for my second placement was quite pivotal for me. Because I wasn't particularly ecstatic at my first one, then I found a school that I really liked.*

> Layla (Core)
> *I'm not quite sure why I preferred my middle school. I think it's one of those things where it's just you know. But I think I was more me in my second school...*

The role of the mentor in school was significant in terms of whether a trainee 'liked' a placement school which aligns with Coldwell and Twiselton's (2019) view that the support, reflection and relationships provided by mentors is vital to shaping a trainee's sense of professional identity and how valued they feel.

Professional Identity as a Teacher

As four participants had secured jobs by the time the final focus group was conducted, at this stage, there was some discussion of future roles and the interview process, as well as feeling valued and supported in a school environment. Louise spoke about the idea of being 'different' in the classroom.

> Louise (School Direct)
> *But I don't think I'm crazy different. And I think it's quite important to be authentic in front of your children so that they know that it's OK to be you and be an individual, like I'm not just going to turn my personality off when I walk in the classroom.*

Jack followed on from this discussion and mentioned the importance of working in a school which allowed you to be yourself.

Jack (Core)
And I mean if you find a school that brings out the things that you don't want or don't like about yourself, I suppose you stay clear of that school.

Sally referred to not feeling valued in her placement school and relates back to the idea of being mis-sold the notion of joining a community. This affected her confidence when looking for teaching posts.

Sally (School Direct)
I think that's the main reason that I didn't like my main placement school, I felt like a student, I felt like a visitor, all the time I felt like I wasn't included.

Layla linked the idea of being valued to a 'feeling'.

Layla (Core)
And I visited quite a few schools before I even applied to one because I was keen to sort of get that feeling that I got when I walked into my second placement school of 'wow I really want to work here'. So yeah, I think it's quite important.

This feeling of being part of a community, belonging and being valued was a recurring theme as trainees negotiated the different communities of practice they encountered during their placements (Colliander, 2018).

In summary, the key findings emerging from the data were that:

- Participants entered their training aware of the challenges of the training route as well as the teaching profession.
- Previous experiences supported participants in assimilating what they saw in classrooms into their professional identity.
- Effective communities of practice supported participants in maintaining motivation through training – participants need a 'safe space' to communicate.
- Workload impacted on participants' stress levels.
- SD participants felt their route was mis-sold and would not choose this route again; all participants identified no differences in the training routes in terms of expectations, workload and experience.
- Relationships with mentors in school impacted on participants' professional identity formation. The effectiveness and quality of mentoring was identified as well as the importance of 'feeling valued'.
- The personal and professional identity need to adapt during training for participants to feel secure entering the teaching profession.

The research revealed that training route is not an indicator of success with regards to the formation of a secure professional identity. There was no marked difference between comments from those on core or SD routes in terms of their professional identity. Professional identity evolves over time, and this study acknowledges that trainee teachers will experience tensions in the development of their professional identity. This study found that tensions arise when the expectations of their training route are not clear to trainees, do not feel appropriately supported in their development by mentors and are struggling to manage their heavy academic and professional workload. Friction can appear when a trainee's personal and previous professional selves are not valued in the formation of their new professional 'teacher' identity. This study did not aim to simplify the process of developing a secure professional identity in trainee teachers, but rather seek to develop an understanding of the views of trainee teachers on two different training routes. Alsup (2006, p. 5) sums up the process of forming a teacher's professional identity as 'difficult, messy and complex', and the findings acknowledge that this is inevitable and, in fact, probably necessary. Referring back to Beijaard et al. (2013, p. 124) model of professional identity formation, this study agreed that the different facets of a person's identity cannot easily be separated from each other and are extrinsically linked and affected by contextual factors.

Even though professional identities are shifting, evolving and being challenged constantly, this study found that if a trainee develops at least one robust relationship (a professional buddy), has effective mentoring and feels valued in the school and in their role, then they can usually rise to the challenge. Teacher educators have a duty to trainee teachers, not to make training simple but to acknowledge the challenges faced by trainees and ensure that their needs are being met to nurture and protect the future workforce.

Conclusion

This research began with the notion that the formation of professional identity is complex and contested. While conclusions were drawn, the conclusions and 'answers' to the research questions are indicators of the possible impacts of the training routes on a trainee's professional identity formation. Elliott and Kushner (2007, p. 161) claim that data 'represent the people – their hopes, fears, aspirations and failures'. Findings represented the feelings and views of participants as they moved through their PGCE training routes and showed that there is no single blueprint for success in developing a robust professional identity. Each participant had a nuanced interpretation of what they needed based on their personal identity as well as a set of reflections on their own professional practice and experience. The recommendations, therefore, should be viewed as discussion points for teacher educators, teachers and policymakers to prompt deeper reflection on the nature and content of teacher training routes to create the right environment for personal growth.

Future studies could adapt the approach taken in this research over a longer period and across multiple institutions and training routes as this would enable the research to focus on professional identity formation beyond the initial training course. Doctoral students interested in the field of professional identity formation or research that explores the impact of policy changes on practice should consider how framing the theoretical and policy debates in their field will allow them to consider the most appropriate methodology and approaches.

For teacher educators, this research questions the impact of relationships and communities during trainees' busy and challenging PGCE year. Findings showed that if there are different routes to becoming a teacher, the key aspect is 'sameness' and a shared experience rather than 'othering' routes such as SD. In focusing on one cohort of trainee teachers, in one institution, the PGCE course was viewed from the perspective of the trainee teachers at the start of their journey to being a professional entering the teaching profession. Identifying the demands of building relationships in schools and the impact of effective mentoring enabled reflection on the realities of training as a teacher and provided evidence regarding the conflict that exists between the trainees' idea of what they need to succeed and the reality. Alongside the existing body of work on professional identity, this study offered a focus on the significance of a relationship in supporting trainee teachers in developing a secure professional identity.

Moving Forward

In the past decade, the government has introduced several reforms to teacher education, including the Carter Review (DfE, 2015), the Teacher Recruitment and Retention Strategy (DfE, 2019) and the introduction of the Core Content Framework (CCF), the Early Career Framework (ECF) and the new suite of National Professional Qualifications (NPQs) (DfE, 2021). The most recent reform was a review of Initial Teacher Training (ITT) provision, the ITT Market Review, which resulted in established and new providers having to apply to be accredited to deliver teacher education with some well-established teacher education providers losing accredited status. These reforms are set against a backdrop of an ongoing teacher supply crisis. This research highlighted that the training route was not significant to the formation of a professional identity but that what was important was professional relationships, feeling valued and high-quality mentoring. These factors *can* be developed, nurtured, and maintained despite yet more policy change that threatens to add further pressure, bureaucracy, and accountability in schools (Skerritt, 2021). This study considered how teacher educators can support trainees to move from *becoming* a primary school teacher to *being* a primary school teacher.

References

Alsup, J. (2006). *Teacher identity discourses: Negotiating personal and professional spaces*. Lawrence Erlbaum.

Avalos, B. (2011). Teacher professional development in teaching and teacher education over ten years. *Teaching and Teacher Education*, *27*(2), 10–20.

Baxter, P., & Jack, S. (2008). Qualitative case study methodology: Study design and implementation for novice researchers. *Qualitative Report*, *13*(4), 544–559.

Beauchamp, C., & Thomas, L. (2011). New teachers' identity shifts at the boundary of teacher education and initial practice in. *International Journal of Educational Research*, *6*(13), 17–32.

Beijaard, D., Meijer, P., & Verloop, N. (2003). Reconsidering research on teachers' professional identity. *Teaching and Teacher Education*, *20*(2), 107–128.

Beijaard, D., Meijer, P. C., & Verloop, N. (2013). The emergence of research on teachers' professional identity: A review of literature from 1988 to 2000. In C. J. Craig, P. C. Meijer, & J. Broeckmans (Eds.), *From teacher thinking to teachers and teaching: The evolution of a research community*. *Advances in research on teaching* (Vol. 19, pp. 205–222). Emerald Group Publishing Ltd. https://doi.org/10.1108/S1479-3687(2013)0000019013

Bell, S., & Olsen, R. (2016). Estimates of external validity bias when impact evaluations select sites nonrandomly. *Educational Evaluation and Policy Analysis*, *38*(2), 318–335.

BERA. (2018). *Ethical guidelines for educational research*. British Educational Research Association. BERA.

Braun, V., & Clarke, V. (2006). Using thematic analysis in psychology. *Qualitative Research in Psychology*, *3*(2), 77–101.

Buchanan, R. (2015). Teacher identity and agency in an era of accountability. *Teacher and Teaching*, *21*(6), 700–719.

Bullough, R. V., Jr. (2005). Being and becoming a mentor: School-based teacher educators and teacher educator identity. *Teaching and Teacher Education*, *21*(3), 143–155.

Burn, K. (2007). Professional knowledge and identity in a contested discipline: Challenges for student teachers and teacher educators. *Oxford Review of Education*, *33*(4), 445–467.

Carter, M., & Francis, R. (2001). Mentoring and beginning teachers' workplace learning. *Asia-Pacific Journal of Teacher Education*, *29*(3), 249–262.

Cohen, J. L. (2009). Getting recognised: Teachers negotiating professional identities as learners through talk in. *Teaching and Teacher Education*, *26*(2), 473–481.

Cohen, L., Manion, L., Morrison, K., & Bell, R. (2011). *Research methods in education* (7th ed.). Routledge.

Coldwell, M., & Twiselton, S. (2019). The 2019 general election and the teaching profession in England. *People, Place and Policy*, *13*(2), 71–74.

Colliander, H. (2018). The experienced newcomer – The (trans)forming of professional teacher identity in a new landscape of practices. *Teaching and Teacher Education*, *69*(1), 168–176.

Conroy, J., Hulme, M., & Menter, I. (2013). Developing a 'clinical' model for teacher education. *Journal of Education for Teaching*, *39*(1), 557–573.

Department for Education. (2015). *Carter review of initial teacher education (ITE)*. https://www.gov.uk/government/publications/carter-review-of-initial-teacher-training

Department for Education. (2019). *Teacher workload survey 2019 research report*. Department for Education.

Department for Education. (2021). *Initial teacher training (ITT) rarket review*. https://www.gov.uk/government/publications/initial-teacher-training-itt-market-review-report

Duncan, M., & Watson, R. (2010). Taking a stance: Socially responsible ethics and informed consent. In M. Savin-Baden & C. Howell-Major (Eds.), *New approaches to qualitative research: Wisdom and uncertainty*. Routledge.

Eisenhardt, K. M. (1989). Building theories from case study research. *Academy of Management Review*, *14*(4), 532–550.

Elliott, J., & Kushner, S. (2007). The need for a manifesto for educational programme evaluation. *Cambridge Journal of Education*, *37*(3), 321–336.

Foucault, M. (1981). Questions of method: An interview with Michel Foucault. *Ideology and Consciousness*, *8*(1), 3–14.

Gee, J. P. (1999). *An introduction to discourse analysis: Theory and method*. Routledge.

Gee, J. P. (2000). Identity as an analytic lens for research in education. *Review of Research in Education*, *25*(1), 99–125.

Hamilton, L., & Corbett-Whittier, C. (2013). *Using case study in education research*. SAGE.

Hill, T. (1994). *Developing a career in primary education*. David Fulton Publishers.

Hobson, A., Ashby, P., Malderez, A., & Tomlinson, P. (2008). Mentoring beginning teachers: What we know and what we don't. *Teaching and Teacher Education*, *25*(1), 207–216.

Jackson, A., & Mazzei, L. (2012). *Thinking with theory in qualitative research: Viewing data across multiple perspectives*. Routledge.

Javadi, M., & Zavea, K. (2016). Thematic analysis and its pitfalls. *Journal of Client Care*, *1*(1), 33–39.

Kervin, L., & Turbill, J. (2003). *Teaching as a craft: Making links between pre-service training and professional practice*. Faculty of Social Sciences: Papers.

Khalid, F. (2014). The impact of teaching practice experience in shaping pre-service teachers' professional identities. *Mediterranean Journal of Social Sciences*, *5*(20), 423–434.

Korthagen, F., & Evelein, F. (2016). Relations between student teachers' basic needs fulfilment and their teaching behaviour. *Teaching and Teacher Education*, *60*(1), 234–244.

Korthagen, F., Loughran, J., & Russell, T. (2006). Developing fundamental principles for teacher education programs and practices. *Teaching and Teacher Education*, *22*(8), 1020–1041.

Lewis-Beck, M., Bryman, A., & Futing Liao, T. (Eds.). (2004). *Convenience Sample. The SAGE encyclopaedia of social science research methods*. SAGE.

Lindgren, U. (2005). Experiences of beginning teachers in a school-based mentoring programme Sweden. *Educational Studies*, *31*(3), 251–263.

Loughran, J., & Menter, I. (2019). The essence of being a teacher educator and why it matters. *Asia-Pacific Journal of Teacher Education*, *47*(3), 216–229.

Machi, L. A., & McEvoy, B. T. (2016). *The literature review: 6 steps to success* (3rd ed.). Corwin.

Maclure, M. (1993). Arguing for yourself: Identity as an organising principle in teachers' jobs and lives. *British Educational Research Journal*, *19*(4), 311–322.

Manchester Metropolitan University. (2016). *The beginnings of school-led teacher training: New challenges for university teacher education*. http://www.esri.mmu.ac.uk/resgroups/schooldirect.pdf

Mason, J. (1996). *Qualitative researching*. SAGE.

Menter, I., Elliot, D., Hall, J., Hall, S., Hulme, M., Lewin, J., & Lowden, K. (2011). *A guide to practitioner research in education*. SAGE.

Mertens, D. M. (1998). *Research methods in education and psychology. Integrating diversity with quantitative and qualitative approaches*. SAGE.

Miles, M., & Huberman, M. (1994). *Qualitative data analysis: An expanded sourcebook*. SAGE.

Moore, M., & Hofman, E. (1988). Professional identity in institutions of higher learning in Israel. *Higher Education*, *17*(1), 69–79.

Punch, K. (2009). *Introduction to research methods in education*. Sage.

Rawlings-Smith, E. (2020). Techniques for mentors to support early career teachers' reflective practice. *Teaching Geography*, *45*(2), 53–55.

Reinharz, S. (1992). *Feminist methods in social research*. Oxford University Press.

Robson, C. (2011). *Real world research*. John Wiley and Sons.

Rubin, H. J., & Rubin, I. S. (2005). *Qualitative interviewing*. SAGE.

Schön, D. (1983). *The reflective practitioner: How professionals think in action*. Basic Book Inc.

Silverman, D. (2010). *Doing qualitative research: A practice handbook* (3rd ed.). SAGE.

Skerritt, C. (2021). Pressure, bureaucracy, accountability, and all for show: Irish perspectives on life inside England's schools. *British Journal of Educational Studies*, *69*(6), 693–713. https://doi.org/10.1080/00071005.2020.1839014

St Pierre, E., & Jackson, A. (2014). Qualitative data analysis after coding. *Qualitative Enquiry*, *20*(6), 715–719.

Thomas, G. (2016). *How to do your case study* (2nd ed.). SAGE.

Thompson, N., & Pascal, J. (2012). Developing critically reflective practice. *Reflective Practice*, *13*(2), 311–325.

Van Heugton, K. (2004). Managing insider research: Learning from experience. *Qualitative Social Work*, *3*(203), 203–221.

Van der Wal, M., Oolbekkink-Marchand, H., Schaap, H., & Meijer, P. (2019). Impact of early career teachers' professional identity tensions. *Teaching and Teacher Education*, *80*(1), 59–70.

Wenger, R. (1998). *Communities of practice: Learning, meaning and identity*. Cambridge University Press.

Wenger-Trayner, E., & Wenger-Trayner, B. (2015). Theory. In E. Wenger-Trayner, M. Fenton O'Creevy, S. Hutchinson, C. Kubiak, & B. Wenger-Trayner (Eds.), *Learning in landscapes of practices* (pp. 13–29). Routledge.

Wright, V., Loughlin, T., & Hall, V. (2018). Exploring transitions in notions of identity as perceived by beginning post-compulsory teachers. *Research in Post-Compulsory Education*, *23*(1), 4–22.

Yin, R. (2013). *Case study research: Design and methods* (5th ed.). SAGE.

Chapter 10

Convergence, Change, Consciousness and Confidence: The Impact of Initial Teacher Training Policy on Confident, Career Changing Practising Teachers

Nicholas Garrick[a] *and Jane Andrews*[b]

[a]Lighting Up Learning, UK
[b]University of the West of England, UK

Abstract

In illustrating and reflecting on my use of constructivist grounded theory methodology, this chapter explores findings of a study involving perceptions of learning of eight career changing trainee teachers enroled across four one-year primary or secondary postgraduate initial teacher education (ITE) programmes in England. Through four sets of unstructured interviews over the course of 10 months, qualitative findings suggest that this group of trainee teachers experience a similar learning process of convergence, change, consciousness and confidence. Diagrammatic modelling of data plays a key role in enacting a constructivist approach to grounded theory by demonstrating coding relationships through constant comparison leading to theory generation. Along with other observations, significant findings include how career changers without prior education experience may adapt and adopt new, professional identities with more confidence more quickly than those with extensive prior education experience, and, alternative teaching placements that occur in the 'middle' of a postgraduate course may have a significant effect in a career changers perceived confidence in 'being a teacher'. Recommendations for ITE programmes, future teacher recruitment policy and researchers employing grounded theory are included. Recommendations for postgraduate researchers in education are scattered throughout this chapter.

Keywords: Career changer; postgraduate; initial teacher education; constructivist grounded theory; diagrammatic modelling

Critical Perspectives on Educational Policies and Professional Identities, 157–170

doi:10.1108/978-1-83753-332-920241010

Introduction

In essence, this chapter's rationale is a novel contribution to constructivist grounded theory (CGT) in how data can be visualised to expose, document and explain extant theory. In addition, one of the significant findings from Nicholas' CGT doctoral study is expanded upon with the interplay between English initial teacher education (ITE) policy and his findings explored. The chapter is written from the perspective of Nicholas in the first person, and concludes with thoughts from Jane, his primary supervisor. Initially, the chapter sets out the policy context in relation to ITE, leading to an introduction of the study with positionality, methods, ethics, participant samples, use of CGT and prompted monologues explained. Following this, the chapter provides a worked example of CGT in action and explores the use of 'diagrammatic modelling' as means of visualising grounded theory, a new way of transparently demonstrating theory construction. Conclusions and reflections from both authors feature at the end of this chapter.

Policy Context of ITE

To contextualise, recruitment and retention of both primary and secondary school teachers in England continues to be of national concern, in part due to the continued rise in teacher vacancies (GOV.UK, 2023). Such discourse continues within the recently enacted Early Career Framework (ECF) (DfE, 2019) which seeks to address recruitment and retention variance in the English ITE landscape. It aims to connect ITE with the development of recently qualified teachers by enhancing national standards of teacher training through the inclusion of mentoring, support and further training post-qualification. An aspiration of the ECF is to redress the challenges of recruitment and retention, in part created through the diversification of ITE routes over the past 20 years. This includes a purposeful targeting of specific demographics, ages and experiences of potential trainee teachers, most notably through introducing school-based training routes. The 1998 Green Paper paved the way for such routes, stating how 'more flexible courses for initial teacher training [are needed as a] boost to employment-based routes into teaching' (DfE, 1998, p. 43). It continued with how 'innovative practice in school-led initial teacher training [should] be attractive to a wide range of applicants - particularly more mature career changers' (*ibid*, 1998, p. 46). This opening up of routes into teacher training for career changers meant that people working in schools who are not trained teachers, such as behaviour support or teaching assistants, could bolster the teaching workforce without leaving a paid role or returning to university full-time. As explored in detail in my thesis, the Green Paper went on to propose 'a shift in funding trainee teachers directly on school-based routes might again attract a more diverse range of applicants, namely those unable to train unpaid on more 'traditional' routes' (Garrick, 2021, p. 13). However, some 25 years later, and despite targeting different groups of potential teachers, the content and format of English postgraduate school-based ITE programmes has changed little, and from the time of researching to the present day, there is scant research or evidence into how career changing trainee teachers experience teacher training routes in England (Wilkins, 2017; Wilkins & Comber, 2015; Wilkins et al., 2012).

Introduction to the Study

My study explored perceptions of learning of eight career changing primary or secondary postgraduate trainee teachers in England over the course of one academic year. Participants were met four times during their programme, with the first being an initial 'participant profile' session where rapport was established, consent re-established and background information sought. Equally spaced out, three 'prompted monologues' followed, approximately two to three months apart. At the time, I was an experienced ITE recruiter and programme leader for school-based routes, and it was widely accepted among my peers when recruiting, career changers with prior school experience – particularly school support staff – were deemed more desirable candidates in becoming teachers, as opposed to those without, due to being familiar with contemporary schools and, therefore, 'experienced'. Out of the eight participants of this study, four had a school background, while four had little or no recent school experience.

Methodologically, my constructivist approach to grounded theory meant that I chose to visually document the grounded methodology to posit theory throughout the thesis, documenting it as it was 'discovered'. Buckley and Waring (2013) model CGT as a spiral, Cho and Lee (2014) as interconnected loops and Charmaz (2014) as a constellation of methods. The metaphors above suggest continually revisiting and reviewing research stages: taking an iterative approach to coding and literature reviews and making links back to previous data sets that may not have made sense at the time. Charmaz (2014) points out the importance of resisting the application of existing or emerging theories too early, but to use them combined with iterative literature reviews (Thornberg, 2012) to inform theory construction in the latter part of the process as verification and validation tools. For this reason, I decided to complete the prompted monologues (a form of unstructured interview explained in the next section) before simultaneously coding data and engaging in iterative literature reviews. Having considered several forms of interpretivist methodologies from experience-centred narrative (Squire, 2008) to case study (Hitchcock & Hughes, 1995), CGT as defined by Charmaz (2014) suited my approach best due to helping avoid unconsciously bringing insider knowledge as an ITE practitioner. The CGT methodology features several aspects such as the 'non-assuming researcher', reflexivity, 'in-vivo' coding (Charmaz, 2014, p. 343; using participants' own words as codes), journaling and diagraming, all explored below in this chapter.

Ethically, as per the BERA (2018) Ethical Guidelines for Ethical Research, participants involved were anonymised and required to choose their own pseudonyms as references in the research. Following standard research ethics procedures enshrined in BERA (with the overarching aim of 'do no harm'), I chose to align the 'prompted monologues' after their self-assessment periods within their course structures to avoid interfering with their experience or adding workload or burden.

The Prompted Monologue: An Ontological and Epistemological Construction

In terms of method, ontological and epistemological beliefs led me away from predefined structured interview questions and towards giving participants opportunities to share what they deemed important as a 'prompted monologue' (PM). A self-created term, 'prompted' refers to verbal suggestions that do not contain 'content' which might steer a participant in a specific direction, i.e. pre-defined questions. While 'monologue' describes an uninterrupted consciousness of thought, the purpose of a prompt without specific content or terminology, is designed to open up a space for the participant to respond using their own words and interpretation, uninterrupted. I would encourage postgraduate researchers to have the confidence to adapt and redefine aspects of known research methods and methodologies, such as 'prompted monologues', to make research approaches more relevant to the context of your study. Within the context of my study, PM was inspired by Charmaz's (2014) reference of the unstructured interview within a grounded theory study. She describes it as:

> intensive interviewing... [a] gently-guided, one-sided conversation that explores research participants' perspective on their own personal experience with the research topic. (Charmaz, 2014, p. 56)

As Charmaz suggests, the role of the intensive interviewer is to encourage, listen and learn; the PM embodies that. To be successful, a 'non-assuming researcher' requires a specific mindset that requires being comfortable with resisting an interpretation of a participant's words in the moment, enabling them to do this themselves (McNamee & Gergen, 1992). A 'not-assuming' mindset means:

> ... that our understandings, explanations, and interpretations [in therapy] not be limited to prior experiences or theoretically formed truths, and knowledge. (ibid, 1992, p. 28)

Despite my study not being one of clinical therapy, McNamee and Gergen's interpretation enhanced my understanding of being a 'non-assuming' researcher. To be clear: 'not assuming' does not relate to an absence of knowledge on my part, and, nor do I claim *objectivity* as a researcher within the field of ITE or anything about the programmes or individuals involved in this research. What 'non-assuming' does relate to is the notion of 'in the living', a translation of in-vivo (exact, precise, documented words shared by participant as enacted into the research prompt) in an attempt to stay as grounded as possible, as exemplified in Table 10.1.

Table 10.1. Extract From a Transcript.

Interview Number	Time Stamp	Line Number	Transcript
2	0:23	5	We are all learning so much at the moment, that it feels like being *thrown in the deep end.* I like it.

The use of 'thrown in the deep end' as a grounded code used to develop theory with regard to ownership identity formation, is a direct enactment of the ontological and epistemological influences of my methodology. By using participant's exact phrases, I aim to be as grounded and theoretical as possible by drawing links and connections to this in the form of diagrammatic modelling. The 'non-assuming' mindset, enabled by the use of PMs, is highly pertinent to the CGT exploration of this study in that I chose to enact an 'in-vivo' approach through the methodology and method. The following section explores a key finding of my research most relevant in contributing to CGT, and a novel form of visualising grounded theory, in the exploration of career changing, postgraduate trainee teachers' perceptions of learning, 'diagrammatic modelling'.

Diagrammatic Modelling

As a new contribution to knowledge, in the saturated field of ITE and Newly Qualified Teachers, *diagrammatic modelling* offers a novel way of clearly documenting the construction of a grounded theory. CGT can be seen to be obfuscating or elusive (Tolhurst, 2012), and yet my experience is the opposite of this. When mapped authentically, with coding clearly exposed, and the journey to theory laid bare, I would suggest that many criticisms of CGT are due to a conflation of debates relating to the relative merits or qualitative or quantitative and mixed-methods research and this serves to obscure what grounded theory seeks to achieve. As a means to mitigate criticisms, a key contribution of my research and most relevant in contributing to CGT exploration of career changing, postgraduate trainee teachers' perceptions of learning, is how I documented emergent coding to confirmed theory. The systematic approach to documenting grounded theory visually through diagrammatic modelling not only challenges criticisms but also exposes the development of potential grounded theories. To demonstrate, the next section shares how diagrammatic modelling was the principal vehicle for understanding the importance of the middle placement for career changing trainee teachers on the development and transition into 'being' teachers.

The Importance of a 'Middle' Placement and Identity Development

One of the key contributions from my research was the significance of the 'middle' placement. To expand, as part of the ITE standards (Department for Education, 2021), all trainee teachers must have at least two professional placements. These must be two contrasting school settings; one longer term 'home' school placement and a shorter 6-week (minimum) 'alternative' placement in a consecutive age range during their one-year programme; preferably in a consecutive key stage, i.e. Key Stage Three and Four. In England, it is compulsory to be educated from the year one turns 5-years-old to 18-years-old, with five formal key stages until age 18. It is within these key stages that trainee teachers must be placed. The five compulsory key stages are organised into two phases: primary and secondary with a third 'tertiary' phase. The primary phase consists of the Early Years and Foundation Stage (ages 4–5), Key Stage One (ages 5–7) and Key Stage Two (ages 7–11). The secondary phase has Key Stage Three (ages 11–14) and Key Stage Four (ages 14–16). After this, it is compulsory for young people to 'stay in full-time education, for example at a college, start an apprenticeship or traineeship or spend 20 hours or more a week or volunteering, while in part-time education or training' (Department for Education, 2022).

For many trainee teachers on postgraduate courses, the alternative placement occurs in the middle of an ITE programme and should take place in a consecutive phase within the key stage they are training to teach. For example, if a teacher is training to be a 'primary' teacher and is placed within a Key Stage Two class as their longer term placement, they are likely to be placed in a Key Stage One class as their 'alternative' placement and usually in a different setting for contrast. From my research, alternative teaching placements that occur in the 'middle' of a postgraduate course have a significant effect in a career changer's perceived confidence in 'being a teacher'.

My research findings suggest that postgraduate career changing trainee teachers go through a process of identity change during their training. I conceptualised these consecutive phases as *convergence*, *change*, *consciousness* and *confidence* with the middle placements usually occurring between *change* and *consciousness*. I noted how participants' technical language developed as they moved into *consciousness*. Their language became more professional, almost jargonistic, away from everyday terms. Words like 'planning', 'teaching' and 'learning' used in earlier PMs became more sector specific with featured acronyms such as 'sequencing objectives', 'pedagogy' and 'AfL' (Assessment for Learning). This notable change in language, and therefore, perceived learning, occurred after the alternative, middle placement. This suggests that an enforced change of context, and the resulting change in professional relationships, compelled participants to reflect on what they had learnt and 'now know'. In applying knowledge to a different context, they were challenged to articulate learning in concise and professional ways to new, 'experienced others' outside of their 'home' school. Having said this, for some participants, the alternative ITE placement occurred too early in their opinion, as the new knowledge became confused when applied to a new context and did not consolidate learning, but complicated it, potentially leading to a different teacher identity in the latter stages of their training.

To explain how I noted the difference in professional identity formation, I explore my approach to visualising data. In order to enact a CGT, connections are made between and across data through journaling (or 'memo-ing' in CGT terms) and 'diagramming' (Charmaz, 2006). The diagraming approach aims to draw out a 'relative power, scope, and direction of the categories' (2006, p. 118), and 'sharpens the relationships amongst the theoretical categories' (2006, p. 121). It could be said that Fig. 10.1 (below) is more aligned with Clark's (2003) 'situational maps' which have the aim of tracking a journey to help expose an emergent theory. Fig. 10.1 (below) visualises the journeys of each participant throughout their teacher training, indicated by a coloured line from the start of their ten-month ITE programme to the end.

Using PMs as reference points, I was able to track each participant's identity journey individually as well as make relational observations. As seen in Fig. 10.1 below, each PM is named using the confirmed theory from that stage of the research derived from the process of codifying original data, finding relationships between initial and secondary coding to create a unifying category, summarising the experiences of career-changing initial trainee teachers involved in the study. The confirmed categories of each PM helped to form the grounded theory of *Convergence, Change, Consciousness and Confidence.* Using existing research on identity construction to help form emergent categories, participant data were mapped accordingly helping to expose different stages of identity construction per participant. For example, in PM1 and PM2, as I mapped focused codes and with original participant data, I saw correlations between the stage of identity and their 'newness' to teaching. Using in-vivo codes from original data, emergent categories of exploring, transitioning and developing were used to group participants' experiences together.

In PM3, the mapped focused codes seemed to become more aligned to everyone experiencing a 'developing' sense of professional identity formation yet subtle differences remained. In conducting literature reviews throughout the study (a significant principle of CGT), Young and Erickson's (2011) reflections on the stages of 'being a teacher' echoed my findings. Reinforced by Lamote and Engels' (2010) earlier study, they suggest that there may be three stages to adopting a professional teaching identity within the latter stages of teacher training programmes. *Imagining*, *becoming* and *being* were useful categories to consider when establishing subtle differences of participant experiences within the *developing* phase. Combining the three stages with emerging categories from participant data, *Being Ready, Being a Teacher* and *Being and Belonging* were established as seen in Fig. 10.1.

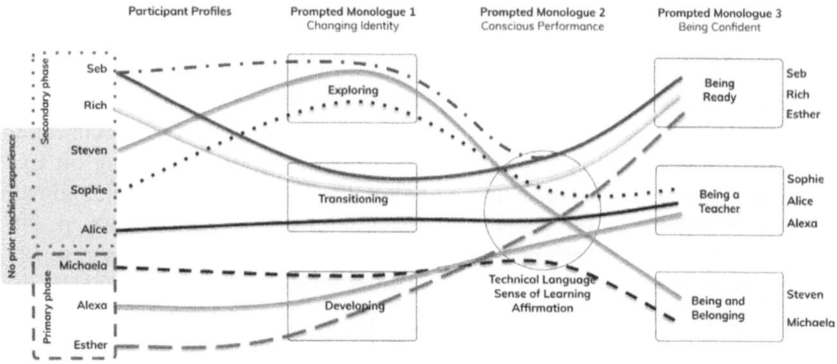

Fig. 10.1. Visual Mapping of Participant Journeys Through Four Phases of Research Mapped Using Formation of Professional Identity Consistency.

Through using diagrammatic mapping, I noticed that connections between participants seemed to change from one prompted monologue to another, however there was one point where all participants seemed to converge; their journeys crossing (indicated by the circle in Fig. 10.1). This mid-year point aligned to PM 2, represented a potential awakening of being *conscious* of the need to 'perform' teaching competencies while on the alternative teaching placement. As mentioned, ITE policy, both at the time of researching and current, states that all trainee teachers must have at least two teaching placements during their teacher training programme. Usually, within a one-year postgraduate model, training comprises a long-term school placement (A) where they spend most of the training, and an alternative, 6-week minimum 'alternative' (B) placement in the middle. Different ITE programmes offer varying approaches, such as AB, BA or may offer more than two placements, e.g. ABC. The purpose of the statutory B placement is to enable trainee teachers to apply newly acquired knowledge without the familiarity of peers and mentors of the A placement. During prompted monologue 2, which occurred during or just after the B placement, all participants discussed a conscious awareness of a need to perform, and demonstrate teaching capabilities to those that do not know them, both teacher and students alike in their alternative placements. This *Conscious Performance* may have been triggered for several reasons, however one common factor emerged: all participants were cognisant of the need to return to their home school having 'made progress', validated by mentors of B placements.

At this point, it is important to distinguish that the four teacher training programmes featured within my study coincidentally included an 'ABA' approach to placements. My research highlighted how the returning to familiarity (A), having experienced difference (B), for some participants, seemed to accelerate a need/desire to consolidate teaching knowledge, or at minimum highlighted possible alternative pedagogies. The awakening of *Professional Consciousness* may also be a result of a heightened emphasis on the 'quality' (not quantity) of evidence required for participants' ITE assessments and in putting what they have learnt into practice. Seemingly, the need for participants to self-identify how they may have improved from A to B correlated with more frequent observations from mentors and programme leaders as they entered the last 'qualifying' third of their programmes. As a result, participants reported how having confidence in one's mentor is critical, particularly at a stage where participants discussed how their own professional *consciousness* awakened.

Observations of the alternative B placement and timing within the programme seemed to be reinforced by a spiral metaphor repeatedly used by some participants. The metaphor did not relate to going around in circles as such, but in returning to an experience or knowledge with a perceived deeper understanding of it, as explained by one participant in particular: Rich. Eager to stress that his new learning was not just a return to something he had done before, Rich noted that his learning from the alternative B placement was an upward spiral, something he had hoped he would obtain from the change of professional context. In the extract below, I noted in my field journal that he 'drew' an upward spiral with his forefinger in the air as he spoke:

> And I think that's [revisiting his understanding of the Teachers' Standards] something that, you know, when I first had that [a skill noted by a mentor in his previous placement], I was like, 'yeah, of course'. Of course they are, but that's become very apparent and that's the spiral that I was kind of kind of, um, yeah, aiming for. (Rich, 3:124)

The 'spiral' of learning may have also contributed to what appeared to be a consistent, steep learning curve for all participants from PM 2 to 3, placements B and A. The step change from participants using general language to describe their teaching to more technical and pedagogically related terminology was notable. The continued development of how participants described what and how they were learning became even more nuanced in PM 3 with *professional consciousness* seemingly leading to a sense of professional identity, as discussed in the developed grounded theory, below.

Identity Convergence, Change, Consciousness and Confidence

As per the national 2011 DfE Teachers' Standards (referenced in my research; subsequently updated (Department for Education, 2021)), all teachers, including trainees, must demonstrate how 'appropriate self-evaluation, reflection and professional development activity is critical to improving teachers' practice at all career stages' (*ibid*, 2021, p. 7). However, despite Beauchamp and Thomas (2009) contributing to evidence that formed to the Teachers' Standards in 2011, there is no mention in guidance for school leaders or ITE providers (Department for Education, 2011, 2021), nor within the ITE Inspection Framework and Handbook (Ofsted, 2022), of how ITE programmes should actively seek to develop an awareness of a changing professional identity in career changing trainees in their early stages. That is not to say that they do not recognise identity formation because it is not referenced in guidance or standards. However, if the four stages of *convergence, change, consciousness* and *confidence* are born out to be consistent (through further studies with greater sample sizes), then this might suggest that this experienced group of professionals would benefit from being professionally required to frame their learning as an iterative, developing process from the onset (as opposed to just evidencing that they can demonstrate standards in isolation). Such expectations are implied in current policy applicable to all teachers, whether trainees or not, but not expected, stating how teachers must 'take responsibility for improving teaching through appropriate professional development, responding to advice and feedback from colleagues' Department for Education (2021, p. 13).

With the above in mind, it is interesting to note where participants start and 'end' their learning journeys as explored in Fig. 10.1 (above), with Steven's journey being the most changeable. However, when reviewing this, I realised how it did not seem to represent the subtleties of the PM 3. In the way that Fig. 10.1 is presented, the 'exploring' of teacher identities of PM 1, were visually 'in line with' with the '*being ready*' [to teach] of PM 3. This was not the case and would have unfairly represented the difference between Seb's *Being Ready* to teach and Steven's *Being and Belonging*, as noted in the extracts below when they are reflecting on the final weeks of their placements.

> Yeah. Even I think you sort of how everything at this point just falls into place a lot quicker. Okay. (Seb, 4:2)

> So it's just been a lot of, again, … integrating in the department and getting involved there. (Steven, 4:36)

Therefore, noting the subtle differences in extracts above, Fig. 10.2 (below) was produced in order to better represent the differences of *Being Ready, Being a Teacher*

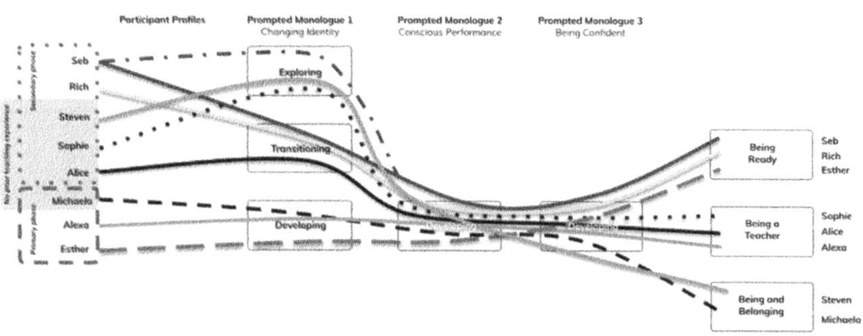

Fig. 10.2. Visual Mapping of Participant Journeys Through Four Phases of Research Mapped Using Coded Categories as Differences of Developing Identity.

and *Being and Belonging* within the *Developing* stage (related to Young and Erikson's (2011) stages of professional identity formation as discussed previously).

Now, in Fig. 10.2, participants within the *Being Ready* category (Seb, Rich and Esther) are more in line with the *Transitioning* identity phase, i.e. at the end of their course they continued to discuss how they were *Transitioning* into *Being Ready* to teach. Sophie, Alice and Alexa seemed to be more in line with the *Developing* identity stage and saw themselves as *Being a Teacher*, while Steven and Michaela seemed to be moving out of *Developing* an identity, seeing themselves as *Being and Belonging* to the teaching profession.

Through using the diagrammatic approach, I was able to refine my grounded theory that career changing trainee teachers experience a similar learning journey of *convergence*, *change, consciousness* and *confidence,* and how an awareness of professional identity formation is integral to this journey. Without visual representations, I do not believe I would have been able to tease out the subtle differences in professional identity formation as distinctly.

Conclusion

As an exploration of career changing trainee teachers, my research showed how they are a complex group of trainee teachers and, in recognition of previous personal and professional experiences, may need greater flexibility with respect to retraining professionally as teachers. Training to teach, unlike other careers which might be dependent on a set body of academic knowledge (e.g. engineering, medicine or law), means that the social, economic and cultural capital (Bourdieu, 1986) of those choosing to train is diverse and complex. With this in mind, prioritising career changers with education experience over those without, when recruiting candidates, may not necessarily yield more confident Newly Qualified Teachers (NQTs). In addition, the seeming importance of a mid-year alternative placement (ABA), and the impact that an experienced in-school mentor may have, should be considerations for ITE programme leaders, particularly when matching to career changers. Hargreaves and Fullan (2000) suggest that school leaders should consider 'deep contextualisation' when selecting in-school mentors, particularly when pairing with career changers to avoid judgementoring (Hobson & Malderez, 2013). Perhaps if the skills, dispositions or mindsets of ITE in-school mentors were more purposefully aligned to those of postgraduate career changers, it might lead to closer, more personalised collaborations (Gorgon, 2020), a potential area for further research.

In addition to substantive contributions, the novel illustrative approach to CGT and my methodological approach centring on prompted monologues is an important tenet of this research. The visual representations of data, whether one references Situational Mapping (Clark, 2003), Diagraming (Charmaz, 2014) or Diagrammatic Modelling (Garrick, 2021), is a useful way to interrogate grounded data through a policy lens, in this case, the experience and learning of postgraduate career changing trainee teachers evaluated against English ITE Teachers' Standards. Associated with this, is perhaps a need for ITE providers to draw trainees' attention to the possibility of learning 'spirals', revisiting concepts previously thought to be 'secure', as a new understanding of the area challenges preconceived notions. In addition, and according to Wilson and Deaney (2010), a lack of understanding of career changers' prior experience and skills on the part of ITE providers might contribute to why so 'many career changers find the transition [into teaching] difficult and even leave teaching during ITE or after only a few years in post' (*ibid*, 2010, p. 170). I suggest, therefore, that it is beneficial for those involved in teacher training to explore and acknowledge how a process of *convergence*, *change*, *consciousness* and *confidence* may provide a framework for addressing the needs of this group of trainee teachers throughout postgraduate ITE programmes in England, and perhaps further afield.

With the contributions above, and with the chapter title in mind, I propose that current ITE routes, and early career recruitment as enacted policy, may need further interrogation if it is to have a significant impact on recruitment and practice, particularly if career changers are going to continue to be part of the solution to the Department for Education policy regarding retention of teachers in England.

Lessons From a Supervisor's Perspective

As second author for this chapter (JA), I reflect now on one of my experiences of being part of the discussions that took place at each stage of the doctoral process Nicholas went through in his exploration of career changers and their evolving identities as trainee teachers. The most notable feature of the study for me as a supervisor was how Nicholas paid great attention to how he would manage his positionality in relation to the study. Professional doctoral students research contexts they know well as an insider and this can raise challenges related to how far and where, in the study, they use that insider knowledge and whether it is placed in the foreground or background. Nicholas' choices to use grounded theory and to apply an intensive listening approach to conducting prompted monologues with his research participants, both explored in this chapter, demonstrate a thoughtfully rationalised approach to addressing the insider researcher's challenge.

References

Beauchamp, C., & Thomas, L. (2009). Understanding teacher identity: An overview of issues in the literature and implications for teacher education. *Cambridge Journal of Education*, *39*(2), 175–189.

Bourdieu, P. (1986). The forms of capital. In *Handbook of theory and research for the sociology of education* (pp. 241–258). Greenwood Press.

Buckley, C., & Waring, M. (2013). Using diagrams to support the research process: Examples from grounded theory. *Qualitative Research*, *13*(2), 148–172.

Charmaz, K. (2006). Grounded theory. In G. Ritzer (Ed.), *Encyclopaedia of sociology*. Blackwell.

Charmaz, K. (2014). *Constructing grounded theory*. SAGE.

Cho, J. Y., & Lee, E. (2014). Reducing confusion about grounded theory and qualitative content analysis: Similarities and differences. *Qualitative Report, 19*(32), 1–20.

Clark, A. (2003). Situational analyses: Grounded theory mapping after the postmodern turn. *Symbolic Interaction, 2*(6), 553–576.

Department for Education. (1998). *Teachers: Meeting the challenge of change.* Education in England. [online]. http://www.educationengland.org.uk/documents/gp1998/teachers-change.html. Accessed on October 27, 2023.

Department for Education. (2011). *Teachers' standards* [online]. https://www.gov.uk/government/publications/teachers-standards. Accessed on October 27, 2023.

Department for Education. (2019). *A framework of core content for initial teacher training (ITT)* [online]. https://www.gov.uk/government/publications/initial-teacher-training-itt-core-content-framework. Accessed on October 27, 2023.

Department for Education. (2021). *Teachers' standards* [online]. https://www.gov.uk/government/publications/teachers-standards. Accessed on October 27, 2023.

Department for Education. (2022). *School leaving age* [online]. https://www.gov.uk/know-when-you-can-leave-school. Accessed on October 27, 2023.

Garrick, N. (2021). *Experiencing initial teacher education as a career changer in England: A constructivist grounded theory exploration of trainee teachers' perceptions of learning.* [online]. https://uwe-repository.worktribe.com/output/7020678/experiencing-initial-teacher-education-as-a-career-changer-in-england-a-constructivist-grounded-theory-exploration-of-trainee-teachers-perceptions-of-learning. Accessed on October 27, 2023.

Gorgon, L. (2020). *Creative approaches to nurturing resilience of trainee teachers.* [online]. Impact. https://impact.chartered.college/article/creative-approaches-nurturing-resilience-trainee-teachers/. Accessed on October 27, 2023.

GOV.UK. (2023). *School workforce in England* [online]. https://explore-education-statistics.service.gov.uk/find-statistics/school-workforce-in-england. Accessed on October 27, 2023.

Hargreaves, A., & Fullan, M. (2000). Mentoring in the new millennium. *Theory Into Practice, 39*(1), 50–56.

Hitchcock, G., & Hughes, D. (1995). *Research and the teacher: A qualitative introduction to school-based research.* Routledge Falmer.

Hobson, A., & Malderez, A. (2013). Judgementoring and other threats to realizing the potential of school-based mentoring in teacher education. *International Journal of Mentoring and Coaching in Education, 2*(2), 89–108.

Lamote, C., & Engels, N. (2010). The development of student teachers' professional identity. *European Journal of Teacher Education, 33*(1), 3–18.

McNamee, S., & Gergen, K. (1992). *Therapy as social construction.* SAGE.

Ofsted. (2022). *Initial teacher education (ITE) inspection framework and handbook.* https://www.gov.uk/government/publications/initial-teacher-education-ite-inspection-framework-and-handbook/initial-teacher-education-ite-inspection-framework-and-handbook. Accessed on October 27, 2023.

Squire, C. (2008). Experience-centred and culturally-oriented approaches to narrative. In M. Andrews, C. Squire, & M. Tamboukou (Eds.), *Doing narrative research.* SAGE.

Thornberg, R. (2012). Informed grounded theory. *Scandinavian Journal of Educational Research, 55*(1), 1–17.

Tolhurst, E. (2012). Grounded theory method: Sociology's quest for exclusive items of inquiry. *Forum for Qualitative Social Research, 13*(3). article 26. https://www.qualitative-research.net/index.php/fqs/article/view/1860/3432

Wilkins, C. (2017). 'Elite' career-changers and their experience of initial teacher education. *Journal of Education for Teaching, 43*(2), 171–190.

Wilkins, C., Busher, H., Kakos, M., Mohamed, C., & Smith, J. (2012). Crossing borders: New teachers co-constructing professional identity in performative times. *Professional Development in Education, 38*(1), 65–77.

Wilkins, C., & Comber, C. (2015). 'Elite' career-changers in the teaching profession. *British Educational Research Journal, 41*(6), 1010–1030.

Wilson, E., & Deaney, R. (2010). Changing career and changing identity: How do teacher career changers exercise agency in identity construction? *Social Psychology of Education, 13*, 169–183.

Young, J., & Erickson, L. (2011). Imagining, becoming, and being a teacher: How professional history mediates teacher educator identity. *Studying Teacher Education, 7*(2), 121–129.

Section 3

Challenging Education Policy and Practice

Chapter 11

Changing the Narrative of Mental and Emotional Health Training in an FE Context: Explorations of Transformational Learning[1]

Georgie Ford[a] *and Richard Waller*[b]

[a]Winterstoke Hundred Academy, UK
[b]University of the West of England, UK

Abstract

This doctoral study arose from a need for policy and training change across further education (FE), to create competent practitioners and a whole college mental and emotional health training framework. Policy cites FE as key to supporting student mental health but there is a significant lack of training and research output supporting this ambition. As a mental health and well-being specialist, I became immersed in the context of FE to design, deliver and evaluate a whole college training model.

The study predominantly utilises qualitative methodology following constructivism as a theoretical framework. Utilising Goleman's (1995) and Mezirow's (2000) theories, the study seeks to redefine professional development by introducing transformational learning through Mental Health First Aid and Emotional training. A mixed-method approach ensures a demonstration of impact, specifically the confidence and knowledge of FE staff.

Thematic analysis allows for the contextualisation of staff experience and explores to which FE roles mental and emotional health support should belong. This enables prescribing of key elements for a whole college training

[1]This chapter has been developed using extracts from the thesis, Ford, G. I. (2022) *Changing the narrative of mental health in the context of FE – Whose role is it anyway?* [Thesis] Faculty of Arts, Creative Industries and Education, the University of the West of England, Bristol.

Critical Perspectives on Educational Policies and Professional Identities, 173–190

doi:10.1108/978-1-83753-332-920241011

approach. A diverse range of pastoral and academic staff demonstrate, via interviews and focus groups, a significant belief that FE mental and emotional health support cannot and should not solely be the responsibility of pastoral staff; this is an outdated model requiring regeneration. This research provides recommendations for FE practice; concluding with the recommendation that affective training must allow opportunity to explore pre-existing schemas and development of new constructions and conceptualisations; those in education require urgent opportunities to create new meanings of mental and emotional health. The study recommends a regeneration of the labelled 'whole' approach, including universal mandatory training for all FE staff.

Keywords: Mental health; emotional health; schemas; transformational learning; training

Introduction, Context and the FE Challenge

Georgie Ford (GF) is the lead author of this chapter, which is based upon her PhD study. Richard Waller (RW) was Georgie's lead supervisor and is second author here. Where the first person is used to explain the background or process of the study, this is from Georgie's perspective.

To understand the rationale for this doctoral study, an outline of the complexity of the further education (FE) policy context is necessary. As an educational mental health specialist, GF witnessed significant local and national disparity within FE cultures and provision of mental health training for staff. The study accesses staff participants and wider bodies including the Association of Colleges (AoC) to further enhance its contextual authenticity. FE has been described as key to supporting the mental health crisis of students (FE News, 2021), yet no national training framework exists to guide the sector. Historical literature describes whole approaches to mental health as vague and diluted (Weare & Nind, 2011) and notices significant focus upon resource development for schools and higher education. These settings present differing contexts of adolescents yet it is not uncommon for FE to be omitted by policy and resource (Duckworth & Smith, 2019), leaving the sector to create autonomous solutions in the absence of structured guidance. This ambiguity of mental and emotional health training and development culminates in staff without evidence-based boundaries within academic roles (Hughes & Panjwani, 2018). Academic FE roles are increasingly complex, there is a novel dimension arising that requires necessary upskilling. A distinct lack of a contextually appropriate training model does not enable or empower FE staff to support a now inevitable part of FE (Smith, 2021). The COVID-19 pandemic has escalated young people's need for mental and emotional support in their place of study (Young Minds, 2020) and training cannot be solely purposed for pastoral teams, especially when it is known that the first point of contact is often an academic tutor. FE academic staff provide significant pastoral support on an ad hoc basis as a response to visible emotional and mental health presentations of young people meaning that a pastoral and academic separation is outdated (Sunderland, 2021). Training methodologies require redefinition and regeneration; FE-based action research can inform this. FE is a marginalised sector with minimal exploratory output and existing literature searches on FE mental health training reveal little of relevance or are tentative explorations that require expansion. FE colleges are described as sidelined educational institutions (Sales, 2021). Paradoxically, the mental health policy context of FE is developing rapidly, a pace that is unmatched throughout literature. This study created an evidence-based training model to respond to limited evidence and concerns about sector parity, and goes some way to creating parity with other sectors, which can be built upon subsequently by other work.

Literature Review and Rationale

The lack of literature focusing on this topic area was a compelling rationale for this study. FE is often omitted (FE News, 2021) within literature and has been a poorly understood, under-researched, under-funded and under-valued part of the education system, often labelled as the 'Cinderella sector' (Wren, 2023). FE News (2021) suggest that the sector should engage in collective learning, building its wealth of knowledge and expertise and the capacity of its working members to research and innovate. The sector is under-represented in comparison to its school and higher education counterparts (Thorley, 2017) that have access to mental health models, such as THRIVE (Wolpert et al., 2019).

Reviewing literature in this field was of key significance to this study. The work of Creswell (2007) is beneficial to a new doctoral researcher, encouraging exploration and authentic understanding of a literature review purpose. Literature searches revealed crucial issues had been repeatedly raised about FE mental health many years ago (Roeser & Midgley, 1997; Warwick, 2008). Sources summarised suggestions of FE staff training, but concerningly, this did not translate into a tangible model (Shelemy et al., 2019). Minimal action research has been conducted to instigate change and contribute towards the literature gap and wider understanding of the situation. Therefore, the literature review and topic selection became crucial to this study to claim originality and drive innovative movement and policy. This doctoral study raises pertinent questions regarding research failures to explore modern-day complexities of the FE academic staff role in student emotional mental health and illness. Conceptually, emotional literacy is not novel to education, but the focus remains on children, rather than the emotional competency of staff. Salovey and Mayer (1990) penned the term in their emotional intelligence article before further exploration by Goleman (2004). There is a wealth of reading surrounding emotional literacy in primary and secondary schools and models such as emotionally healthy schools arise from this, but FE remains neglected. Education focuses on the delivery of emotional literacy programmes for students due to its correlation with increasing academic performance (Meher et al., 2021).

Action Research to Change the Narrative

This research encapsulates GF's passion for educational change combined with prolonged engagement in the FE policy context to conduct participatory action research (Bradbury & Reason, 2005). The study followed 3 key stages:

(1) Problem identification across the FE sector locally and nationally.
(2) Development and implementation of a transferable training model.
(3) Evaluation (qualitative and quantitative) and recommendations for practice.

A whole FE staff emotional and mental health training model was developed and implemented (over the course of one academic year) based upon sector voice and engagement. The training model was evaluated via interviews, a focus group and training surveys generating both qualitative and quantitative data. Data analysis included thematic analysis of 1:1 interviews and a focus group, plus the quantitative analysis of descriptive statistics reported from evaluations of training. The developed model was the result of iterative reflective action cycles and was informed by consistent prolonged FE sector engagement. The study aimed to evaluate the model authentically via the experience of staff participants and was designed using a graduated approach of universal and targeted training based upon the premise that these are strong in combination (Adi et al., 2007). Each programme was designed according to the principles of transformational learning theory (TLT) (Mezirow & Taylor, 2009) to allow staff participants the opportunity for discourse and reflection during training. The research investigated whether participants' pre-existing frames/structures regarding mental health can be reformulated to make new meaning, thus transforming habits of the mind (Mezirow, 2000). In the cognitive, rational perspective, transformative learning is a process by which previously uncritically assimilated assumptions, beliefs, values and perspectives are questioned and thereby become more open, permeable and better validated (Mezirow, 2000). If our existing habits of mind are challenged by an event or information which is discrepant with what we believe, we are led to critical self-reflection and potentially to a revised way of viewing ourselves and the world around us. There are numerous examples of this built into the training packages within this model. Discourse plays a critical role in Mezirow's (2000) understanding of transformative learning theory. Ideas and evidence from others help us to consider our views in a novel way. Transformative learning takes place when this process leads us to open our frame of reference, discard a habit of mind, see alternatives and thereby act differently in the world (Mezirow, 2000).

Universal training was made mandatory for all staff, the first example of this approach in the United Kingdom's FE sector, and targeted training provided upskill workshops in prominent mental and emotional health challenges including anxiety, loneliness and self-esteem. Universal training comprised adult Mental Health First Aid (MHFA) training and emotional and cognitive literacy training to provide a baseline level of knowledge and confidence to FE staff. MHFA is a national evidence-based offering and emotional literacy was designed by GF in response to the study college's contextual needs and the COVID-19 pandemic.

Organisations must now begin to understand their unique staff requirements in the response to mental and emotional health. In this study, an action research design surveyed staff attitudes prior to training implementation. These responses translated into the design of a whole college training model to embed mental and emotional health support into everyday culture, responding to suggestions that a pastoral and academic divide is outdated. This study does not suggest that academics are responsible for mental health support but that they should be prepared adequately due to the inevitability of mental health conversations (Sunderland, 2021).

The rationale for this doctoral study has been outlined and this following segment of this chapter introduces the research design, shown below Fig. 11.1.

Study Participants

This research study attracted a broad sample of FE staff from a leading college in the southwest of England. At some level, 615 participants took part in this study. This number represents some 59% of the college's 1,038 staff.

Method	Number of Participants
Whole college survey	362
MHFA (Universal and mandatory training)	58
Emotional literacy (Universal and mandatory training)	203
1:1 Interviews (Targeted and voluntary training)	13
Consolidatory focus group	13

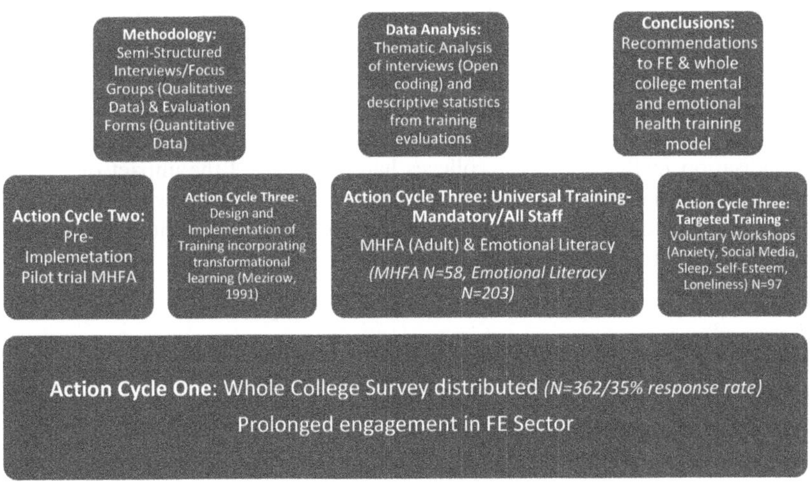

Fig. 11.1. Research Map.

Research Questions

This study included five key research questions critical to this topic area.

- Is a whole college training model of universal and targeted training appropriate for the integration of mental and emotional health support for staff within an FE environment?
- How can a whole college training offering within an FE environment improve clarity for aligning mental and emotional support within FE?
- Does job role impact participation in a whole college mental health framework?
- Can transformational learning increase confidence towards inclusivity of mental and emotional health support within FE?
- Do FE colleges require an MHL who holds responsibility for facilitation of a whole college training model?

Action Cycle 1: Pre-Implementation Fact-Finding, Problem Formulation and Action Planning

The purpose of the initial cycle was to learn as much about the problem prior to designing and implementing a training model and to understand staff requirements. This action cycle fulfils a significant element of prolonged engagement (Lincoln & Guba, 1985) and remained continuous within my role. To be wholly informed to design training, the debate of FE mental and emotional health support and training was approached holistically to local and national context. A whole staff survey during this cycle ensured the voice of the study college, gathering both quantitative and qualitative data, and 99.4% of respondents requested mental and emotional health training and believed this was necessary in FE. This survey included 10 questions. This cycle began with membership to two national policy groups: (AoC Mental Health Policy Group and Mental Health in Schools' network). These networks provided a unique opportunity to collaborate with FE professionals in a problem-solving space. During this engagement, colleges were beginning to train staff sporadically using MHFA without guidance or operationalisation methods and FE colleges had not tracked the impact or explored any consequential transformations. Therefore, due to the knowledge and reflections of this action cycle, GF decided to include MHFA in parity with what was already being utilised throughout FE.

Action Cycle 2: Pre-implementation Trial of MHFA

Action cycle one demonstrated that MHFA was beginning to improve knowledge and confidence across FE, and indicated that a pilot trial of MHFA in the study college would be appropriate to acquire impact insights and assess my role as an internal MHFA instructor. This was a cycle of inquiry and pilot evaluations allowed for adaptations to delivery, environment and the course materials. From this pilot, I acted to ensure that training was scheduled on days such as insets and timetable-free days to ensure participation. Taylor et al. (2014) observes a failure of previous programmes to be adaptable to staff time and pressures. This study gained consent to use MHFA course evaluations as descriptive data and the pilot demonstrated that participants understood these. Staff trained during this pilot cycle reported increases in confidence and knowledge, however, reflectivity within this action cycle highlighted a lack of emotion-based material within MHFA. This was a significant milestone in the research study. While MHFA demonstrated impact, it was clear that to address the complexity of mental health, a second mandatory training model was required to provide transformational opportunities focusing on emotions and self-awareness to provide holistic understanding to all staff.

Action Cycle 3: Development and Delivery of Training Programmes

Action was taken to deliver the result of engagement and understanding during the previous cycles by designing and implementing a training model with two mandatory programmes. MHFA is nationally recognised and was delivered by GF during the study according to the principles of transformative learning theory (Mezirow, 2000). Action cycle two demonstrated on a pilot sample that MHFA training could increase confidence by allowing staff an opportunity to refine existing, inaccurate schemas of mental health and illness, suggesting that TLT was an appropriate delivery style. This training model acknowledges that all staff are likely to possess individual, personal meanings and stereotypes of mental health that must be addressed. The second universal training programme of emotional literacy was designed as a result of prolonged engagement, reflectivity and pilot training evaluations resulting in an acute recognition of staff requirements. This training programme endeavours to educate self-awareness of emotion, self-regulation and communication according to the principles of TLT. Action cycle 2 in combination with literature exploration provided an in-depth understanding of how to facilitate a TLT environment. The research delivered five cohorts of MHFA within the study college and over 10 sessions of emotional literacy. Effectively, this cycle resulted in the design and implementation of a proposed whole college training model with two mandatory programmes and a selection of targeted workshops to be offered across the duration of one academic year. Data were collected via semi structured 1:1 interview (qualitative), confidence and knowledge measures on evaluation surveys (quantitative) and a focus group to triangulate data.

Action Cycle 4: Consolidatory Focus Group

Qualitative data documented rich experiences of the model and it was critical to triangulate all data collection methods in the form of a final focus group to further ensure the authenticity of participant voice. As a group, participants suggested the key themes arising from their journeys for the final focus group discussion to ensure that recommendations were naturally occurring and honoured staff voice. These were the significant policy development areas that they felt required addressing. The final themes for discussion are presented in the Table 11.1. These themes were in alignment with the themes occurring from thematic analysis on the 1:1 semi-structured interviews.

Ethics and Transferability

This study adhered to the British Educational Research Association's ethical guidelines (BERA, 2018) and the impact upon participants and the study college was a paramount consideration. Ethical approval was received from the appropriate university committee and study college group. Due to a dual researcher role, this study maintains solid ethical practice to protect identities and avoid moral conflict. Although complete anonymity cannot ever be guaranteed (Sikes & Piper, 2010), no additional information was stored and participants were anonymised. Sim and Waterfield's (2019) guidance for informed consent was implemented alongside of awareness of the potential ethical dilemmas present in focus groups. No participants were subject to unnecessary harm and this research was not achievable without human participants due to the focus on human description, experience and assessment of transformation. Qualitative research produces rich accounts of thick description (Geertz, 1973), and this is vital to provide a profound understanding of required training within the sector.

This study cannot claim generalisability and instead aims for transferability for FE colleges to individualise according to context, demographics and geography. Transferability refers to the transfer of findings to another context and the researcher can judge how feasible that transfer is. The training model encourages colleges to adapt to their individual and unique settings (Lincoln & Guba, 1985). Its design allows for adaptability and transferability for colleges with or without a Mental Health Lead to ensure parity of FE support and training. Future doctoral

Table 11.1. Final Focus Group Themes.

1. Staff well-being and support
2. Delivery methods of training
3. Universal and targeted approach
4. Clarity of job role/boundaries
5. Emotional literacy – transformational learning
6. MHFA – Impact
7. Continuation of training model
8. Awareness/Confidence
9. Lockdown and COVID-19

candidates researching from within can take value from concepts of transferability that could be overlooked in favour of a traditionalist generalisability stance. Generalisability may not be appropriate in the context of mental health in education due to the varied nuances of each institution and their resources. Many frameworks allow for and encourage, qualitative rigour (Maher et al., 2018).

Findings

Post-training, participants completed evaluative questionnaires, a focus group and interviews to create a holistic report of their experiences from each training programme. Confidence and knowledge were measured numerically through evaluative surveys and compared before and after training; participants rated themselves on a 10-point scale. Each training cohort demonstrated at least a three-point increase in both confidence and knowledge suggesting that MHFA training increases these areas and is appropriate training as a minimal expectation within a whole college training model.

> I think what Mental Health First Aid did for me was gave me a much wider level of knowledge as well as then utilising the workshops to draw it all together. The default position is "I'm fine" but it encourages you to ask, "How are you really?"

Qualitative data added human experience to the quantitative and provided evidence of transformational learning. Participants referred to the transformation of knowing how to address suicide and correcting existing incorrect schemas. Additionally, participants appreciate exploring the differences between mental health and mental ill health and topics such as self-harm.

> It's now less of a shock for self-harm, it's more of a "oh okay, yeah I can talk about it". It's just become another thing, like anxiety. It's become normalised.

The impact of training and schema regeneration were apparent in the results of this study. Mental health in education is now a significant policy area and it is unlikely that this will change. Professional development should be designed to observe the pertinent consideration that affective learning should subscribe to TLT principles to encourage and create opportunities for discourse, reflection and new schema creation. An additional benefit of this is a signal that emotions and mentalities are part of the cultural conversation within education, not a tokenistic training addition.

Self-awareness during emotional literacy training was a key journey for many participants and was a recurring transformational theme during thematic analysis. Ninety-one percent of staff reported that they felt more confident in the key principles of emotional literacy (n = 203) and 93% reported a developed ability to listen actively and empathise with emotions. Qualitative data also revealed developing self-awareness and reflective behaviours indicating that investment in staff emotional development valuable; one participant suggested:

> I think the other thing it also did for me personally is it reinforced to me that actually, you need to treat people differently, and I think it raised that awareness of me. It just gave me an increased level of tolerance and a greater understanding that, sometimes, people need things differently from how I may need them.

Discussion

Emotional Health; A New Trajectory for FE

A significant lesson from this research was the critical necessity to implement emotional understanding as a multifaceted element of mental health. Originally, there was no plan to address emotional health, simply mental health. However, significant reflection and a global pandemic demonstrated that they are inextricably linked and to increase understanding, staff must view these in parallel. This meant significantly refining the study and the inclusion of an additional training programme alongside MHFA as a universal and mandatory offering. Emotional literacy training was designed and delivered by GF and included knowledge-based delivery about labelling basic human emotions, opportunities to discuss pre-existing schemas and methods to encourage emotional self-awareness.

The study training is designed to equip staff participants to purposefully label the emotions that they often are problem-solving with young people. Goleman (2004) acknowledges self-awareness as a crucial principle of emotional intelligence and cognitive ability to increase interpersonal relationships. Creating emotionally literate FE environments could improve the quality of relationships and subsequently authentic communication between staff and students, making this the norm. Emotional literacy training in this research included self-regulatory skills, to encourage staff to recognise their emotional frame before considering that of others. Educational staff are not exempt from what Ekman (1992) describes as reactive emotions including fear and anger, both cited by FE staff returning from the pandemic to academic roles. Therefore, self-awareness and regulatory skills are vital to the reintegration and recovery of society and education. If staff are key to supporting students' mental and emotional health, they must be sufficiently skilled in their emotional behaviours. Research frequently presents the importance of emotion in human behaviours and relationships (Antoniou, 2005). In summary, to confidently recognise mental and emotional health difficulties and deliver appropriate support, academics must be adequately trained and, more significantly, report competence.

The doctoral research upon which this chapter is based encapsulates Goleman's (2004) concepts that emotional capabilities are not innate talents but learnt capabilities and part of this study implemented and explored these principles. This policy area is consistently gaining momentum and significant room exists for new researchers to inform its direction. There was an urgent need for change within FE; a mental health staff training model was required that explored staff conceptualisations and beliefs of mental and emotional health. Researching from within was vital to the development of this so that it could be designed, implemented and tested by those engaged and experiencing the sector during a time of significant mental health challenge.

Transformational Learning – A Training Style for Mental and Emotional Health Delivery

According to TLT, adults learn effectively when their frames of reference are challenged (Mezirow, 2000). This is significant for the design of educational CPD and the focus of the research underpinning this chapter. A frame of reference encompasses the habits of the mind (ways of thinking, feeling and behaving) and points of view (values and beliefs). Mezirow (2000) defines four techniques in which learning occurs and these were embedded within the universal and targeted training in this study:

(1) Elaborate on existing frames of reference.
(2) Learn new frames of reference.
(3) Transform habits of the mind.
(4) Transform points of view.

The research investigated whether participants' pre-existing frames of mental health can be reformulated through different training programmes to make new meanings, transforming the habits of the mind (Mezirow, 2000) resulting in increased confidence and less ambiguity. Transformative learning is a process by which previously uncritically assimilated assumptions, beliefs, values and perspectives are questioned and thereby become permeable, and better validated (Mezirow, 2000). If existing habits of mind are challenged by new knowledge within training which is discrepant with what we believe, we are led to critical self-reflection and potentially to a revised way of viewing ourselves and the world. The training in this study allowed staff to explore and question current beliefs and knowledge about mental and emotional health.

The choice of TLT in educational CPD is courageous due to the emphasis on human exploration and refinement of historical conceptualisations. There is a lesson here for new doctoral researchers. Educational CPD is often a taught, instructional session often perceived as a mandatory exercise. Change agency is possible from within to research and consequently innovate. Mental health within educational settings can be a sensitive subject with several ambiguous policy recommendations (Hughes & Panjwani, 2018). Mental health is a personal experience and to create competence and confidence, implicit conceptualisations and biases require exploration through training.

Educational authors have observed a paradigm shift towards the adult and refer to a change in adult attitudes aligning with positive behaviour in schools

(Dix, 2017). To improve mental health knowledge and emotional literacy, opportunity is required to explore an adult's prior experience and existing knowledge. This doctoral research proposed a transformation of the 'whole' approach and a reconsideration of 'affective' (emotional) education to include the transformation of cognitive mechanisms. This is an ambiguous step for educational development. It requires and encourages potentially sensitive conversations; however, this exploration is crucial to empower staff to engage with confidence in conversations about emotions and mental health. This is achieved with a trained facilitator (MHFA instructor) in a safe and neutral training space. The educational field has shied away from this style of in-depth learning, but qualitative data within this study demonstrates these transformations to be advantageous; encouraging emotional authenticity and validation of one another's feelings, vital skills that can be role modelled within the classroom.

Redefining Mental and Emotional Conceptualisations

Expansion of the understanding of mental illness and its distinction to mental health is necessary. The terms are frequently used interchangeably within FE. The whole college survey distributed prior to model design demonstrated that all respondents requested training and did not report competence to support mental health challenges. Sixty-three percent of staff reported prior mental health training, yet when asked how confident they would be in assisting a learner with a mental health crisis, only 5% of staff reported feeling extremely confident to do so. This suggests prior training was not relevant or fit for purpose. The need for mental health training within the sector was explored in the survey and only one respondent thought there was no need for this meaning the purpose of this study was clear. Two respondents used the 'did not know' option meaning that 99.4% of the respondents identified a need for further training within FE. Thus, it is crucial that staff have opportunities to increase competence. This study agreed with Conrad and Barker's (2010) research suggesting that social meanings are overlooked. Social meanings refer to our own perceptions of what mental health and illness are. It cannot be assumed that educational staff understand the distinction between these two terms.

MHFA contains exercises that encourage discussion of existing schemas and language and to define the concepts of mental health and mental illness. Participants are encouraged to engage in discourse around these constructs while examining language that contributes to inaccurate perceptions of mental ill health. Interview data suggested that the opportunity to link judgemental language to prior opinions was useful to understand schema formation. MHFA invites participants to engage in the mental health continuum, an exercise demonstrating that mental health and mental illness are not linear. This exercise demonstrates that you can be diagnosed or experience symptoms of mental illness but still maintain good levels of well-being which many do not comprehend in the absence of training. MHFA encourages listening activities to learn authentic and non-judgemental listening; a critical opportunity for FE staff to examine their values and attitudes about mental health and illness.

Recommendations for Policy Change

This study provided numerous recommendations for FE policy change, the most significant are detailed below.

Universal Training Should Be Mandatory for All FE Staff

This training model presents a suggested model of mental and emotional health training that should be offered to all FE staff including cleaners, facilities staff and administrators. There are supplementary considerations to this recommendation within the study. Universal training is a minimum training standard that supports FE staff in the basic comprehension of mental and emotional health leading to evidence-based responses whilst simultaneously improving knowledge and confidence; significant staff concerns about supporting mental health are evident within FE. Universal training encourages staff to challenge existing, historical frames of reference based upon individual personal experience, providing opportunity and a neutral, safe space for critical reflection and discussion. Knowledge provided through training means we continuously reconstruct new experiences and learn to extend existing constructions. Staff in FE roles are not devoid of existing perceptions, schemas and values constructed from a variety of past experiences and universal training addresses these safely. FE must now acknowledge that culture is a transmitter of constructions, and these are often inherited from an array of past experiences (Lincoln & Guba, 1985). This research data demonstrates significant impact; participants reported a developed ability to reflect and acknowledge constructions that differ to their own entrenched beliefs. Therefore, the design of the model is appropriate for FE mandatory training. If colleges are not equipped or resourced sufficiently to implement the training model, then universal training is adequate in isolation as an initial stage to commence building a whole college approach. The training programmes recommended by this research for universal (mandatory) implementation are:

i. Two Day Adult MHFA
ii. Emotional and cognitive literacy (2 hour workshop).

CPD Requires Regeneration

Mental and emotional health training requires empathetic delivery methodologies; FE leaders must consider that affective development should differ from traditional classroom education and requires diversity of approach. Emotions and mental health do not lend themselves to a taught instructional methodology. The current study demonstrates that adult attitudes can be transformed and refined in optimal environmental conditions. FE has a duty to acknowledge its role in exploring the perceptions and schemas of its staff via transformational training. As a minimum, some conditions for transformational learning should be created in the delivery of mental and emotional health training. This research highlights the importance of beliefs, attitudes and perceptions and staff must be trained to challenge existing cognitions and create new knowledge constructions that result in confident staff support methods, boundaries and signposting. Ultimately, training is key to removing concerns of ambiguity of role voiced by staff during prolonged engagement in action cycle 1.

Transformational learning can enhance how human beings view themselves and the world around them. Central to TLT is the critical concept of empathy (Mezirow, 2000), a construct emphasised in emotional literacy training. FE establishments must consider that traditional development processes are not appropriate for meeting the complexity of young peoples' mental and emotional health needs. Traditional methods are no longer workable to support the complexity of emotional and mental health. Changing the paradigm to focus on staff development instead of student prevention in isolation promotes autonomy, well-being, clarity of job role and early intervention skills. It is unproductive to teach new concepts, such as empathy, in the absence of a context and environment to encourage its development. In the absence of transformational learning and facilitation, staff are unable to apply new concepts and knowledge. Transformational learning can contribute to, and inspire, a growing research body within FE; the more the constructs and assumptions about mental health are shared, the more researchers and their output will reach a consensus about the validity of research in this field (Hammersley, 2007). Training should facilitate environments that are safe spaces to explore interpersonal relationships, role boundaries and perceptions of mental health. This developmental opportunity is a powerful tool to change perceptions and attitudes of academics towards mental health training and define what has become an ambiguous role through providing evidence-based boundaries. Training within this model actively encourages discussion and feedback exchange between participants and, due to the nature of this type of training, this is one the study's most successful elements. This element of the study alone creates empathy between staff and is a catalyst for peer support and interaction, a method to increase staff well-being.

Recommendation – A Whole College Training Approach Includes a Universal (Mandatory) Layer, a Targeted (Voluntary) Layer and a Specialist Layer

Whole college approaches to mental and emotional health must mean exactly that, evidence-based training opportunities encompassing all staff. If mental and emotional support are inevitable to modern FE roles, then training can no longer be reserved for pastoral staff alone. FE colleges are a critical front line service in the support of young people at a crucial period of adolescence (Sutherland, 2021). If genuine FE whole college stances are not implemented, we neglect those who make a difference in student lives. The current research does not suggest that all staff should reach specialist level, but that staff train to feel confident to navigate difficult conversations. This study provides a critically required holistic method to regenerate the whole approach to reflect the modern FE context rather than a division in which academic staff support only teaching and learning, a shift that is required within FE.

Impact of Research and Reflection on Lessons Learnt

This research did not have scope to explore the actions and transformations in practice post-training but recommends that this is a key follow-up to any mental and emotional health training. There is significant scope in this area for FE research-based activity to further explore existing theoretical ideology that could further enhance affective training deliveries. The impact of this doctoral research study was unexpected, and as time went on, the interest of policymakers and wider FE community grew. This gave further voice to many within the FE sector experiencing similar challenges. Since the doctoral research reported here began, it has been presented at the London International Conference for Education, published in the International Journal for Cross-Disciplinary Subjects in Education and assisted in the winning of a Gold Carnegie Award from Leeds Beckett University. The study college is currently the only FE college to hold this award.

One of the largest lessons to arising from this study is the importance of people in any establishment. People and educational communities of staff desire to learn and understand mental and emotional health because the benefits are twofold. This research signals that if FE is to become central to the support of its young population, there are significant preparatory mechanisms that must be considered first. Perhaps the most significant of these is that emotional and mental health must become part of organisational culture. No longer is taught, instructional CPD appropriate or effective to achieve this. To truly embed emotional authenticity within cultures, training must be provided that allows staff to challenge misperceptions and potentially inaccurate schemas. Staff must be equipped to navigate uncomfortable conversations and emotional distress; this is a learnt skill. Some policymakers may argue that education is not the place for these often-uncomfortable training experiences but then we must argue whether in that case, education is the place to be 'key' for mental health support as is so often cited. Since the publication of the doctoral research, the study college has trained over 400 staff in MHFA and the emotional literacy CPD continues in termly training sessions. In addition, the study college is the first in the United Kingdom to begin training its staff in Suicide First Aid; a 'pioneering' move according to FE Week (2023). However, the study college continues in its mission to facilitate evidence-based CPD that arises as a result of findings and evidence from its research, a mechanism to secure the transformations of staff and increase confidence and knowledge. This topic is significant, and it is not difficult in mental health and change agency to achieve beyond the realistic scope and parameters of a doctoral study. Future researchers selecting this topic will benefit from a neutral critical source to maintain boundaries and to ensure realistic scope. The nature of this work will continue in further action research cycles (Bradbury & Reason, 2005) long after this study and continuously be seeking situational and policy improvements. For new doctoral candidates, one of the greatest lessons learnt throughout this study was that reflection is the greatest thing you can do for the quality of your research. It is tempting to want your research to follow the linear plan you have doubtless created, however, the best research is slightly messy and follows the trajectory of authenticity to your cause; instinct is a useful tool in research.

References

Adi, Y., Killoran, A., Janmohamed, K., & Stewart-Brown, S. (2007). *Systematic review of the effectiveness of interventions to promote mental wellbeing in primary schools: Universal approaches which do not focus on violence or bullying*. National Institute for Clinical Excellence. https://www.ncbi.nlm.nih.gov/books/NBK73674/. Accessed on April 20, 2019.

Antoniou, A. S. (2005). *Emotional intelligence and transformational leadership*.

Bradbury, B., & Reason, P. (2005). *Handbook of action research* (Concise pbk edition ed.). Sage Publications.

British Educational Research Association. (2018). *Ethical guidelines for educational research* (4th ed.). https://www.bera.ac.uk/researchers-resources/publications/ethical-guidelines-for-educational-research-2018

Conrad, P., & Barker, K. K. (2010). The social construction of illness: Key insights and policy implications. *Journal of Health and Social Behavior*, *51*, S67–S79. Accessed on November 21, 2019.

Creswell, J. W. (2007). *Qualitative inquiry and research design: Choosing among five approaches* (2nd ed.). Sage Publications, Inc.

Dix, P. (2017). *When the adults change, everything changes: Seismic shifts in school behaviour*. Crown House Publishing.

Duckworth, V., & Smith, R. (2019). *Further education in England: Transforming lives (summative report)*. UCU.

Ekman, P. (1992). Are there basic emotions? *Psychological Review*, *99*(3), 550–553.

FE News. (2021). *Building an FE research community of practice*. Accessed on April 21, 2021.

FE News. (2023). *The Pioneering College brave enough to tackle suicide head-on*. https://feweek.co.uk/the-pioneering-college-brave-enough-to-tackle-suicide-issues-head-on/. Accessed on June 27, 2023.

Geertz, C. (1973). *The interpretation of cultures: Selected essays*. Basic Books.

Goleman, D. (1995). Emotional intelligence. *Why it can matter more than IQ*. Bloomsbury Publishing.

Goleman, D. (2004). *Emotional intelligence and working with emotional intelligence* (1st ed.). Bloomsbury Publishing Plc.

Hammersley, M. (2007). The issue of quality in qualitative research. *International Journal of Research and Method in Education*, *30*, 287–305.

Hughes, T., & Panjwani, B. (2018). Student mental health. *The role and experiences of academics.* studentminds.org.uk/uploads/3/7/8/4/3784584/180129_student_mental_health__the_role_and_experience_of_academics__student_minds_pdf.pdf. Accessed on September 5, 2019.

Lincoln, Y. S., & Guba, E. G. (1985). *Naturalistic enquiry* (1st ed.). Sage.

Maher, C., Hadfield, M., Hutchings, M., & de Eyto, A. (2018). Ensuring rigor in qualitative data analysis: A design research approach to coding combining NVivo with traditional material methods. *International Journal of Qualitative Methods, 17*(1).

Meher, V., Venkateswar, B., & Bankira, S. (2021). An analysis of emotional intelligence and academic performance V. *Shanlax International Journal of Education, 9*(2), 108–116.

Mezirow, J. (2000). Learning to think like an adult. Core concepts of transformation theory. In J. Mezirow, & Associates (eds.), *Learning as transformation. Critical perspectives on a theory in progress* (pp. 3–33). Jossey-Bass.

Mezirow, J., & Taylor, E. (2009). *Transformative learning in practice: Insights from community, workplace, and higher education.* Jossey-Bass.

Roeser, R. W., & Midgley, C. (1997). Teachers' views of issues involving students' mental health. *The Elementary School Journal, 98*(2), 115–133.

Sales, P. (2021). *BTEC debacle shows we are still too often forgotten.* TES News. BTEC debacle shows we are still too often forgotten | Tes Magazine. Accessed on March 1, 2021.

Salovey, P., & Mayer, J. D. (1990). 'Emotional intelligence', imagination. *Cognition and Personality, 9*(3), 185–211.

Shelemy, L., Harvey, K., & Waite, P. (2019). Supporting students' mental health in schools: What do teachers want and need? *Emotional and Behavioural Difficulties 24*(1), 100–116. https://www.tandfonline.com/doi/abs/10.1080/13632752.2019.1582742?needAccess=true&journalCode=rebd20

Sikes, P., & Piper, H. (2010). Ethical research, academic freedom and the role of ethics committees and review procedures in educational research. *International Journal of Research and Method in Education, 33*(3), 205–213.

Sim, J., & Waterfield, J. (2019). Focus group methodology: Some ethical challenges. *Quality and Quantity, 53*, 3003–3022.

Smith, J. (2021). In S. Mallon, & J. Smith (eds.), *Preventing and responding to student suicide: A practical guide for FE and HE settings.* Jessica Kingsley.

Sunderland, M. (2021). *Schools, colleges and universities are essentially now front-line services.* https://www.fenews.co.uk/exclusive/schools-colleges-and-universities-are-essentially-now-front-line-mental-health-services/. Accessed on February 10, 2022.

Taylor, J. A., Phillips, R., Cook, E., Georgiou, L., Stallard, P., & Sayal, K. (2014). A qualitative process evaluation of classroom-based cognitive behaviour Therapy to reduce adolescent depression. *International Journal of Environmental Research and Public Health, 11*(6), 5951–5969.

Thorley, C. (2017). *Not by degrees. Improving student mental health in UK Universities.* Institute for public policy research. Not by degrees: Improving student mental health in the UK's universities | IPPR. Accessed on September 3, 2020.

Warwick, I. (2008). Supporting mental health and emotional well-being among younger students in further education. *Journal of Further and Higher Education, 1*, 1–13. https://www.tandfonline.com/doi/abs/10.1080/03098770701560331. Accessed on September 13, 2019.

Weare, K., & Nind, M. (2011). Mental health promotion and problem prevention in schools: What does the evidence say? *Health Promotion International*, *26*, 29–69. https://pubmed.ncbi.nlm.nih.gov/22079935/. Accessed on August 14, 2019.

Wolpert, M., Harris, R., Hodges, S., Fuggle, P., James, R., Wiener, A., & Munk, S. (2019). *THRIVE Framework for system change*. CAMHS Press.

Wren, A. (2023). Further education: The cinderella of the education sector? In *University of cumbria learning, education and development research centre (LED) lightning talk*. 8 February 2023, Online. (Unpublished).

Young Minds. (2020). *The Impact of Covid-19 on young people with mental health needs*. https://youngminds.org.uk/about-us/reports/coronavirus-impact-on-young-people-with-mental-health-needs/. Accessed on December 1, 2020.

Chapter 12

'It's Our Job to Take the Limits Away': Exploring the Beliefs and Practices of High Expectation Teachers[1]

Julie Smith[a] *and Richard Waller*[b]

[a]Wyedean School, UK
[b]University of the West of England, UK

Abstract

This study explores the beliefs of 'high expectation teachers', and the practices through which teachers aim to build an inclusive learning environment in addition to the ways they develop strategies that do not rely on pre-determined ability labelling. The study is a case study design focused on one phenomenon, that of the beliefs and practices of high-expectation teachers, and one bounded case illustrates the phenomenon. The case is specific and bounded by time and location. It emphasises uniqueness through the in-depth exploration of the participants' experiences. Following the use of thematic analysis to analyse data collected through questionnaires, interviews and focus groups, the phenomena of high teacher expectation remained only partially scrutinised in terms of social justice. Therefore, the social concerns raised throughout this study are also explored through the theories of Bourdieu, to make sense of the wider issues of inequality inherent in this study. Habitus is helped by, and helps shape, pedagogical action. Findings include the requirement to recognise that in education, socially advantaged interests and voices dominate in terms of social mobility agendas. Furthermore, teachers are only granted space in the public domain through technical competency. Teachers must however be emotionally

[1]This chapter has been developed using extracts from the thesis, Smith, J. A. (2020). 'It's our job to take the limits away': A case study approach to exploring a culture of teacher expectations in an English secondary school. [Thesis] Faculty of Arts, Creative Industries and Education, University of the West of England, Bristol.

Critical Perspectives on Educational Policies and Professional Identities, 191–208

Published under exclusive licence by Emerald Publishing Limited
doi:10.1108/978-1-83753-332-920241012

committed to different aspects of their jobs, as their sense of moral responsibility lies at the core of their professional identity.

Keywords: Teacher expectation; ability labelling; social justice; social mobility; case study; barriers

Introduction

Research on teacher expectation – the ways that teachers assimilate information about students as they form their expectations about academic performance, attitudes and social development – was studied over half a century ago by Rosenthal and Jacobson (1968). Research since then on teacher expectation has focused primarily on the occurrence of inaccurate teacher expectations in a range of classroom contexts, and their relationship with students' academic achievements, family background, motivation and engagement as well as teacher characteristics and beliefs (De Boer et al., 2018). Despite these studies establishing an association between teacher expectation and academic achievement, relatively little work has been done on teacher expectation interventions. One approach to addressing teacher expectation through interventions is to instruct them to exhibit behaviours associated with high-expectation teachers. The practices of high-expectation teachers, as defined by Rubie-Davies et al. (2015), have been used in most recent such studies: their intervention study focuses on the beliefs and practices of high-expectation teachers including student grouping, positive classroom climate and the instructional practices of questioning, goal setting and feedback.

The average effect of teacher expectations on student performance has been found to be relatively small, although students who are prior lower attaining in terms of academic achievement and students from low-income families and minority groups seem to be more susceptible to the detrimental effects of low teacher expectations (De Boer et al., 2018). Consequently, this chapter is based on a doctoral study which aimed to offer greater insight into teaching beliefs and strategies understood as creating a culture of high expectation and, additionally, to explore the barriers to creating this environment.

Developing the Theoretical Framework

Our concern with basing teaching activities on pre-determined ability labelling initially led to engaging with the work of Hart et al. (2004) who define ability labels more broadly. In line with our own thinking, the authors reject the fallacy of fixed ability for a more optimistic view of human educability; one which is responsive to the natural propensity of human beings to learn and change over time (Hart et al., 2004).

Clarifying our position that the notion of 'fixed ability' is fallacious resulted in focusing on teachers' own constructions of learners' abilities. This could avoid an over-reliance upon pre-determined ability labelling for individuals or groups of students (Hart et al., 2004). When the lack of student success is explained by a lack of ability on their part, a teacher is more likely to limit their attempts to encourage the student to succeed (Rubie-Davies et al., 2015). In contrast, when teachers believe that all students can learn, they are more likely to produce learning gains from them (Dweck, 2006).

Our research is driven by a social justice agenda, and a belief in human educability in contrast with the predictability of ability labelling. Thus, the social concerns raised throughout this study led to exploration of Bourdieu's (1977, 1984, 2002) theories with the aim of understanding the wider issues of inequality inherent here. This lens has been helpful in trying to understand wider issues of inequality, particularly how habitus is aided by, and helps shape, pedagogical action. Through a Bourdieusian lens, we can see how and why education tends to reproduce social division, providing an additional, more complex understanding of the phenomenon studied. As in any field, education is comprised of objective relations and structures, and these are complex and dynamic. Family background also exerts significant influence in social reproduction and has consequences for the likelihood of student success (Schirato & Danaher, 2002).

Social Mobility

When designing this research, we initially believed that exploring the beliefs and practices of high-expectation teachers as defined by Rubie-Davies et al. (2015) could lead to possible ways of building a more inclusive learning environment. Education is supposed by government (SMC, 2018) to have a transformative potential that can overcome social background, disadvantage and injustice, and school experiences can be seen as operating outside the structures and interactions involved in social reproduction (Hoskins & Barker, 2019). Upon reflection, as the research progressed, it became clearer that the aim of educational research as problem-solving is of limited use when exploring systemic social issues, in that education cannot compensate for an inherently unequal society (Bernstein, 1970).

Biesta et al. (2019) suggest there is an ongoing need for educational research to identify problems and, in that sense, to create them: both teachers and students in this study are clear there are barriers to teaching and learning hindering the creation of a culture of high expectation. This research exposes hidden assumptions and engages in a conversation about what is worthwhile and important in both education and society more broadly (Biesta et al., 2019). As De Boer et al. (2018) suggest, biased teacher expectations seem to be the product of student characteristics, including socio-economic status. This deficit model is reflected in policy as successive UK governments have adopted policies designed to promote and advance both intragenerational and intergenerational social mobility (SMC, 2019).

Policy texts encourage the view that young people should have high aspirations, assuming that relatively low progression rates into further and higher education among disadvantaged young people are due to a poverty of aspiration on their part. Despite both political focus and significant expenditure, there is little sign that low-income groups are making progress relative to their peers (Hoskins & Barker, 2019). Friedman and Savage (2017) refer to social mobility as a chimera, as our current version of meritocracy has failed to impact on class inequalities. In fact, it may have exacerbated them. In a highly competitive education system, those who can maximise their existing advantages are best placed to succeed (Friedman & Savage, 2017). Our research is underpinned by the concept that the current policy of social mobility as fairness results in a deficit model of working-class achievement (Brown, 2013). The concept of social mobility also dismisses the effects of structural inequality, as individual failure is constructed as a fair outcome of a meritocratic education system (Hoskins & Barker, 2019), rather than inequalities in either 'starting positions' or opportunities or for advancement.

Policy focus has for some time been on lifting aspirations for those from socially disadvantaged backgrounds, rather than addressing inequalities in life-chances (Harrison & Waller, 2017; Roberts, 2022). Policy debate becomes reduced to what working-class students and families lack, assuming that giving them more of what the middle-class already have will reduce this deficit (Brown, 2013). This is exemplified most recently in the latest Ofsted framework which references cultural capital, and charges schools with ensuring students are given the knowledge they need to 'succeed in life' (Ofsted, 2019). Brown (2013) posits that there needs to be greater political commitment to confront longstanding questions of distributional justice and social inequalities in life-chances. Underlying structures, such as those related to status hierarchies, family networks, social background and relative poverty appear to have a greater impact on health, opportunity and life chances than any reforms designed to encourage social mobility (Hoskins & Barker, 2019).

The Complexities of Creating a Culture of High Expectations for All: The Impact of Socio-Economic Factors

Educational attainment in England is highly stratified by social class (Paterson, 2022). A close correlation exists between socio-economic background and educational attainment, with those from the lowest socio-economic backgrounds experiencing lower educational attainment (Clifton & Cook, 2012). Children from low socio-economic backgrounds tend to be 'behind' middle-class children academically even when starting school, suggesting a strong impact of social factors external to education in reproducing educational inequality. These attainment gaps widen, rather than narrow, as children progress through school suggesting that schooling does not overturn inequalities in attainment outcomes. Inequalities have recently been illustrated by growing evidence that students from less well-off households have been impacted most by partial school closures during the COVID-19 pandemic (COSMO, 2022).

The socio-economic gap regarding educational attainment has focused government attention on issues of equality of opportunity, social justice and social mobility (Francis et al., 2017). Inequality is exacerbated by the neoliberal assumption within our educational system that choice, competition and markets lead to efficient and effective schools. However, these forces may create even more inequalities than previously existed (Apple, 2012). Neoliberal values contradict those of the post-war welfare state, which was established to ensure basic citizenship rights were removed from the insecurities of market forces. Apple (2012) and Ball (1993) suggest middle-class parents have become skilled in exploiting market mechanisms in education and in bringing their social, economic and cultural capitals to bear in them: affluent parents are more likely to be able to decode and use marketised forms to their own benefit.

Social class has been shown to have significant effects on educational outcomes and life chances (Demie & Lewis, 2011). Working class students are less likely to attend popular, 'successful' schools than their middle-class peers, less likely to achieve good GCSE grades, and are less likely to progress to higher education (Brown, 2013). Demie and Lewis (2011) found this underachievement is connected to low parental aspiration, low-literacy levels, feelings of marginalisation within the community, lower levels of parental education and the lack of support necessary to break the cycle of poverty and disadvantage. They suggest the main contributor to this underachievement is the government's failure to recognise that some groups in society have needs that are not being met. Specifically, working-class boys continue to be one of the lowest attaining groups in the English qualification system. Aspiration remains a key focus in educational policy for this group; within this narrative, working-class families are often blamed for their 'failure' to act responsibly regarding their education (Harrison & Waller, 2017). However, for working-class students in education, embracing 'successes' as defined by middle-class aspirations requires difficult identity negotiations; for many working-class boys, the losses inherent in this shift may be larger than the gains (Reay, 2002).

Methodology: Why Case Study?

The research is a case study design based on the methodology described by Stake (2005). It focuses on one phenomenon, that is, the beliefs and practices of high-expectation teachers. We have selected one bounded case, the organisation in which Julie Smith (JS) works, to illustrate the phenomenon. The case is specific, and bounded by time, location and policy context. The term 'bounded' means the case is separated out for research in terms of time, place or some physical boundaries. In other words, it is possible to create limits around the object of study.

This research emphasises uniqueness through in-depth exploration of the participants' experiences. Kushner (2017) suggests that case study is a form of organisational analysis, in that any organisation is a case. Within this bounded system are the relationships between people and events, and within those are differing perspectives. Kushner's (2017) definition is relevant as the positions on what makes a 'high expectation' teacher are contradictory, and not universally agreed. Kushner also comments on the importance of understanding the organisation that is being researched, as the organisation is where democratic social contract is experienced: we relate to the state through its institutions, and organisations provide the context within which these interests play out. If the organisation can be understood like that, case study can be seen as a democratic methodology for its capacity to legitimise difference and foster debate. These debates are apparent in both the differing definitions of the beliefs and practices of high-expectation teachers, and the problems that practitioners in this case study inhabit, in contrast to solutions inhabited by organisational leaders and policymakers (Kushner, 2017).

Ethical Considerations

Before any fieldwork could commence, ethical approval was required from the university, and a successful application was made as per BERA (2018) guidelines. Recommended amendments were incorporated into topic guides and participant information sheets prior to distribution.

Asymmetry of Power

This case study explored teacher expectations from the perspectives of both students and teachers alike. The research offered privileged knowledge of both groups, particularly given JS's position within the institution being studied (Mercer, 2007). Consequently, there were issues of potential asymmetry of power over 'the researched'. We believe all social research intrudes in people's lives to some extent and agree 'qualitative research often intrudes more' (Punch, 2009, p. 50). Therefore, the perception of young people as competent social actors informed the approach, and JS aimed to be respectful of their views, listening attentively and actively, managing emotions where appropriate (Brockbank & McGill, 2012). JS embraced the uncertainty surrounding issues of dependence and independence, regarding all participants as individuals, and being open and vigilant to their human complexities.

Ethical Issues Surrounding Conducting Research With Children

There have been major changes in the way research with children has been construed and approached, leading to a greater concern with children's perceptions, attitudes, beliefs, view and opinions (Alves et al., 2022; Punch, 2002). This includes the United Nations Convention on the Rights of the Child (1990), wherein children have the right to both having their views heard and to freedom of thought. Punch (2002) suggests that research involving children differs from that involving adults, and issues such as developing rapport, not imposing the researcher's views, the research context and clarity of questions need to be considered, along with the more frequently addressed issue of children's vulnerability to unequal power relationships. We believe that developing rapport with students is one way of helping mitigate these power imbalances (Oakley, 1981), which resonates with a sociology of childhood suggesting children's agency needs to be considered relationally, while perceiving children in context (Punch, 2016).

The initial invitation to students to be involved in the study aimed to stimulate thinking and discussion about the topic of teacher expectations as well as helping to build rapport by generating enthusiasm. JS's position as an insider researcher was also helpful here as a sense of familiarity supported the relationships developed. Time was taken to develop a rapport with the group and to respond to any questions and make any clarifications where necessary (Oakley, 1981).

Being an Insider-Researcher in an Educational Setting

Cain et al. (2019) suggest that the usefulness of research lies in its potential to improve the quality of schooling by informing practitioners' thinking, reflection and organisational learning, and as a platform for teachers to engage in critical conversations. Research engagement is a continuum from superficial to deep engagement, which may include conducting research as a practitioner (Cain et al., 2019). However, undertaking research as a teacher, particularly an insider-researcher, can raise certain tensions and dilemmas. One benefit to being an insider-researcher is ease of access to potential participants, although this can make it hard to tell where research stops, and the rest of life begins (Scott, 1985). Given JS's familiarity with the context of the research, links between situations and events could be understood and the implications of following avenues of enquiry assessed.

Pre-existing relationships between colleagues may mean respondents have greater trust in the researcher, offering the potential for both gathering different data and having insights and understandings into the organisational culture. Nevertheless, JS's familiarity with the setting may have led to pre-conceived assumptions about the data and the studied phenomenon (Mercer, 2007), and a risk of presenting colleagues in an unrealistically favourable light. We are also mindful personal identities are not unitary or fixed but formed through social interactions (Sikes, 2006), and that they are constructed from the categories people choose to explain themselves. JS chose to focus on the participants' words, embracing the complexities and contradictions inherent within these despite this risk in order to reflect the self-reporting of the researched.

Context and Methods

The school in this study is a non-selective, stand-alone academy in England, with mixed gender entry from ages 11–18. The first phase of data collection for the case study began with questionnaires administered to both students and staff. The benefits of a questionnaire method at this stage were that responses to the questionnaires enabled a broader understanding of teacher and student views of teacher expectation within this context, partially as questions were both open-ended and closed. Students and teachers were invited to explore their thoughts further in a focus group or in an interview; the semi-structured format of both the focus groups and interviews allowed participants to be more expansive in their responses, which allowed for questions for clarification or to explore ideas in more detail. All Year 9 students were invited to participate in the study; out of a total of approximately 200 students, 33 responses were recorded. All members of staff were invited to participate, and out of a total of 70, 13 responses were recorded. All names were anonymised using a random name generator.

We chose to analyse the data using reflexive thematic analysis (Braun & Clarke, 2012). Although there is debate over whether thematic analysis is a method, the approach to thematic analysis developed by Braun and Clarke (2012) locates it in a qualitative paradigm. Through this qualitative lens, the subjectivity of the researcher is integral to the analytical process. Themes are developed from coding following detailed engagement with the data, and rigour is achieved through a systematic and thorough approach. Although a strength of this approach is that it is flexible, it is not atheoretical, and treating it is such would limit its interpretative power (Braun & Clarke, 2012). As thematic analysis can be used to analyse a range of data types, it was suitable for the case study approach in this study, which included a range of methods of data collection.

The main research questions considered were:

(1) What are teachers' and students' perceptions of teacher expectations in the workplace?
(2) What strategies do teachers and students believe teachers use to create a culture of high expectation?
(3) What are the perceived barriers to creating a culture of high expectation?

Research Findings

Research question 1: What are teachers' and students' perceptions of teacher expectations?

The data from participants showed that teachers hold the view that students can achieve their best given the right support. There is also awareness that academic success looks different for different learners, and that teachers' expectations should not be dependent on students' prior attainment; their role is to support students to 'catch-up'. Teachers also believe that one purpose of school is to enable students to achieve goals of their own choosing, whether these goals are academic or vocational. Participants drew on notions of transformability, suggesting students' capacity for learning can be enhanced instead of relying on predetermined notions about ability (Hart et al., 2004).

Students commented that teachers expected them to try their hardest, believing in a causal link between student effort and attainment. Many believed that if they have tried their hardest, their attainment is of less importance to teachers since they have 'done their best'. Students also believe there are further requirements to being successful at school beyond their attainment, naming character traits such as kindness, helpfulness and good behaviour as particularly desirable. However, teachers and students alike were clear that barriers to teaching and learning hindered the creation of a culture of high expectations.

Research question 2: What strategies do teachers and students believe teachers use to create a culture of high expectations?

i. The use of questioning in the classroom
   Several teacher participants expressed commitment to the practices of dialogic teaching, classroom conversation and use of teacher questioning as important classroom tools for furthering student confidence and understanding and developing positive teacher–student relationships. Questioning was sometimes used to build student confidence, and to promote diversity and inclusivity in the classroom, signalling that all voices are valued. Here, the research findings are similar to those of Rubie-Davies et al. (2015), who comment on the benefits of effective questioning and use of classroom dialogue to maximise student learning. The findings of Davies et al. (2017) are also supported, as they espouse using dialogic teaching to extend student thinking, and to facilitate students' participation in discussions about their learning.

   Students referred to this classroom practice less frequently, believing that teachers expect them to produce meaningful answers and sometimes to think of their own questions, but there is contradictory evidence implying that students feel they are receiving unwarranted attention when a teacher directs questions to them: as student 'Jordan' stated 'my teacher always asks me the questions. I don't really like it because I feel like she's targeting me'.
ii. The role of feedback
   The research supports findings that the role of feedback is a practice that high-expectation teachers use to create a culture of high expectation (Rubie-Davies et al., 2015). Teachers stated that they use feedback to set students' goals, clarify misconceptions and to fill gaps in student knowledge. Feedback is also used to reinforce positive teacher–student relationships, to acknowledge student effort and to build student confidence (Hattie, 2011). Verbal feedback is considered valuable, both in terms of student learning preference and as a means of reducing teacher workload, impacting positively on student learning. Students also acknowledged the importance of teacher feedback, perceiving it as indicative of teachers' efforts to improve their work: 'Lauren' commented 'I feel that the teachers in certain subjects strive further to help their students improve their work, maybe marking their books regularly or staying back at lunch to help them'.
iii. Strategies teachers use to improve student motivation
   Several teachers suggested they use praise and positive language to encourage and motivate learners and in building their confidence. Some commented that motivation and feedback are bidirectional and explained how they ensure that students experience success to build confidence. Thus, many teachers scaffold learning to support struggling learners. This research supports the findings of Wray et al. (2000) and Rubie-Davies et al. (2015), who suggest that providing a framework and scaffolding for learning can improve understanding of new concepts.

Students did not refer to their motivation in relation to teaching strategies; instead, they referred to motivation in relation to behaviour. These comments were sometimes positive, as summarised in responses to research question 1: Students perceive motivation and a positive work ethic as key to academic success: 'if you put your mind to it and listen and compete the work I feel you can do well at school' ('Maddie') and correspondingly, both teachers and students perceive a lack of motivation as a barrier to academic success: as teacher 'Joshua' commented, 'some students are more motivated, some have a higher degree of self-efficacy and believe that their effort will pay off, others have lower self-esteem and self-belief which I think impacts on their focus and independent work'.

iv. The importance of classroom relationships

Many respondents commented on the importance of classroom relationships. Several teachers acknowledged the importance of positive and healthy peer relationships in the classroom; students also mentioned the importance of peers in making progress in academic work. Although some preferred to work with friends, most students preferred to work with those who valued their own academic work and were keen to progress. Many teachers saw positive relationships with students as pivotal to success in the classroom, believing that openly caring about students as both individuals and academic learners was important to their academic progress. Several students expressed a desire to be 'known' by teachers and valued understanding and acknowledgment of their academic goals and limits. Students sometimes expressed discomfort when they felt teachers judged them prematurely, before a relationship had chance to develop: 'when there are more vocal people in the class, I'm not sure that the teacher understands that I really want to do well in that subject' ('Georgia').

This research supports the work of several authors (Nias, 1989; Rubie-Davies et al., 2015) who comment on the importance of a 'warm', friendly classroom climate, in which the quality of teacher–student relationships can foster academic success. Students may be more motivated if they believe that the teachers care about them.

Research question 3: What are the perceived barriers to creating a culture of high expectation?

Teachers and students perceived that there are barriers to creating a culture of high expectation. Teachers believed that students' academic progress is hindered where some parents and carers have to cope with other burdens. Where students have fewer clear boundaries at home, those students find the enforcement of boundaries at school a greater challenge. Students are disadvantaged by a lack of resources including access to books and computers, or by a lack of educational aspiration in their families. These findings agree with writers including Blandford (2018), who comments that disadvantaged students are, on average, two years of learning behind non-disadvantaged peers by the end of secondary school. Some teachers believed barriers to creating a culture of high expectation include students' poor behaviour, motivation, resilience and self-regulation. These findings resonate with the research literature, wherein student motivation is a major determinant of student achievement (Dweck, 2006).

Some students also expressed frustration with the poor behaviour of peers, sometimes attributing this to the level of pace and challenge in the classroom. Although this can be framed in terms of work being 'too easy', it was sometimes considered too challenging, resulting in lesson materials being inaccessible to them. Students were often reflective about their own behaviour, demonstrating awareness that a barrier to their learning is 'chatting to other people' ('Caitlin'), that they 'talk too much' ('Sophie') or 'find it hard to be sensible' ('Lewis'). Students' levels of academic self-concept and belief about their academic abilities were considered by several teachers and students as a further barrier to their learning. Some teachers believed that students have a fear of failure or labelled themselves as already failing. Several suggested that low self-confidence can be exacerbated when students compare themselves to their peers.

Although authors such as Archer et al. (2018) suggest this form of competitive individualism can be magnified by attainment grouping, students and teachers alike commented that students ranked each other regardless of the groupings they are placed in. Such rankings may be compounded in this case study as students are taught in a combination of attainment groupings and mixed groupings. Several students commented that the teaching group they are placed in is irrelevant, if the work they are given is pitched appropriately for them: 'I like working in sets because everyone's at the same level' ('Sol'); 'when the teacher speaks, it's for everyone, not for the people who are the best, or clever' ('Lewis'). Most staff teaching in attainment groupings believed that mixed attainment groups would create further barriers to progress, given difficulties facilitating sufficient challenges for higher-attaining students.

Francis et al. (2017) find that while small achievement gains may be made by placing higher-attaining students in sets, the impact on previously lower attaining students is negative. Teachers of mixed attainment groups commented on the benefits of working with students of varied prior attainment, since their talents and abilities can be celebrated, and aspiration can be modelled to a wider range of students. Grouping was related to behaviour by both teachers and students. Teachers were sometimes concerned with the impact of large class sizes, suggesting this narrows the range of teaching and learning strategies they would prefer to use, and that large class sizes allow more opportunities for off-task behaviour. Most students, of varying levels of prior attainment, seemed concerned with avoiding disruptive behaviour. Both here and in the literature, there is a belief that students in lower attainment groupings are more likely to exhibit disruptive behaviour (Archer et al., 2018).

Archer et al. (2018) assert that the legitimacy of setting is maintained through misrecognition. Students come to understand themselves and others as deserving their set allocation on the basis that setting is reflective of their 'natural' abilities, and segregation is necessary to protect the experiences and attainment of 'higher' 'ability' students from the 'distracting' presence of 'others'. Teachers were apprehensive about the prospect of mixed-attainment teaching, fearing middle-class parental complaints, perhaps unsurprisingly given that socially advantaged interests and voices tend to predominate within debates around setting (Crozier et al., 2011).

A Bourdieusian Perspective

When re-reading the case study data, it seems teacher and student comments concerning barriers to creating a culture of high expectations relate to Bourdieusian ideas about different types of capital. Since more middle-class forms of cultural capital are valued over others, social inequality is further entrenched. Through a Bourdieusian perspective, academic capital is the product of the combined effects of cultural transmission by the family and the school (Bourdieu, 1977, 1984). Consequently, if students' cultural capital is similar to that as defined by the school, they are in an advantageous position (Bourdieu, 2002). In terms of economic capital, several teachers commented that student progress in school is hindered when parents and carers are coping with other burdens.

There are certain indications in the data wherein teachers recognise schooling presents fewer barriers for students possessing middle-class cultural capital: some believed that certain students have fewer clear boundaries at home; therefore, they find coping with their enforcement at school more challenging. Teachers tend to come from relatively privileged backgrounds and are perhaps predisposed to favour students who share their values and attitudes (Schirato & Danaher, 2002). Students' levels of academic self-concept and belief about their academic abilities are considered by several students and teachers as a barrier to their learning. Some teachers believed that students have a fear of failure or label themselves as already failing. However, language used by both students and teachers within this case study reflects the language of meritocracy and the ethos that students can achieve highly in terms of academic success if they possess the necessary work ethic.

Jensen (2010) argues this concept denies the role of privilege in individuals' success and does not engage with the effects of class, social hierarchy or wealth. The physical embodiment of cultural capital, 'habitus', is also supported in the study. Students expressed the idea that they 'belong' in certain sets, therefore, reproducing the cultural arbitrary of the dominant (Archer et al., 2018; Bourdieu & Passeron, 1977). Teachers also commented on how students rank and judge each other, with some suggesting there is a correlation between students placed in a lower attaining set and self-belief in their potential. Some participants' comments referred to the discomfort created when students' ability-identity is at stake, particularly among the high-academic attainers. In the initial thematic analysis of the data, most teachers and students seemed to believe that mixed attainment teaching would not remove the social hierarchies inherent in school structures, and that students would continue to rank and judge each other regardless. We found students' comments on attainment grouping reassuring, in that most seemed less concerned with the groupings they were placed in than being 'known' by the teachers and being placed in the set where they 'belong'. However, through a Bourdieusian lens, students may be oblivious to the way social reproduction operates: this type of domination involves at least some sense of below conscious complicity, or symbolic violence, on the part of the subjugated. Processes of misrecognition wherein attainment grouping allocation is deemed natural makes this possible (James, 2015).

In response to research question 2, some teachers are perceived as trying to create a culture of high expectation, despite the barriers. Most students and teachers eschewed the values of individualism and marketisation of education in favour of commitment to the social justice values of comprehensive education. They committed to a social justice agenda, believing that success looks different for different learners. Teachers actively aimed to develop and harness the power of social cohesion in their classrooms, and some students' comments exemplify their role in creating an atmosphere of trust and collegiality.

Implications for Practice

Sharing the behaviours, characteristics and beliefs associated with high-teacher expectations (Rubie-Davies et al., 2015) may be beneficial to classroom practitioners interested in exploring these within their own contexts. However, there is an additional, more complex understanding of this phenomenon. Therefore, we suggest that in terms of practice, there needs to be:

- A recognition that in education, socially advantaged interests and voices dominate social mobility agendas (Archer et al., 2018). Social cohesion is therefore a challenge as inequality rises from an education system tailored to white, middle-class values (Bourdieu & Passeron, 1977), and until we value the diversity of heritage in all its forms, we cannot hope for greater equity for our students.
- A notion of the teacher's voice that addresses the right to speak and be represented. These voices have been encouraged and granted space in the public domain only through technical competency (Goodson, 2014). As the voices of teachers in this case study illustrate, teachers must be able to be emotionally committed to different aspects of their jobs, as their sense of moral responsibility is at the core of their professional identity (Nias, 1989). Hence, in terms of professional identity, the culture of professional development should be one of critical self-reflective practice, in which teachers become aware of and make public their process of learning with others.

One possible way teachers could develop social cohesion is through the careful consideration of student attainment grouping. There are well-documented challenges with all forms of grouping, but attainment grouping seems to provide no overall benefit in terms of student success, and furthermore exacerbates existing social inequalities (Francis et al., 2017). Nevertheless, setting in an equitable way presents challenges for schools. We are also mindful of the importance of context and believe that the application of research evidence is for the practitioner to decide, using their knowledge, thinking and astute judgement (Kvernbekk, 2016).

The recommendation here would be that a form of 'high-integrity' setting could be implemented.

Strategies such as: making setting as subject specific as possible, grouping students by attainment rather than perceived effort, regularly testing and moving students between sets and using a lottery system when assigning borderline students to sets may help mitigate the consequences of attainment grouping (Francis et al., 2017). Schools, however, are often deterred from implementing more equitable grouping practices by perceptions of middle-class parental and student preferences for attainment grouping (Crozier et al., 2011). A further complication raised in this study is that most teachers currently teaching in attainment groupings believe that mixed attainment groupings would create further barriers to progress.

Learning From Research Design

This research project began with an idealistic notion that exploring one definition of high-expectation beliefs and teaching practices could lead to the creation of a culture of high expectation. The reality is far messier. In addition to the contradictory definitions of what makes a 'high expectation' teacher, research discourse related to teachers tends to be prescriptive, rather than serious study of, or collaboration with, those prescribed to or portrayed. Furthermore, although the research questions did not ask for parental views of teacher expectation, this could have been a fruitful avenue for exploration, particularly as the deficit discourse in terms of expectation is not explored through parental voice. Similarly, it can be a challenge for schools to listen to and to access student voice authentically amidst the everyday pressures of school life. Although we paid close attention to power asymmetries throughout the study, we cannot really claim that the research is fully participatory; giving students the opportunity to become co-researchers rather than participants may have addressed some of these concerns.

Final Reflections

Blandford (2018) challenges the assumption that academic achievement is paramount and suggests that there are many other measures of success, in which students discover and are celebrated for a particular talent, or a passion for something new. The ability to make choices should be a fundamental right and accessible to all as a result of social justice (Blandford, 2018). This presents a challenge in today's economic and political climate. At the time of writing, almost one in three children are living in poverty, and UK inflation continues to remain at a high level, with a 40-year high of 9.6% recorded in October 2022 (ONS, 2023). Despite this economic context, by 2024–2025, after accounting for the specific costs facing schools, school spending per pupil will be 3% lower than in 2010 (Sibieta, 2022).

Britain's high-status professions remain dominated by those from privileged backgrounds; people from traditionally working-class backgrounds earn on average £6,800 less than colleagues from professional and managerial backgrounds (Friedman & Savage, 2017). Although students in this study feel that they can 'get ahead' on merit, it could be suggested that British society is profoundly unfair. Education is crucial to social change, and indeed social reproduction, but cannot be considered in isolation if we are to tackle the challenge of disadvantage. Education must be freed from its current constraints so that educators can develop every child's personality, talents and abilities to the full (UNCRC, 1990), and to take the factors limiting them away.

References

Alves, H., Gibbs, L., Marinkovic, K., Brito, I., & Sheikhattari, P. (2022). Children and adolescents' voices and the implications for ethical research. *Childhood, 29*(1), 126–143. https://doi.org/10.1177/09075682211061230

Apple, M. (2012). *Can education change society?* Routledge. https://doi.org/10.4324/9780203083550

Archer, L., Francis, B., Miller, S., Taylor, B., Tereshchenko, A., Mazenod, A., Pepper, D., & Travers, M. C. (2018). The symbolic violence of setting: A bourdieusian analysis of mixed methods data on secondary school students' views about setting. *British Educational Research Journal, 44*(1), 119–410. https://doi.org/10.1002/berj.3321

Ball, S. J. (1993). Education markets, choice and social class: The market as a class strategy in the UK and the USA. *British Journal of Sociology of Education, 14*(1), 3–19. http://www.jstor.org/stable/1392976

Bernstein, B. (1970). Education cannot compensate for society. *New Society, 26*, 344–351.

Biesta, G., Filippakou, O., Wainwright, E., & Aldridge, D. (2019). Why educational research should not just solve problems but should cause them as well. *British Educational Research Journal, 45*(1), 1–4. https://doi.org/10.1002/berj.3509

Blandford, S. (2018). *Born to fail? Social mobility: A working class view.* Catt.

Bourdieu, P. (1977). *Outline of a theory of practice.* Cambridge University Press. https://doi.org/10.1017/CBO9780511812507

Bourdieu, P. (1984). *Distinction: A social critique of the judgment of taste.* Routledge and Kegan Paul.

Bourdieu, P. (2002). Habitus. In J. Hiller, & E. Rooksby (eds), *Habitus: A sense of place* (pp. 27–34). Routledge. https://doi.org/10.4324/9781315253701

Bourdieu, P., & Passeron, J. C. (1977). *Reproduction in education.* Society and Culture. Sage.

Braun, V., & Clarke, V. (2012). Thematic analysis. In H. Cooper (Ed.), *APA handbook of research methods in psychology* (pp. 57–71). APA books.

British Educational Research Association. (2018). *Ethical guidelines for educational research.* https://www.bera.ac.uk/publication/ethical-guidelines-for-educational-research-2018

Brockbank, A., & McGill, I. (2012). *Facilitating reflective learning: Coaching, mentoring and supervision.* Kogan.

Brown, P. (2013). Education, opportunity and the prospects for social mobility. *British Journal of Sociology of Education*, *34*(5–6), 678–700. https://doi.org/10.1080/01425692.2013.816036

Cain, T., Brindley, S., Brown, C., Jones, G., & Riga, F. (2019). Bounded decision-making, teachers' reflection and organisational learning: How research can inform teachers and teaching. *British Educational Research Journal*, *45*(5), 1072–1087. https://doi.org/10.1002/berj.3551

Clifton, J., & Cook, W. (2012). *A long division: Closing the attainment gap in England's secondary schools*. IPPR. https://www.ippr.org/files/images/media/files/publication/2012/09/long%20division%20FINAL%20version_9585.pdf

COSMO. (2022). *COVID-19: A generation-defining challenge*. https://cosmostudy.uk/

Crozier, G., Reay, D., & James, D. (2011). Making it work for their children: White middle-class parents and working-class schools. *International Studies in Sociology of Education*, *21*(3), 199–216. https://doi.org/10.1080/09620214.2011.616343

Davies, M., Kiemer, K., & Meissel, K. (2017). Quality Talk and dialogic teaching—an examination of a professional development programme on secondary teachers' facilitation of student talk. *British Educational Research Journal*, *43*(5), 968–987. https://doi.org/10.1002/berj.3293

De Boer, H., Timmermans, A. C., & Van Der Werf, M. (2018). The effects of teacher expectation interventions on teachers' expectations and student achievement: Narrative review and meta-analysis. *Educational Research and Evaluation*, *24*(3–5), 180–200. https://doi.org/10.1080/13803611.2018.1550834

Demie, F., & Lewis, K. (2011). White working-class achievement: An ethnographic study of barriers to learning in schools. *Educational Studies*, *37*(3), 245–264. https://doi.org/10.1080/03055698.2010.506341

Dweck, C. (2006). *Mindset: How you can fulfil your potential*. Random House.

Francis, B., Archer, L., Hodgen, J., Pepper, D., Taylor, B., & Travers, L. (2017). Exploring the relative lack of impact on research on 'ability grouping' in England: A discourse analytic account. *Cambridge Journal of Education*, *47*(1), 1–17. https://doi.org/10.1080/0305764X.2015.1093095

Friedman, S., & Savage, M. (2017). The shifting politics of inequality and the class ceiling. *Renewal*, *25*(2), 31–40. https://journals.lwbooks.co.uk/renewal/vol-25-issue-2/article-8905/

Goodson, I. F. (2014). Investigating the life and work of teachers. *Estonian Journal of Education*, *2*(2), 28–47. https://doi.org/10.12697/eha.2014.2.2.02b

Harrison, N., & Waller, R. (2017). Success and impact in widening participation policy: What works and how do we know?. *Higher Education Policy*, *30*(2), 141–160. https://doi.org/10.1057/s41307-016-0020-x

Hart, S., Annabelle, D., Drummond, M. J., & McIntyre, D. (2004). *Learning without limits*. OUP.

Hattie, J. (2011). *Visible learning for teachers: Maximising impact on learning*. Routledge. https://doi.org/10.4324/9780203181522

Hoskins, K., & Barker, B. (2019). Social mobility: The potential of a genealogical approach. *British Educational Research Journal*, *45*(2), 238–253. https://doi.org/10.1002/berj.3499

James, D. (2015). How Bourdieu bites back: Recognising misrecognition in education and educational research. *Cambridge Journal of Education*, *45*(1), 97–112. https://doi.org/10.1080/0305764X.2014.987644

Jensen, T. (2010). Warmth and wealth: Re-imagining social class in taxonomies of good parenting. *Studies in the Maternal*, *2*(1), 1–13. https://doi.org/10.16995/sim.86

Kushner, S. (2017). *Evaluative research methods: Managing the complexities of judgement in the field*. Information Age Publishing.

Kvernbekk, T. (2016). Evidence-based educational practice. In G. W. Noblit (Ed.), *Oxford research encyclopaedia of education* (pp. 1–20). OUP.

Mercer, J. (2007). The challenges of insider research in educational institutions: Wielding a double-edged sword and resolving delicate dilemmas. *Oxford Review of Education*, *33*(1), 1–17. https://doi.org/10.1080/03054980601094651

Nias, J. (1989). *Primary teachers talking: A study of teaching as work*. Routledge. https://doi.org/10.4324/9780203032527

Oakley, A. (1981). Interviewing women. In H. Roberts (Ed.), *Doing feminist research* (pp. 30–61). Routledge and Kegan Paul.

Office for National Statistics. (2023). *The cost of living, current and upcoming work: February 2023*. The cost of living, current and upcoming work – Office for National Statistics. ons.gov.uk

Ofsted. (2019). *Education inspection framework*. https://www.gov.uk/government/collections/education-inspection-framework

Paterson, L. (2022). Education and high-status occupations in the UK since the middle of the twentieth century. *British Journal of Sociology of Education*, *43*(3), 375–396. https://doi.org/10.1080/01425692.2022.2026763

Punch, S. (2002). Research with children: The same or different from research with adults? *Childhood*, *9*(3), 321–341. https://doi.org/10.1177/0907568202009003005

Punch, K. F. (2009). *Introduction to research methods in education*. Sage.

Punch, S. (2016). Exploring children's agency across majority and minority world contexts. In F. Esser, M. S. Baader, & T. Betz (eds), *Reconceptualising agency and childhood: New perspectives in childhood studies* (pp. 183–196). Routledge.

Reay, D. (2002). Shaun's story: Troubling discourses on white working-class masculinities. *Gender and Education*, *14*(3), 221–234. https://doi.org/10.1080/0954025022000010695

Roberts, N. (2022). *The pupil premium (England)*. House of Commons Library. https://researchbriefings.files.parliament.uk/documents/SN06700/SN06700.pdf

Rosenthal, R., & Jacobson, L. (1968). *Pygmalion in the classroom: Teacher expectation and pupils' intellectual development*. Holt, Rinehart and Winston.

Rubie-Davies, C. M., Peterson, E. R., Sibley, C. G., & Rosenthal, R. (2015). A teacher expectation intervention: Modelling the practices of high expectation teachers. *Contemporary Educational Psychology*, 40, 72–85. http://doi.org/10.1016/j.cedpsych.2014.03.003

Schirato, T., & Danaher, G. (2002). *Understanding bourdieu*. Sage. https://doi.org/10.4324/9781003118305

Scott, S. (1985). Working through the contradictions in researching postgraduate education. In R. Burgess (Ed.), *Field methods in the study of education* (pp. 115–130). Falmer Press.

Sibieta, L. (2022). *School spending per pupil in 2024 to remain 3% below 2010 levels in real-terms once you account for actual costs faced by schools*. Institute for Fiscal Studies. https://ifs.org.uk/news/school-spending-pupil-2024-remain-3-below-2010-levels-real-terms-once-you-account-actual-costs

Sikes, P. (2006). On dodgy ground? Problematics and ethics in educational research. *International Journal of Research and Method in Education*, *29*(1), 105–117. https://doi.org/10.1080/01406720500537502

Social Mobility Commission. (2019). *Social mobility in great britain: State of the nation 2018 – 2019*. https://www.gov.uk/government/publications/social-mobility-in-great-britain-state-of-the-nation-2018-to-2019

Stake, R. E. (2005). Qualitative case studies. In N. K. Denzin, & Y. S. Lincoln (eds), *The Sage handbook of qualitative research* (pp. 443–466). Sage.

UNCRC. (1990). *The united nation convention on the rights of the child*. https://www.unicef.org.uk/wp-content/uploads/2016/08/unicef-convention-rights-child-uncrc.pdf

Wray, D., Medwell, J., Fox, R., & Poulson, L. (2000). The teaching practices of effective teachers of literacy. *Educational Review*, *52*(1), 75–84. https://doi.org/10.1080/00131910097432

Chapter 13

Context, Consciousness and Caution: Teachers of History in England and the Exploration of Sensitive and Controversial Issues in Practice[1]

Sarah Whitehouse and Verity Jones

University of the West of England, UK

Abstract

This chapter is about primary and secondary school teachers of history in England, and how they negotiate policy in order to teach sensitive and controversial issues which feature as part of the history curriculum. We present research conducted in two phases that used a bounded case study (Stake, 1995) as a methodological approach. In Phase One, two focus group interviews were undertaken; in Phase Two, six unstructured individual interviews were conducted. Participants were teachers of history in England from Key Stage 1–5 (children aged 4–18 years).

Thematic analysis was used to analyse the data which were informed by reflections on positionality and being a socially conscious researcher (Pillow, 2010). Three key policies were explored as part of this research: the National Curriculum (DfE, 2013), the Teachers' Standards (DfE, 2012) and the Prevent Duty (DfE, 2015). Research findings demonstrate how the context of the school is fundamental in how teachers enact policy in relation to their practice, particularly in light of political changes in society. Self-surveillance was identified as a key strategy, adopted in the teaching of sensitive and controversial issues. We frame this context around Kitson and McCully's (2005) theoretical continuum which indicates that there is a reluctance by

[1]This chapter has been developed using extracts from the thesis, Whitehouse, S. (2020). Context, consciousness, and caution: Teachers of history and the exploration of sensitive and controversial issues in practice. [Thesis] Department of Education, University of the West of England.

Critical Perspectives on Educational Policies and Professional Identities, 209–227

doi:10.1108/978-1-83753-332-920241013

some teachers to engage with the teaching of sensitive and controversial issues due to concerns with policy enactment.

The findings of this research illustrate that policy impacts on teachers in numerous ways. Policy was demonstrated to be ambiguous for teachers, and recommendations are made relating to policy and the need for clearer guidance for teachers to support them with their practice.

Keywords: Surveillance; pedagogy; sensitive and controversial; history education; teachers and policy

Introduction

This chapter draws on Sarah's doctoral research which is about teachers of history in England from Key Stages 1–5 (age 4–18) and their experiences of teaching sensitive and controversial issues. Both of us (Sarah and Verity) have since used the findings from this research to extend combined projects that explore anti-racist pedagogy (see https://respectprojectbristol.org/).

In this chapter, we reflect on three key policies that have informed our ongoing work: the Teachers' Standards (DfE, 2012), the National Curriculum (DfE, 2013) and the Prevent Duty Strategy (DfE, 2015). These policies have shaped the current education practice and provided new challenges for teachers when engaging with sensitive and controversial issues in the classroom. This research considered how teachers may be categorised in relation to the teaching of sensitive and controversial issues, and how they often adopt a protectionist stance due to surveillance and the impact of policy.

In this thesis, there were four research questions; however, for the purpose of this chapter, we have decided to focus on research question 2 which was: How does policy impact on the teaching of sensitive and controversial issues? To answer this research question, we will draw on data from focus groups and interviews. Data will be presented in relation to individual policy but also how the findings align with the work of Kitson and McCully (2005) and Magill (2016) which further demonstrate the complexity of policy and its impact on teachers' practice.

This chapter will first draw on literature pertaining to the teaching of sensitive and controversial issues in history before outlining the policy context for this study. The focus will then move to considering how teachers can be categorised in relation to how they approach the teaching of sensitive and controversial issues. The discussion will then move to outlining both the methodological approach and methods used in the research. Details of the participants in the study will also be provided and how data were analysed. The findings and discussion will then be presented before concluding comments.

Literature Review

Davies (2017) states that the study of history is essential for living in a democratic society and that sensitive and controversial issues emerge within the teaching of history. They argue that this is essential if children are to be able to make links with the past and the present. Similarly, Cowan and Maitlas (2017, p. 32) argue discussing sensitive and controversial issues as part of education is a crucial part of any history curriculum.

For the purpose of this chapter, sensitive and controversial issues refer to discussions that may provoke an emotional response. Goldberg et al. (2019) note that children are going to meet sensitive and controversial issues before and after they leave school; therefore, schools have a duty to support them in developing their understanding of such issues. Barton and Mc Cully (2007, p. 13) state that if a democratic society depends on 'the ability of citizens to take part in reasoned discussion then. . .it is our job as educators to develop this ability in our students'. This implies that taking part in discussions which are sensitive and/or controversial should enable children to be critically reflective, to question claims of neutrality and to be tolerant of uncertainty. In the case of sensitive and controversial issues within history, this would also require the ability to prepare children to question constructions of the past. We will now consider how three policies influence what past is discussed, and how the discussion of controversial issues is presented within these.

The National Curriculum for History (DfE, 2013)

The content of the National Curriculum for History (DfE, 2013) creates both challenges and opportunities for teachers when teaching sensitive and controversial issues. The National Curriculum (DfE, 2013, p. 64) for History aims for children to be able to 'understand that different versions of the past may exist', and 'how interpretations of the past have been constructed'. Maddison (2017) suggests that National Curriculum (DfE, 2013) provided opportunities for children to study a range of different topics; this unquestionably created opportunities and challenges for teachers to engage with the teaching of sensitive and controversial issues.

The Teachers' Standards (DfE, 2012)

While the National Curriculum (DfE, 2013) presents the breadth of educational content, it is the Teachers' Standards (DfE, 2012) that outline clear expectations all teachers must meet to be an effective classroom practitioner. Presented in two parts, there are eight standards in Part One which relate more directly with teaching and accountability. Part Two of the Standards focus on teachers' professional values. An important part of Part Two of the Standards is the requirement to uphold British Values which are characterised as, 'not undermining fundamental British values, including democracy, the rule of law, individual liberty and mutual respect, and tolerance of those with different faiths and beliefs' (DfE, 2012, p. 2).

These Standards (DfE, 2012) both guide and shape teachers' practice. Gove (2011) stated that the revision of the standards (DfE, 2012) was part of an initiative designed to be used as a performance management tool by head teachers. Lander (2016) suggests that radical changes to the teaching profession since 2010 have resulted in a school-led system that fosters a neoliberal ideology which is framed around the marketisation of education. With a greater focus on exams, the context neglects opportunity to foster a more holistic approach to education and the teaching of sensitive and controversial issues. Part Two of the Standards (DfE, 2012), with their focus on the teaching of British Values, could be viewed as an opportunity to develop teachers' practice in relation to sensitive and controversial issues. However, this could raise some challenges for teachers. Lander (2016, p. 276) argues that as a consequence of Part Two, teachers have become marginalised and a performativity agenda is in place as British Values are assessed by Ofsted (the English education inspectorate authority). Furthermore, there can be an overlap between history and British Values, and Mansfield (2019) suggests that the teaching of these values has fallen to teachers of history. It is particularly contentious because much of the discussion in classrooms relating to British Values has implications for both teachers and children as teachers are now expected to prevent extremism through their teaching.

Many of the skills within the teaching of history can be used to construct different interpretations of the past and an understanding of different perspectives; this has some overlap with the teaching of British Values curriculum. Lander (2016, p. 329), however, suggests that there has been a lack of training in supporting teachers on how best to deliver British Values, which has resulted in 'nostalgic imperialist constructions of Britishness'. Lander (2016) argues that this potentially leaves teachers vulnerable because their naïve interpretations of Britishness can result in contentious discussions.

The Prevent Duty (DfE, 2015)

In February 2015, the UK government published a new Counter Terrorism and Security Act (2015) in which teachers had a legal duty to recognise children who would be potentially vulnerable to extremism and to prevent them from being part of terrorist activity. This combined with the requirements for teachers to teach fundamental British Values (as set out in the Teachers Standards DfE, 2012) has, as Smith (2016, p. 298) states, 'changed the face of education policy'. While the full extent of these changes has yet to be realised, the statistics for referral to Channel (the UK government's anti-radicalisation scheme) are noteworthy. Dickens (2015, p. 8) reports that 50% all the referrals of children in 2015 came from teachers, a 42% increase from 2012 to 2013.

Guidance included in the Prevent Duty (DfE, 2015, p. 5) states that:

> It is not intended to stop debating controversial issues. On the contrary, school should provide a safe space in which children, young people and staff can understand the risks associated with terrorism and develop the knowledge and skills to be able to challenge extremist arguments.

This guidance, on the one hand, encourages teachers to discuss sensitive and controversial issues. However, on the other hand, it implies that sensitive and controversial discussions may lead to comments that could be viewed as alarming. This is supported by Mansfield (2019) who argues that there is a tension for teachers who are expected to promote British Values while they monitor pupils for pejorative comments which could indicate that children are vulnerable to extremism. Elton-Chalcraft et al. (2016, p. 1) argue that because of this policy, teachers are seen as 'state instruments of surveillance'.

The National Curriculum (DfE, 2013), Teachers Standards (DfE, 2012) and Prevent (DfE, 2015) are significant policies that were designed to shape teachers' practice in relation to the teaching of sensitive and controversial issues. However, these policies provide little by way of detail as to how the teaching of sensitive and controversial issues should be accomplished. For insights into practice, we must look to the history teacher.

Categorisation of History Teachers

This section will introduce research by Kitson and McCully (2005) and Magill (2016) who categorised teachers by the way they approached the teaching of sensitive and controversial issues. In both cases, the link between policy and the context they inhabit is of importance.

Kitson and McCully's (2005) research took place in Northern Ireland, which had experienced recent conflict. Their research focused on what historical topics teachers had included in their teaching. They also considered why some topics had been excluded from the curriculum, and what justification was used in determining these choices. Within the research, they identified three categories of teacher: the 'avoider', 'container' and 'risk taker'. The research found that teachers' prior experiences linked directly with these categories. Characteristics of the 'avoider' included the avoidance of teaching topics which could be potentially sensitive or controversial and a belief that the purpose of teaching history was for children to get better at the subject. The teacher as a 'container' found that although controversial issues were taught, they were contained to avoid contentious debate. Topics were taught as directed in schemes of work and did not focus on topics relevant to the learners. The teacher as 'risk taker' fully embraced the difficulties and complexities of teaching history. They were able to make links between the past and present and looked to develop opportunities which challenged children's pre-existing ideas.

Magill (2016) builds on the earlier work by Kitson and McCully (2005). She presents a model which examines the relationship between history taught in school and the recovery of historical memory in Spain. Magill (2016) identifies the same categories of teachers as Kitson and McCully (2005) – avoiders, containers, risk takers – and adds a fourth category of 'activists'.

Magill (2016, p. 260) argues that 'history as an uncontested body of knowledge was a major tool for legitimizing the state, under Franco, the goal of education was not the liberation of the individual but the subordination of the individual'.

Therefore, Magill (2016) argues that the teaching of history needs to link past and present if children are going to develop their historical understanding and awareness of contemporary society. She questions to what extent children can really understand the present if they do not critically question the past. This is supported by McCully (2012, p. 151) who argues that 'history teachers must not collude with social amnesia by avoiding sensitive aspects of the past' or present the past as truth rather than considering different interpretations of it.

Returning to the categories that Magill (2016) identified, avoider, container, risk taker and activists, the avoider category has been adapted from the earlier work of Kitson and McCully's (2005) research to include 'natural avoiders' and 'reluctant avoiders'. Magill (2016) found that both types of avoider tended to select topics that would not be considered to be sensitive and controversial. By contrast, reluctant avoiders embraced the complexity of teaching but were constrained by several factors such as peer pressure, fear of reprisal and lack of support from their schools. The natural avoiders rejected the complexity and difficulties of teaching sensitive and controversial issues within history. The 'containers' did not purposefully avoid teaching topics but did not seek out opportunities to teach sensitive and controversial issues.

The risk takers in Magill's (2016) research tended to create opportunities to tackle the teaching of sensitive and controversial issues in the classroom. While they fully embraced the complexity and difficulties of teaching sensitive and controversial history, they actively encouraged the use of critical thinking skills with children in the classroom. The fourth category of 'activists' were like the risk takers in that they sought out opportunities within the curriculum to teach controversial issues. However, the activist sought to take a standpoint in the classroom which enabled them to share with children their own strongly held views. These four categories of teacher can be seen to be the product of a profession under surveillance.

Surveillance

Caluya (2010) and Page (2016) claim that surveillance has become embedded in all aspects of society and because of this, surveillance is situated within the context of power. Caluya (2010) uses the term 'pedagopticon' to describe how teachers' awareness of their pedagogical decision-making may be viewed by others. Caluya (2010) argues that there has been a 'rhizomatic growth' of surveillance in its many forms. This metaphor recognises both the potential for the positive and negative aspects of surveillance – in this case surveillance as a multi-directional web of connections to protect individuals or a pervasive weed rooted in covert behaviour. The implication of the latter is that teachers can be even more accountable for what happens in the classroom. For Foucault (1977), the panopticon became the central metaphor for surveillance in modern society, a potential gaze that creates self-discipline among citizens, workers and the institutionalised. Page (2016) argues that there is a move towards a post-panopticon which can help understand surveillance within the context of schools and classrooms.

Page (2016) reasons that surveillance within the context of education is not new and has taken various forms which they categorise as vertical, horizontal and self. Vertical surveillance could refer to surveillance in the form of school inspections and strategies of senior leaders within schools – such as watching back CCTV, undertaking teaching observations and learning walks. Page (2016) also suggests that vertical surveillance may include the actions of students who use mobile phones to record teachers. Horizontal surveillance concerns other teachers in terms of peer observation in classrooms but also more routine forms of surveillance such as informal staffrooms conversations. Horizontal surveillance also includes parental surveillance, which operates directly or through parental networks and collective action (Posey-Maddox et al., 2014). Self-surveillance is enacted through reflective practice and self-monitoring. Page (2016) argues that teachers are consciously aware of how their practice may be viewed by various stakeholders.

Page (2016) argues the notion of self-surveillance is perhaps the form and practice that most defines the surveillance of teachers as distinct from the context of Foucault's (1977) panopticon. Foucault (1991) argues that the gaze moves 'inside' and discipline becomes internalised to produce 'docile bodies'. Self-surveillance activities that teachers engage with, Page (2016) argues, is a form of surveillance that 'panopticism cannot account for in contemporary surveillance'. In this context, teachers are the active agents and willing participants within the surveyed space.

Having outlined the policies related to the teaching of sensitive and controversial issues and how teachers can be categorised in relation to teaching these issues, we will now turn to the insights provided by teachers of 4–18 year olds.

Methodology

Due to the aims and objectives of this research project, the interpretivist paradigm was chosen as the central epistemological position. Mack (2010) states interpretivism emphasises the ability of the individual to construct meaning of their research. This construction is attributed to the fact that social reality is viewed from multiple perspectives and is interpreted differently by individuals and social groups (Mack, 2010). Case study was adopted as a methodology as it assumes an in-depth understanding and deep immersion with the subject (Flyvberg, 2006; Stake, 1995; Yin, 2014). Thomas (2016) describes interpretivist research and a case study approach as natural partners, as they each seek for rich, intensive understanding of the phenomena being researched. Stake (1995) suggests that a case study provides the opportunity to study the particularity and complexity of an issue.

The participants in the research project were selected through purposeful sampling. Emails and information were sent out to teachers who were either known through our informal history networks or were contacts or colleagues of teachers (see Table 13.1 below).

Table 13.1. Contextual Information About the Participants.

Name	Teaching Experience	School Context	Age Phase	Focus Group	Individual Interviews
Sammy	More than 10 years	Large inner-city academy[a]	Secondary	1	No
Rebecca	Less than 5 years	Large semi-urban academy	Primary	1	Yes
Charlie	Less than 5 Years	Large urban academy	Primary	1	Yes
Mike	Less than 5 Years	Large urban academy	Secondary	1	Yes
Nate	Less than 5 years	Large urban academy	Primary	1	Yes
Emma	Less than 5 years	Independent urban school	Secondary	2	No
Kate	More than 5 years	Independent urban school	Primary	2	No
Jim	Less than 5 years	Large, suburban academy	Primary	2	Yes
Robert	More than 10 years	Large inner-city school	Secondary	No	Yes

[a]An academy refers to a group of schools in England that receive funding directly from the government and are managed by an Academy Trust.

The data collected involved using two methods, focus groups and individual interviews. Focus group discussions are a particularly rich source of data collection. Aurine et al. (2016) define the focus group as a method of understanding and describing an issue from the perspectives of the participants; they are an opportunity for multiple participants to interact with others through dialogue. Unstructured individual interviews were used which sought to understand the subjective feelings, thoughts and experiences of the participants individually – this method allowed for data collection while seeking to understand individual perspectives which were contextualised within their experiences (Aurine et al., 2016). Table 13.1 outlines contextual information about the participants who were part of this study, using alternative names for participants to anonymise those taking part.

Thematic analysis was adopted and drew on the work of Clarke and Braun (2017, p. 297) who suggest that this approach can provide an 'accessible and systematic approach' to generate themes from qualitative data. This allows for the generation of a critical framework which can 'interrogate patterns within personal and social meanings … and to ask questions about the implications of this' (Clarke & Braun, 2017, p. 297).

Braun and Clarke (2006) suggest that there are five key stages to thematic analysis:

(1) Become familiar with the data;
(2) Generate initial codes;
(3) Search for themes and potential themes;
(4) Review themes and check for examples that do not fit;
(5) Refine themes, generate propositions and look for complexities common with a thematic approach.

This five-step guidance provided by Braun and Clarke (2006) gave a robust guide that was used to support thematic analysis of both the focus group interviews and the individual interviews in Phase One and Two, respectively.

Thomas (2009) states that ethics is about the conduct of a researcher's work. So, an attentive and reflexive approach was adopted as the research unfolded and was guided by the BERA ethical guidelines (2014). The principles of being a socially conscious researcher (Pillow, 2010) who acknowledged the importance of listening to and representing the voices of the participants, committing to ethical principles through all decision making, and recognising social justice with education was adopted. Data were anonymised and presented within themes. It was important that teachers' identity was protected as teachers shared some challenges from their practice which could compromise their professional standing.

Findings and Discussion

The policies highlighted in this chapter have been: The Teachers Standards (DfE, 2012), the National Curriculum for history (DfE, 2013) and the Prevent Duty (DfE, 2015) as these policies shaped the context for this research which influences the categorisation of teachers when teaching sensitive and controversial issues. The policy context was overlapping and, therefore, themes were identified across the data and included:

- Exploring and Defining the Terms 'Sensitive' and 'Controversial';
- Reflections from Classroom Practice;
- History as an Opportunity to Discuss Controversial and Sensitive Issues;
- Disclosure Dilemma;
- Strategies for Developing the Teaching of Sensitive and Controversial Issues;
- Influential Factors that Impact on Teachers' Decision-making in the Classroom;
- Constructions of Childhood;
- The Influence of Parents;
- Unexpected Discussion;
- The Significance of the School Context.

As this chapter emphasises policy context, the data will be presented under each policy and how this influenced teachers' practice. Please refer to Table 13.1 for details about pseudonyms used to protect teacher identity.

National Curriculum (DfE, 2013)

During the focus group interviews, the participants provided four specific examples of content that had the potential to be sensitive and controversial: The Bus Boycott and The Slave Trade in Bristol (Charlie), World War 1 (Nate) and Guy Fawkes (Sammy). In the case of Charlie, the events that he cited had a particularly strong local connection. This illustrates that controversial and sensitive issues can be identified for teaching to local and time-specific contexts. It is worth noting that none of these events or individuals are explicitly mentioned within the National Curriculum (DfE, 2013) at the key stage that the teachers were working at (Key Stages 2, 3 and 4). This suggests that the curriculum has flexibility within its content and that individual teachers do select content that can engage with sensitive and controversial issues that are relevant to the context they are being taught in.

Teachers Standards (DfE, 2012)

The Teachers Standards (DfE, 2012) were seen to pose some challenges for teachers, especially during the United Kingdom's Brexit vote in 2016 (a vote to leave the European Union which affiliates countries across Europe in political, social and economic issues). Both Nate and Charlie – who were Year 6 teachers (10–11-year-olds) – found this a difficult time as they were unsure how, or if, they should respond to children's comments and questions about politics. Nate commented that 'I just didn't think I could answer', and Charlie stated that he could not 'form an opinion towards them [children] or anything'. This response was indicative of the polarised feelings towards the Brexit vote that teachers were negotiating in the classroom at the time and reflected wider political unrest.

Magill (2016) identified how some teachers in her research were identified as 'activist'. These teachers explicitly selected sources avoided different perspectives and promoted their own viewpoint; this could be seen as exploiting children's vulnerability and is not the position that Charlie and Nate took. However, what Charlie and Nate acknowledged was teachers' powerful position of influence with the point of which vulnerability and exploitation occurs being unclear. While the Teachers Standards (DfE, 2012) may be clear, Charlie and Nate's experience shows that the application of them is more difficult in practice. This predicament also raises questions about self-surveillance and protectionism which will be considered later in this chapter.

In terms of teaching British Values, Lander (2016, p. 329) suggests that there has been a lack of training in supporting teachers, and this potentially leaves teachers vulnerable. Lander (2016) argues that naïve interpretations of Britishness may cause contentious discussions both inside and outside of the classroom.

While Charlie and Nate did not refer explicitly to a lack of training, Charlie's experiences of teaching British Values provided an interesting insight into how he approached it, protecting his position by using a purchased ready-made resource available online through a popular educational website.

Charlie used the phrase 'I don't have to worry...[they] packaged it up very objectively' when using such resources. This implied that he had shifted his personal responsibility and therefore presented a protected, container position. This contrasted with his previous comments regarding the Brexit referendum where Charlie presented avoidance tactics. Through the purchased resource, he felt he had ensured that he did not express his personal beliefs and so he was upholding the Teaching Standards (DfE, 2012). Nate was reflexive of his choices and did question the use of this ready-made resource. He recognised 'a naïve interpretation of Britishness', Lander (2016, p. 67) regarding the delivery of British Values. This supports the idea that a naïve perspective of British Values can be presented in the classroom and indicates that some teachers are aware of it.

The Prevent Duty (DfE, 2015)

Robert discussed how he perceived how his role of teacher had changed in light of training in the Prevent Duty (DfE, 2015). He recalled how he had not had training of this kind in his previous teaching career and that he was not happy about it. One reason for his concerns stems from the underlying ethics of the policy and this training. He commented:

> We're almost being like East German informant type people
>
> And whereas if we saw a vulnerable kid, we'd look out for them and like talk to them, like talk to their parents. Now it's shop them to the police

Robert's comments indicate that he views the reporting of vulnerable children as being like an 'informant'. His position seems to echo Elton-Chalcraft's (2016) concerns when she uses the term to describe teachers as 'state instruments of surveillance'. These comments demonstrate how Prevent Duty (DfE, 2015) has impacted on his practice. Robert uses state control as a metaphor for current legislation which implies that he is uncomfortable being in the role of the surveyor of children's comments. Being so openly opposed to official policy could be viewed through an activist lens, and while Robert does not fit Magill's (2016) category of activist, he does indicate that he is aware of surveillance in his school.

We will now consider how the three policies (National Curriculum DfE, 2013; Prevent Duty DfE, 2015; Teachers Standards DfE, 2012) shape teachers practice in relation to how they shape their discussions around sensitive and controversial issues. We will frame this around the Kitson and McCully (2005) and Magill's (2016) categorisation of teachers: risk takers, containers, avoiders and activists.

Risk Takers

Kitson and McCully (2005) and Magill's (2016) research found that the teachers they identified in this category confronted uncomfortable truths and challenged children's misconceptions and preconceptions. The teachers sought to develop a critical stance in the classroom where children could understand the complexities of the past rather than being presented with a simplistic narrative. From the focus groups, examples of risk taking were provided; these included using images with the intention to shock, expecting children to be upset in order to engage with historical empathy, considering how a particular issue is approached, and the way in which counter narratives were presented to the hegemonic position by the teacher playing the role of devil's advocate (taking on an alternative position to their own and/or their student's for the sake of argument and discussion).

Emma used images in her teaching of the Holocaust and the Vietnam War. She deliberately selected emotive images in her teaching to provide uncomfortable truths. Kate recognised that teachers have a choice in how they approach the teaching of sensitive and controversial issues. This implied that the same issue could be taught in different ways, some more risky than others. Sammy provided an example of choice regarding the teaching of the British Empire. She felt that the emphasis on celebrating the Empire is an expectation by the UK government. Sammy spoke of how teaching British Empire in this way did not challenge uncomfortable truths but instead provided a simplistic explanation of the past. Part of her rationale for adopting a riskier approach with multiple perspectives was because of her sense of self and acknowledgement of her political position being 'a bit lefty'. Here, her politics were informing her choice of approach.

A further risk-taking strategy can be seen regarding how Mike used the strategy of devil's advocate to counter children's responses when confronted with a sensitive and controversial theme. In this instance, Mike commented that his responses to children's comments were reactive rather than being planned or politically informed. With this strategy, he was able to provide different perspectives indicating that Mike felt this was a useful way of generating discussion. However, due to the unplanned nature and potential for reactive comments, this strategy may have left Mike in a vulnerable position because his comments may not have been supported by evidence.

Containers

Teachers who are considered 'containers' Kitson and McCully (2005) and Magill (2016) do not encourage children to fully engage with the issues being taught and they contain the possibility of emotive or upsetting discussions. This indicates a contrast to the Risk Takers section where we discussed strategies of risk taking in the form of teacher's position and resources used: this could facilitate unplanned, emotional responses. However, it could be argued that without taking the risk of challenging uncomfortable truths, children are at risk of not being able to understand the past because of the choices that teachers make. We previously problematised Charlie's use of commercially made resources to discuss Brexit. Of particular interest were the comments made about the use of a commercial company who mass produce teaching resources. Charlie suggested that the responsibility for the discussion had been shifted to the resource maker, and therefore, he could absolve himself of any responsibility. His use of the words 'appropriate', 'objectively' and 'easier' were key indicators that Charlie felt this was a more straightforward way of teaching about British Values, and this enabled him to be more confident in his teaching. However, Charlie neglected to consider that he had selected this resource due to his trust in these commercially available resources. As a result of this trust, he had considered this resource to be 'objective'. Charlie's lack of questioning of the use of this resource in teaching has the potential to limit learning and may indicate a quick fix to a solution rather than providing an opportunity for children to engage critically with a discussion about British Values. Without questioning the content of resources can potentially place the teacher in a vulnerable position. Not all participants were comfortable with this approach, and Nate recognised that the selection of sources needed careful consideration.

In addition to containment through the choice of resource, Jim reflected on how he contained learning through the negotiation of children's questions. Jim articulated how his teaching about flags raised the possibility to develop a deeper teaching opportunity about colonialism. While Jim's intention had been to teach about flags and their associated country, the children were very curious and appeared to want to know more about the relationship between flags and Great Britain (as many flags have part of Great Britain's flag embedded in their own). This was unplanned, and his comments-initiated containment of the discussion. He used the words 'loose' and 'loosely' to demonstrate the tokenistic discussion that occurred in the classroom around the topic in question. Jim was tentative in expanding this discussion. While Jim recognised that this was an opportunity to engage with a deeper discussion, it also indicated two types of containment, planned in the case of Charlie with the use of commercially made resources and unplanned in the case of Jim and flag identification.

Avoiders

While some participants used strategies of containment in their research, Kitson and McCully (2005) and Magill (2016) identified categories of avoider. Within Magill's (2016) research, she identified teachers who were 'natural avoiders' and 'reluctant avoiders'. Magill (2016) found that both types of avoider tended not to teach or chose topics that would be uncontentious. Reluctant avoiders acknowledged the complexity of teaching sensitive and controversial issues. However, they were reluctant in facilitating these because of external factors. By comparison, the natural avoiders rejected the complexity and difficulties of teaching history and provided a simplistic approach. In the doctoral research, Rebecca provided an example of this when she commented that she avoided sensitive and controversial issues because she did not want to 'confuse' or 'worry' children in her Year Two class (6–7-year-olds). She felt that the children were unable to 'process and understand' at this age.

Rebecca's concerns seem to stem from the fact that she felt her class would not be cognitively able to understand sensitive and controversial issues. Rebecca's rationale for avoidance was from a protectionist position where she used child development as a factor in her decision-making. This indicates that there is a potential relationship between avoider and protectionist.

Emma provided a further example of avoidance when she commented that teachers may use homework to avoid discussions of sensitive and controversial issues in the classroom. She suggested that teachers may shift the responsibility to parents. She gave the example of her son's school where each year children are given homework that involved identifying a country, a flag and a culture. Emma felt strongly that discussion around identity, including culture, should take place in school with the teacher and should not be avoided.

Emma and Rebecca's comments provide examples of when teachers may use strategies of avoidance. This resonates with Magill's (2016) category of natural avoiders. During the research, no explicit mention of reluctant avoiders was noted within the teaching of history. However, when Nate and Charlie refer to the teaching of British Values in the context of Brexit, they imply this reluctance regarding the sharing of their personal political views.

Activists

While risk takers, containers and avoiders have been discussed, Magill (2016) identified a further category of teachers as 'activist'. In her research, activists presented a one-sided view that related specifically to their value position. Activists did not seem to be wary of reprisal and seemed to be aware that they could manipulate children's thinking. However, in returning to Part Two of the Teachers' Standards (DfE, 2012), it clearly states that teachers should have 'mutual respect and tolerance' while ensuring 'that personal beliefs are not expressed in ways which exploit pupils'. The activist position would seem to oppose these Teachers Standards (DfE, 2012). In interviews, Sammy openly shared her own value position and actively encouraged children to recognise this in the sources she used within her teaching. However, this contrasts with Magill's (2016) research as Sammy recognised that her own beliefs influenced her teaching, but they were not more important than engaging with the teaching of history. In this example, Sammy's practice did not oppose the Teachers Standards (DfE, 2012).

Jim explored his recent experience of teaching about current affairs which he described as a sensitive and controversial issue through the teaching of British Values. Jim decided to use *First News*, a weekly newspaper designed for 7–14-year-olds which can support learning in the classroom. He focused on an article and video clips about Donald Trump (then President of the United States):

> I didn't want my own negative views superseding and clouding over what the facts are so, to go on 'First News', that to me although it could be seen as having some bias,

Jim justified the use of an article about Trump as he did not want to disclose his 'negative' views about the President. This suggests that Jim would have found it difficult to share a neutral viewpoint. Jim explicitly selected and used external sources that supported his views. Media coverage in the United Kingdom at this time did not present Trump in a positive light. It should be noted that there is a potential tension here. Jim did not provide alternative narratives around Trump to the children which are an essential consideration in the teaching of controversial issues. This example has some of the characteristic noted in Magill's (2016) research which identified the category of activist. Magill (2016) suggests that activists present information that is in line with the teachers' own strong views without concern for giving a balanced discussion. Jim described his school as one which has the support of parents. Activists identified in Magill's (2016) research taught in contexts where parents were likely to hold similar views to the teacher, so there was less fear of reprisal. In Jim's context, this could indicate that the parents may have also shared similar opinions about Trump or that they had trust in the teacher and were likely to support him.

Surveillance

In the literature review, we referred to the work of Caluya (2010) and Page (2016) and considered how surveillance is embedded within school practice. Page (2016) provides a model of surveillance: vertical (referring to Ofsted and SLT), horizontal (referring to peer, parents and children) and interpersonal or self-surveillance (self-monitoring and reflective practice). While Page's (2016) work discusses more general aspects of teachers practice, surveillance has a particular importance within the teaching of sensitive and controversial issues.

Sammy was happy and confident in sharing her own values with the children that she taught. However, she acknowledged that she needed to restrict this in some ways and 'keep it out'. This suggests that she was conforming to professional expectations and not engaging in anything that may have been considered inappropriate or extreme. Traits that could be considered verging on activism were silenced, resulting in Sammy self-surveying her comments in line with the Teachers' Standards (DfE, 2012).

Nate undertook a similar strategy of not sharing all political viewpoints by not responding to children's questions that asked him to reveal his political position when discussing Brexit. He too engaged in self-surveillance in front of the children. Teachers in this study also presented their use of devil's advocate as a surveillance strategy (Stradling, 1985). This protection comes in three forms: first, the teacher is able to protect themselves by not disclosing their own views; second, the teacher is able to challenge children's comments without fear of a known position; third, if children or parents have concerns about what has been discussed, then the teacher can say that they were playing the role of devil's advocate. This strategy can be used to create a mirage where the teacher can be protected, thus simultaneously acknowledging and deflecting the power of surveillance. Self-surveillance does not happen in a vacuum, and Nate recognised that his practice was shaped by both vertical (the head teacher) and horizontal surveillance (the parents). The lens of surveillance can be used to further explore the experiences of Jim through his teaching of Trump.

Jim decided to use a social media platform to share his teaching about Trump.

> I shared on social media …. 'Oh, after reading First News, my class has been a hive of political discussion, a buzz with political discussion' something like that. And they [a national newspaper] reshared it, and the editor reshared it and said, 'it's great how young minds get some… [knowledge of current affairs]
>
> It was Saturday and I was feeling relaxed, I didn't have my school head-on…

The act of sharing seems to raise tension in Jim's thinking. On the one hand, he shared news about how the discussion was political, but in earlier comments, he stated that the child's letter lacked any political focus. Jim first described how the letter written at home was a bit of extra writing and 'not a political…' task, and this seems to contrast with the focus of the lesson in which, unquestionably, the content was political, gaining facts about a world leader for non-fiction writing. Jim was aware of how his professional identity changed between home and school. The use of the words 'didn't have my school head-on' indicates that even though Jim was messaging about his work, he did not seem to think of this in a professional context. He refers to feeling 'relaxed', and as a consequence, he makes decisions that he may not have done if he had been at school.

Jim's sharing of information ended up with a journalist writing an article about Jim and the school with the letter written by a child (at home) as a piece of homework appearing in a popular online paper. Jim did not seem to have any regrets about using social media to share class news, and this form of social media is encouraged by his school. However, what is shared and in what context has implications on how teachers' professionalism may be framed, and this raises questions about who decides what is appropriate to be shared on social media. In this instance, the children, the teacher and the parents did not seem to be concerned about the content of the discussion that had taken place in the class or the media coverage that followed. However, there were some concerns about the political nature of Jim's social media messages by the Multi Academy Trust (MAT); Jim commented:

> [the problem was management thought we were] looking like were taking sides in a political] discussion

> [it gave the] school maybe some publicity that we didn't want and almost landed me in quite hot water. Yeah, I think there were conversations about that higher up

The MAT expressed some apprehensions about the repercussion of Jim's social media messages. One concern was that Jim had not followed the press coverage protocol once the message had reached an online newspaper. A further concern was that senior leaders within the MAT did not think that the school should be seen to be taking sides in current political debate. In this example, the actions of the MAT could be viewed as a form of vertical surveillance (Page, 2016).

Conclusion

This chapter has sought to highlight tensions within the teaching of sensitive and controversial issues in the classroom and how the National Curriculum (DfE, 2013), Teacher's Standards (DfE, 2012) and Prevent Duty (DfE, 2015) impact on teachers' practice. These policies are competing and overlapping which adds to the complexity of teaching history, and they impact on teachers' practice at numerous levels. The research illuminated the pressures that teachers face when teaching sensitive and controversial issues and how they adopt protectionist strategies to ensure that they fulfil their professional responsibilities while adhering to policy. The teachers in this research can be categorised in line with Kitson and McCully (2005) and Magill's (2016) research; however, these categories are not fixed but fluid and subject to change as a result of policy and school context – shifting from avoider to activist dependent on the topic and context. The polices considered here are ambiguous, leaving teachers walking a precarious tightrope as they navigate tensions in their classroom practice. Through this work, we have identified that teachers require greater support and training in how to teach sensitive and controversial issues, along with how to protect themselves in what can be a vulnerable environment. We have used insights from this research to inform our ongoing exploration of anti-racist pedagogy, another sensitive and controversial issue.

References

Aurine, J. D., Heath, M., & Howells, S. (2016). *The how to of qualitative research.* Sage.

Barton, K., & Mc Cully, A. (2007). Teaching controversial issues… where controversial issues really matter. *Teaching History*, *127*.

BERA. (2014). *Ethical guidelines for educational research.* BERA.

Braun, V., & Clarke, V. (2006). Using thematic analysis in psychology. *Qualitative Research in Psychology*, *3*(2), 77–101.

Caluya, G. (2010). The post-panoptic society? Reassessing Foucault in surveillance studies. *Social Identities*, *16*, 621–633. https://doi.org/10.1080/13504630.2010.509565

Clarke, V., & Braun, B. (2017). Thematic analysis. *The Journal of Positive Psychology*, *12*(3), 297–298.

Cowan, P., & Maitlas, H. (2017). *Understanding and teaching Holocaust education*. Sage.

Davies, M. (2017). Teaching sensitive and controversial issues. In M. Davies (Ed.), *Debates in history teaching* (2nd ed.). Routledge.

Department for Education. (2012). *The teachers' standards*. DfE. https://www.gov.uk/government/publications/teachers-standards

Department for Education. (2013). National curriculum in England: History programmes of study. https://www.gov.uk/government/publications/national-curriculum-in-england-history-programmes-of-study

Department for Education. (2015). The prevent duty. In *Departmental advice for schools and childcare providers*. DFE. https://www.gov.uk/government/publications/protecting-childrenfrom-radicalisation-the-prevent-duty

Dickens, J. (2015, November 8). Ofsted wants more anti-extremism training. Schools Week. In J. Metzler & L. Woessmann (Eds.), *The impact of teacher subject knowledge on student achievement: Evidence from within-teacher within-student variation* (Vol. 99, No. 2).

Elton-Chalcraft, S., LanderRevell, V. L., Warner, D., & Whitworth, L. (2016). To promote, or not to promote fundamental British values? Teachers' standards, diversity and teacher education. *British Educational Research Journal*, *33*(1). University of Cumbria.

Flyvberg, B. (2006). Five misunderstandings about case- study research. *Qualitative Inquiry*, *12*(2), 219–245.

Foucault, M. (1977). *Discipline and punish: The birth of the prison*. Allen Lane.

Foucault, M. (1991). *Discipline and punish – The birth of the prison*. Penguin.

Goldberg, T., Wagner, W., & Petrović, N. (2019). From sensitive and historical issues to history teachers' sensibility: A look across and within countries. *Pedagogy, Culture and Society*, *27*(1), 7–38.

Gove, M. (2011). Speech: The moral purpose of school reform. https//www.gov.uk/government/speeches/Michael-gove-on-the-moral-purpose-of-school-reform. Accessed on December, 2019.

Kitson, A., & McCully, A. (2005). You hear it for real in school. Avoiding, containing and risk taking in the history classroom. *Teaching History*. The Historical Association 120.

Lander, V. (2016). Introduction of fundamental British values. *Journal of Education for Teaching*, *42*(3), 274–279.

Mack, L. (2010, October). The philosophical underpinnings of educational research. *Polyglossia*, *19*.

Maddison, M. (2017). Primary history: Current themes. In I. Davies (Ed.), *Debates in history teaching* (2nd ed.). Routledge.

Magill, C. (2016). Approaches to teaching the Civil War and Franco dictatorship in contemporary Spain. In D. Bentrovato, K. V. Korostelina, & M. Schulze (Eds.), *History can bite*. V&R Unipress.

Mansfield, M. (2019). Confusion, contradiction and exclusion: The promotion of British values in the teaching of history in schools. *The Curriculum Journal*, *30*(1), 40–50.

McCully, A. W. (2012). History teaching, conflict and the legacy of the past. *Education, Citizenship and Social Justice*, *7*(2), 145–159.

Page, D. (2016). Conceptualising the surveillance of teachers. *British Journal of Sociology and Education*. https://www.researchgate.net/publication/307890090_Conceptualising_the_surveillance_of_teachers

Pillow, W. (2010). Confession, catharsis, or cure? Rethinking the uses of reflexivity as methodological power in qualitative research. *International Journal of Qualitative Studies in Education*, *16*(2), 175–196.

Posey-Maddox, L., Kimelberg, S., & Cucchiara, M. (2014). Middle-class parents and urban public schools: Current research and future directions. *Sociology Compass*, *8*(4).

Smith, H. J. (2016). Britishness as racist nativism: A case of unnamed 'other'. *Journal of Education and Teaching*, *42*(3), 298–313.

Stake, R. E. (1995). *The art of case study research*. Sage.

Stradling, B. (1985). Controversial issues in the curriculum. *Bulletin of Environmental Education*, *170*, 9–13.

Thomas, G. (2009). *How to do your research project: A guide for students in education and applied social sciences*. Sage.

Thomas, G. (2016). *How to do your case study* (2nd ed.). SAGE.

Yin, R. (2014). *Case study research design and methods* (5th ed.). Sage.

Chapter 14

Counter-Terrorism Measures in the Classroom: The Importance of Professionalism, Agency and Autonomy When Enacting the Prevent Duty

Max Weedon[a], *Kathy Mansfield Higgins*[a] *and Ciaran Burke*[b]

[a]No Institutional Affiliation, UK
[b]University of the West of England, UK

Abstract

The Prevent policy was singular and 'simple': to prevent individuals from getting drawn into terrorism, to identify and stop this process before it begins. In the context of the global war on terror and the shadow of terrorist attacks in the United States and England, this was an increasingly growing issue within the media and the broader public discourse. A central institution charged with enacting Prevent in the United Kingdom were education institutions (schools, colleges and universities), the rationale being that these places of learning house individuals during impressionable and vulnerable times and the Prevent policy can protect these individuals.

This chapter will provide an alternative critical discussion on Prevent by framing it as the securitisation of the UK education sector. As such, Prevent is a form of surveillance and a mechanism of power over educators and learners which carry counterproductive consequences for both. In doing so, this chapter will question how education professionals balance their professional identity and their new role in supporting and enacting the Prevent duty. Through developing a new multi-level 'Critical Realist World Systems Model', this chapter will provide a conceptual discussion of Prevent policy more broadly and how education professionals navigate the friction between their professional values and legal obligations. This chapter draws on a range of theoretical traditions to begin to question a well-established security policy within English and Welsh educational institutions providing a conceptual starting point to examine similar and future policies.

Critical Perspectives on Educational Policies and Professional Identities, 229–246

doi:10.1108/978-1-83753-332-920241014

Keywords: Prevent; surveillance; Foucault; critical realism; securitisation; professional identity

Introduction

In 2006, the Blair Labour Government introduced the first Prevent policy, Preventing Violent Extremism. The provision was designed to stop individuals becoming radicalised and to stop these individuals becoming terrorists, as such it was intended as a pre-emptive strategy. It was trailed as a pilot of only 1 year during 2007–2008 and then expanded until 2011 when it was revised and relaunched by the then Coalition government. In July 2015, the Counter-Terrorism and Security Act came into force which included a statutory duty on specified authorities to have 'due regard to prevent people from being drawn into terrorism'... (HMG, 2015, p. 2). Perhaps one of the most significant changes to the original strategy, which had sought to address all forms of terrorism and violent extremism, was the addition of 'non-violent extremism, which can create an atmosphere conducive to terrorism and can popularise views which terrorists can exploit' (HMG, 2015, p. 2). Clearly, this addition presents challenges to all required to deliver this policy within any context of civil rights and particularly of the right to hold views that others may find offensive or extreme, but nonetheless are completely legal points of view. The government went on to issue Prevent duty guidance for all institutions in England and Wales, which Kundnani (2012) argues requires educational, health and social service professionals to implement counter-terrorism measures within their normal duties. Since then, thousands of public servants have undergone compulsory Prevent training, including across the education sector, and Ofsted inspections prioritise how the Prevent duty has been prioritised by staff.

This chapter is a critical, reflective account of research into the impact of the Prevent security policy which mandates a duty of surveillance on educational professionals in England and Wales. It examines how this central government policy affects teachers/lecturers perceptions of their roles and impacts their professional identity and practices. This chapter is based on research from the lead author's doctorate entitled: 'Counter-Terrorism Measure in the Classroom: Exploring the Perceptions and Experienced of Educational Professional Enacting the Prevent duty in Bath and Bristol'. Through the research process, a unique multi-level conceptual model, the Critical Realist World Systems Model (CReWS), was developed. The research used a form of critical realist methodology and the methods used included a questionnaire and semi-structured follow-up interviews with education professionals working in primary, tertiary (Further Education) and higher education in the Bath and Bristol areas.

This chapter begins with an examination of the justification for the adoption of the Prevent policy, followed by considerations on whether it is in fact a counter-productive measure in achieving its aspirations. With this background, it then describes the research approach detailing the development of the CReWS model and empirical processes. This chapter focuses on one aspect of the broader findings from the research on examining how professionals engage with Prevent policy. The chapter concludes with a discussion concerning how and why individuals engage in a range of actions as they negotiate the friction between professional values and legal obligations.

Safeguarding the Vulnerable: The Epidemiological Justification for Prevent

A central rational underpinning Prevent is a discourse of safeguarding vulnerable individuals (Coppock & McGovern, 2014; Heath-Kelly, 2017). As such, the policy assumes that all individuals are potentially vulnerable to radicalisation. This vulnerability extends to young people studying in the UK education system. DeMause (2002) and Lifton (2007) frame this vulnerability and the assumption that these young people may harm themselves or harm society based on problematic conceptualisations of a mental health crisis and well-being for young people. As such, we have witnessed the justification of a pre-emptive securitising approach in UK education under the guise of 'safeguarding' and risk management.

In their analysis of Prevent policy, Coppock and McGovern (2014) examine documentation providing guidance on identifying and 'safeguarding' 'vulnerable' children and young people in schools from being drawn into terrorism. They report a problematic construction of 'childhood vulnerability' and equally problematic practices for 'child protection' and 'safeguarding' in the Prevent duty. As such, there are questions to be asked concerning how Prevent defines and supports vulnerability. This is further problematised as these definitions fall under Foucault's (2008) concept of a 'regime of truth' termed effectively as a discourse which is understood to be true and therefore protected from critique. There is a clear need for an exploration of how educational professionals understand and apply these concepts and recommendations for best practices. Such an examination will provide a greatly needed critical account of a powerful discourse.

Governmentality, Freedom of Speech and Surveillance: Could Prevent Be Counterproductive?

Lemke (2002) writes that 'Governmentality' provides a conceptual lens to understand the techniques and strategies by which a modern society is rendered governable. The concept was first introduced by Foucault (1991) to account for how the state shapes individual identities and practices (Li, 2007, p. 5). Foucault applied Bentham's notion of the 'panopticon'; this was a form of prison architecture which allowed prison guards to monitor prisoners without their express knowledge of when they were and were not being monitored. The point is that prisoners were disciplined and re-shaped rather than punished (Foucault, 1975). Foucault argues that this form of constant surveillance inculcates a consciousness of being constantly observed/judged; the panopticon is internalised leading to self-regulation, a process Foucault (1975) terms 'panopticism'. This form of surveillance is highly successful as it works on the principle that you do not know when you are being observed; therefore, you act like you are always being observed. In this context, Prevent can be conceived of as a form of governmentality practised through counter-terrorism measures (Aradau & Van Munster, 2007; Mythen & Walklate, 2006). Individuals are constantly observed, or feel they are, throughout their educational lives (and elsewhere), to the point where state regulations are internalised and become their own regulations. Such a process is discussed by Elton-Chalcraft et al. (2017); they contend that through Prevent education, professionals are transformed into instruments of state surveillance, fundamentally changing their professional roles and identities.

Previously, Bryan (2017) applies the concept of governmentality when demonstrating how Prevent regulates its subjects from a distance, replacing Foucault's prison guards with teachers and other educational professionals. For Bryan, The Prevent policy is designed to produce 'governmentable subjects' or what Foucault termed 'docile bodies' (1975), importantly not just in terms of students but also of education professionals, who themselves internalise state regulations in the process of applying Prevent duty. O'Donnell (2016) outlines the broad implications of Prevent for educational professionals. These include shifts in: the curriculum, freedom of speech, critical enquiry, the nature of pedagogical relationships. These are alongside the personal integrity of both students and educational professionals being compromised or questioned. The problematic lack of transparency/confusion regarding the criteria used for Prevent assessments, as discussed above, prevents nuanced understanding and application of the policy. For O'Donnell (2016), what is presented as 'safeguarding' is effectively surveillance leading to pedagogical, testimonial and epistemic injustices (O'Donnell, 2017).

Revell and Bryan (2016) examine how UK head teachers approach appraisals in light of Prevent. The authors are particularly interested in the policy's requirements for teachers to actively uphold fundamental British values (FBV) (Department for DfE Department for Education, 2011) and to promote them both inside and outside of schools (Department for DfE Department for Education, 2014). Their study reported confusion among head teachers concerning how these standards should be achieved which led to anxiety around whether educational professionals were meeting professional demands/standards. Habib (2016) contends that schools provide an opportunity for students to build resilience against radicalisation. However, we argue that schools are not currently providing such a context. Critics maintain that opportunities for Muslim students to express critical thinking against radicalisation are reduced under the Prevent duty (Brown, 2010; Puar, 2017), rendering a 'chilling' effect on academic freedom (McCormack, 2016), with some suggesting this has the potential to radicalise the British Muslim population (Dudenhoefer, 2018).

In 2018, the UK Home Office published statistics relating to the number of individuals referred through Prevent in the past year (April 2017 to March 2018). The data show that approximately 95% of the referrals to Prevent were deemed unnecessary, with only 394 from the 7,318 referrals being classified as requiring Channel support, a governmental deradicalisation programme (Home Office,

2018). The large amount of unnecessary referrals reported by the Home Office could be read as counterproductive in that the time and resources it takes to process the referrals takes that time and resources away from investigating legitimate threats. In addition, unnecessary referrals risk creating alienation and anger in those falsely referred and their communities. Such consequences demonstrate the need to talk to educational professionals to account for why these unnecessary referrals are happening, in an effort to avoid them in future and avoid counterproductive consequences of Prevent.

Thinking Differently About Prevent

The 'regime of truth' underpinning Prevent is one that arguably exemplifies Foucault's concept of 'power/knowledge' in action. It became clear, however, that the existing research corpus is significantly limited in terms of the relative scarcity of empirical studies of Prevent. This project's research questions, and its methodological approach(es), have been formulated in response to such findings, in order to productively advance, and nuance, extant critical-theoretical work on Prevent by expanding the empirical evidence base for the policy's enactment on the micro/meso levels. There is no standard methodology for research in the field of education policy, as Malen and Knapp (1997, p. 419) point out: 'there are multiple metaphors and models but no "grand theories" of public policy generally or education policy more specifically'. As such, this research developed a CReWS model to provide a multi-level heuristic thinking tool to research Prevent. Such conceptual innovation was necessitated due to Prevent's unprecedented nature and impact, in terms of the securitisation of the United Kingdom's education sector at a scale never before witnessed.

The Prevent policy can be conceived of as what Foucault (1980) terms a 'dispositif'. In Foucauldian terms, a 'dispositif' refers to mechanisms and knowledge structures which maintain and strengthen the exercise of power within society. Prevent can be viewed in these terms as having multidisciplinary roots that stretch into the fields of security, military, politics, criminology and psychiatry: a dispositif that is bolstered by neoliberal and neoconservative ideologies. Any attempt at understanding Prevent fully thus requires a multidisciplinary, pluralised methodology. This contention sparked the inspiration to develop a new conceptual model, one fit for the task at hand. The CReWS critical paradigm evolved over the course of the project, with different theoretical 'toolkits' privileged at different times, depending on their relative utility to the analytical task at hand. By locating the research in a stratified critical-realist paradigm, a wide variety of epistemological and methodological approaches are available with which to productively interrogate the focus of the research. At a basic level, the CReWS theoretical model – illustrated in Fig. 14.1 – represents a combination of critical-realist meta-theory (incorporating a pluralist approach to theoretical tool-kits) with Wallerstein's (1974) world systems theory.

Wallerstein's world systems theory is a multidisciplinary, macro-scale approach to world history and social change. It posits a capitalist world

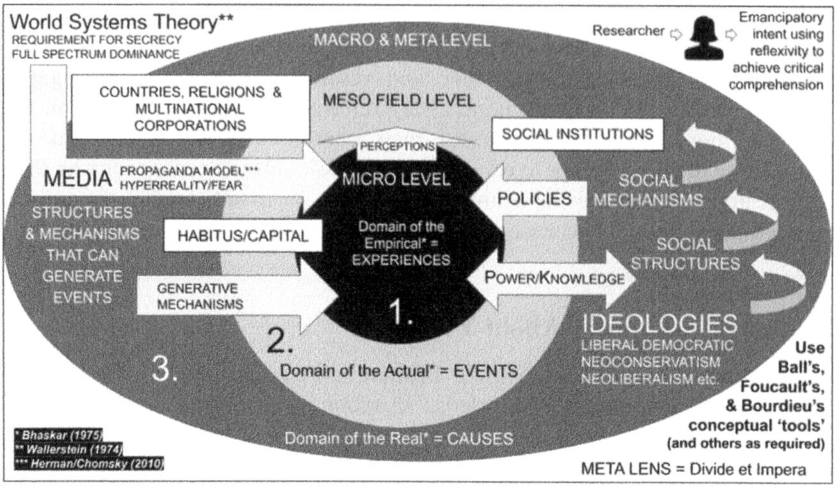

Fig. 14.1. The Critical Realist World Systems Theoretical Model (CReWS).

economic system in which some countries and multinational corporations benefit to the detriment of others. World systems (and not nation states) should, therefore, form the basis of social analysis as a framework for studying reality. Using world systems theory allows us to contextualise Prevent, a policy which emerged as a direct result of geopolitical events, within the global field of power relations on a systemic (macro) level and bring these insights to bear when analysing Prevent at the individual (micro) and institutional (meso) levels. Critical realism is a meta-theory with a meta-ontological approach which allows for a stratified conception of reality that attempts, ultimately, to diffuse the ongoing tension between positivist and interpretivist camps. The critical-realist approach combines ontological realism, where reality is considered intransitive and independent of our perception and knowing, with epistemic relativism; it insists upon a stratified ontology of the social order, with upwards and downwards causality between higher and lower level strata (Archer, 2020). This stratified ontological reality encourages a pluralistic approach to generating knowledge that draws on a range of ontological, epistemological and methodological concepts or 'tool kits'. Deployed in combination, as with the pluralist CReWS model, these 'tool kits' excavate a range of often-interconnected insights that may not be evident in a more traditional, singular approach.

This model outlines the benefits on drawing on a range of theoretical concepts in an effort to provide an opportunity to consider the range of different elements within Prevent. As an illustrative example, we would like to briefly outline how two such theoretical concepts can work by discussing the synergy between Foucault and Bourdieu. As Bang (2014) argues, Foucault and Bourdieu provide complementary approaches when analysing power. As discussed above, Foucault's unpacking of the mechanisms of power and the consequences leading to docile bodies are central to critically examining Prevent. Where Bourdieu's (1992) concept of habitus as a set of durable dispositions points to the longevity of such attitudes and practices. The habitus can be informed and moulded by relations and power structures which are accepted but also harmful to that individual, through the process of symbolic violence (Bourdieu, 1992). As such, through examining the subtle mechanisms and power and durable outcomes, combining these two thinkers provides the conceptual account of a 'docile habitus'. The core argument and rationale for this model has been to begin to critically examine and challenge education policy and subsequent practices, we need to equip ourselves with a wholistic and plural account of the problematique.

Data Collection

The following sections outline the research methods used to collect, analyse and interpret the data. A mixed-method approach combining mainly qualitative with limited quantitative research (Johnson & Turner, 2003) was determined to be most appropriate to evaluate education professionals' views of the Prevent duty and their reported enactment practices. The mixed methods approach included: an online survey and subsequent in-depth in-person interviews. All research was conducted within the BERA (2018) ethical guidelines, and all ethical clearance was sought and secured before data collection began.

Survey

An online survey was designed to measure participant's knowledge, attitudes and behaviours concerning Prevent (Rattray & Jones, 2007). Open questions and Likert-type scale questions were used to collect data to provide an opportunity for participants to elaborate on answers. Employing a random sample, the survey attempted to reach as many participants as possible who met the main selection criteria that they were professional educators who taught in an English school, college or university. The link to the online survey was disseminated through a combination of advertising in local multi-educational trusts' bulletins and emailing to the lead author's existing professional networks. The intention of this combined access approach was to gain a broad range of attitudes, experiences and practices within the sample. Recruitment resulted in a sample size of 75 education professionals.

Semi-Structured Interviews: Gaining Insights Into Professional Identity

In order to elicit the desired rich data concerning education professionals' perceptions and experiences of enacting Prevent, individual semi-structured interviews were employed.

Prospective interview participants who indicated they were interested in a follow-up interview were contacted via the email address they supplied when completing the survey. An additional selection criteria was included requiring all potential participants to work in the Bristol or Bath area. This decision was taken for a range of reasons. The study was limited in terms of financial resources and timescales, as interviews were conducted face-to-face geographical proximity ensured access. Including participants from two larger South West urban centres increased levels of anonymity for participants. This felt particularly important given the focus of the research. In addition, it created an opportunity for a wider exploration of the 'Prevent' experience across the sector, rather than privileging responses to a particular set of institutions in one sub-sector. Eighteen participants met the geographic criteria of the study indicated when completing the online survey that they would be interested in a follow-up interview, resulting in an interview sample of $n = 17$ (with one having moved out of the area). Interview participants were from a range of 10 different educational institutions. All schools in the study (by chance outcome) were academies or independent state-funded schools. This was not a deliberate choice, and unsuccessful efforts were made to try to gain representation from the private sector and non-academised state schools.

Counter-terrorism and counter-extremism are sensitive, highly charged areas of investigation. As such, participants likely held substantive concerns around privacy. To address this, individual interviews were favoured above focus groups. The individual interview provided a level of privacy to participants which created an atmosphere for more frank, authentic responses, offering the researcher a deeper understanding of the sensitive issues at hand and leading to more reliable research findings. In contrast to asynchronous data collection methods such as surveys, interviews are an interactive experience between the interviewer and participant and offered a greater insight into the participant's subjective attitudes, experiences and practices (Flick, 2009). Interviewees were thus encouraged to discuss subjects related to the Prevent duty – their own perceptions, experiences, meanings and ultimately the 'reality' of the policy for them – on their own terms supported by the flexibility of the semi-structured interview format.

Participants were also given the opportunity to review their interview transcript accuracy. Along with adding to levels of trustworthiness through member checks (Lincoln & Guba, 1985), this process provided participants with an increased level of trust and confidence in the research process. Reviewing their transcripts reduced the chance of their words being misunderstood or misrepresented. A degree of follow-up was possible, with participants providing clarification on particular points or inaudible moments on the recordings, when necessary, thus strengthening the reliability of the data.

Data Analysis

Data analysis involved a hybrid approach, combining deductive and inductive reasoning as 'complementary processes' (Gravetter & Forzano, 2015, p. 46), with an open attitude towards new theories emerging from the raw data. This corresponds to the critical-realist analytical method, which encourages the combination of deductive and inductive modes of inquiry and theorising. Initially, Braun and Clarke's (2006) thematic analysis was employed. The data were first grouped according to the research questions and the themes identified in the literature review. Interview responses were reviewed iteratively to identify data relevant to the research questions and to look for insights and patterns. This approach supported the creation of a typology of education professionals' policy work and policy positions towards Prevent. Thematic analysis fits into the critical-realist paradigm as an approach that allows theoretical flexibility (Braun & Clarke, 2006), which can help to bridge the quantitative (positivist) and qualitative (interpretative) divide (Boyatzis, 1998). It is 'open' in that it allows for the incorporation of other qualitative approaches (Willig, 2013), such as critical discourse analysis (CDA) and Foucauldian discourse analysis (FDA) which were further applied within this study.

Findings and Discussion

This study focuses on attitudes, experiences and practices of teaching staff who are tasked with enacting the Prevent duty within their own teaching space. Through the expansion of Prevent in 2015, there was a significant broadening of criteria beyond violent terrorism to include civil disobedience and membership of a range of social justice groups. Research participants viewed this expansion as problematic as it directly impacted their role and practice if they were to meet their professional obligations within the Prevent duty. This new responsibility was misaligned to many participants understanding of their professional identity and reasonable autonomy they had previously enjoyed within their own classroom. A review of the relevant literature suggests that Prevent does not face significant opposition among those tasked to enact it (Busher et al., 2017). However, we contend that this depiction of either agreement or acquiescence leading to unproblematic enactment stems from a relative lack of empirical studies examining experiences and practices of front-line educational professionals. To address these issues, this study focuses entirely on the experiences and views of a sample of these professionals, revealing a range of more nuanced responses and positions than has previously been presented.

Four key findings emerge from an analysis of the study data:

(1) Educational professionals are not monolithic in their enactment of Prevent. Rather, professionals adopt a fluid and diverse range of positions in fulfilling their legal duty.
(2) Educational professionals deploy 'Prevent-friendly' strategies, avoiding controversial subjects to comply with the 'hidden curriculum' of Prevent.
(3) Educational professionals are subject to 'soft coercion': oppressive managerial and performativity techniques which are understood as perceived threats to livelihood.

(4) Students are subject to a permanent socio-technical surveillance infrastructure that exists beyond the control of the teacher in the classroom and extends into the world beyond the school gates.

This chapter concentrates on the first finding examining the fluid and diverse range of positions that professionals adopt in fulfilling their legal duty to unpack how practice can challenge policy. The data demonstrated that the Prevent duty was routinely perceived to be in contrast with professionals' values, especially in terms of ethical relationships with students, therefore risking individuals' own professional identity:

> I think the role of the teacher is becoming the role of the teacher brackets counsellor, and police officer [. . .] my job title is 'teacher', it's not 'teacher of deradicalisation strategies'. (Participant Q)

In response, professionals established strategies to navigate their legal responsibility of enacting Prevent while maintaining professional values and standards. Professionals challenged Prevent's 'top-down' policy by becoming policy actors, using translation processes in order to create and protect space within the legal framework to retain as much of their professional agency and classroom autonomy as possible. Stemming from this range of professional responses, this research developed a new taxonomy of policy enactment work, derived from respondents' real-life experiences with three distinct categories of policy actors identifiable: *legitimators*, *assimilators* and *doubters*.

A New Taxonomy of Policy Enactment Work

Due to the agentic response and application of professionals to the Prevent duty, the effective dual role of 'both receivers and agents of policy' (Saunders, 1987, p. 108), this research went beyond previous representations of academic identity (Fanghanel, 2007; Whitchurch, 2008, 2009). Instead this research built on Ball et al.'s (2011) conception of 'policy actors', those who reinterpret, translate or ignore elements of policy to resist perceived or expected negative outcomes. In the context of this study, professionals cited 'good teaching' and 'common-sense' as the rationale for their pedagogical choices that potentially stood at odds with their Prevent duty responsibilities. This study develops Ball et al.'s typology, modulating it for the education sector and the Prevent policy specifically based on the empirical data collected.

Within each conceptual group (legitimator, assimilators, doubters), educators demonstrated professionalism and an autonomous response to enacting Prevent. Individual attitudes and practices were driven by a combination of institutional context and individual/professional and personal identity. The three groups map a spectrum of most to least supportive of the Prevent duty: *legitimators* view the policy most positively and *doubters* most negatively. Membership of groups was not mutually exclusive but rather professionals shifted between groups.

Participants could behave outwardly assuming a pro-Prevent *(legitimator)* position 'defensively' in terms of workplace behaviours – to ensure job security, for example – while simultaneously espousing viewpoints more typically ascribed to *assimilators* and *doubters*. Strategies for Prevent enactment are marked by high levels of contextual agility and contingent flexibility.

Legitimators

Legitimators expressed the least doubts concerning the Prevent policy seeing it as a legitimate outcome from national security concerns. They follow the official regulations and guidance. As such, they legitimate the official narrative. *Legitimators* were often in leadership roles and displayed a 'common-sense' attitude towards combating terrorism. A key element of the legitimator discourse is they acknowledge and accept the narrative of the ever-present threat of terrorism. The head of a primary school offers an archetypal legitimator perspective:

> the whole Middle East politics have been part of our thinking for twenty or thirty years so when Prevent came in it wasn't a new risk (Participant O)

Legitimators expressed few concerns about the securitisation of education, but this was minimal compared to participants in other groups. However, as noted above, a single individual may adopt multiple, even competing, strategies at the same time. This can be demonstrated through the testimony of one interviewee, a line manager of 30 lecturers. On the one hand, this participant testified that he had implemented Prevent scrupulously, having made 10 referrals thus far – identifying him as a *legitimator*. Yet in the same interview, he presented a performative element of enacting Prevent policy in order to support his career progression, or at the least be shielded from job loss. Further than this subtle criticism of Prevent, he was also critical of Prevent for politicising educational roles and enforcing what he viewed as illiberal surveillance practices. We can see here how individuals can occupy more than one conceptual group; importantly, we maintain that his reluctant membership as a *legitimator* stems from perceived coercion from his institution and, ultimately, the state. However, even enthusiastic *legitimators* disclosed substantial doubts about Prevent in terms of policy design and application, if not rationale. As one *legitimator* remarked:

> Prevent has the potential to be applied to four-year-olds and 30-year-olds and that's too wide a spectrum for one strategy to be managed properly without problems. [. . .] I looked at what it could do for children and I thought it could do good stuff for children, but I could see if you were 25 and at university and exploring that you could feel pressurised[.] (Participant A).

Assimilators

Members of this group presented the most diverse set of strategies to address their perceived issues with Prevent. In Ball et al.'s (2011) typology, they could be described as:

- Policy 'narrators' – making meaning from the official Prevent discourse through reinterpreting and recontextualising the policy.
- Policy 'translators', putting their professional autonomy into practice by subtly altering aspects of Prevent where they deem this to benefit students which more appropriately align to their professional identity.
- Policy 'critics' sought to preserve a counter-discourse. In these ways, educators attempted to transform the enactment of Prevent into practices that were more congruent with their values and professional identity.

The findings presented numerous examples of creative resistance towards the policy and ethos of Prevent. Participants emphasised using a range of reflexive pedagogical approaches: teaching critical-thinking skills, open debating in a nurturing classroom atmosphere, modelling behaviour and so on. One participant emphasised the need for teachers to demonstrate agency and act as role models rather than simply reacting to trigger words or behaviours in a punitive, Prevent-led response:

> I will model a good way of being a collaborative human being, in an equitable society [...] having a sensible conversation with the child about why they hold that belief [...] sorting it out on a relatively ad hoc basis just using wisdom and sensitivity[.] (Participant J).

The agency and autonomy a teacher had to question Prevent was dependent on their experience and expertise. Often, *assimilators* discussed avoiding any immediate labelling of students because of 'trigger' remarks they made or views they held. One experienced respondent explained:

> If I take the word of a 14-year-old, and then say 'I am concerned about what this kid has said' am I not potentially criminalising that kid? [...] as soon as someone puts a label on you it changes the landscapes of your beliefs...as someone puts a label to it [...] it adds some kind of kudos to your belief[.] (Participant J).

This teacher said he used 'common-sense' and inclusive strategies, engaging respectfully with students to encourage trust in the classroom, to understand context and possible motivation for 'referrable' remarks, instead of escalating the situation by making a referral. This approach stands in contrast to that of the *legitimator* discussed above, who disclosed that he had made 10 referrals while being subtly/internally critical of the policy. In an attempt to avoid formal referrals if at all possible, *assimilators* routinely expressed a commitment to upholding the rights of the young people in their care and their families.

Besides re-framing the policy requirements to different degrees, other respondents reported the 'chilling effect' Prevent has on frank discussion of so-called 'risky' topics (Coppock & McGovern, 2014). In particular, self-regulation is an assimilator response to the perceived panoptic gaze of Prevent:

> I was avoiding certain areas, not many, but one or two debates that might have come up in a course where you are talking about the civil rights movement, and the sort of movements where people are protesting, protest music, that sort of stuff [...] I definitely had to change that and rethink it when Prevent came out[.] (Participant D)

Despite classroom autonomy and agency, educational professionals cannot escape, nor actively dismantle, the oppressive surveillance culture instantiated by Prevent in the classroom.

Doubters

This final group of respondents was the most outspoken concerning their unease at enacting the policy. Importantly, their presence offers a rebuttal to the current critical consensus that the Prevent policy has been adopted without significant resistance from education professionals. This research demonstrates that a critical mass of educators carry significant doubts about the policy and the primary role they play in being required to enact it.

Doubters openly discussed their thoughts on the issues within Prevent and declared themselves reluctant to become part of the securitised educational landscape the duty instantiates. They presented Prevent as coercive to professionals in that they risked their job security if they did not comply with the expectations of the policy. As one interviewee explained:

> 'It's like an obligation that I have to do this training and this training means I am now trained to identify extreme people, and I'm in a position where I can't say no, if I say no, I'm not going to have a job[.] (Participant C)

The requirement to teach Fundamental British Values (FBV) is a mainstay of the Prevent curriculum. Though this element was an issue for all participants, it was a particular issue for *doubters*. Indeed, for some, the issue of FBV compelled a reactive shift to adopting the *doubter* stance. One secondary headteacher, generally an *assimilator* with *legitimator* responsibilities incumbent to their managerial role, stated that they embedded FBV into the Personal, Social, Health and Economic (PSHE) education programme, thus allowing 'opt outs' by students who might be offended by certain topics. This headteacher met their obligation to enact and by extension legitimate the Prevent policy but also found a way to protect students from the risk of potential Prevent referral in the controversial area of 'British' values, thus by implication displaying *doubter* values.

Another approach from who could be described as an 'overt' *doubter* was to engage in a performative acknowledgement. This participant commented that in the context of being reviewed by Ofsted, he *would probably have to do some crazy* 'nod' *to the requirement to teach British* 'values'. Compliance here was entirely performative and acknowledged as such. In addition, *doubters* asserted their own agency based on values and pedagogical practices developed through their professional experience over the years. Members of this group reinterpreted the requirements of Prevent initially speaking to the child and their family rather than making immediate referrals if a child made 'suspect' opinions known.

Conclusion

As it stands, existing literature on the Prevent duty appears to offer a consensus that there is little opposition from professionals to the policy or its implementation. The CReWS model outlined above demonstrates the need to embrace complexity and question assumptions, particularly those which reinforce existing power relations and fail to problematise policy. The empirical findings offer a compelling counterpoint to this assumption pointing to the need for further research. Crucially, the existing 'consensus' does not take into account the opinions of front-line educators, professionals tasked with enforcing Prevent nor the strategies staff employ to curtail the negative impact of the policy while meeting the legal duty. This research demonstrates that their voices must be heard in order to provide a more nuanced assessment of the duty in practice.

This study supports the existence of the widespread belief that education professionals' job security is directly tied to their compliance with Prevent, even as enactment of the policy is perceived by many as a direct challenge to professional values and standards. Maintaining professional values is of utmost importance to the educators interviewed in this study. Despite the potential risk to their livelihoods, many educators act to counter the harmful effects that they believe that Prevent can have on their students. Though at the macro-level, the organisation itself had no choice but to be Prevent-compliant; it also supported the officers' condemnation of the policy. Similarly, educational professionals tread a fine line in balancing their legal duties and professional ethics, with many offering a 'soft' challenge to the Prevent policy while formally obeying its mandate.

Study respondents were unanimous on one crucial point: Prevent has the potential to encourage classroom practices that are detrimental to educators and to their charges. Almost all study participants expressed concerns about harm as a potential result of enforcement. This included, for example, fears that students could perceive implementation of the policy as discriminatory, generating distrust and leading to the breakdown of friendships, fracturing wider societal bonds and causing alienation. This could increase the risk of anomie and radicalisation that the policy seeks to avoid.

While each of the three groupings agreed on this point, the corresponding arguments for this position varied. *Doubters*, for example, staunchly believed that existing practices were sufficiently robust to monitor and protect their students and opined on this at length. *Assimilators* reinterpreted and translated Prevent policy to blend its requirements into their practices, equating to a model of harm reduction. *Legitimators* tended to emphasise that, although Prevent could be harmful in a general sense, this was not the case in their own organisations which, in their view, used a 'light touch' approach to what they saw as legitimate enactment of policy.

In summary, Prevent has become an unavoidable part of life in the education sector, an addition to the regulatory landscape of top-down policies and requirements made of educational professionals. Folded into this formal, authoritarian environment Prevent has added a layer of securitisation to education where navigating Prevent 'effectively' (i.e. to minimise its potential harms) perhaps becomes a foundational element of professional values. This chapter focused on the combination of professionalism, agency and autonomy in the context of professionals meeting their legal obligations under Prevent. These findings demonstrate that individuals straddle different positions (responses and practice) based on a range of factors. In terms of future practice and a new generation of educators, it is clear that these individuals need to retain criticality to construct a response to policy, that aligns to their values and also meets statutory responsibilities.

Post-Script... What Does This Mean for Doctoral Researchers?

This is a challenging section for us as authors to write as sadly Max, our first author, passed away before this section was written. As such, we are forced to consider what Max learned through the process and what other doctoral researchers can learn from this chapter and the broader work on which it is based. There are two areas I think that future researchers can learn, especially within the theme of this final section in the edited collection:

(1) If a theory or conceptual framework does not adequately meet your needs, then one may need to be developed. The CReWS model provides an innovative account of social space in which to examine Prevent. Here, we can see the combination of a range of theorists and theoretical frameworks which work together to provide a more critical tool in which to conduct social inquiry. Importantly, Fig. 14.1 outlining the CReWS is not finished; it tells the reader to add conceptual tools as required. This is very much in the spirit of this model in that it was developed because current tools were not up to the task but also no one is saying that this model is the end of the conversation; it is a heuristic device and one which can and hopefully will be developed by others. At the doctoral stage, researchers are fledgling academics but such innovative ways of examining the social world are welcome and needed.

(2) The other area is to embrace complexity and nosiness of real life. The findings outlining the three 'types' of participant could have been presented in neat categories but in reality we are often more than one thing and so while it is challenging to empirically demonstrate this, such endeavour provides a richer and more nuanced glimpse into the social world. Yes, it makes it messy and challenging to articulate at times on the page or in a viva exam, but it is also when we look at these nuances that we understand power and resistance to power – in this it was Prevent but there are many, many instances where this is equally as true and needed.

References

Aradau, C., & Van Munster, R. (2007). Governing terrorism through risk: Taking precautions, (un)knowing the future. *European Journal of International Relations*, *13*(1), 89–115.

Archer, M. S. (2020). The morphogenetic approach; critical realism's explanatory framework approach. In P. Róna & L. Zsolnai (Eds.), *Agency and causal explanation in economics* (pp. 137–150). Springer, Cham.

Ball, S. J., Maguire, M., Braun, A., & Hoskins, K. (2011). Policy actors: Doing policy work in schools. *Discourse: Studies in the Cultural Politics of Education*, *32*(4), 625–639.

Bang, L. (2014). Between the cat and the principle: An encounter between Foucault's and Bourdieu's conceptualisations of power. *Power and Education*, *6*(1), 18–31.

BERA British Education Research Association. (2018). *Ethical guidelines for educational research*. BERA. https://www.bera.ac.uk/wp-content/uploads/2018/06/BERA-Ethical-Guidelines-for-Educational-Research_4thEdn_2018.pdf. Accessed on July 18, 2010.

Bourdieu, P. (1992). The purpose of reflexive sociology. In P. Bourdieu & L. Wacquant (Eds.), *An invitation to reflexive sociology* (pp. 61–217). Polity.

Boyatzis, R. (1998). *Transforming qualitative information: Thematic analysis and code development*. Sage.

Braun, V., & Clarke, V. (2006). Using thematic analysis in psychology. *Qualitative Research in Psychology*, *3*(2), 77–101.

Brown, K. E. (2010). Contesting the securitization of British Muslims: Citizenship and resistance. *Interventions*, *12*(2), 171–182.

Bryan, H. (2017). Developing the political citizen: How teachers are navigating the statutory demands of the Counter-Terrorism and Security Act 205 and the Prevent Duty. *Education, Citizenship and Social Justice*, *12*(3), 213–226.

Busher, J., Choudhury, T., Thomas, P., & Harris, G. (2017). *What the prevent duty means for schools and colleges in England: An analysis of educationalists' experiences*. University of Huddersfield Repository. http://eprints.hud.ac.uk/id/eprint/32349/. Accessed on July 24, 2019.

Coppock, V., & McGovern, M. (2014). 'Dangerous minds'? Deconstructing counter-terrorism discourse, radicalisation and the 'psychological vulnerability' of Muslim children and young people in Britain. *Children & Society*, *28*(3), 242–256.

DeMause, L. (2002). The childhood origins of terrorism. *Journal of Psychohistory*, *29*, 340–348.

DfE Department for Education. (2011). *Teacher's standards: Guidance for school leaders, school staff and governing bodies* (p. 14). https://assets.publishing.service.gov.uk/government/uploads/system/uploads/attachment_data/file/665520/Teachers__Standards.pdf. Accessed on July 24, 2019.

DfE Department for Education. (2014). *Promoting fundamental British values as part of SMSC in schools* (p. 5). https://assets.publishing.service.gov.uk/government/uploads/system/uploads/attachment_data/file/380595/SMSC_Guidance_Maintained_Schools.pdf. Accessed on July 24, 2019.

Dudenhoefer, A. (2018). Resisting radicalisation: A critical analysis of the UK prevent duty. *Journal for Deradicalisation, 14*, 153–191.

Elton-Chalcraft, S., Lander, V., Revell, L., Warner, D., & Whitworth, L. (2017). To promote, or not to promote fundamental British values? Teachers' standards, diversity and teacher education. *British Educational Research Journal, 43*(1), 29–48.

Fanghanel, J. (2007). Local responses to institutional policy: A discursive approach to positioning. *Studies in Higher Education, 32*(2), 187–205.

Flick, U. (Ed.). (2009). *The sage qualitative research kit: Collection*. SAGE Publishing.

Foucault, M. (1975). *Discipline and punish: The birth of the prison* (Trans. from the French by A. Sheridan). Vintage Books.

Foucault, M. (1980). In C. Gordon (Ed.), *Truth and power, power/knowledge: Selected interviews & other writings 1972–1977* (Trans. from the French by C. Gordon, L. M. John Mepham, & K. Soper). Pantheon Books.

Foucault, M. (1991). Governmentality (Trans. from the French by R. Braidotti and rev. by C. Gordon). In G. Burchell, C. Gordon, & P. Peter Miller (Eds.)., *The Foucault effect: Studies in governmentality* (pp. 87–104) (2011). University of Chicago Press.

Foucault, M. (2008). *The History of Sexuality (1976–2018)* (Translated from the French by R. Hurley). Pantheon Books.

Gravetter, F. J., & Forzano, L. A. B. (2015). *Research methods for the behavioural research*. Wadsworth.

Habib, S. (2016). *Teaching & learning britishness: Encountering and negotiating discourses of identities and belongings through critical pedagogy*. PhD, Goldsmiths. University of London.

Heath-Kelly, C. (2017). The geography of pre-criminal space: Epidemiological imaginations of radicalisation risk in the UK Prevent Strategy, 2007–2017. *Critical Studies on Terrorism, 10*(2), 297–319.

Home Office. (2018). *Individuals referred to and supported through the Prevent Programme, April 2017 to March 2018*. https://assets.publishing.service.gov.uk/government/uploads/system/uploads/attachment_data/file/763254/individuals-referred-supported-prevent-programme-apr2017-mar2018-hosb3118.pdf. Accessed on July 24, 2019.

Johnson, B., & Turner, L. A. (2003). Data collection strategies in mixed methods research. In A.Tashakkori & C. Teddlie (Eds.), *Sage handbook of mixed methods in social and behavioral research* (pp. 297–319) (2010). Sage.

Kundnani, A. (2012). Radicalisation: The journey of a concept. *Race & Class, 54*(2), 3–25.

Lemke, D. (2002). *Regions of war and peace*. Cambridge University Press.

Li, T. M. (2007). *The will to improve: Governmentality, development, and the practice of politics*. Duke University Press.

Lifton, E. J. (2007). A clinical psychology perspective on radical Islamic youth. In T. Abbas (Ed.), *Islamic political radicalism: A European perspective* (pp. 25–41) (2007). Edinburgh University Press.

Lincoln, Y. S., & Guba, E. G. (1985). *Naturalistic inquiry*. SAGE Publications.

Malen, B., & Knapp, M. (1997). Rethinking the multiple perspectives approach to education policy analysis: Implications for policy-practice connections. *Journal of Education Policy*, *12*(5), 419–445.

McCormack, T. (2016). Academic freedom in an age of terror? In C. Hudson & J. Williams (Eds.), *Why academic freedom matters: A response to current challenges* (2016). Civitas.

Mythen, G., & Walklate, S. (2006). Criminology and terrorism: Which thesis? Risk society or governmentality? *British Journal of Criminology*, *46*(3), 379–398.

O'Donnell, A. (2016). Securitisation, counterterrorism and the silencing of dissent: The educational implications of prevent. *British Journal of Educational Studies*, *64*(1), 53–76.

O'Donnell, A. (2017). Pedagogical injustice and counter-terrorist education. *Education, Citizenship and Social Justice*, *12*(2), 177–193.

Puar, J. K. (2017). *Terrorist assemblages: Homonationalism in queer times*. Duke University Press.

Rattray, J., & Jones, M. C. (2007). Essential elements of questionnaire design and development. *Journal of Clinical Nursing*, *16*(2), 234–243.

Revell, L., & Bryan, H. (2016). Calibrating fundamental British values: How head teachers are approaching appraisal in the light of the Teachers' Standards 2012, Prevent and the Counter-Terrorism and Security Act, 2015. *Journal of Education for Teaching*, *42*(3), 341–353.

Saunders, M. (1987). Perceptions on TRIST: Implications for INSET. *Research Papers in Education*, *2*(2), 106–125.

Wallerstein, I. M. (1974). *The modern world-system I: Capitalist agriculture and the origins of the European world-economy in the sixteenth century*. Academic Press.

Whitchurch, C. (2008). Shifting identities and blurring boundaries: The emergence of third space professionals in UK higher education. *Higher Education Quarterly*, *62*(4), 377–396.

Whitchurch, C. (2009). The rise of the blended professional in higher education: A comparison between the United Kingdom, Australia and the United States. *Higher Education*, *58*(3), 407–418.

Willig, C. (2013). *Introducing qualitative research in psychology* (3rd ed.). Open University Press.

Chapter 15

Home Language Literacy Learning as an Extracurricular Activity by Pupils and Parents: Do the Findings Warrant a Case for Introducing Home Language Policy for Primary Education in England?

Shamsudin Abikar[a], *Helen Bovill*[b] *and Jane Andrews*[b]

[a]Bristol City Council, UK
[b]University of the West of England, UK

> Shackle a people, strip them bare, cover their mouths: they are still free. Deprive them of work, their passports, food and sleep: they are still rich. A people are poor and enslaved when they are robbed of the language inherited from their parents: it is lost forever. (Baker, 2011, p. 45, citing the Sicilian poet Buttitta, 1972)

Abstract

Despite the fact that almost two million learners in state-funded schools in England learn English as an additional language (DfE, 2020), there is no official policy for developing home languages (HLs), even though the use of HL in classrooms for academic purposes is linked to academic attainment (Smyth, 2012). Cummins' (1976) language interdependence hypotheses were employed as the analytical framework for the original study underpinning this chapter, as it showed the benefits of HL in the classroom. The study included 13 Somali-origin pupils in a Key Stage 2 class (8 boys and 5 girls – 10–11 years) and their 7 parents. Parents and pupils were separately taught HL literacy once per week for 24 weeks as extracurricular activities. HL literacy pre- and post-assessments, semi-structured interviews with pupils and parents and a researcher reflective diary were used for data collection (Abikar, 2020). The data from HL assessments when comparing the pre- and

Critical Perspectives on Educational Policies and Professional Identities, 247–263

doi:10.1108/978-1-83753-332-920241015

post-assessments showed improvement in areas assessed, except for writing. The semi-structured interview data demonstrated that learning HL literacy was beneficial for: social and spiritual identity, cognitive skills needed in the classroom and fostering communication between the family, relatives and the wider community. Additionally, positive attitudes to learning HL were evident within the study findings. The study strongly highlighted that it would be beneficial for pupils if there were strategies which would help them to maintain their HL; thus, this chapter will argue the case for the introduction of a HL policy for primary education in England. Overall, the study made recommendations for policymakers to introduce HL literacy sessions for the benefit of pupils.

Keywords: Home language policy; language interdependence hypotheses; academic attainment; KS2 class; Somali-origin pupils; Somali parents

Introduction

What is 5 ku-dar 4?

Assuming that you are an English monolingual, how would you confidently answer this question? It appears simple, straightforward even, yet you might not be in a position to provide answers confidently. This is because out of the 5 words, only one word, *ku-dar* (Somali language), is unfamiliar. You should potentially be capable of solving the above problem if told that 'ku-dar' means 'add'.

Now, if the process of correctly answering this simple question requires knowing a language, other than English, and its concept – can you imagine the challenges faced by learners of English as an additional language (EAL) in English schools where the medium of instruction is English? This chapter will explore research conducted for an educational doctorate, where acquisition of English was explored for Somali learners in a primary school in Bristol. This was considered in relation to how support for the learners' heritage language might benefit them in acquiring stronger skills in English language and literacy. The research was conducted through extracurricular teaching and activities with a small group of Somali children and their families. The aims of this research were (a) enhancing the English literacy attainment of the children through learning Somali heritage language literacy and (b) developing Somali heritage language literacy among the children's parents to inculcate them with the confidence to support their children's literacy skills (grammar) at home in both Somali and English languages.

In this chapter, the term *home language* (HL) is used to mean the language used by the learners' parents in their origin home country (Riagáin, 2018) – in this case Somalia language; *the study* refers to the doctoral dissertation undertaken by the first author; and the terms *child*, *children*, *pupil* and *learner* will be used interchangeably (except where explicitly indicated) to mean the participants of the study. Likewise, *HL literacy* means the reading, comprehension, writing and speaking skills of HL. The following section will explore the EAL learners and

HL issues, in particular to advance arguments for HL policy in England. Moreover, by using Cummins' (1976) language interdependence hypotheses as a framework, this chapter will advance the argument about the importance of HL in academic attainment. This chapter was co-authored by the second author, Helen Bovill, and third author, Jane Andrews, who have been the Director of Studies and Doctoral Supervisor, respectively, for the first author. Finally, as the focus of this chapter is the centrality of HL policy for classroom activities, only the children's data from the study, rather than parents, will be the focal point.

Setting the Scene: EAL and HL

At the time of this study, there were 8.1 million pupils in state-funded schools in England in 2018, of which 1.6 million were identified as EAL learners (DfE, 2020). To understand English proficiency of pupils with EAL, in the spring of 2018 information concerning EAL pupils' first language was generated by consulting school census data submitted by schools to the Department for Education (DfE). These data indicate that 36% of pupils with EAL were assessed as being fluent in English and a further 25% as competent (DfE, 2020). To determine the English proficiency, one of the characteristics used by the census was the length of time in an English school. Furthermore, the census claimed that 87% of EAL learners in years 7–11 who had attended an English school since the reception class were recorded as competent or fluent in English. It would have been meaningful to report on pupils' proficiency in their HL as well. However, this fact was overlooked by the census in its '*First Language*' section which focused, instead, on listing first languages only and providing data on proficiency in English according to those first languages.

The term EAL may sometimes be conflated with the term 'bilingual learner'. Slabakova (2016) defined bilingualism as the skill of mastering two languages with minimal proficiency. EAL is often used as a broad term and may mean learners whose language and culture differ from majority students in a country (Conteh, 2015). The DfE (2020, p. 4) defines EAL through the following:

> A pupil is recorded as having English as an additional language if she/he is exposed to a language at home that is known or believed to be other than English.

The definition above seems to paint a picture of a child living in two worlds: home where they use HL and school where they use English. HL can be regarded as a precondition for belonging to a particular group as Tajfel (1978) noted that it relates to sharing cultural values and emotional significance with that group. If the community aspect of the group is disrupted, negative consequences may ensue. Montrul (2010) emphasised that disadvantages can be associated with children losing their HL up to the age of 4, as this stage is when a child's metalinguistic ability is developing. Thus, losing HL at an early age can negatively impact the emergent literacy learning in classrooms.

During his career at primary schools, the first author, as a practitioner fluent in Somali and English, regularly observed how the Somali origin pupils quickly lost their HL proficiency when they began school. For instance, in 2015–2016 academic year, he met a Year 1 pupil who started school late in her Reception Class before that year. Prior to school, she was fluent in HL, and how she used to express herself was above average for a Somali child of her age. During the Muslim festival 'Eid', the first author greeted her '*ciid wanaagsan*' – '*happy Eid*'. She replied '*heh?*' the first author repeated the greeting. He then reverted into English. '*How come just last year you were fluent in the Somali language, and you knew no English; and now you do not know what I am saying in Somali?*' She giggled and elaborated, '*my mum cannot understand me!*' (Abikar, 2020). This means that her communication with her mother, whom she came to the United Kingdom with at the same time, has been disrupted because of her second language development at the cost of her HL at that early age. Montrul (2008) reaffirms that children who have yet to reach their late childhood are likely to lose their HL in a second language (L2) dominant environment. This is because their HL acquisition might have been incomplete. The rate with which HL decline occurs, such as the above pupil demonstrates, can be alarming; this is only one of the many examples from the study and further data are explored below.

Cummins (2000) studied loss of Gaelic in a Scottish context and recounted how, for reasons including lack of political will and lack of learning materials, the Scottish pupils faced dilemmas in terms of using their HL in schools. He continued further to explain that this circumstance became reversed as educators found that students who used Gaelic became good readers of English when '…they had a basic grounding in Gaelic grammar and literature' (Cummins, 2000, p. 173). From Cummins' work, it may be evident that HL needs maintenance as well as stimulating. Cummins' (1976) language interdependence hypotheses provide a helpful framework to make sense of understanding the performance in classrooms by children operating in two languages. The interdependence hypothesis postulates that the proficiency gained in one language can be transferred to a second language if sufficient exposure of the second language is observed. This means that when children learn concepts in HL literacy, they may be in a better position to transfer that concept to the English literacy.

The following section will explore two policies to contextualise the positioning of HL in education in England: The Bullock Report (1975) and the National Curriculum of England (NCE) (DfE, 2013). These two landmark policies are chosen because they show different conceptualisations of HL within education policy discourse, and they represent a change in thinking between 1975 and 2013. These policies contribute to our understanding about the existence of inequality in classrooms with regard to language hierarchies and provide background to how pupils developing EAL in, classrooms may be having a different experience in terms of their languages being recognised and supported today, compared to 40 years ago. These two policies also help to demonstrate that change in this context is slow, perhaps even stagnant.

Exploring the Changing Policy Perspectives on HLs

Bullock (1975) Report

Countries that host migrants usually devise strategies for developing migrant children's language skills. The history of such provision in the United Kingdom can be usefully traced to the Bullock Report (1975) when *Sir Alan Bullock* was commissioned by the then Secretary of State for Education and Science to investigate teaching in schools of reading and developing English language skills. Among recommendations reported by Bullock (1975) was how to help children acquire the ability to use language in different contexts. To realise this, Section 5.1 of the Bullock Report suggested (a) educating parents with the process of language development and (b) enhancing the teacher's skill and knowledge in accurately supporting the child's language needs. These recommendations can conceivably be assumed as an inherent aspect in classroom learning since they highlight two crucial facts that concurrently enhance the child's academic achievements, the place of the parent/primary carer and the teacher within this.

Furthermore, Bullock (1975) stipulated that in order for teachers to be in a position to monitor the competence of children's language progress, they must retain the ability of examining the verbal interaction of the class in terms of an explicit understanding of the operation of language. This appears to be logical because auditing activities in the classroom, in this case, the child's language progress, requires the teacher's skill to allow them to consider a variety of classroom verbal interactions. Nonetheless, in the case where the teacher and the learner operate in different languages, explicit or mutual understanding is a challenge. Moreover, in 5.10 of the Bullock Report, recommendations are made that all children should be helped to acquire as wide a range as possible of the uses of language, to help parents understand the process of language development in their children and to take their part in it and parents and teachers to work together to promote the child's language skills (Bullock, 1975). For the latter, Bullock (1975) explained that it helps teachers' measured attention to the child's precise language needs and their inventiveness in creating situations which enhance this. Teachers' inventiveness is a critical element in classrooms, yet the teacher's inventiveness should not be confined in certain contexts, with consideration also given within the context of EAL learners.

Perhaps the most important aspect of the Bullock Report for this chapter is its suggestions for maintaining the child's culture and language.

> No child should be expected to cast off the language and culture of the home as he [*sic*] crosses the school threshold, nor to live and act as though school and home represent two totally separate and different cultures which must be kept firmly apart. The curriculum should reflect many elements of that part of his life which a child lives outside of school. (Bullock, 1975. p. 286)

Despite Bullock's recommendation of a role for HL in the 1970s, it is yet to be realised and reflected in the English education policy.

The National Curriculum of England (NCE)

The National Primary Curriculum in England, which was introduced in 1988 and revised in 2013 (DfE, 2013), clearly instructs the advancement of English language to support classroom learning, where English is the medium of instruction. Thus, one can question the extent to which EAL students who are newly arrived in the United Kingdom are capable of understanding the classroom instruction when unfamiliar language is used to make sense of content in the form of the same new language. This dilemma may then further negatively impact the EAL learner's academic attainment. This may place the EAL learners under pressure which is exacerbated 'through language policies that clearly positioned English as the prestige language...' (Keh & Stoessel, 2017, p. 110).

To promote the inclusion of EAL learners, the NCE (DfE, 2013) Section 4.5 instructs teachers of the need for understanding the difference between additional needs, EAL learning and special educational needs and disability. The section continues by advising that activities for EAL should be planned in age-appropriate ways and should take account of the length of time in the country alongside previous education and ability in other languages.

Section 4.6 emphasises EAL student need in relation to advancing communication skills in English. Consequently, the NCE (DfE, 2013) clearly gives preference to and prescribes the use of English over other languages. Since children spend an average of six hours in school every day, the school environment is highly influential in their developing language skills and prescribing English over other languages makes the maintenance of HL literacy by the EAL child potentially untenable. The foremost task of teachers is instructed within the NCE to be advancing the communication skills in English by pupils whose language is different than English. This is explored in this chapter and shown to be difficult to achieve without also prioritising HL. Because languages used by the child and teacher are different, effective mutual understanding may become difficult if not impossible. In many cases in schools in England, there is just one teacher and sometimes a teaching support assistant for a class size of 30 children. Thus, it can easily be understood that advancing the communication skills through planning and executing teaching opportunities in English for all these EAL learners with divergent levels of English proficiency can be a difficult if not impossible task to achieve. This chapter does not offer solutions to this complex problem, but it does offer suggestions to incorporate HL learning alongside the medium of English whenever possible. The following section will clarify the first author's doctoral study and methodology.

Introduction to the Doctoral Study

The doctoral study examined the perception of learning HL in extracurricular activities. The first author was motivated to complete this study because of his philosophy that he would be in a better position to inspire a community of learning (pupils and parents learning HL literacy together at home) as well as for his professional development (understanding how HL and L2 reinforce each other). A desire to support EAL learners in general also drove motivation for this study. Observations of pupils who are newly arrived, as well as those who were born in England and use an HL, often demonstrated grammatical mistakes when writing English. In the case of those newly arrived, grammatical mistakes may have begun to occur because of higher concentration upon acquisition of English. After a period of time trying to master the English language, it was noted that pupils began to lose mastery of their HL. This is a phenomenon known as subtractive bilingualism (Baker & Jones, 1998).

Participants of the study were 13 Year 4 pupils, who are 8–9 years old (8 boys and 5 girls) in a primary school in England, and 7 of their parents (all mothers). Participant children's pseudonym names and gender are noted in the Table 15.1.

All participants were of Somali origin. Following a process of gaining voluntary informed consent, guided by the BERA guidelines (2018), the pupils and parents were separately involved in learning the reading, writing, listening and speaking of HL interventions for 45 minutes per week over 24 weeks, at the first author's school. The reasoning for separately involving the pupils and the parents was not a pedagogical decision but one of timing and convenience. The first author's availability to teach the children was Thursdays after school; and the separate availability of parents was on Wednesday mornings when they drop off their children.

Table 15.1. Participants' Pseudonym Names, Abbreviations and Gender.

Pseudonym	**Abbreviation**	**Gender**
Ali	PU01	Boy
Farah	PU02	Boy
Ahmed	PU03	Boy
Maryam	PU04	Girl
Fatha	PU05	Girl
Ubah	PU06	Girl
Gelle	PU07	Boy
Leyla	PU08	Girl
Liban	PU09	Boy
Ikram	PU10	Girl
Abdullahi	PU011	Boy
Muallim	PU012	Boy
Ibrahim	PU013	Boy

To help demonstrate the voluntary nature of participants' engagement with the research, about 4 weeks before the end of the study, four pupils: Fatha, Liban, Ikram and Ibrahim opted to discontinue their involvement for personal reasons. Thus, their data are not available in post assessment. This withdrawal from the study also helps to demonstrate that power relations were mediated well within the study, in that these four pupils felt confident to let the first author know of their desire to withdraw from the study, free from consequence. As a person of Somali origin, the first author had worked at the school since 2004 and developed a good working relationship with previous and current parents and students, and lessening power imbalances was an important consideration. The four participants who opted to discontinue the study demonstrate a sense of equality in the research relationship that might not have been achieved by an outsider.

According to the BERA guidelines (2018), research participants can be regarded as vulnerable when they possess characteristics such as being from an asylum-seeker background, having limitations in their understanding of academic research or the fact that English is not their first language. Thus, since the participants of the study possessed these qualities, they could be considered as vulnerable participants. This understanding inspired the first author to treat the study participants not just, according to Aldridge (2016), as objects of the research but as active citizens with important contributions to offer. Ways in which this was achieved were, as well as the above exercising of freedom to withdraw, by the first author acting as one of the participants and learning HL literacy together. An example of dispersing power relations is found when pupils were quick to correct the first author's HL typing errors without worry of consequence.

Prior to the study, participants were involved in pre-HL literacy assessments of reading, writing, listening and speaking. The aim of the assessments was to obtain a base line with which to gauge whether HL literacy improvement occurred after HL literacy intervention. For reading, the participants (pupils and parents separately and on a one-to-one-basis) read 100 words from a Somali language non-fiction text called '*biyaha*' ('*water*'), which the first author had prepared. Victoria State Government's (2023) conversion chart provided a systematic way of calculating the percentage of correctly read words. For example, if a reader mispronounced 4 of the 100 words, then 100/4 = 25. This means 1 out of 25 words was incorrect and is noted by the ratio 1:25. Table 15.2 displays ratios and their corresponding percentage of accuracy, based on these calculations.

The extracurricular activities with the children ran for 45 minutes at a time, one session a week over 24 weeks. The extracurricular activities took place on school premises. The number of children slightly fluctuated over these weeks, but most sessions were attended by most of the 13 children. A total of 30 lessons – 15 for the pupils and 15 for the parents – were delivered. They consisted of (a) Somali alphabet, short vowels, long vowels, double consonants and consonant-vowel-consonant (CVC) words and how to blend letters; (b) grammar topics such as using capital letters, full stops, pronouns, articles, verbs, adjectives, adverbs and

Table 15.2. Reading Calculation.

Calculation	Text	Easy		Medium		Hard	
Total words (100)/ incorrect	The hundred	1: 200	99.5%	1:17	94%	1:9	89%
100/4 = 25 Incorrect = 1: 25	words to be tested.	1: 100	99%	1:14	93%	1:8	87.5%
1:25 = 96% correct		1:50	98%	1:12.5	92%	1:7	85.5%
		1:35	97%	1:11.75	91%	1:6	83%
		1:25	96%	1:10	90%	1:5	80%
		1:20	95%			1:4	75%
						1:3	66%
						1:2	50%

Adopted from Victoria State Government (2023).

active and passive sentences; and (c) reading parts of non-fiction (the banana tree, stories of Prophet Mohammed (Peace Be Upon Him- PBUH), the African continent and the Islamic calendar) and fiction stories (the clever policeman and the Noor) Somali texts.

Following the extracurricular activities post-HL literacy assessments of reading, writing, listening and speaking were conducted with 9 of the 13 original children, as 4 had opted to discontinue the study at this point. In addition, a qualitative method was used as the aim of the study was to generate theory by analysing the impact of HL literacy on participants. Children's perspectives on the intervention were collected using semi-structured interviews. Each child was interviewed once. The interviews were conducted in English; although they were given the choice of English or HL, they chose English. Each child was interviewed for circa 8–10 minutes, a short time span which is in keeping with their likely level of desired attention due to their ages. Interviews took place on school premises and were conducted to get an understanding of the potential impact of the extracurricular activities upon the children.

The study adopted descriptive statistics to the quantitative HL literacy assessments as Holcomb (1998) noted that it is a clear way of organising and summarising data for interpretation. Additionally, the study was not large enough to generate meaningful inferential statistics. The qualitative interviews were analysed by using Braun and Clarke's (2006) six steps thematic analysis: familiarising with the data, generating the initial codes, searching for themes, reviewing themes, defining and naming the themes and, finally, producing the outcome or the report. In addition to the interviews, a research reflective diary was used to offer the opportunity to regularly update the records. The participants' semi-structured interview data indicated that children perceived that learning HL was important for their identity awareness, developing their cognitive skills and communication. Due to space limitations the cognitive skills theme will be focused upon, alongside the development of positive attitudes to learning HL.

Findings From Semi-Structured Interviews and HL Assessments: Importance of HL for Cognitive Advantage and Positive Attitudes to Learning

This section reports the interview and HL literacy assessment data of the study. The interview was conducted in English. However, for the pre- and post-HL literacy assessments, children had to use HL to capture their level of HL skills.

The study found that children were in a better position to transfer the concepts learned in Somali to English and vice versa:

> *Muallim*: I am now able to translate from English to Somali.

Also, it could be the case that the children may find learning HL literacy easier than English literacy in the first instance.

> *Muallim*: The thing that is good about the Somali language is because it is my first language. All my ancestors learned Somali. It is my first language, and it is easier than English.

Another child added:

> *Gelle*: I learned grammar... which is easier than learning English grammar.

From above, it can be deduced that children are in a position to assess their HL learning in comparison to English literacy, and this assessment ability may then help them with their classroom activities by transferring concepts from HL to English and vice versa. For instance, during the study, Ubah (reading HL text) loudly murmured that for Somali language,

> *Ubah*: in order to form an adverb, a word comes before the adjective (**si** tartiib- slow**ly**) whereas the English adverb, the 'ly' is the suffix of the word.

This demonstrates that the child was using particularly complex understandings of grammar and was able to relate back and forth between both their HL and English. Participants of the study showed motivation to learn HL during the study and learned it rapidly, as demonstrated by the pre- and post-HL reading assessment data (Chart 1) below.

The findings indicated that pupils' language skills in reading, comprehension, listening and speaking improved when compared with the base line scores of the pre-study assessments. Due to space limitation, the reading data will be presented in Chart 1 since it is indicative of the progress that children made in all areas of HL literacy except the writing where no one achieved the minimum score of 10%. Similarly, in terms of space limit, pupils' names were substituted by letters and numbers (Fig. 15.1).

All pupils participated in a pre-reading assessment; however, only nine pupils participated in the post-assessment. PU05 left for Somalia, PU09 and PU10 were busy with other activities outside school and PU13 withdrew from the study without giving a reason.

Further demonstrations of learning success are explored in the qualitative interview responses and through the children's enthusiasm for learning and sharing the learning with parents, for example,

> *Fatha*: you know I challenged my mother whether she knows the Somali short and long vowels and she said she did.

On another occasion, during the semi-structured interview, I requested a child to provide answers in English and he replied,

> *Ali*: Somali ayaan rabaa (I want to speak in Somali)

Though this utterance does not directly demonstrate improved cognitive ability, it does demonstrate a renewed enthusiasm for the HL and a positive attitude to learning. An enthusiastic learner is likely more engaged with the

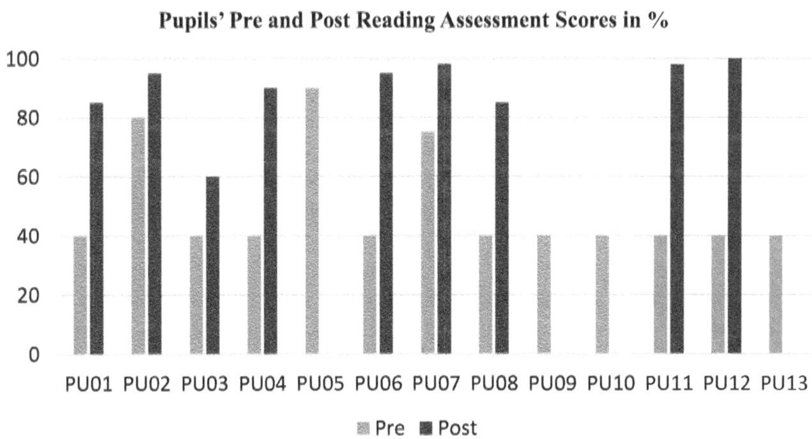

Fig. 15.1. Pupils' Pre- and Post-reading Assessment Data. Adapted from Abikar (2020).

process as demonstrated by Wood (2017, p. 23), who notes that 'positive cognitive engagement ... approaches learning activities with enthusiasm'. Additionally, the children realised that they possessed an empowering tool in their use of their HL potentially not yet shared by others in the community, such as their older siblings who were not part of the study. An interesting dynamic emerged where the participants felt they could share their knowledge gained from using HL in the intervention with others in the community, acting as their teachers. This is demonstrated in the following extracts.

> *Leyla*: Mr Shamsudin, my brother tried to read the Somali sheets you gave us yesterday. He could read them but, the word 'jeer' the 'ee' he read it as the English 'ea'. Then I told him that 'ee' is sounded like English alphabet 'a'.

The children in the study also felt empowered to teach HL literacy to their peers at mosque where they learn the *Quran*, as demonstrated by the following:

> *Gelle*: I want to teach it (HL literacy) to people who go to my mal'amad [the mosque where children go to learn the Koran].

These positive learning moments demonstrate that the children were enabled to gain confidence in their learning and wanted to function as useful members of the Somali society.

During the study, the first author experienced how pupils' conceptual understanding was expanded as they appeared to have gained confidence in transferring HL to English and vice versa, for example,

> *Muallim*: I am now able to translate from English to Somali.

Conceptual understanding was expanded in this instance due to gaining confidence in both their HL and English; this is because:

> ...children who benefit from literacy and concept development in their mother tongue are more likely to succeed in learning additional languages... (Phillipson & Skutnabb-Kangas, 2013, p. 510)

If the participants of the study demonstrated such positive attitudes towards their confidence in translating HL to English in such a brief time as this study, it is reasonable to consider the question: how would their performance in classroom be if HL literacy was used alongside English as a medium of instruction in the longer term? Additionally, the benefit of learning HL extended beyond the participant children to their peers from other minority communities in the classroom. For example, a Year 4 child (of non-Somali origin) once disclosed to the first author that he read a bilingual (English and Somali) book to one of the participants of the study. Thus, the first author observed:

> The study appears to have positively impacted on a pupil who neither shares cultural nor linguistic identity with the Somali-origin pupils (Research diary).

Although it was not the scope of this study to observe how learning of Somali language HL could extend to the children from other communities, these observations are useful to note as further areas of research. The above is a powerful observation which depicts the realities hidden from view when policymakers construct policy which does not take account of the richness of the multicultural and multilingual reality in England.

The Case for HL Policy

The first author's thesis demonstrates how HL literacy learning by participants contributed positively to their well-being by enhancing their confidence, motivation, self-esteem and positive attitude to learning. The thesis also demonstrated the need for HL policy in classrooms, if the aim of England's primary curriculum is introducing children to the essential knowledge that they need in order to be educated citizens (DfE, 2013).

The data from the study show the intrinsic part that HL literacy plays in the child's life inside the classroom (Smyth, 2012). This has long been understood by education practitioners, children, families and researchers but has not been enacted by policymakers in England. As discussed earlier in this chapter, the conceptualisation of HL within education policy appears to be less strong today than it was four decades ago. Use of HL may increase self-confidence and provide a secure environment for children fostering positive attitudes to learning, particularly if they are displaced from their native country. The doctoral study demonstrated that grasping the concept of English grammar by using their newly learned Somali grammar concepts fostered a desire in participants to share this HL literacy with their peers, family and communities.

In the context of migration, in most cases, the learner is expected to use a language other than their HL. The learning they receive is likely to differ from the learning experience of children learning in their native country. The learner may lack meaningful language signs as the new language can be unfamiliar to their brain (Benjamin, 2014). This, then, may create difficulty for the child to express themselves and constitute as barriers for their understanding of both their HL and acquiring the new language (in this case English). Barriers that presented from the doctoral study for both understanding HL and acquiring the new language of English were a lack of HL literacy input at home as parents were found to be proficient in HL speaking skills but less confident in writing and reading. This is eclipsed, however, by the dominance of English at school in all areas of literacy, often at the total expense of HL. Outside of the classroom, this is compounded by, for example, interacting with friends in English and older siblings too who are also subject to losing their HL proficiency and struggling to acquire English for the same reasons as the participants of this study.

Due to potential differences in ethnicity between the child and peer group and the child and teacher, the child may find it a challenge in associating themselves with the new environment (school). Thus, this may force the child to feel alienation in the classroom. The newly arrived child may experience a delayed learning process, caused by the unfamiliar medium of instruction which might necessitate extra support. These barriers can establish an environment in which the child may feel embarrassed by the consequence of their inability to perform what their peer groups are able to do (Jackson, 2014).

Challenges to the Introduction of HL Policy

In the above section, we have discussed the importance of HL literacy for the children's performance in the classroom, in the family and the wider community. However, despite this, a concrete HL policy is absent in England.

Bullock's Report (1975) was a helpful example in terms of preserving the child's culture as it clearly discouraged expectations of the newly arrived child to abandon their language and culture when they begin their school journey. It also emphasised that the reality of the child's life outside of school should be reflected in the curriculum. From the report, it is evident that keeping both the HL and dominant language prominent in the curriculum should be the expectation, if the aim is to advance the English language skills in classroom this current study concurs.

However, the contemporary reality is that we live in a complex and unpredictable world. The findings of the doctoral thesis illustrate the potential benefits and opportunities of focusing on the HL of pupils who have EAL, and that these are being missed in policy and could be capitalised upon if a HL policy was adopted. This has far-reaching consequences beyond the immediacy of the primary classroom. For example, participants of the study did not only think about their current HL status but pondered the dilemmas they might encounter in the future if they would not be in a position to communicate with relatives back in Somalia.

Thus far, despite almost 50 years since the Bullock Report (1975), no concrete measures have been adopted in English policy regarding the importance of maintenance of HL. In a time where anti-immigration sentiment can be seen to be increasing (Peresman et al., 2021), the argument for policy change regarding the importance of HL in schools becomes both more important to resolve and more difficult to enact. Maintenance of HL alongside acquisition of English is in line with England's multicultural reality (Panayi, 2014). However, Adam (2014) postulated that since the mid-nineteenth century, education and politics have been intertwined, and how they are organised reflect the social and political ways of viewing how the world works; therefore, political will is needed if such policy is to be enacted.

Conclusion

This chapter evolved from the first author's doctoral study, which strongly proposes for the introduction of HL policy in England to enable teaching HL alongside English. It is argued that such policy would establish priorities and developments which are necessary for effective HL education. This is because the Primary NCE (DfE, 2013) suffers from the lack of HL enrichment which would empower EAL learners. Also, this policy if introduced would raise the awareness of English schools' obligations towards HL. As the example given at the beginning of this chapter about solving a simple arithmetic problem and the doctoral study discussed here, it can be seen to be in the best interests of EAL learners in England to benefit from an HL policy introduced by the UK government.

NCE (DfE, 2013) rightly prescribes the promotion of the whole student: their spiritual, moral, cultural, mental and physical development. Likewise, it instructs schools to prepare students for opportunities, responsibilities and experiences for later life. If that is the aim, then it is actually inconceivable not to consider the multi-ethnic reality in England's classrooms where almost two million students are EAL learners. The doctoral study has highlighted that EAL pupils consider HL literacy learning as an integral resource for their identity and a tool for academic achievement.

As the responsible entity, as well as the institute that safeguards the well-being of children in England's schools, the Government of England needs to reflect more fully than it currently does in policy, the fact that education is for all and not only for an indigenous segment of society. Introducing a HL policy would be a step towards establishing priorities and developments necessary for EAL learners' social and academic attainment. Finally, to end the chapter, we would like to share some of our reflections on the first author's doctoral journey.

Lessons Learned From the Viva Team: Doctoral Student, Director of Studies and Second Supervisor

During the study, the pupil participants were keen to demonstrate what they had learned in the interventions delivered. They discussed this with the researcher conducting the study, Shamsudin Abikar. Shamsudin came to us (his doctoral supervision team) with this request and between us all we arranged for the participants and those of their parents that could make it, to attend a language seminar being hosted by Jane Andrews, the Second Supervisor. This was part of Jane's own research. Both the Director of Studies and the Second Supervisor attended this event, where the pupils enacted a play, first in Somali language and then in English. This was a rich and rewarding display of the wider benefits of research. The children were proud to present what they had learned, and the parents delighted to hear it. The academic audience were impressed with the enthusiasm for learning conveyed. As part of this day, the Director of Studies, Helen Bovill, conducted a 'what it is like at university' session with the participants who were evidently proud, overawed and enthusiastic to think about this potential step in their life. These demonstrate the unintended consequences of research and how a project can grow in many ways.

As a Doctoral Researcher, I (Shamsudin Abikar) learned that before embarking on a doctoral journey, one needs to be mentally prepared for what it might bring, and it is important to be well-organised. Furthermore, despite working with Somali origin pupils for more than a decade in this particular school, I could not help but realise how little I knew about their emotions towards their HL. Prior to the study, I was anxious about choosing the topic as I was a little wary of whether participants would be interested in the study. However, I proved myself wrong when participant children demonstrated their strong feelings towards learning their HL. This study also helped me to learn more about the power of relationship building. This included: relationships between me the children and parents, as well as relationships between children, between parents and between children and parents.

References

Abikar, S. (2020). *Developing Somali heritage language through extra-curricular activities: A case study exploring perceptions of Somali origin primary pupils and their parents*. Doctoral Thesis. https://uwe-repository.worktribe.com/output/5261105/developing-somali-heritage-language-through-extracurricular-activities-a-case-study-exploring-perceptions-of-somali-origin-primary-pupils-and-their-parents. Accessed on February 10, 2023.

Adam, P. (2014). *Policy and education–Foundations of education studies*. Routledge.

Aldridge, J. (2016). *Participatory research–Working with vulnerable groups in research and practice*. Policy Press.

Baker, C. (2011). *Foundations of bilingual education and bilingualism* (5th ed.). Multilingual Matters.

Baker, C., & Jones, S. P. (1998). *Encyclopaedia of bilingualism and bilingual education*. Multilingual Matters Ltd.

Benjamin, A. (2014). *Focus on text–Tackling the common core reading standards–Grades 4 – 8*. Routledge.

BERA. (2018). *Ethical guidelines for educational research* (4th ed., pp. 1–41). British Educational Research Association.

Braun, V., & Clarke, V. (2006). Using thematic analysis in psychology. *Qualitative Research in Psychology*, *3*(2), 77–101.

Bullock, A. (1975). *A language for life*. https://education-uk.org/documents/bullock/. Accessed on June 19, 2022.

Conteh, J. (2015). *The EAL teaching book, promoting success for multilingual learners* (2nd ed.). Learning Matters.

Cummins, J. (1976). *The influence of bilingualism on cognitive growth: Synthesis of research findings and explanatory hypotheses*. Working Papers on Bilingualism, No. 9. Ontario Inst. for Studies in Education, Toronto. Bilingual Education Project. https://files.eric.ed.gov/fulltext/ED125311.pdf. Accessed on December 28, 2022.

Cummins, J. (2000). *Language, power, and pedagogy–Bilingual children in the crossfire*. Multilingual Matters.

DfE. (2013). *The national curriculum in England framework document*. www.gov.uk/dfe/nationalcurriculum. Reference: DFE-00177-20. Accessed on December 25, 2022.

DfE. (2020). *English proficiency of pupils with English as an additional language*. www.gov.uk/government/publications. Reference DfE-00052-2020. Accessed on December 27, 2022.

Holcomb, Z. C. (1998). *Fundamentals of descriptive statistics*. Pyrczak Publishing.

Jackson, E. L., Jr (2014). *The modern princess–The 21st century guide to fairy tale relationship*. iUniverse LLC.

Keh, M. L., & Stoessel, S. (2017). How first is first? Revisiting language maintenance and shift and the meaning of L1/L2 in three case Studies. *International Multidisciplinary Research Journal, 11*(2), 101–114.

Montrul, S. (2008). *Incomplete acquisition in bilingualism: Re-examining the age factor*. John Benjamins Publishing Co.

Montrul, S. (2010). Current issues in heritage language acquisition. *Annual Review of Applied Linguistics, 30*, 3–23.

Panayi, P. (2014). *An immigration history of britain–Multicultural racism since 1800*. Routledge.

Peresman, A., Carroll, R., & Bäc, H. (2021). Authoritarianism and immigration attitudes in the UK. *Political Studies*, 1–18.

Phillipson, R., & Skutnabb-Kangas, T. (2013). Linguistic imperialism and endangered languages. In Bhatia, T. K., & Ritchie, W. C. ed. *The handbook of bilingualism and multilingualism* (pp. 495–516). Blackwell Publishing Ltd.

Riagáin, P. (2018). *Measures of language proficiency in censuses and surveys–A comparative analysis and assessment*. Springer International Publishing AG.

Slabakova, R. (2016). *Second Language acquisition*. Oxford University Press.

Smyth, G. (2012). *Helping bilingual pupils access the curriculum*. David Fulton Publishers.

Tajfel, H. (1978). Introduction. In Tajfel, H. ed. *Differentiation between social groups–Studies in the social psychology of intergroup relations* (pp. 1–23). Academic Press Inc.

Victoria State Government. (2023). *Literacy teaching toolkit: Running records*. https://www.education.vic.gov.au/school/teachers/teachingresources/discipline/english/literacy/readingviewing/Pages/examplerunning.aspx. Accessed on August 18, 2023.

Wood, R. (2017). *The influence of teacher–Student relationship and feedback on students' engagement with learning*. Cambridge Scholars Publishing.

Chapter 16

Reviewing the Collection's Contribution and Value of Practice-Based Doctoral Studies

Meg Maguire

King's College London, UK

The Value of Practitioner Research – the Value of Doctoral Studies

The act of education practitioners researching their own practice is not a new phenomenon. It has always been valued for its capacity to illuminate the groundedness of practice through attending to the voices of those doing the work, those enacting the policies and those dealing with any consequences on a daily basis. In the 1970s in England, there was a powerful turn towards the 'teacher as researcher' movement led by Lawrence Stenhouse who argued for:

> …the betterment of schools through the improvement of teaching and learning. Its characteristic insistence is that ideas should encounter the discipline of practice and that practice should be encountered by ideas. The teacher research movement is an attack on the separation of theory and practice. (Stenhouse, 1975, p. 3)

Quite simply, the idea was that if teachers were more centrally involved in researching in schools, it would be their 'problems' that would be explored; it would be their 'questions' that would be investigated; it would be their 'reflections' that would lie at the heart of the work. In this way, teachers would be a driving force for reform and 'betterment'. Rudduck (1987, p. 5) also claimed that practitioner research could play a key part in making research more democratic through incorporating the expertise and knowledge of professionals, thus enriching research work more generally.

> (…) there is an urgent need to analyse the structures that govern the production and distribution of research knowledge and the right to engage in research acts. Teacher research is, at one level, a

Critical Perspectives on Educational Policies and Professional Identities, 265–272

doi:10.1108/978-1-83753-332-920241016

> means of countering the hegemony of academic research which teachers are often distanced by.

This collection of practitioner research includes contributors who are involved in education in different phases, stages, institutions and disciplinary settings, such as health education and sports science and extends beyond the work of school teachers – though they are here too. What is interwoven between all these accounts is a concern with theory and practice, conceptual and empirical work, the power of the 'voice' of educational professionals and a strong desire to transform aspects of their work. Where this unique collection 'breaks' with the 'practitioner-researcher' movement lies in its *co-production* between experienced practitioners who have pursued research degrees, writing with, against and alongside their supervisors *and/or more experienced academic researchers*. The manner in which the co-production process is managed here offers an excellent model that others could employ to help develop the academic writing of early career researcher colleagues, aiding them to make the early steps in publishing following postgraduate research.

These chapters have their origins in the research projects undertaken by educational practitioners who have been undertaking doctorates at the University of the West of England. As Manison and Rosenberg put it:

> Professional doctorates, representing several years of the writer's life and often written alongside the demands of the professional 'day job' are frequently referred to as a journey, and a journey that will peak, trough and shape-shift along the way. (Manison & Rosenberg (in this collection))

However, these journeys all have a range of different beginnings as well as endings. For some there is the chance to change jobs, for others the insights that make their 'day job' more enriching, and for others there may be the move into more academic work – writing and publishing. One concern that many of us share is that frequently, after the completion of doctoral studies, when the cap and gown have been put aside, all that work, neatly bound, goes onto a shelf in the university library or to the online research repository – and rarely gets shared or revisited. So, in this co-produced collection, what we get is a chance to revise the ending and ensure that these studies get disseminated more widely in a manageable and accessible form.

Critical Perspectives on Educational Policies and Professional Identity: Learning From Doctoral Studies

The book is organised around a set of three core themes that engage with questions based on various 'Constructions of the Professional and Society', 'Approaches to Becoming, Being and Developing as Education Professionals' and aspects of 'Education Policy and Practice'. While these themes are useful in threading links between the different doctoral studies, the studies themselves draw on diverse contexts and different methodologies that are engaging and sometimes provocative. So while the overarching themes do work to set a frame for the studies, there are many overlaps and intersections with studies in different sections which add significantly to the sum of the parts of the book.

For example, Alex Morfaki, Helen Bovill and Nicola Bowden-Clissold's chapter on the early years setting highlights the ways in which professional hierarchies can work to 'silence' the voices of some practitioners – something that will probably characterise many occupational settings. In terms of identity matters, what this work also does is 'trouble' any simple notion that professionals are a homogenous group of equals. It reveals how power/knowledge plays out in professional settings – another factor of practice that is sometimes sidelined but is reflected in many of the studies in this collection. Sally Moyle and Richard Waller's chapter that looks at nurse education through photographic prompts also deals with hierarchies (differences in power and position). In their chapter 'gaps' between the Emergency Nurse Practitioner, the nurse and the doctor are characterised as third spaces – described as 'a "boundary zone" where two cultures meet, hybrid identities take shape and new discourses are created' (Verbaan & Cox, 2014, p. 2). While this is clearly the case in this health setting, this 'boundary gap' characterises other professional settings and can produce tensions and opportunities for professional development, for example, in the university workforce where there are many hybrid identities and crossovers between administrative and academic roles.

Manison and Rosenberg's chapter takes a different turn to explore how some working class and middle class women come to choose a professional occupation in the first place – their case study is primary school teaching as a career. Their claim is that the symbolic violence done to women in their homes and as they grow up in schools and community settings, etc. produces limits and constraints on what counts as an 'appropriate job' for women. Their chapter provides a powerful sociological lens on the being and becoming of the professional through its concentration on the role of social class in shaping occupational outcomes. And of course, one obvious question is how do these influences and symbolic violences shape the decision-making and career-choosing in other feminised divisions of labour – for example, nurses and nurse educators? Manison and Rosenberg represent their findings in poetic form – and as an aside, sometimes it can be in doctoral studies that imagination and creativity get more space than in other research environments. There may not always be many larger-scale funded projects that choose – or are able to choose – this form of illustration. (However, see the work of Laurel Richardson as an example of this, e.g. Richardson, 1995, 2003).

The fourth and last chapter in this section looks at the complexities of professionalism for sports lecturers in further education (FE). Jacob Bacon and Tessa Podpadec write about a culture of instrumentalism that seems to pervade the sports sector where tutors stressed 'grades, retention numbers, as opposed to the development of the student'. In contrast to other chapters in this section, professionalism is seen as set within dominant neoliberal discourses that accent performativity and outcome rather than alternative processes to engage and enthuse young people. One question that emerges from this chapter (and study) is to ask how much this picture represents other disciplines in other settings in education? Discourses of professionalism frequently centre on expertise, knowledge, integrity and commitment; normative education policies highlight attainment, accountability and the need for reform, all discourses that are closer to an outcomes approach rather than one that attempts to work with and reflect the learners' interests – a reworking of the construct of professionalism perhaps?

'Interrogating Approaches to Becoming, Being and Developing as Education Professionals' starts with an exploration of teaching and learning as a complex process and the need to work as flexible, nuanced professionals who can deal with 'in the moment' judgement-making. This chapter by Ben Knight with Neil Harrison lays out dominant policy approaches in English Initial Teacher Education that stress sets of standards and competencies rather than any reflexive approaches towards learning and how it occurs. In teacher education, normative policies that influence teaching and the teachers' identify seem to be incompatible with the messiness and situatedness of what is actually involved. In this setting, what is constructed as being 'professional' likewise can become a form of instrumentalism and policy compliance where complexity, sensitivity to settings and students, as well as criticality and reflexiveness are disregarded and discounted by policymakers in favour of a 'one size fits all' approach.

Some of these arguments are also reflected in the chapter by Juliet Edmonds who looked at primary school teachers with responsibility for leading on science education. One key finding was that those teachers with greater science capital were more empowered and able to exert more agency and thus shore up their professional identity – knowledge as power perhaps? In my view, the role of disciplinary capital in lending authority and confidence to professional identities is another useful 'take-away' from this collection and an aspect that does not seem to get much attention in the wider literature. In Andy Goldhawk's chapter, the focus is with the professional development of FE lecturers and their middle managers. Continuing professional development (CPD) is a contentious and contested matter in all phases of educational provision. Goldhawk argues that the mandated provision that he explored 'locates the teacher within a complex web of organisational managerialism' (Lloyd & Davis, 2018, p. 92). Again, neoliberalism and an instrumental approach to reform are evidenced in this grounded perspective that seems to characterise and capture many institutional approaches towards CPD provision. This finding would have relevance in other sectors of educational provision too.

Karan Vickers-Hulse and Marcus Witt work in initial teacher education and this is the setting for their chapter (and the one that follows it). Vickers-Hulse and Witt make an argument for identity that develops through a growing connection with the profession and while they recognise that identity is a complex and highly contested concept, they trace its development over time on different routes into teaching. This chapter sits well alongside that of Manison and Rosenberg and their detailing of influential and gender-binaried discourses about 'a suitable job for women' – and a mapping of changes over the training routes in Vickers-Hulse and Witt's work. One comment from Louise, a participant in this study, who said she had found some of her courses to be linear; 'we're going to take you, we're going to mould you, we're going to train you' – another illustration of instrumentality in educational policymaking and professional practice. The final chapter in the second section by Garrick and Andrews also looked at teacher education but from the perspective of older participants who were changing their careers to become a teacher. Here the focus was with their learning, although their identities were involved in this process. Nicholas Garrick and Jane Andrews say, 'Training to teach, unlike other careers which might be dependent on a set body of academic knowledge (e.g. engineering, medicine or law), means that the social, economic and cultural capital of those choosing to train is diverse and complex'.

The third main organising theme in this collection is 'Challenging Education Policy and Practice'. Five chapters look at aspects of current policy work. Georgie Ford and Richard Waller look at the FE sector and argue that there is a growing need for more support for students' mental health and that staff need more sensitive and reflexive education (for instance, through CPD) to help them do this work and to embed emotional authenticity. This aspect is not present in current forms of more instrumental approaches to professional development in this area – and issues to do with mental health are increasingly being shown to be a major challenge across all phases and sectors of education provision. The second chapter, led by Julie Smith with Richard Waller, takes a proposition – that encouraging high expectations by teachers for their learners will raise attainment – and shows how more complex this 'common sense' policy drive can be in practice. Such findings are precisely the point of practitioner research, to uncover aspects of policy and demonstrate that things are much 'messier' on the ground!

The next chapter is extremely timely – it focuses on how primary teachers actually navigate and work with/against policies in order to teach controversial and sensitive issues in the history curriculum, in ways that match their ethics and integrity. They describe 'teachers walking a precarious tightrope as they navigate tensions in their classroom practice'. What emerges from their analysis based on some high-stakes and controversial school policies is a useful typology of teacher tactics in the face of controversy. These tactics range from being avoiders, risk takers, containers and activists. This typology will resonate with many teachers in different disciplines who work in contentious arenas. Indeed, Sarah Whitehouse with Verity Jones highlights the relationship between their policy context and wider aspects such as the need for anti-racism/racial literacy in schools.

I now want to move to the final chapter where Shamsudin Abikar, with Helen Bovill and Jane Andrews, looked at school-home languages policy. They make an argument for a 'missing' policy and for the inclusion of developing home languages in the primary classroom. The value here is in signalling a space where more policy work is needed – and much policy work concentrates (understandably) on critical and scholarly appraisals of policies currently being enacted. More work could usefully be done on policy gaps and perhaps too, small-scale policy innovations, being undertaken by committed practitioners in their own settings drawing on their own capital/s perhaps?

Another chapter has taken a contentious piece of policy for exploration. Max Weedon, Kathy Mansfield Higgins and Ciaran Burke took the Prevent Duty in schools for their chapter's topic (the penultimate chapter) which has some obviously overlaps with the chapter by Whitehouse and Jones. Prevent is a mandated policy and so schools (and teachers) have to be compliant with what is outlined in the text and legislation. Perhaps unsurprisingly, the authors found that 'individuals straddle different positions (responses and practice) based on a range of factors'. They also raised some of the complexities involved in 'doing policy' that might not be believed in or valued by different teachers. They argued that educationalists need to 'retain criticality' in order to manage these conflicts in their professional lives holding onto their values and managing compliance simultaneously. This is certainly not as easy as it may sound – and one wonders about the experiences of those teachers who are leaving the profession in their droves after a short period of time in the classroom!

Here I have exchanged the order of the two last chapters in order to revisit a point made at the start of this piece and at the very end of this chapter about the value of doctoral studies for researchers. This is what they write:

> The findings outlining the three "types" of participant could have been presented in neat categories but in reality we are often more than one thing and so while it is challenging to empirically demonstrate this, *such endeavour provides a richer and more nuanced glimpse into the social world.* Yes it makes it messy and challenging to articulate at times on the page or in a viva exam but it is also *when we look at these nuances that we understand power and resistance to power* – in this it was Prevent but there are many, many instances where this is equally as true and needed.

And, for me, in a nutshell, this sums up the key purpose of the practitioner-researcher.

Takeaways From 'Critical Perspectives on Educational Policies and Professional Identity: Learning From Doctoral Studies'

Some of the key takeaways from this book lie in the way in which issues such as a creeping instrumentalism shape the work of the educational professional seems to be fairly wide spread across all sectors. While this may be a characteristic of contemporary normative policy texts and legislation, teachers holding more complex and situated values will often wrestle with/against this pressure to conform to what is being demanded. Writing of the messiness of policy processes, Ball (2021, p. 63) claims that 'it is practitioners who are left to solve the resulting inconsistencies and contradictions, suffering criticism if they cannot'. And this tension is a perspective that comes across in many of the chapters in this collection. Another aspect that comes across powerfully is the complexity of being and becoming an educational professional – the gaps, the hybrid formations, the changes over time as well as some foundational influences that shape occupational choice and identity formation.

I would like to offer two more perspectives that arise from this rich collection of different works on identities and policy analysis. First, one aspect that comes across strongly in all the chapters is the way in which the studies focus on the work being done in various settings to *interpret*, *enact* and sometimes *disrupt* policy shifts. It seems evident from reading these research accounts that being a practitioner-researcher (in whatever the setting – FE, early years, health or teacher education) is itself a form of policy work. Through exploring discourses of power and instrumentalism, it is possible to discern attempts to construct the teacher in particular ways – ways that frequently get interrupted by professional training or practice settings and contextualised experiences. Accounts that illustrate the ways in which educationalists are notionally positioned by various policies that they see as problematic and attempt to ameliorate and rework less than positive outcomes are also testimony to the spaces that still exist for some disruption and challenges to reforms that sit less well with other (professional) values such as an ethics of care and commitments, respect and integrity.

Second, not all reforms are necessarily good of themselves and democratic societies depend on their professional (and other) communities to point out inconsistencies and to 'speak power to truth' when necessary. Professionals' familiarity with specialised knowledge and practices and with their capacity to deploy theoretical insights (as evidenced across this collection) empowers them to question and challenge the status quo. As MacLure (2010, p. 277) writes 'the value of theory lies in its power to get in the way'. And the chapters in this collection really do get in the way – of 'commonsense', unreflexive policy approaches, of issues related to social justice as well as giving 'sight' and 'voice' to the practice worlds of educational professionals. In doing this work, this collection positions practitioner-researchers as partners in the co-production of knowledge that needs sharing and dissemination if it is to effective critical thought and maybe more appropriate reforms or policy gaps/needs – and one tactic is through a book like this one!

References

Ball, S. J. (2021). *The education debate* (4th ed.). Policy Press.

Lloyd, M., & Davis, J. (2018). Beyond performativity: A pragmatic model of teacher professional learning. *Professional Development in Education*, *44*(1), 92–106.

MacLure, M. (2010). The offence of theory. *Journal of Education Policy*, *25*(2), 277–288.

Richardson, L. (1995). Narrative and society. In Van Maanen, J. Ed. *Representation in ethnography*. Sage.

Richardson, L. (2003) Poetic representation of interviews In Gubrium, J. F. and Holstein, J. A. (eds), *Postmodern interviewing*. Sage.

Rudduck, J. (1987). Teacher research, action research, teacher inquiry: Whats in a name? In J. Rudduck, D. Hopkins, J. Sanger, & P. Lincoln (eds), *Collaborative inquiry and information skills, British library research paper 16*. British Library.

Stenhouse, L. (1975). *An introduction to curriculum research and development*. Heinemann.

Verbaan, E., & Cox, A. M. (2014). Occupational sub-cultures, jurisdictional struggle and third space: Theorising professional service responses to research data management. *The Journal of Academic Librarianship*, *40*(3–4), 211–219.

Index

Printed and bound by CPI Group (UK) Ltd, Croydon, CR0 4YY

13/09/2026

14961026-0006